EUROPEOPLE

14070.

341
EUROPEAN.

COPENHAGEN

DENMARK

THE NETHERLANDS

The Hague

GERMANY

Bonn

Brussels

BELGIUM

LUXEMBOURG

Luxembourg

UNITED KINGDOM

London

Paris

FRANCE

Dublin

REPUBLIC OF IRELAND

ITALY

Rome

GREECE

Athens

Madrid

SPAIN

PORTUGAL

Lisbon

EUROPEOPLE

A Guide to
the Nations of
the European Community

TONY GRAY

Macdonald

A Macdonald Book

First published in Great Britain in 1992 by
Macdonald & Co (Publishers) Ltd
London & Sydney

ISBN 0 356 20251 8

Typeset by Leaper & Gard Limited, Great Britain
Printed and bound in Great Britain by
BPCC Hazell Books
Aylesbury, Bucks, England
Member of BPCC Ltd.

A CIP catalogue record for this book is available from the British Library.

Macdonald & Co (Publishers) Ltd
165 Great Dover Street
London SE1 4YA

A member of Maxwell Macmillan Publishing Corporation

CONTENTS

Sources and Acknowledgements   vii
The New Neighbours   1
The European Community I: How It Started   5
The European Community II: How It Works   15
The Belgians   27
The British   57
The Danes   95
The Dutch   117
The French   147
The Germans   191
The Greeks   237
The Irish   271
The Italians   303
The Luxembourgers   349
The Portuguese   363
The Spanish   393
The European Community III: How It's Going   445
Community Chronicle   457
Vital Statistics   464

For Michael and Chris
and Vicki and Paul

SOURCES AND
ACKNOWLEDGEMENTS

To acknowledge all the sources I have used in assembling this book would be completely impossible. For a start, I have lived and worked for protracted periods in three of the twelve Community countries (Ireland, the United Kingdom and France), and have spent fairly long periods working in two others (Italy and Denmark). I have also spent some time in the other seven, as a tourist, and I have talked to many old colleagues who have worked in various parts of the Community as journalists, and incorporated some of their views. While doing the research for this book, I consulted dozens of the thousands of books that litter every room in our home, and numerous encyclopaedias, gazetteers, and other books from my local library at Kew and in the Richmond Reference Library.

However, as soon as I started to work on the book in earnest, I began by consulting Robert Elphick, spokesman for the Commission of the European Community in London and an old Fleet Street hand like myself, and he has been extremely helpful. Not only did he supply me with all the European Community statistics, and guide me through them, but he also read the book in copy form and made many helpful suggestions. I hasten to make it clear at this point that while Bob Elphick supplied me with many of the facts and statistics I have used in the book, he cannot in any way be held responsible for any conclusions I have drawn from them, or for any comments I have made on anything.

Statistics, which for one reason or another were not available from the European Commission, I have taken from material supplied to me by the press and public relations offices of the various embassies and other representatives of the Community in Britain and elsewhere in Europe. Where there were inconsistencies, I have taken as a firm guideline a little booklet published by the Commission of European Communities, *A Journey Through the EC*. It was published in 1988 and it has not since been updated, and some of its statistics only go as far as 1985, but I felt it better to rely on one standardized work than try to thread my way through statistics often based on different periods, and frequently couched in different languages. In addition it gives a set of comparative statistics not yet available for any later period.

I would also like to thank Gavin Scott, an old friend and fellow journalist, who read the chapters on Spain and Portugal and made some invaluable suggestions. Gavin is currently Bureau Chief and a senior editor with *Time* magazine in Chicago; he spent about nine years covering Spain and Portugal for the magazine and subsequently spent another five or six years as Bureau Chief in Rio de Janeiro, covering Latin America. I am very grateful too, to an old Fleet Street friend, the much-travelled Carolyn Martin, for her advice on European cooking.

My thanks are also due to Robert Hale Ltd and the David Grossman Literary Agency for permission to quote some passages from Susan Thackeray's *Living in Portugal*; to the Octopus Publishing Group and Paul Reynolds, Literary Agent, New York for permission to quote from William Shirer's *The Rise and Fall of the Third Reich*; to Hamish Hamilton and the Agenzia di Rosemary Liedl in Milan for permission to quote from Luigi Barsini's *The Italians*; to Barrie and Jenkins and the Random Century Group for permission to use material from Jan Morris's *Spain*; and to Harper Collins, Publishers and Random

House in New York for permission to quote from *Hellas* by Nicholas Gage.

In addition, I am extremely indebted to my agent, James Hale and to Alan Samson of Macdonald for the support they gave me when I approached them with a germ of an idea which grew into this book.

TONY GRAY
September 1991
Combals, St Gervais sur Mare, France

THE NEW NEIGHBOURS

On 31 December 1992, the United Kingdom is going to join eleven other European nation-states as we all become full members of a properly functioning European Community Single Market. Few of us new neighbours know very much about one another. We may speak a few words of another language – some of us indeed may even speak a few languages fluently and feel perfectly at home in many of the towns and cities and villages of some or all of the other eleven member-states. But how much do we really know about them?

When, for example, did Belgium become an independent state? And with a king? Where on earth did the Belgian royal family come from? And they had an empire too once, didn't they? And didn't somebody say on TV the other night that Belgium has three legislatures, one for the north, one for the south and one for Brussels? And two languages, French and Flemish? And what about the Walloons? Who are they, when they're at home?

And Holland? Is it Holland or the Netherlands, and if so why? And wasn't Holland at one time somehow connected with Spain? And isn't Curaçao in some way connected with Holland and those other Malay states? Did tiny, ineffectual Holland really have an overseas empire once, like Britain? And wasn't there something

1

about the last time a serious invasion attempt was made upon Britain when the Dutch navy got as far up the Thames as Gravesend, or was it Greenwich, in the sixteenth or was it the seventeenth century? And what about Portugal? Wasn't it Portugal, or was it Spain, from which Columbus set off to find a new route to the Far East, and in the process discovered America? And didn't Portugal, by far the poorest country in the European Community, once have an empire almost as great as the British Empire? What happened? And is there a lesson there for us somewhere?

Even Margaret Thatcher didn't seem too sure of the facts. When, in 1990, she argued that Britain was different because there were the interests of the royal family to be taken into account, had she forgotten — or did she never know — that Spain, Holland, Belgium, Luxembourg and Denmark also have royal families?

Most of us have no clear idea of how the European Community came about, or how it operates. We have a vague notion that there is a European Parliament which sometimes sits in Luxembourg — or is it Bonn? — and sometimes in Strasbourg, but we don't know whether it has any power to legislate for the Community as a whole, or for that matter, any power to legislate for us, or even what is its basic purpose.

Most people would probably guess that CAP means Common Agricultural Policy, but what about FAST (the European Programme for Forecasting and Assessment of Science and Technology), ESPRIT (the European Strategic Programme for Research and Development of Information Technology), BRITE (Basic Research in Industrial Technologies for Europe) and all the hundreds of others? And who foots the bill for this fast-breeding bureaucracy?

So, having sorted out a few of these puzzling questions to my own satisfaction, it occurred to me that it might be very useful to write a light-hearted, informal introduction to the twelve members of the European Community: a basic in-fill on some essential facts about the origin of the people, their languages, customs, beliefs, food and drink, etc. with a glance at their history and geography, and an introduction which would provide, in perhaps an oversimplified but easily assimilated way, a layman's guide as to how the Common Market came about.

But primarily this book is about the plain folk of the new European Community and all the things that have gone into making them the kind of people they are.

THE EUROPEAN COMMUNITY I:

How It Started

THE WEALTH OF A NATION

In any federation of nation states such as the European Community, it is useful to have some indication of the relative wealth of the different states. But how do you measure the wealth of a nation? Economists do it by comparing figures which give some indication of the total annual income of all the people and the total earnings of all the industries and services in the country. As no two economists agree entirely on how exactly this figure is reached, or indeed on anything else, I shall play safe and cite the 1990 edition of the *Macmillan Encyclopaedia*:

> *Gross national product (GNP)*, a measure of the total annual output of a country, including net income from abroad; it provides a measure of the economic strength of that country. GNP can be calculated in three ways, based on income, output, or expenditure. If income is used as the basis, all incomes accruing to residents of the country as a result of economic activity (excluding, for instance, pensions) are summed (national income is thus synonymous with GNP calculated in this way). On the basis of output, the value added to a product at each stage of production is summed. If expenditure is used, the value of all consumption products is calculated. All three methods should give the same result. *Gross domestic product* (GDP) is GNP excluding net income from abroad and gives some indication of the strength of industry within a country.

I thought it as well to clear up this point right at the start, since both terms are used throughout the book.

THE EUROPEAN COMMUNITY I:

How It Started

The idea of a federation of European states is usually attributed to Sir Winston Churchill who called for 'a kind of United States of Europe' immediately after World War II when it became clear that the devastation in Europe caused by two world wars within twenty years could not possibly be tackled without some sort of communal effort.

It had also become clear to a great many of the people who thought about it that national pride and a blind, fierce feeling of patriotism had been one of the contributory causes of both world wars, and that if a European Community co-operating on economic, political and social issues could be created, the fear of future wars within Western Europe could be greatly reduced, if not altogether eliminated,

And the very fact that final victory in both wars was not achieved until the intervention of the United States – the most powerful economic and industrial federation in the world with, at the time it entered World War I, the manpower and the industrial capacity to produce the weapons needed to end it – made

7

people in Europe wonder whether the time had not come for a similar federation in Europe, both as a safeguard against possible future wars and as a bulwark against the threat from one of the other great world powers, the Soviet Union and its satellites.

Understandably, it was the smaller, weaker nations who were the first to think along these lines. In 1948, Belgium and Luxembourg — who already had a fiscal union dating from between the wars — together with the Netherlands established the Benelux customs union, and started to consider what, if any, form of combined defensive measures might be devised to protect them from attacks by any of the stronger nations by which they were surrounded.

The Organization for European Economic Co-operation (OEEC) had already been set up in 1947, on the suggestion of General Marshall, the US Secretary of State, to co-ordinate and control the distribution of US aid — the so-called Marshall Plan. The OEEC was an intergovernmental organization; all its decisions had to be unanimous, and were then expected to be implemented by the member-states themselves, though this didn't always happen.

Meanwhile pressure for a federal Europe continued, and culminated in the formation of a European Congress at The Hague in May 1948, which eventually led to the first attempt at a Council of Europe, set up in 1949. Basically the initial Council consisted of an intergovernmental Committee of Ministers, directly responsible to their own separate governments, but attached to a Consultative Assembly which was little more than an international debating society. There was no supranational element in its constitution, and it fell far short of satisfying the federalists, who continued their pressure for a supranational organization with power to take corporate decisions on almost every aspect of life in Europe, including defence, which had been one area specifically excluded from the terms of reference of the Council of Europe.

The Soviet Union had already started to solve the immediate short-term — and most people believed also the long-term — problem of any resurgence of German aggression by dividing the country into two halves, with, eventually, from 1961, a wall running straight through Berlin and an almost impenetrable Iron Curtain cutting Eastern Europe off from the West.

Most serious economists in France and West Germany considered the revival of the coal and steel industries to be absolutely basic to any programme for overall economic recovery. The French were understandably nervous of any scheme which might restore West German industrial power; and equally, West Germany was convinced that economic recovery and international acceptance could be gained only through the revival of its industrial base.

Between them, Jean Monnet, head of the French economic recovery programme, and Robert Schuman, the French Foreign Minister, came up with a bright idea: the pooling of all steel and coal resources in Western Europe under one single authority. The suggestion was eagerly welcomed by the Benelux countries, West Germany and Italy, and in April 1951 the Treaty of Paris created the European Coal and Steel Community (ECSC), which came into force in July 1952 and set the pattern for the whole European Community.

The key factor, which made it such a unique step forward in the federalization of Europe, was that all executive power was vested in an organization which represented the best interests of the Community as a whole, and could not be vetoed by ministers representing the various countries involved.

The Schuman Plan, although concerned only with coal and steel, nevertheless set a pattern for European co-operation in one vital industry and created a community with a great number of common interests initially known as Les Six – France, West Germany, Italy and the three Benelux countries.

The success of this fundamental exercise in European co-operation led immediately to attempts to fashion similar supranational organizations to decide on wider matters, including defence, economics and politics, and resulted in the formation of the European Defence Community (EDC) and the European Political Community (EPC).

Britain and France, however, fearful of pressure from the

Soviet Union, had already in 1947 signed a defensive alliance, the Treaty of Dunkirk, and had extended it in 1948 to include the Benelux countries. It was then known as the Treaty of Brussels.

Then came the Soviet blockade of West Berlin in 1948; and the US reaction to that was to seek a closer alliance with the Brussels Treaty allies, which in turn resulted in the North Atlantic Treaty signed in 1949. The question of rearming West Germany had now to be faced.

The war between North Korea, supported by the Communist powers, and South Korea, supported by the Western democracies under US mandate, involved the Americans ever more deeply in European affairs. Proposals were made for the rearming of West Germany, and the highly successful coal and steel co-operative was taken as a role model for a proposed new European Defence Community which would include armed forces from West Germany.

Alarmed at the prospect of her ancient enemy rearming with US approval, the French National Assembly rejected the EDC Treaty in 1954. The result was the development, largely as a result of British pressure, of the Western European Union (WEU), which led to the formation of the North Atlantic Treaty Organization (NATO) in its present form. It was in effect an extension of the Treaty of Brussels, to include West Germany and Italy, and it accepted German participation in NATO as well as the continuing presence of British troops in Germany.

Nevertheless the French government's rejection of the EDC led to the collapse of the proposed European Political Community and very nearly brought down the European Coal and Steel Community.

The next attempt to put the whole package together again was made in April 1956 by Paul-Henri Spaak, the Belgian Foreign Minister, who set up the European Atomic Energy Community (EURATOM). His Treaty of Rome established a common market with a common external tariff to apply, initially at any rate, only to the original six, but to be extended, in time, to other European countries which might eventually choose to join the Community.

Spaak's Common Market concept also envisaged the free

movement of workers (and not only migratory labourers, but doctors, nurses, dentists, vets and architects, an aim which was achieved by the eighties), as well as of services and capital within the Community and the progressive co-ordination of the economic policies of the member-states to bring increased industrial efficiency and a new level of economic prosperity to the entire region.

General de Gaulle, who became President of France in 1958, was bitterly opposed to Spaak's whole concept, principally because if the Common Market were to be extended to include Britain, which was Spaak's intention, Britain would receive all the Common Market trade benefits while still retaining all its old Commonwealth preferences. De Gaulle, like many of his compatriots, was jealous of the fact that Britain had not surrendered to the Nazis as France did in 1940. And the fact that Britain had been largely instrumental in enabling France to eject the Germans and regain something of her former *gloire* in 1944 only made matters worse.

The result of de Gaulle's opposition to Spaak's plan was the formation in 1960 of the European Free Trade Area (EFTA), a trading partnership between the 'outer' West European countries, including Austria, Denmark, Norway, Portugal, Sweden and Switzerland, designed to increase trade among its members and to cope with Les Six until such time as a sizeable single Western European Community became feasible.

By 1961, Britain, now with Harold Macmillan as prime minister, had decided that the risks of continuing to remain outside the European Community were probably, on balance, slightly greater than those involved in joining it and accordingly in July 1961 applied for membership. De Gaulle instantly vetoed Britain's entry; now on the grounds that the Nassau Agreement between Macmillan and Kennedy, under which the United States had supplied Britain with Polaris missiles, implied a special relationship between the two countries as a result of which Britain's prime interests must be regarded as 'non-European'.

Again in 1967 when Britain reapplied for membership under Harold Wilson's Labour government, the French president said no.

It was only after de Gaulle's resignation and the arrival on the scene of Georges Pompidou of France and Willy Brandt of West Germany that negotiations for the enlargement of the Community were resumed with the British government. By now, Denmark, Ireland and Norway had also decided to apply for membership. On 1 January 1973, the United Kingdom, Denmark and Ireland became full members. The Norwegian people had rejected its government's proposal to join the Community in a referendum held in 1971.

In the United Kingdom, membership of the Community was always felt to be politically explosive. When a Labour government under Harold Wilson came to power it held a referendum to discover whether the British were happy to be members. Roughly two-thirds of the electorate were in favour of membership.

At a summit meeting in Paris in 1972, the Community – now strengthened by three prospective new members – declared itself in favour of creating a European Monetary Union by 1980, but its discussions were seriously hampered by recurring and seemingly insoluble problems, such as Britain's contribution to the Community Budget, which Britain felt had been pitched far too high.

Matters weren't helped by the oil crises of 1973 and 1978 and the world recession which followed them. Greece, in 1981, and Spain and Portugal, in 1986, next became members. The British budgetary problem was finally solved, more or less to everyone's satisfaction, at Fontainebleau in June 1984.

The original Treaty of Rome of 1957 had provided for the creation of a European Parliament to consist of directly elected members representing all the states in the Community, but it was not until 1979 that the first direct elections to the European Parliament took place, and even today there is no agreement on a common method of election. However, a European Parliament does now indeed exist and in February 1984 it approved, with an overwhelming majority, a draft treaty establishing a European Union, the result of which was the Single European Act of February 1986.

This act, the first amendment to the Treaty of Rome signed

nearly thirty years earlier, attempted to bring, within a treaty framework, complete Community control over such matters as science, technology and ecological policies, as well as committing the Community to a measure of political cohesion, an internal market and a common monetary system, or at very least a workable exchange rate mechanism, designed to stabilize currency within the Community. There were considerable delays before the act was ratified by all the member states. Two of them, Denmark and Ireland, put it to the electorate in the form of a referendum even at this late stage, and as a result the Single European Act will not come into full effect until the end of 1992.

The twelve member states — Belgium, Denmark, France, Germany (enlarged to include East Germany after the fall of the Berlin Wall towards the end of 1989 and the reunification of Germany in October 1990), Greece, Ireland, Italy, Luxembourg, the Netherlands, Portugal, Spain and the United Kingdom (including Northern Ireland) — will become one Single European Community on 1 January 1993.

The totally unforeseen reunification of Germany illustrates vividly the extreme difficulty of giving any watertight definition of the institutions which comprise and control the Community since it is evolving all the time, forcing these institutions to change and adapt themselves to cope with each new situation as it arises. It has been like this from the start: as Hugh Arbuthnott and Geoffrey Edwards put it in their *Common Man's Guide to the Common Market* (London: Sheed and Ward, originally published 1987, second edition 1989), the evolution of the Community resembles a building 'in the process of conversion, but without an architectural blueprint of the final result'.

THE EUROPEAN COMMUNITY II:

How It Works

A PROBLEM OF COMMUNICATION

A letter to the editor of the *Spectator* magazine on 3 November 1990 pointed out that it was no wonder that the European Community was experiencing some difficulty in making firm decisions about anything and suggested that one possible explanation might be found in the fact that while the Lord's Prayer consists of only fifty-two words, and the preamble to the Declaration of Independence, which enshrines the basis of the Constitution of the United States of America consists of less than 180 words, the European Community regulations, in one language alone – English – covering the importation and exportation of one small, insignificant food product – caramel – runs to more than 2,500 words.

THE EUROPEAN COMMUNITY II:

How It Works

When you consider the profound and fundamental differences in the ethnic, historical, cultural, economic and social backgrounds of such countries as Germany and Greece, Ireland and Italy, Belgium and Britain, the mystery is not that any attempt at constructing organizations to co-ordinate and control them had to be experimental, tentative and flexible, but that so much agreement on all major issues has been achieved in such a relatively short space of time.

Economic necessity was the initial spur — the need to resolve old enmities and to revive the French and German coal and steel industries destroyed during World War II — and economic development (more and more and better cars and ever better hi-fi systems and more efficient car telephones and bigger TV sets and more powerful personal computers and more luxurious luxury bathrooms and secondary residences and even longer holidays in ever more inaccessible places) will probably provide the glue that will keep the disparate elements of the Community together. And indeed, as is already perfectly clear, it will probably continue to attract other unlikely bedfellows, for example Turkey, whose in-habitants now seem to be only too anxious to forgo at least some of their proud and ancient traditions and customs in return for what they regard as their fair share of Playthings of the Western World.

The European Parliament, which was set up under the Treaty of Rome of 1957, is modelled roughly on the parliaments of the other European member states, with one essential difference: it does not have the power to legislate, which is the principal func-tion of all the other European parliaments. All legislation for the Community is initiated by the Commission, in effect an assembly of ex-MPs, former government ministers, higher civil servants and promising recruits from industry, appointed by the member-states to represent them.

All proposed legislation is discussed at length in the European Parliament and amendments are suggested, but the final decision lies with a third Community institution, the Council of Ministers, an intergovernmental assembly consisting of the ministers or secretaries of state of all the member-nations.

Of the four basic Community institutions – the European Parliament, the Commission, the Council of Ministers and the European Community Court of Justice – the most important, in many ways, is the Commission. The Commissioners are appointed for a four-year term of office, and the President of the Commission for a renewable two-year term. There are two members each on the Commission from the five larger states (France, Italy, Spain, the United Kingdom and Germany) and one each from the seven smaller ones.

Although initially dependent upon their governments for nomination, once they are appointed, the Commissioners enjoy total independence. Their function then becomes narrowed down to the representation and promotion of the best interests of the Community, regardless of their own nationality or political persuasions. They take all decisions on the basis of a simple majority, and they are collectively responsible for all Commission decisions.

They are backed by a vast corps of international senior civil servants, 11,000 strong. With their assistance, the Commission initiates all policy proposals, including draft legislation, but has no power to take any decisions except where specifically delegated, for example in the day-to-day running of the Common Agricultural Policy (CAP). Decision-making is the prerogative of the Council of Ministers.

The secondary function of the Commission is to see that Community policies, once agreed, are implemented throughout the Community. In order to achieve this aim, if member-states fail to comply with Community rules, the Commissioners are empowered to take them to the Community's fourth basic institution, its International Court of Justice in Luxembourg (not confused with the International Court of Justice at The Hague). However, since this court hasn't any real power to enforce its decisions if the country involved decides to ignore it, this is only one of hundreds of fundamental problems for which no solution has yet been discovered.

The Commissioners thus represent roughly the equivalent of the permanent higher civil servants whose task it is to cope with the details of framing and revising legislation in most parliamentary democracies. They are nominated by their governments in more or less the same way as they would be appointed or promoted to such positions at home.

And the Council of Ministers who make the final decisions on all proposed projects or legislation are the ministers and secretaries of state of the twelve member-states — and because of anomalies in the various voting systems, they do not necessarily represent the wishes of the majority of the electorate.

Aware of this weakness, Paul-Henri Spaak, back in the fifties, decided that the European Assembly would be a directly elected assembly. Ideally, he would have liked all the member-states to use the same sort of proportional representational system of election, but certain member-states preferred their own domestic system of voting. Britain, for example, stuck doggedly to the single-seat constituency, first-past-the-post voting system, understandably enough since it has given the Conservative Party an overwhelming majority in Parliament with only a minority support in the country. Other member-states chose to stick to their own varied forms of proportional representation.

Initially the members of the European Parliament were nominated in more or less the same way as the Commissioners were nominated by their governments; it was not until 1979 that the first direct elections to the European Parliament were held.

There were further elections in 1984 and 1989 and today the European Parliament consists of 518 members; eighty-one each from Britain, France, Germany and Italy; sixty from Spain; twenty-five from the Netherlands; twenty-four each from Belgium, Greece and Portugal; sixteen from Denmark; fifteen from Ireland; and six from Luxembourg. It is only fair to Britain to add at this point that in order to achieve some representation of both the Catholic and Protestant viewpoints held in Ulster, a form of proportional representation was used for the Northern Ireland seats in the 1979, 1984 and 1989 European Parliament elections, with a straight majority voting system for the remainder of the UK seats. Once elected, the MEPs act not as national delegates but broadly according to their political affiliations; thus, the British Socialists sit and vote with the German Socialists, and so on.

The Parliament is not permanently in session. It meets for various plenary sessions of about five days at a time each month – except in August – and these days all its sessions are held in Strasbourg. Initially, meetings were divided between Strasbourg and Luxembourg, but because the old Parliament building in Luxembourg proved too small for the MEPs of the enlarged, twelve-strong Community, it now meets only in Strasbourg. The headquarters and Parliamentary Secretariat are nevertheless still situated in Luxembourg, and between plenary sessions, many of the smaller, more specialized parliamentary committees hold their meetings in Brussels, so that inevitably there is a great deal of transportation and duplication of paperwork.

The Parliament is still not empowered to initiate legislation, except on a few minor budgetary items, and its power to call the Executive – i.e. the Council of Ministers – to account is still very limited. On the other hand, a two-thirds majority vote of censure (or vote of no confidence as it is known in Britain) is sufficient to topple the Commission. That this has never happened is probably due to the fact that although the European Parliament has the power to sack the Commission, it has to be the Commission in its entirety, it doesn't have any say in its replacement. That remains a matter for the governments of the individual member-states, and so there is little point in the Parliament attempting to sack the Commission.

So, in the last analysis, the Parliament's functions are advisory and, to a lesser extent, supervisory. The Commission tends to consult the European Parliament about proposed legislation, though neither the Commission nor the Executive (the Council of Ministers) is obliged to accept the European Parliament's decision, or even its advice − a situation which renders it virtually powerless and makes it a highly expensive luxury with which many people believe the Community could easily and profitably dispense.

Some increased powers of co-decision were accorded to the Parliament by the Single European Act but it is still far from being a Parliament like those of the individual member states.

Under the Single European Act, decisions on a number of matters, including for example any further enlargement of the Community, must be taken in consultation with the Parliament, and if Parliament rejects a majority decision of the Council of Ministers, the Council can go ahead with its decision only after securing a unanimous vote on the issue.

Probably the most useful function of the European Parliament is that it provides a forum where both the Commission and the Council − who take their decisions in sessions not open to the public or the press − can from time to time be called to account, and questioned, and required to explain the reasons for their decisions in public.

Thirdly, there is the Council of Ministers: all matters of real moment are finally decided by representatives of the twelve governments sitting in council. Members of the Commission take part in these discussions on an advisory, non-voting basis. Although normally known as the Council of Ministers (singular), meetings of the agricultural ministers, finance ministers, environment ministers and so on — which are known as technical councils, since they are involved with technical details of specific areas of Community co-operation — are so frequent as to be almost continuously in session.

Until 1974, the overall co-ordination of Community policies was the responsibility of the Council of Foreign Ministers, or the General Council. However, from time to time, when there were matters of major importance to be discussed, meetings of the General Council tended to become summits attended by all the heads of state. One such occasion was the meeting in Paris in October 1972, just before the United Kingdom, Denmark and Ireland were due to join the Community.

Since 1974, however, when the European Council was formed to provide a regular opportunity for the heads of the twelve governments to meet on a more regular basis, the European Council has largely taken over the business of making all major decisions on behalf of the Community as a whole, but the Council of Ministers remains the body which gives legal effect to these decisions.

And although meetings of the European Council tend to attract a lot of media attention by virtue of the very presence of all the heads of state, the Council of Ministers nevertheless does all the hard day-to-day decision-making on all the problems that constantly arise.

The President of the Council of Ministers changes every six months, from among the leaders or ministers of the twelve member-states, rotating in alphabetical order, according to the name of each state in its own language. Normally the president chairs all major Council meetings; meetings of the specialised technical councils are chaired by the appropriate minister or secretary of state from the country which happens to hold the presidency.

The President also represents the Council at meetings of the European Parliament, answering questions from the Parliament and reporting on the progress of all Council projects.

The system by which the Council votes was laid down in the various treaties; in general, the treaties envisaged a movement towards majority decisions. However, in practice, where particularly important or sensitive areas are under discussion, there has been a tendency to go for unanimous decisions.

Unanimous decisions would be preferred in such matters as the admissions of any new member-states, or any fundamental change in any of the treaties which, taken together, amount to the constitution of the Community.

When voting on matters not included in the original treaties — such as environmental policy — each member-state's vote is adjusted according to its size and relative importance. Thus, on this particular issue, Britain, Germany, France and Italy are currently each allotted ten votes; Spain eight; Belgium, Greece, the Netherlands and Portugal five each; Denmark and Ireland three; and Luxembourg two. Out of a total of seventy-six votes, fifty-four are required to constitute a majority — it is called a qualified majority — a measure which means that the smaller states cannot be outvoted automatically by the larger ones.

The Council of Ministers, or to be more accurate, the various councils of ministers, including the technical councils, rely to a great extent on work done by the permanent national delegations to the Community. The twelve Brussels-based missions consist of senior officials from the national administrations, most of them resident in Brussels, others commuting back and forth between Brussels and their home-countries. These form the Committee of Permanent Representatives (COREPER), and constitute another vast collection (currently the figure is 15,787) of highly paid *fonctionnaires*, some of whose salaries and expenses must be provided for, somehow, out of the Community Budget. It all amounts to an extremely expensive exercise.

The Council of Ministers also works very closely with the Commission. One of the Commission's prime functions is to mediate in disputes within the Council of Ministers, both in support of its own proposals and in an effort to reconcile opposing national positions. One of its great successes in practice has been the production of package deals containing elements which made the proposed projects acceptable to all the ministers involved.

The President of the Council of Ministers can also achieve more or less the same objective — and indeed some have — by means of skilful political persuasion.

Over and above these three bodies which effectively run the European Community — the Council of Ministers (and from time to time the summit meetings of the European Council); the Commission; and the European Parliament — there is a final Court of Appeal, the Community's Court of Justice, a permanent institution which sits in Luxembourg. Its function is to see that the constitution of the European Community — the treaties upon which it was based, and all the subsequent amendments that have been made to them — are correctly interpreted and uniformly implemented throughout the Community.

The Court consists of thirteen judges, one nominated by each member-state, plus one other, chosen by the four largest member states on a rotational basis, and the thirteen judges elect the President of the Court from among their own members, rather in the way that the College of Cardinals elects one of its number to be Pope. All decisions of the Court are taken in secret; a simple majority vote is final, and no dissenting opinions are subsequently published. The Court also employs six Advocates General, whose job it is to sum up each case before the court in public, and to give expert legal opinion on the issues involved before the judges retire to consider their verdict.

The Community has had its own European Investment Bank (EIB) in Luxembourg since 1958, with the member-states of the Community as its shareholders and the ministers of finance of the member-states as its Board of Governors. It is non-profit-making; its capital, subscribed by the member-states, is 14,400 million ECUs (European Currency Units). The ECU is a Community secondary currency made up of a basket of member-states' currencies, including the pound sterling, despite the fact that the United Kingdom resolutely refused until October 1990 to have anything to do with any form of European Exchange Rate Mechanism.

The European Investment Bank raises funds by borrowing on the international money markets and lends this money to be invested in projects, particularly improvements in the infrastructure of the member-states and of other states with which the Community has agreements, such as, for example the African, Caribbean and Pacific states which were signatories to the Lomé Conventions. In 1990, the Community and other interested states, including the United States, set up a new internationally funded investment bank to perform much the same service for former Iron Curtain countries. It works closely with the European Investment Bank in Luxembourg and may well be a pointer to the shape of things to come.

The Community was initially designed to be self-financing. Its revenue was expected to be based on the Common External Tariff on goods from outside the Community, the proceeds from customs duties, and a proportion of the VAT (value added tax), a common turnover tax which operates in slightly different ways in the different member-states; for example, books, food and children's clothing are zero-rated in Britain, while other countries have separate bands of value added tax, reduced, standard and luxury.

Another source of revenue includes the import levies on agricultural products from outside the Community, basically designed to shore up the income of farmers in the Community under the Common Agricultural Policy (CAP).

In practice, the policy of supporting the European Community farmers' standard of living with subsidies and levies and 'green' currency (under the CAP, when a member-state's currency is devalued, this does not affect the farmer; he continues to be paid at the old rate, in so-called 'green' currency) plus guarantees and quotas, has eaten up nearly three-quarters of the Community's total revenue and has several times brought it close to bankruptcy.

As I write, an agreement to reduce subsidies to farmers by 30 per cent, reached only after months of acrimonious discussions, seems likely to lead to a trade war between the European Community and the members of the General Agreement on Tariffs and Trade (GATT), an organization which represents more than 100 countries including the food-producing areas of

North and South America, as well as Australia and New Zealand. This in turn could lead to an economic war and possibly a world recession.

Despite all the indecision and confusion which has surrounded it since its inception, the European Community has not merely survived but has prospered; and it is now the most powerful single economic unit in the world. As early as 1982 its trade with the rest of the world represented 19 per cent of total world trade, as compared with 14 per cent for the United States and 8 per cent for Japan; it consumes about 25 per cent of the entire world's food products, including products from within the Community itself and it represents the biggest single consumer market with the highest potential spending power in the world. Well over 100 countries worldwide have now sent accredited diplomatic representatives to Brussels, and the Community had forged trading links with Communist China, the Soviet Union and the other Iron Curtain countries long before the Iron Curtain was torn down towards the end of 1989.

But from 1 January 1993 the new Singular European Community — marking the completion of a process started years ago to remove all trade barriers and turn the area into a true Common Market — will embrace and engulf The Twelve — Belgium, Denmark, France, Germany, Greece, Ireland, Italy, Luxembourg, the Netherlands, Portugal, Spain and the United Kingdom — twelve of the most idiosyncratic, awkward, opinionated, argumentative, inventive, cynical, destructive, proud, prejudiced collections of individuals you would be likely to encounter anywhere in the entire world.

It is now time to make their acquaintance, one by one, in the strict alphabetical order, not of the names of the nation-states, but of the people themselves, starting with the Belgians ...

THE BELGIANS

No Man's Land

BELGIUM IN PROFILE

Area	30,518 sq km
Population	9,900,000
Population density	323 per sq km
Women	51.2%
Under 15	19.3%
Over 65	13.7%
Language	Flemish, French, German
Religion	Predominantly Catholic
Labour force	41.7% of population
Employed in:	
Agriculture	3%
Industry	29.9%
Services	67.1%
Women in labour force	38.2%
Unemployment (as % of labour force)	12.6%

Major exports: Machinery and vehicles (25.7%); iron and steel products (13%); textiles and clothing (7%); chemicals (6%)

Main customers: EC (72.9%); USA (5.3%); Switzerland (2.4%); Sweden (1.5%)

THE BELGIANS

There is something of an anomaly in Belgium's current position as commercial and administrative capital of the European Community, headquarters of the Common Market and the North Atlantic Treaty Organization, and centre of a host of other European Community-related agencies such as EURATOM, FAST and CODEST (the European Development Committee for Science and Technology).

Belgium and the institutions situated there preside over what, since the sudden and seemingly total collapse of communism in the Soviet Union and her satellites in Eastern Europe in 1989, has become the most powerful combination of nations — more than half of them very highly industrialized — the world has ever known.

Indeed, there now even seems to be a possibility that the Eastern Bloc countries may want to become associated with the Community in some way, as do some of the other European countries which avoided or postponed joining the European Community until they saw how things were going, so that Brussels may well become the Washington of a future United States of Europe.

The anomaly, of course, is that Belgium didn't even exist as a separate state until 1830. Previously it had been figuratively, and very often literally, a No Man's Land, without even a proper name other than the vague and faintly pejorative one of the Netherlands, or Low Countries, sometimes in association with Holland and Luxembourg and Limbourg, and sometimes alone.

It is now one of the most highly industrialized, efficient, prosperous countries in the world, the dynamic centre of the biggest international trading unit in the world; its comprehensive rail network — the second in Europe after the United Kingdom, whose railroad pioneer George Stephenson was present at King Leopold's side for the inaugural departure of the first train from Brussels in 1835 — and its elaborate motorway system are so well-lit that they are frequently used to identify Europe from Outer Space, and can be clearly seen from the moon.

And yet it's not a country that would appear very high on anyone's list of places to be visited. One trouble is that it's very hard to find its real identity. It's not really famous for anything. It has no Eiffel Tower, no Tower Bridge, no Colosseum, no Parthenon, no Brandenburg Gate, no single feature instantly identifiable in the minds of the muddled masses of package-tourists that swarm all over the entire area of Western Europe every summer; if it's Thursday, then it must be Brussels, and isn't this the place that has a statue of a little boy pissing into a fountain?

Unfair? Unjust? Well, what is Belgium famous for? Happening to be there, in the right place, to provide the foreign fields where other, greater nations could clash in battle — Waterloo, Quatre Bras, Malplaquet, Mons, Ypres and all the others?

It is the only European industrialized nation which has never had its own marque of motor car. Unimportant? Not in a world in which a man's success or failure is almost invariably initially assessed by the sort of car he drives.

Belgium's great painters were all Flemish and are listed as such in most art catalogues for the very good reason that Belgium did not exist as such when they were painting and the Dutch claim a number of the borderline cases. The most famous of them all, Peter Paul Rubens was born in Germany and spent his formative years – from the time he was twenty-three years of age until he was thirty – in Italy. Belgium's two great popular entertainers of recent times, the novelist Georges Simenon and the singer Jacques Brel are believed by most people to be French.

The food in Brussels is as good as that in France, but Brussels has never been famous for its food. And while you can buy better chips at any street corner in any Belgian town than anywhere else, chips are always inescapably associated in the public mind with the British.

Even the Belgian people themselves have no recognizable national characteristic, apart from an inherent dullness which is as common, according to an Irish journalist who spent five years covering the EEC from Brussels, among the French-speaking Walloons who believe themselves to be witty and volatile and versatile, as it is among the Flemish-speaking people from Flanders who seem to take pride in the fact that they know themselves to be pious, taciturn, obstinate and worthy.

Talleyrand said: 'There are no Belgians, never were any, never will be any. There are French, Flemings or Dutch – the same thing – and Germans.'

Voltaire, writing from Brussels, commented: 'As for this dreary city where I am, it is the home of ignorance, of heavy dullness [*pesanteur*], of boredom, of stupid indifference. An old country of obedience, deprived of spirit, satiated [*rempli*] with faith.'

Clive James, the TV journalist, once referred to Belgium as the Canada of Europe.

On the other hand, *The Economist* remarked: 'If the Martian Institute for Fundamental Research were to focus its attention on Planet Earth and wonder where in Western Europe it would find the most effective answer to the economic threat from Japanese technology, there would be no doubt as to its conclusions. The Martians would choose Belgium, and with good reason, because this sturdy little country offers a range of advantages which no other country can equal.'

LAND AND PEOPLE

The Language Barrier

The country now known as Belgium consists of 30,518 square kilometres of land with a 67 kilometre coastline on the North Sea, and land frontiers with the Netherlands on the north, Germany and Luxembourg on the east, and France on the south-west. It is about the size of Wales or Maryland.

The low coastal plain — originally swampland desultorily drained and farmed in the Middle Ages — is now diked off from the sea and very fertile. The central plateau is also highly productive, but the land to the south, in the Ardennes — an ancient European mountain range worn down by time and erosion to a maximum height of 694 metres — is poor. Approximately one-half of the country consists of farming land and forests of no outstanding scenic distinction.

It has a maritime temperate climate like the British Isles, which means that it is usually dull and misty, and often chilly, with a good deal of rain.

When Julius Caesar's Gaul was divided into three parts, Gallia Belgica was one of them; that's where Belgium gets its name. The Romans held a very high opinion of the Belgae as redoubtable fighters; when Mark Antony reminded his listeners at Caesar's funeral of 'the day we overcame the Nervii', he was talking about a hard-fought battle in which the Romans were very nearly defeated by the Nervii, the most warlike of all the Belgian tribes, and lost all but 500 of their 60,000 strong army. Reinforcements came from England where the Belgae had established a settlement near Winchester under a king called Cunobeline (Shakespeare's Cymbeline).

The Belgae were a mixture of Germanic and Celtic Gauls who, some time shortly before Caesar's conquest of All Gaul, had settled in the area between the Seine, the Rhine and the North Sea as well as on the island which was to become Britain; and the Romans gave them the Latin language, which the Gallo-Romans later developed into French, and all the amenities of Roman civilization, plus, some time later, the debatable blessing of the Christian religion. However, for some unknown reason, north of an imaginary line drawn between Boulogne and Cologne (one possibility is that a long-forgotten line of Roman fortifications once lay along this boundary), the influence of the Roman Empire petered out and the people to the north of it continued to use variants of their ancient Teutonic tongue.

This language barrier runs bang through modern Belgium and has resulted in the division of the tiny country into three separate administrative areas: Flemish-speaking Flanders to the north, French-speaking Wallonia to the south, and a bilingual area around Brussels where both languages are spoken — Wallonia comes from a Roman word (Wala) for Romanized Celts. There is even a tiny area near the German border where about 1 per cent of the population speak German.

In effect, in Brussels, certainly since World War II, three languages are spoken: Flemish for patriotic reasons by people who originally came from Flanders; French because it was always the principal language of the city, and also happened to be spoken by many of the Eurocrats representing the various inter-European organizations such as the EEC, NATO, EURATOM, etc. which set up their headquarters in Brussels in the late forties and early fifties; and English because it was the only common language spoken or understood by the armies of international businessmen and bankers immediately attracted to what looked like becoming the capital of a United States of Europe.

The Flemings and the Walloons have remained obsessively determined to ensure that all road signs in their areas are written in the appropriate language, despite the confusion that this causes to the millions of non-Belgian tourists travelling through the country every year, as for example signposts directing you to Braine-le-Château which suddenly disappear to be replaced by signs pointing in the same way but now directing you to Kasteel-brakel (the same place, in Flemish).

Nevertheless, there are probably more bilingual and multi-lingual speakers per square kilometre in Belgium than there are anywhere else in Europe, and probably the world.

Belgium has almost no natural resources: some hard coal which is extremely expensive to mine because of geological faults, some sand, clay and stone quarries, and of course, the land itself — in particular its position at the very heart of Europe — and its people.

HISTORICAL PERSPECTIVE

Wanted: A King

When Charlemagne's Holy Roman Empire of the West was split up at the Treaty of Verdun in 843, no attempt was made to adjust political boundaries along the language boundaries, probably because the official language of Charlemagne's court was Latin, and nobody really cared what the peasants thought about anything. The treaty, which was the result of a quarrel between Charlemagne's sons, created the two separate states of Francia Occidentalis (France) and Francia Orientalis (Germany) — with the Netherlands, briefly known as Francia Media, in between them, to act as a buffer state. Thus Belgium's destiny for the next twelve centuries as the cockpit of Europe, the perpetual No Man's Land between the continent's warring empires, was firmly and formally established.

But the Verdun solution did not last long; the two Francias went their separate ways, and Pope John XII decided to bestow the crown of the Holy Roman Empire on Otto I, King of Francia Orientalis, and the most formidable of the warring Teutonic chieftains plaguing Europe at that period. Thus began the Holy Roman Empire of the German nation.

Right from the start, this empire was under constant attack from three sides. From the south, in Spain and North Africa, came the highly warlike and dangerous Moslems. The eastern frontier was liable to be invaded at any moment by multitudes of savage Magyars, Slavs and Tartars. The western coast was constantly being ravaged by expeditions of Norsemen in search of loot and women. The demand for strong leadership to protect these frontiers gave rise to the feudal system by which the Holy Roman

Empire soon became partitioned off into a multitude of small principalities, organized as fighting units by dukes, counts, barons and even in some cases bishops. These local lords assumed most of the rights and privileges of the Emperor over their own subjects in return for a promise of assistance in times of trouble.

Under this system, Francia Media (the Netherlands) soon devolved into principalities and prince-bishoprics — Liège, Flanders, Brabant, Hainaut, Namur, Luxembourg — each fiercely jealous of its own independence in the face of French or German suzerainty, and each seeking to extend its power and influence by war or by arranging suitable marriages; indeed, under the Dukes of Burgundy who held court at Brussels, in Brabant, during the fifteenth century the whole area of the Netherlands including Holland became known as 'the seventeen provinces'.

And it was as the seventeen provinces that the Netherlands became part of the Holy Roman Empire, following the marriage of Mary of Burgundy to Maximilian of Hapsburg towards the end of the fifteenth century.

Their son was in turn married to the heiress of Spain, and so began a period in which the seventeen provinces became in turn the Austrian and subsequently the Spanish Netherlands, exposed to the tyrannies of both the Austrian and the Spanish Hapsburgs. The latter introduced the Inquisition among other indignities and eventually the Protestant Prince of Orange felt obliged to embark upon a war of liberation.

By 1579, the seventeen provinces were split up, the southern Catholic Lowlands going to the King of Spain and the northern United Provinces — where the Reformation had proved a wild success and Calvinism had become the predominant religion of the region — forming an independent state, later to be known as Holland, or the Netherlands.

Belgium's history as a separate state did not begin until it was invaded and eventually annexed by post-revolutionary France. Napoleon's attempt to dominate Europe was finally and decisively terminated at Waterloo, about eighteen miles south of Brussels, and when the Allies who had defeated him met to carve Europe up yet again in 1815, they amalgamated Belgium and Holland into the United Kingdom of the Netherlands under the Dutch House of Orange, establishing Luxembourg as a separate grand duchy. They did this solely to prevent any further French expansion northwards and without any great regard to the wishes of the people, and of course it proved a disastrous failure.

The tactless Protestant Calvinism of William I, the King of the Netherlands, upset all the Belgians, but particularly the fervently pious Catholic Flemish in the north; you do not endear yourself to your subjects greatly by removing all the schools from church control in a country that is 95 per cent Catholic. His insistence on Dutch as an official language infuriated the French-speaking Walloons, who regarded French as a vastly superior language, and still do. His dislike of free speech and his distrust of a free press enraged all nine million of them because the Belgians, whatever language they happen to speak, have always valued freedom of speech and thought above almost everything else, except perhaps money and food.

By 1828 the younger Liberals and Catholics in William's southern provinces of the so-called United Netherlands had got together in a way that would have been impossible a generation earlier and decided that the time had come for them to show a united front. Catholic and Liberal newspapers started a combined opposition campaign to challenge William's right to treat Belgium merely as an annexed province. A revolution as sudden and unexpected as the 1989 revolution in Romania occurred almost spontaneously, it seemed, on 25 August 1830, when a crowd which had been listening to a patriotic operetta became so overcome with revolutionary zeal that they burst out into the street and began to loot and pillage and set fire to government buildings. Overnight, the bourgeoisie had formed a civil defence committee, declared a state of emergency and formed a civil guard to restore law and order.

Within three days, Brussels was, to its own amazement, under its own military jurisdiction with the Dutch police and military standing by, uncertain what to do, like the Chinese soldiers during the early days of the Tiananmen Square protest, some even allowing themselves to be disarmed. By the time William had reacted to the situation and sent in fresh troops under his son Frederick, it was too late.

After some fighting the troops withdrew and the ancient revolutionary flag of Brabant (black, red and orange like today's Belgian flag), which had been briefly brandished once before during a peasants' revolt in 1789, was raised again.

A provisional government was formed and the revolutionaries, having declared Belgium's independence, were minded to go for a full-blooded republic. Some of the fainter hearts, however, conditioned perhaps by all those centuries under one ruler or another, thought that this might try the patience of Europe's Crowned Heads too far. So they decided instead upon a liberal constitutional monarchy, and began to look around for a suitable candidate to whom they could offer the position of king of the new state.

The final choice was Prince Leopold of Saxe-Coburg, a forty-year-old member of the ruling family of one of Europe's smaller principalities, a family with, however, very good connections: Leopold had been married to Princess Charlotte, heir to the British throne who had died in childbirth, in 1817. He was English by culture — he was, in fact Queen Victoria's uncle — and as a widower he would be free to marry one of the French monarch Louis-Philippe's daughters, which seemed a convenient way of gaining the support of the pro-French Walloons. He was, it is true, a Protestant; on the other hand, any children resulting from this marriage would necessarily, as native-born Belgians, have to be brought up as Catholics. It was a perfect solution to the problem, probably prompted by Britain's Lord Palmerston.

Leopold I was made King of the Belgians on 4 June 1830, with a British guarantee of Belgium's territorial integrity which carried with it an obligation on Belgium to remain neutral in any future war.

The inhabitants of the new state didn't feel one whit different after the revolution; they still thought of themselves as coming from Ghent or Liège or Antwerp, rather than as Belgians. But their new king assumed command of the army, took over the direction of his country's foreign affairs, and succeeded in strengthening his ties with the other Crowned Heads by persuading his English niece Victoria to marry his nephew Albert; he had already arranged a marriage between another nephew, Prince Ferdinand of Coburg-Kohary, and the recently widowed Queen of Portugal. Yet another nephew, Prince Auguste of Saxe-Coburg, was married to the French King's daughter Princess Clementine and his niece Princess Victoria of Saxe-Coburg-Kohary was married to Louis-Philippe's son, the Duke of Nemours, a pretty neat piece of top-level, international nepotism.

By the middle of the nineteenth century Leopold was the most respected monarch in the whole of Europe.

COLONIAL CONNECTIONS

Now Wanted: An Empire

If, even sixty years ago, Belgium would have appeared to be the one country least likely to become the capital of a United European Community, the new state, when it became an independent kingdom in 1830 seemed even more unlikely ever to possess an overseas empire. And yet by 1885, Leopold's son Leopold II had acquired all 2.38 million square kilometres of the Congo, in Africa, an area almost eighty times the size of Belgium. Before long he was making himself one of the richest men in the world by ruthlessly exploiting it for its rubber and ivory, treating its inhabitants with a merciless cruelty that made the name of Belgium stink even in the fairly noisome annals of European colonialism.

He did this with the assistance of a very remarkable man. John Rowlands was born in Wales, worked his way across the Atlantic, changed his name to Henry Stanley and fought on both sides in the American Civil War before becoming one of the most famous journalists of all time. James Gordon Bennett of the *New York Herald* sent him to Africa to find Dr Livingstone, the celebrated British explorer and missionary, which he promptly did and thereafter made Africa his life. He discovered the source of the Congo after a journey that took 999 days and led directly to the carving up of that area of Africa by the European states.

In Belgium, Leopold II was restless; the country was not big enough to contain his fierce energy. He was fascinated by the accounts of Africa brought back by the explorers and sent an emissary to meet Stanley at Marseilles, on his return to Europe in 1878, and offer him a job. The job was to create an empire for Leopold in Africa, no less.

Stanley accepted, returned to the Congo and spent four years obtaining the signatures of some 300 African chieftains to various vague documents and treaties. The chieftains were immediately rewarded with bottles of gin and various of the other products of European civilization and their signatures guaranteed Stanley's boss, King Leopold II of the Belgians, certain concessions in return for the dubious benefit of the 'protection' offered by the flag of Leopold's recently formed philanthropic and Christian African societies.

As early as 1876, to prepare the way for this enterprising adventure, Leopold had invited an innocent-looking collection of explorers, geographers and people interested in Africa in a simple, well-meaning way to a conference at his royal palace in Brussels. The ostensible object of the exercise was to discuss how best they could open up the Dark Continent to the benefits and blessings of European Christian civilization, and thus thwart the plans of less high-minded European colonial powers.

To achieve this aim and also, again ostensibly, to abolish the slave trade and set up sociological research stations in Africa, he proposed an organization known as the International African Association (AIA), and became its first chairman. The flag of the AIA — a gold star on a sky-blue field — was planted by Stanley on African soil and under the cover of this innocent and innocuous-sounding organization, Leopold proceeded to carry out the next stage of his plan.

Stanley was by now setting up a series of stations along the Congo River to serve as centres from which the benefits of Christian civilization were to be distributed to the heathen. These stations would form the nucleus of a series of 'Free Negro Republics', under the auspices of the International African

Association and its equally innocent-sounding offshoot, the Comité d'Etudes du Haut-Congo, generally (and correctly) assumed to be the same sort of well-meaning but ineffective institution devoted to general do-goodery in Foreign Parts.

At the same time, Leopold also set up a company to control and exploit his projected empire in the Congo, under the confusingly similar name of the *Association Internationale du Congo* (AIC), which was an entrepreneurial finance corporation entirely under his own personal control, and of a very different nature.

He next set about trying to gain diplomatic recognition for the AIC; he did this by playing the Great Powers off against one another, representing his enterprise as a brave little effort on the part of one very small and weak neutral European state to save at least a corner of the vast African continent from exploitation by the wicked colonial Great Powers.

He tried the Americans first. When he pointed out to them that Portugal, backed by Britain (both of them nervous of further French expansion in Africa), was laying claim to the mouth of the Congo — which if successful would have been disastrous for his own plans for the area — Congress immediately recommended diplomatic recognition of what they genuinely believed to be a collection of new Negro states to be set up under the protective eye of a Belgian philanthropic Christian institution.

Leopold then turned to France, offering her a 'right of preference' should he ever decide to dispose of his AIC interests in the Congo, and in this way gained a French promise of friendly neutrality and eventual recognition.

This proposal frightened the daylights out of Britain and Germany, who were now prepared to support Leopold's Association of Negro Republics if only to ensure that France would never be able to use it to gain a firmer foothold in Africa. And at an international conference held in Germany in 1884 to discuss the matter, Bismarck as chairman welcomed the new Congo state and praised the King of the Belgians for his work.

The Belgian Parliament made it quite clear that they wanted no part of this deal but they authorized Leopold to take the title of

Sovereign of the Independent State of the Congo, and almost overnight the new monarch of Europe's smallest kingdom turned himself into absolute sovereign of a country the size of Western Europe.

He ruled it personally and without mercy. As early as 1885, a decree made all 'vacant land' in the Congo the property of the estate, in other words, Leopold's own personal property. The term vacant land meant in effect any land that Leopold wanted; because if it was not vacant, it was very easy to make it vacant by pushing the natives out into the bush, or by killing them.

Rubber and ivory, the two most valuable commodities in the Congo at that period — later vast copper reserves as well as uranium and other valuable chemicals were to be found in the area — became state monopolies, and Leopold enjoyed absolute proprietary rights over the whole country.

Leopold's agents, the representatives of a developed power in a very primitive area, resorted to the most horrifying atrocities in order to keep ever-increasing supplies of rubber and ivory coming in. Quotas were set, and African workers who failed to deliver their daily quota were mutilated or shot. Various estimates of the human cost of Leopold's African enterprise have been made; it probably came out at something between 5 and 8 million African lives.

The most brutal practice was that of mutilation. If an African worker did not satisfy his boss, a hand or a foot — or even both — would be hacked off. Africans had never used mutilation as a punishment; this was a purely European innovation — apart from everything else, it saved bullets and gunpowder. To prove their diligence, the white bosses would bring their superiors baskets full of amputated arms and legs, sometimes smoked to preserve them in that humid tropical climate. But that wasn't all: villages were burned, men flogged, women mutilated and children flung to the crocodiles *pour encourager les autres*.

Inevitably news of these goings on leaked out and there were protests from all over the world. The British sent Roger Casement, their consul at Boma, to investigate the matter, and when his report was published, Leopold was forced by the pressure of outraged public opinion to appoint a commission of inquiry to investigate the horrors.

Reforms were instituted, the atrocities ceased (though forced labour didn't) and in the end Leopold had to surrender his Congo Free State to the Belgian government. By this time the Belgian Government had become fully aware of the potential value of the colony and were no longer reluctant to take it over; in any event, in order to get the project off the ground, Leopold had been obliged to spend a great deal of money, which he didn't have. He managed to get it quite easily, simply by cheating the Belgian government.

One ruse was to pretend that he had borrowed 5 million francs from an Antwerp banker and had mortgaged a huge area of the Congo as a security. Reluctant to lose this valuable slice of the Congo, and anxious to avoid the shame of allowing the world to learn of their king's insolvency, the Belgian government gave him 6.5 million francs to pay the debt and tide him over; the debt of course, had been entirely fictitious.

On another occasion, Leopold had suggested to his government that in return for a substantial loan, he would publish a will bequeathing the entire Congo to the Belgian government. After ten years, the government could decide whether to take advantage of his gift or demand repayment of the loan. As the government was now fully aware that Leopold had made almost 3 million francs out of the Congo in the ten years between 1896 and 1906, they agreed enthusiastically to his suggestion of a loan on this basis.

Shortly before the Belgian government annexed the Congo from their king in 1908, when the full horrors of the atrocities had become public, he managed to con them into giving him yet a further grant of 2 million francs as a mark of gratitude for his work in Africa before the sky-blue flag of the AIC with its golden star was finally pulled down and packed away for ever.

The oldest bank in Belgium, the *Société Generale de Belgique*, through its holdings in the Congo copper company *Union Minière* effectively took over the task of running Leopold's empire and ran it with apparent efficiency and enlightenment; the copper mines of Katanga were a model of African paternalism, with hospitals, schools and housing of a far higher standard than anything in neighbouring Northern Rhodesia (now Zambia). But while they were happy enough to take vast dividends from the Congo, the *Union Minière* took no responsibility for the country's political future, and when the African wind of change led to riots in the Congo, Brussels agreed in January 1960 to give the Belgian Congo complete independence *within six months*, making no preparations whatever for what might happen after the withdrawal of the Belgian troops.

What did happen was a mutiny in the Congolese army in June. The European technicians and administrators fled from Leopold-ville to Brazzaville and Belgium had to send its troops back to the Congo. When Moise Tshombe, president of the mineral-rich Katanga province, proclaimed it a separate and independent republic, he was supported by the *Union Minière* whose *respons-ables* maintained that they could not interfere in what was purely a political matter. Despite appeals from the UN and the Belgian government, urging them to pay their taxes into the central government rather than to Katanga, the diehards of the *Union Minière* continued to subsidise Tshombe. It was not until the bitter end two years later that they would agree to come to terms with the central government of the Congo. In offloading their one colony in this thoughtless way, at the cost of thousands of lives, including that of the UN Secretary-General, Dag Hammarskjöld, the new constitutional monarchy at the heart of Europe added a new word to the dictionary, initially used by Trotsky: Belgianiza-tion, meaning the abandonment of all national responsibilities for the sake of purely commercial values.

Leopold's successor, his nephew Albert I, did a great deal to restore faith in the monarchy when in August 1914 the Kaiser dismissed the Treaty of London guarantee of Belgium's neutrality as a mere scrap of paper and demanded a free passage through Belgium for the German army, on its way to invade France. Albert refused, and the Belgian army fought resolutely until the end of October and then retired, still undefeated, to hold a narrow strip

of West Flanders between the Yser River and the French frontier
for the four years of the war. This was 'Free' Belgium, and Albert
had his headquarters at Veurne and made nearby De Panne his
capital. A committee of ministers ran the country as best they
could on his behalf from a government in exile at Le Havre,
France.

Leopold III, who succeeded Albert the 'soldier king' in 1934,
after his father had been killed in a climbing accident, didn't do
nearly as well. When on 10 May 1940 the Germans invaded the
Low Countries, he surrendered in less than a month, leaving the
Allies' northern flank completely exposed. He spent the entire
period of the German occupation as a fairly comfortable prisoner
of war in his own Laeken Palace in Brussels. When the Allies
invaded Europe, he was deported to Germany and didn't return to
Belgium for over five years, during which period Belgium was
ruled by a regent, his brother Prince Charles.

Despite his obvious unpopularity, he continued to refuse to
abdicate, living in exile in Switzerland until 1949, when in a
plebiscite 57 per cent of the population voted 'that the King
Leopold III should resume the exercise of his constitutional
powers' and 42 per cent voted against him.

Leopold considered this gave him a sufficient mandate and
returned from Geneva to Brussels, ignoring all the strikes and
protest marches and demonstrations all over the country, until
three demonstrators were killed at an anti-Leopold meeting in
Liège, and 100,000 demonstrators began to march on the
capital. When civil war seemed inevitable, he agreed to step down
and on 1 August 1950 he finally abdicated in favour of his son
Baudouin.

Baudouin himself abdicated for one day in 1990 on a matter of
conscience, when it became clear that his government was about
to pass legislation on the subject of abortion, which he, as a
Catholic, could not countenance. So when the bill had been
passed, in his absence, so to speak — since a king who has
abdicated could not be required to sign any state documents —
he returned to the throne.

Strange people, the Saxe-Coburgs.

DEVELOPMENT DIRECTIONS

From Blue Nails to Cobalt

In Belgium, agriculture still dominates almost half the total area of the country, but today employs only 2.45 per cent of the workforce, as against 6 per cent in 1966 and about a quarter around the turn of the century.

Throughout the more industrialized nations of the European Community, agricultural workers have been leaving the land and crowding into the cities at the rate of about half a million a year. Fortunately, however, intensive farming methods, the latest agricultural machinery and the efficiency of the modern Belgian farm worker have combined to produce a situation in which each agricultural worker in that tiny country now produces enough to feed eighty people.

Belgian farmers and market gardeners between them could provide more than 80 per cent of the country's entire food requirements, but of course it doesn't work like that these days. Belgium imports a great deal of food from all over the world – 70 per cent of it from other Common Market countries – and exports a great deal of its own farm produce – about 85 per cent – to the European Community.

The Belgians claim that the idea of intensive cultivation under glass was a Belgian invention. This may well be true because glass manufacture was among the country's earliest industries in the more commonly accepted use of the word industry. They also claim to have discovered endives, or chicory as it is called in Britain (the Flemish is *witloof*, meaning white leaf) and hold a minor record for the world's largest production of azaleas.

Long before Belgium became a nation, its cities were becoming well known all over the world, as trading centres. In *The Canterbury Tales*, written in the fourteenth century, Geoffrey Chaucer wrote:

> A good WIF of beside BATHE ther was,
> But she was ever somewhat def, allas.
> In cloth-makyng she had such judgement
> She passed them of Ypris and of Ghent.

Bruges had been a centre for the wool trade from the time of the Romans, and Flemish cloth was famous for both its texture and its colour; by the eleventh century the demand for Flemish woven material was so great that wool had to be imported from England, and almost every town in Flanders had a textile industry. Concentration on industrial production also had the consequence that as more and more people left the land — far earlier in Belgium than anywhere else in Europe — food had to be imported. The merchants who arrived there from Venice and Florence, from Spain and Germany and Brittany to trade the fashionable and consequently expensive Flemish textiles for grain from Germany, wine from France, spices from the East, upset the whole rural social system.

Feudalism in Europe had been based on the peasants, who were tied to their seigneurs' estates as serfs, producing food and cloth and performing other services in return for protection. They supplied only as much as their overlords' households demanded and they themselves required but they were not freemen and probably wouldn't have wanted to be.

The merchants had no such ties, nor did they occupy any real niche in the feudal pattern, and consequently they were accepted from the first as freemen, and their trading posts were given the status of free ports. Before long they had organized themselves into guilds strong enough to negotiate with the lords of the local manors; and among the many deals they made was one for the release from serfdom of certain skilled craftsmen. The weavers and shearers, the dyers and fullers of the cloth trade, known as 'blue nails' because working with the wool turned their hands blue, became freemen as soon as they left his lordship's service to go and work in the factories for the merchants. By the thirteenth century, taking into account the assistance given by the wives and children of all the freed craftsmen, possibly half the entire population of Flanders worked in industry, an extraordinarily high proportion for the Middle Ages.

Flanders was therefore probably the first industrialized area in Europe, in the sense that the textile craftsmen went to work in factories instead of weaving and spinning in their own homes, though the real industrial revolution didn't happen until machinery was invented to do the work that had previously been done by hand.

When it did come along, towards the end of the eighteenth century, the Industrial Revolution caught on far more quickly in Belgium than it did anywhere else in Europe, apart of course from the country where it started, England.

Feeding the growing communes engaged in cloth manufacture and metal-working — another Belgian specialty — led to a large-scale clearance of forests and the draining of the Flemish marshes; and the Belgian industries' dependence on raw materials and food from abroad made the country extremely sensitive to such upsets as wars, riots or revolutions.

And, naturally enough, the workers in Belgium's industries took a leaf from their betters' book and formed their own guilds; as early as the thirteenth century strikes began to become common as the 'blue-nails' clashed with the 'good folk' (the ruling classes) in an effort to get better working conditions.

In the face of worldwide competition, Belgium began to produce more tapestries, more linen, more lace and more glass, and specialized in printing and engraving — Caxton's first printed English book was produced in Bruges in 1475 — and the country has been closely associated with the development of printing ever since.

Belgium was not only the first continental European country to build its own railway system in 1835 but, like Britain, it pioneered railway systems all over the world: the Paris Metro, the Compagnie Internationale des Wagons-Lits et des Grands Express Européens, and the Orient Express were all Belgian ideas, as was the first railway in China, designed by Emile Franqua and Jean Jadot, both Belgians. More recently, the Metro in Metro-Manila is a Belgian enterprise; and so is the railway between Rabat and Casablanca in Morocco.

And though Belgium never had its own marque of car, its metal-working industry, the most important industrial sector with over 20 per cent of total national production, assembles more than a million motor cars a year, 93 per cent of which are exported, mostly within the Common Market.

Beer, glass, diamonds (both industrial and 'cut in Antwerp' for fashion wear), chocolate, paints, varnishes, resins and photo-chemical and pharmaceutical products are all high among Belgium's principal export products.

Which leaves cobalt. With the help of its former colony Zaïre (a part of what was once the Belgian Congo), Belgium is now one of the world's biggest producers of cobalt. Important? Yes, a bit. Cobalt is the metallic chemical element used in making most alloys, particularly those essential to jet engines and gas turbines, as well as in the manufacture of high-speed precision machine tools, as a pigment for making paint, as a radio isotope used in the treatment of cancer, and, industrially, as an isotope tracer. It's one of the elements the world can least do without, and Belgium controls 70 per cent of the entire world's production.

So what price Little Belgium now?

With 3,734 kilometres of railroad track and 15,350 kilometres of main roads, including the nine international motorways which pass through it, not to mention probably the most congested air corridors in Europe, it is perhaps not surprising that the entire country is heavily polluted with exhaust fumes. More especially when you consider that with 323 people to every square kilometre of territory, it has, next to the Netherlands, the highest concentration of humans for the amount of land available in Europe; the whole country is as crowded as the British industrial Midlands or the Ruhr Valley in Germany were sixty or seventy years ago. Most of Belgium's big cities are close together; Antwerp, Charleroi and Ghent are within forty-eight kilometres of Brussels, and Bruges is only ninety-six kilometres away from the capital.

Through the country flow several great rivers, the Meuse, the Scheldt, the Waal and their tributaries and canals, and it is this feature which made the area a natural outlet and market-place for the commercial traffic of Northern Europe, and initially attracted the interest of the area's neighbouring states in the Middle Ages.

Navigable waterways total 1,517 kilometres, about half of which can accommodate ships carrying more than 1,350 tonnes.

They link the principal industrial areas with neighbouring countries and with such seaports as Antwerp, Ghent and Zeebrugge. Antwerp alone handles 77 per cent of the maritime exports of the Belgian–Luxembourg Economic Union, with 300 shipping lines carrying goods to over 800 overseas destinations. Economic union between Belgium and Luxembourg was achieved as early as 1921. This agreement is still in force, within the European Community, the two territories being regarded as a single unit as far as customs and excise duties are concerned, and the Belgian franc is the official currency of both countries.

Brussels National is one of the busiest airports in Europe, Sabena, the Belgian international airline, has a telecommunications system which is among the most efficient in the world.

'Radio and television play a major role in the spread of culture,' says a government hand-out. Maybe. Is anybody greatly comforted by the knowledge that the capital city in the new European Community has twenty different TV stations and that thanks to an extensive cable network, Dutch, English, French and Italian transmissions are capable of being received by around 3 million Belgian TV sets?

AFFAIRS OF STATE

Compulsory Franchise

Belgium is a hereditary, constitutional, parliamentary monarchy much as Britain is, except that Britain has no constitution and the monarchy has far less power than in Belgium, where the king was initially commander-in-chief of the armed forces, though no longer actively so since 1949, and is still more or less effectively in charge of foreign affairs.

However, although the king reigns and enjoys considerable rights and responsibilities, he does not rule. He implements decisions of the legislative authority by royal decree, but no act of monarchy can be effective until countersigned by a minister. Equally, no ministerial decision can have any legal force until countersigned by the king.

The king may dissolve or prorogue parliament, he can appoint ministers of state, even from outside parliament (though only with parliament's approval), and he may dismiss them, whether they come from within or without parliament. He can accept or refuse to accept a minister's decision, and he appoints civil servants, magistrates and diplomats, though his prime duty is always to act as head of state.

Legislative power resides with parliament, which consists of two elected houses – the House of Representatives (212 members) and the Senate (178 members) – and no bills can become law until they have been approved by both houses and promulgated by the king. Election to these houses is on the basis of universal suffrage for both men and women over eighteen years of age – on a proportional representational, single vote system – and everybody is obliged to vote. Failure to turn up at the polling booth, unless you happen to be in possession of a medical certificate exonerating you, is an offence entailing a nominal fine approximately equivalent to five pounds. Once appointed, the judiciary are independent of the legislature.

So far as foreign policy is concerned, Belgium goes along with the big league. Belgium has always voted for European unity, the Atlantic Treaty Alliance, détente, disarmament and the development of European co-operation. It was among the founders of the United Nations Organization and the first Chairman of the UN General Assembly was the Belgian statesman, Paul-Henri Spaak.

The headquarters of NATO is situated in Belgium and the country commits 2.24 per cent of its GNP to defence, with conscription for 10–12 months for young men of military age. The total strength of its armed forces is about 97,000 (out of a total population of about 9.8 millions), two-thirds of these being professional soldiers.

Since 1970, the Central Government has devolved some of its powers to the communities and even to the regions. Thus the Flemish, French and infinitesimal German-speaking communities manage their own cultural affairs. The Flemish, Walloon and Brussels regions also look after most of the social, economic and administrative matters in their own areas, as indeed do the nine provinces, through the nine Provincial Councils, also elected by universal suffrage.

What all this adds up to, in Belgium, is a reassuring amount of genuine democracy.

Belgium has a working population of over 4 million or 42.6 per cent of its total population. The labour force is one of the most highly trained in the world, and seven out of ten workers belong to a union, but there are very few strikes; in an average year, fewer than three man-hours per worker are lost. The working week is established by law at forty hours but most Belgians work only a thirty-eight-hour week, with an annual holiday of four weeks on *double* pay.

Medical facilities are among the best in Europe with the number of hospitals, doctors, dentists and nurses per head of the population well above the European average (for example, Belgium provides one hospital bed per 107 inhabitants as against the UK's one per 133 and Greece's one per 167, and one physician for every 371 inhabitants as against one for every 494 in France and one for every 795 in Ireland).

Since the nineteenth century Belgium has had a comprehensive social security system based on the principle that well-being must be shared by all. It covers family allowances (Belgium was the first country in the world to provide child allowances for all families with dependent children), student grants, health insurance, unemployment benefit and retirement pensions. Contributions provide about three-quarters of the capital, one-half coming from the employers, and one-quarter from the employee; the remaining quarter is paid by the state.

Almost alone in the Community, Belgium has a system of child allowances, sickness insurance and old age pensions for the self-employed, which aims at achieving uniformity between industrial employees and the self-employed.

CULTURE AND LEISURE

Miniatures and Mercator

Both religious freedom and absolute freedom of education are guaranteed by the Belgian constitution. Approximately 60 per cent of the population are Catholics, but ministers of the Anglican and other more evangelical Protestant Churches as well as of the Jewish and Islamic faiths are paid by the state.

Between the ages of two and a half and eighteen, Belgian children attend kindergarten, nursery, primary and secondary schools, as well as specialized establishments for technical and vocational education or to study music and the arts. The country has two educational networks: the state system, which accounts for 43 per cent of the country's 2.2 million students, and the free system (predominantly Catholic) with 57 per cent of the total. This double-layer system is necessarily expensive.

There are eight universities, the best known of them in Ghent (Dutch-speaking), Liège (French-speaking) and Louvain (a Catholic university founded in 1425).

The most famous of a number of works by artists from Brabant, Hainaut and Limbourg for the French court is probably the exquisite series of miniatures, *Les Trés Riches Heures du Duc de Berri*, by the Limbourg brothers. Flemish painters specialized in miniatures and Jan van Eyck is probably the best-known miniaturist, though it is now generally agreed, even among Belgians, that he was not, as was once claimed, the inventor of oil painting. Among his pupils were Petrus Christus and Rogier van der Weyden. The influence of Flanders was paramount in the religious paintings of Germany, Portugal, Spain and Naples in the fifteenth and sixteenth centuries and the School of Bruges attracted men like Hans Memling from Mainz and Hieronymus Bosch, now claimed by the Dutch.

Modern Belgian painters include James Ensor, the forerunner of Expressionism, and the Surrealists Paul Delvaux and René Magritte. César Franck is the only internationally well-known Belgian composer.

Flemish literature includes the world's first eye-witness reports on the royals, Froissart's chronicle of the goings-on at the Burgundian court in Brussels. The poet and dramatist Maurice Maeterlinck won a Nobel prize for literature, Georges Simenon gave us a Belgian detective as celebrated as Sherlock Holmes if a bit more taciturn, and Georges Hergé created the strip cartoon Tin-Tin.

Belgium has also contributed more than her fair share to the sciences. Mercator, a geographer from Rupelmonde near Antwerp, gave seamen the first simplified, cylindrical projection of the world upon which navigators could plot their voyages accurately, using the compass to establish direction for the first time. On a Mercator projection, the directions are invariably impeccable, but the areas are often outrageously wrong; for example, Greenland looks roughly the same size as Africa.

In more recent times, Belgium has made distinguished contributions in various aspects of cancer research, particularly in the development of the interferon protein. Three Belgian scientists have been Nobel prizewinners: Professors Claude and de Duve in 1974 for physiology and medicine, and Professor Prigogine for chemistry in 1977.

Belgium throughout history has on the whole, though, been more famous for its visitors than its natives. Among the most distinguished of them: Erasmus, the Dutch scholar; the Englishman, William Caxton, who printed his first book in Bruges in 1475; Breughel the Elder, Durer and Holbein, the artists; and Sir Thomas More, the writer who made the gardens of his lodgings at Antwerp the background for his *Utopia*.

Belgian architecture is undistinguished; the Grand Place in Brussels where the ornate headquarters of the ancient guilds are situated is worth seeing if you happen to be in the capital, but is hardly worth making a special trip for, and there are better examples of medieval architecture and crusaders' fortresses elsewhere in Europe.

The Belgians eat a lot. 'We don't think a meal is worth eating unless there's a lot of it,' is a common comment. Beefsteak, and chips washed down with beer is probably the favourite national dish. For special occasions, everybody drinks wine, though the country produces hardly any.

Southern Belgium is France's best foreign customer for the wines of Burgundy. The Flemish have always preferred claret, imported by sea from Bordeaux to Antwerp. But all sorts of wines are available throughout Belgium.

Beer is the national drink and most of the Belgian beers are lager-type, mainly mass-produced. Specialties include the heavy half-wheat, half-barley Gueuze and Lambic, and a cherry-flavoured Kriek so bitter that it is usually sipped through a lump of sugar.

Belgian food is extremely good and extremely rich — like a combination of French regional cuisines, Périgord, Provençale, Armoricaine — and meals in cities like Brussels are about as expensive, or as cheap, according to the way you look at it, as they are in any capital city. In fact, one of the effects of the New Singular Europe, even before it has come into official existence, has been a general levelling out of prices and standards all over the western part of the continent.

Soup, particularly *chervil*, is popular all over Belgium and in some restaurants is served in bowls large enough to make a meal in itself. The Ardennes region is celebrated for its distinctive pâté and smoked ham, and also provides many varieties of game, including wild boar, venison and hare. Beer is used a great deal in cooking, and seafood specialities include young (*au vert*) eels, oysters from Ostend and trout from the Ardennes. You can buy chips at every street corner and also *gaufres* (*wafel* in Flemish), a form of pancake with a wide choice of fillings.

Pigeon-fancying, of all things, is extremely popular with the Belgians and several journals devoted to that bizarre sport are published. Brass bands, more a leisure activity than a sport, and archery are also among the top pastimes in Belgium, as well as cycling. The Belgians are very nearly as keen on cycling as a competitive sport as the French, and cycling champions enjoy the same status with schoolboys as football champions do in England.

Football is also popular, principally as a spectator sport.

On the other hand, if you happen to live in Belgium, on mainland Europe, with half a dozen of Europe's trunk motorways running through your country, you can indulge in any sport that appeals to you. You can get into your car and drive to the Alps for a weekend's skiing, or take your sailboard down to Lake Maggiore, or go to Amsterdam for the strip clubs and the sights of the red light district, and be back home in time for work on Monday morning.

THE BRITISH

Not a Very United Kingdom

BRITAIN IN PROFILE

Area	244,111 sq km
Population	56,600,000
Population density	232 per sq km
Women	51.3%
Under 15	19.5%
Over 65	14.8%
Language	English, Welsh, Gaelic
Religion	Mainly Protestant, but 35% Catholic in Northern Ireland
Labour force	48.1%
Employed in:	
Agriculture	2.6%
Industry	32.4%
Services	65%
Women in labour force	42.1%
Unemployment (as % of labour force)	12.1%

Major exports: Machinery and transport equipment (34.4%); manufactured goods (26.5%); mineral fuels (21.6%); chemicals (11.3%)

Main customers: EC (47.9%); USA (14.4%); Canada (2.3%); Australia (1.7%); New Zealand (0.5%)

THE BRITISH

It has to be the British. There simply isn't another word for the people of the United Kingdom as a whole, not that it ever has been a whole, nor even particularly united for that matter.

The Welsh Celts were not conquered by the Anglo-Norman kings of England until 1282 and even then could only be ruled from a string of stout castles built along the Welsh border. The Welsh resented the English then and they resent them still, and would happily break away if they could make an independent Wales a viable proposition. In the meantime, they try to get their own back, whenever they can, on the Rugby football field, or by burning down English holiday homes in Wales.

The Scots were mostly Celts who had emigrated there from Ireland; nobody seems to know for certain where the Picts, who were already there, had come from; they were probably pre-Celtic aboriginals. Together, they constantly rebelled against all attempts to rule them from south of the border.

Then, on the death of Queen Elizabeth I in 1603, they suddenly found themselves being ruled from London willy-nilly, and by one of their own Scottish Stuart monarchs. King James VI of Scotland was the only son of Mary, Queen of Scots, who had been executed for her part in a plot to assassinate Elizabeth, and take her place on the throne. He became King James I of England when he succeeded Elizabeth.

The Scottish Nationalists are still pressing for an independent parliament of their own, and even the most conservative of Scots are in favour of some measure of devolution.

Apart from England itself, the only other ostensibly 'loyal' part of this not very United Kingdom is the area known as Northern Ireland. This consists of six of the counties of Ulster, the predominantly Protestant area which the Unionists pressured Lloyd George into partitioning off from the rest of Ireland in 1921 after the Easter Rebellion of 1916 and the War of Independence of 1919–21. It contains about 1 million Protestants, the descendants of Cromwellian soldiers and Lowland Scottish settlers, of whom a vociferous and recalcitrant minority are violently pro-British and anti-Catholic, plus about half a million Catholics, most of whom believe they would be happier under a Dublin government.

The 'state' of Northern Ireland proved a disastrously unviable proposition economically and could only be maintained with the aid of massive subsidies from Westminster. Politically it has always been intrinsically unstable, and since the present troubles flared up in 1969, it has required the presence of up to 50,000 armed police and British soldiers to keep the peace. The cost, up to August 1989, the twentieth anniversary of the arrival of the troops in Belfast and Londonderry, added up to 2,700 lives (British and Irish, from bombs, bullets, hunger strikes and other abominations) in what at times amounts to almost total civil war.

Until May 1973, Northern Ireland had its own parliament with a limited autonomy, but all efforts by successive British prime ministers to persuade the Ulster Unionists to give the Catholics a fair share in running the place failed abysmally. Consequently, since 1973, the 'province' – as the Ulster Unionists insist on calling it, through it is only two-thirds of a province – has been under direct rule from Westminster, and a solution to the Irish Question seems to be as far away as ever.

But whereas in Northern Ireland you will find plenty of people who are proud to call themselves British, it is not easy to find many

people in England who will admit that they are English.

Ask anyone you meet in a pub and you're likely to get an answer like: 'Good God, no. My father was Irish and my mother's family originally came from Cornwall'. I had forgotten to add that the Cornish people don't regard themselves as English either, but as pure Cornish, a totally separate race; this goes back to the time of the arrival of the Anglo-Saxons when pockets of Celtic Ancient Britons survived and maintained an independent existence in Wales and Cornwall. In all the years I've lived in London, I can only think of one man I met who admitted being English and proud of it, and he always added: 'By that I mean of course Anglo-Saxon. Not a drop of Norman or Danish blood, so far as I'm aware.'

And yet the English, as well as the British in general, have so many things of which they can be so proud, and justifiably.

The greatest empire the world had ever seen, the empire on which the sun never set, did not last very long certainly, and the winds of change which swept it all away left in their wake many problems as insoluble as Ireland's; all over Africa and India, in Cyprus and Aden and Israel, in the Middle East, the Persian Gulf and Hong Kong. Everywhere the British ever set foot really, apart from North America, where the rebels had the only decisive victory ever achieved in war waged on Britain from inside or outside the empire. And apart from Australia and New Zealand of course, both too far away for any untoward interference from Whitehall.

Perhaps their natural reluctance to acknowledge any guilt over such matters also makes the British a little reticent in claiming credit for achievements about which any other nation would certainly boast. Or it could be that they feel it is unnecessary to boast about things which are so clearly capable of speaking for themselves?

I'm not thinking of the spread of Norman culture, the glories of cathedrals like Salisbury, Ely, Canterbury, York and Winchester, nor of landmarks on the road to democracy like the Magna Carta, habeas corpus, the Mother of Parliaments and Hampden and Pym, nor of the dreaming spires of Oxford, nor the splendours of English literature from Spenser and Shakespeare to Dickens and

Wordsworth, nor even of the fact that, until the day before yesterday almost, no innocent man need ever walk in fear of the unarmed British Bobbies, so-called after the founder of the force, Sir Robert Peel.

I'm not even thinking of Britain's ability to produce an endless succession of indomitable characters, from Boadicea to Churchill (and indeed many would include Thatcher), or of the nation's ancient valour which may stem from the fact, as many of her enemies have argued, that the British may lose hundreds of battles and yet they never lose a war, because they never accept defeat. At Waterloo, Napoleon remarked: 'This man Wellington is so stupid that he does not know when he is beaten and goes on fighting.'

I'm thinking about more recent developments, since the Industrial Revolution in fact. You could perhaps even include the Industrial Revolution, which started in England, except that it could be argued that, by and large, the results of the Industrial Revolution have not been altogether and universally beneficial to humankind. Britain's contributions, however, to the comfort and convenience of humanity in developed societies in the wake of that event have been spectacular.

Let's just take a few at random. The railway train, the jet aircraft, radar, television, the hovercraft, the fax machine, etc., etc. You could go on almost indefinitely.

Or firsts. The first to fly the Atlantic, the first to climb the highest mountain, the first to introduce the concept of the Welfare State, the first civilian police force, the first mass-circulation popular daily newspaper, the first four-minute mile, the first ... again, you could go on indefinitely.

Or bests. For example, the Rolls-Royce/Bentley, unquestion-ably the best motor in the world. Other countries have built faster, flashier, more sporty models, but nothing to touch a Roller for sheer comfort, style, quality, reliability and class. The Savile Row suit, another quality product, is instantly recognizable anywhere and impossible to obtain anywhere else. Purdy guns, Burberry raincoats, Marks and Spencer, the BBC; the list of British bests is endless.

But if the British do not boast about all these achievements because they feel that they are so obviously outstanding as to require no further endorsement, how do we explain their failure to follow up the innovations of their own inventors? Why, when the British invented television, did they allow its development to be taken out of their hands first by the Americans and later by the Japanese? Why, having invented the jet aeroplane engine, did they allow the Americans to dominate the production of large passenger-carrying planes?

Possibly, they were prisoners of their own past, trapped in a sort of instinctive conservatism of thought. How else could you explain why the British, having taken the huge step of developing the jet engine from nothing, should then balk at taking the next logical step? Which was, of course, the possibility of positioning the engines anywhere on the plane, rather than in the traditional position, close to the centre of gravity, where the engines had to be situated in planes that actually flew instead of being hurtled through the air by the thrust of the jets?

The French immediately grasped the significance of this, and stuck the jet engines on to the tail of their Caravalle, in a position where they were readily accessible for repair and maintenance. The Americans mounted theirs on fins under the wings of their 707s and DC8s, in an equally convenient place for removal or repair.

Pioneers always pay a heavy penalty for coming in first, of course, because once something has been invented it is comparatively easy to see its shortcomings and to improve on it. In this way, the British have constantly lost out on their own innovations to other nations.

The fax machine is a good example of the way in which the British will invent something and then allow others to exploit it. It was originally developed in England, as a convenient means of transmitting the complete layout of a newspaper page by wire, between London and Manchester, but when the print unions started to create difficulties about accepting this innovation, the British immediately sold the idea to the Japanese and the rest is history. But the original idea was 100 per cent British.

A problem which sorely besets the British is their extreme reluctance or perhaps their inability to speak other languages. This didn't matter all that much in the great days of the expansion of British colonialism; in any event, it wasn't as prevalent then as it is today.

Many of the Victorian travellers who did the Grand Tour could manage to make themselves understood in several European languages, and a great many of the Indian civil servants and military administrators spoke a number of Indian languages and dialects very fluently. The same was true of West and South Africa.

It is perhaps only since the end of World War II, and the foisting of some form of American English on most of the rest of the world as part of the price of a share in American aid that the British, by and large, have lapsed into a sullen inability to cope with foreign languages. Once American English had become the *lingua franca* of a world recovering from a debilitating war, it was possible for British tourists, businessmen and even, I suspect, diplomats to get through their day by repeating, very loudly and at frequent intervals: 'If you don't understand me, then please take me to someone who does.'

Recently, however, this system has broken down completely, for the reason that most Europeans and Asians, including many Japanese, have become completely fluent in English. An English salesman who used to be able to conduct enough business to get by in English or some form of pidgin English, now finds that his clients are perfectly capable of talking to him in his own language without losing control of the situation, whereas he is quite incapable of meeting them even half-way on their ground.

The average British businessman's ability to grasp foreign languages was described as 'frightening' in a survey carried out by the British Institute of Management, published in March 1991. According to this survey fewer than half of the 3,000 sample businessmen tested could understand a simple business letter written in French and only 14 per cent could understand a letter written in German. Only one in twenty could make out a letter in Spanish.

Their ability to reply was even more abysmal. Less than a quarter felt that they could write back in French, only 9 per cent felt that they could cope in German and only 2 per cent said they could manage a reply in Spanish. The survey was called *Bonjour Europe*!

Another big change which has overtaken the British in a couple of generations is in their attitude to foreigners and indeed, to abroad, generally.

While, a century or so ago, their betters went on Grand Tours or wintered in Nice or Cannes or Tuscany, sketching the landscape and practising their French and Italian by chatting with all the people with whom they came in contact, the lower middle classes and what used to be called the working classes were perfectly happy to spend their holidays at some dismal resort somewhere along the bleak British coast.

Now they travel the world, booking package tours to the Seychelles, safari trips into the African bush, or cruises down the Nile, and buying up cottages and chalets and châteaux in the Dordogne, the Costa del Sol and the Algarve. They have the same insatiable appetite for travel as their Victorian predecessors from a very different slice of society but, unlike them, they rarely mix with the natives other than in the capacity of waitresses, waiters and shop assistants. Consequently, they learn absolutely nothing about the people among whom they elect to spend their vacations or their retirement years, mixing resolutely and almost exclusively with other English tourists and fellow-retirees.

The English class system, as it has developed in the affluent society of the second half of the twentieth century, is another curiously British institution. Most countries have their aristocracy, their bourgeoisie, their artisans and their peasants, but in no other country I believe is the middle class divided into so many wafer-thin sub-strata, recognizable only to those within that slice and to those immediately next to it on either side. Thus there are members of what might be described as the lower lower middle class and members of the upper upper working class who are absolutely indistinguishable from one another but who nevertheless believe themselves to be as different socially as they imagine the Duke of Westminster to be from his dustman.

This difference manifests itself in all sorts of small things, like the schools attended by their children, the precise model and registration plates of the motor cars they drive, the relative expensiveness of their kitchen equipment, and the toys which they buy, not actually for their children, but so that their children can carry the tradition of fine class distinction on into the next generation. In this enterprise, naturally, they are greatly assisted and encouraged by shops and stores, by the newspapers and magazines and above all, by the ads on the telly.

In the last analysis, probably the finest thing about the British is that they are in general a fair-minded, honest and basically liberal people. Honest to an amazing degree.

When I came to live in London first in 1959, I was staggered by the fact that the newspaper-seller outside Charing Cross station could leave his pitch for a cup of tea at rush hour knowing that his clients would take their *Evening Standard, Star* or *News*, and deposit exactly the right amount of money in the cardboard box he had left there for that purpose, even if necessary depositing a half-crown coin, and taking the correct change from the pennies and sixpences and shillings already there. No newspaper-seller would have been able to do that in Dublin then, nor in Paris, nor in Rome. (At best, people would have helped themselves to free copies of the paper, but, more likely, someone would have stolen the day's takings.)

As well as honest, the British are fair-minded, almost to a fault. Their national game of cricket is based on a sense of fairness not present, so far as I know, in any other sport.

Over the years, politicians have learned how to play on this innate British fairness of mind. When the Catholic writer Hilaire Belloc decided to go into politics as a Liberal MP for Salford, he was advised by his supporters and his campaign manager to make no reference at all to the fact that he was a Catholic, since this might alienate a predominantly Protestant electorate.

But Belloc was a better politician than any of them. He stood up and began his first campaign speech by announcing: 'Gentlemen, I am a Catholic. As far as possible, I go to Mass every day. This (taking a string of rosary beads from his pocket) is a rosary. As far as possible I kneel down and tell these beads every day. If you reject me on account of my religion I shall thank God that he has spared me the indignity of being your representative.'

After a moment or two of stunned silence, there was a burst of deafening applause. And the fact that he was elected with an overwhelming majority says far more about the essential fair-mindedness of the British than any other example I can bring to mind.

LAND AND PEOPLE

True Blue Ancient Britons

The United Kingdom consists of one very large island which comprises England, Scotland and Wales, and part of a smaller island separated from it by about 100 kilometres of rough Irish Sea — it's basically the Atlantic, split apart by encountering the island of Ireland and meeting again in the middle of the narrow space which cuts off the latter from Great Britain.

The total UK area of 244,111 square kilometres also includes six of the counties of Northern Ireland still run by Westminster, hundreds of islands all around the coast, as well as two offshore groups north of Scotland (the Shetlands and the Orkneys), the Scilly Isles to the south-west of Cornwall, and the Isle of Wight just across the Solent from Southampton. There are also the tiny Isle of Man in the Irish Sea and the Channel Islands in the English Channel between Devon and Normandy. Both the Isle of Man and the Channel Islands are largely self-governing and outside the European Community except for customs purposes and for certain aspects of the Common Agricultural Policy.

If you were to draw a diagonal line from the border between Devon and Cornwall to England's North Sea border with Scotland, you would find all the mountains in the British Isles roughly to the north of that line, up the spine of England, in Cumbria (the Lake District), in Wales, Ireland and Scotland and in the Scottish Isles. The mountains are all very old, and none of them is very high. The highest peaks are between 1,000 and 1,342 metres high. South of this line, most of the land is extremely fertile and has been extensively farmed for centuries.

English, basically Anglo-Saxon, with words borrowed from Latin and Greek, Norman and modern French, Danish, and a very few from Gaelic, is spoken universally, though a couple of forms of Gaelic, the ancient language of the Celts, are still spoken in Wales and in parts of Scotland. Accents and dialects vary widely; what Prince Charles refers to as 'a hyse' would be called 'a howse' by most middle-class people, 'a hoose' by a Scot and 'an 'ass' by the Cockneys.

In prehistoric times this whole area was part of the Eurasian continent, and even as comparatively recently as 18,000 years ago a wide plain joined England and the Low Countries. The Thames and the Rhine probably met in the centre of this plain, and flowed northwards as one river to join the ocean.

But there had been signs of life in the area that became Britain even earlier than that. Part of the skull of a woman found in the Thames Valley established that she came from Pithecanthropic Neanderthal stock and had lived there over 150,000 years ago, in one of the sub-tropical intervals between the successive Ice Ages.

These intervals proved highly important to Britain's future because it was this recurring pattern of sub-arctic and sub-tropical conditions which led to the decay of the forests which, buried under the weight of the centuries, were to turn into the rich seams of coal upon which the country's industrial supremacy in the nineteenth century was based.

Subsequently, other minerals were discovered, and in the late sixties and early seventies of this century, considerable natural gas and oil deposits were found under the North Sea off the eastern coast of England and the northern coast of Scotland, with the result that the United Kingdom is virtually, or could be, completely self-sufficient in energy terms.

By far the most impressive relic of the Megalithic Age in Britain is the immense stone circle at Stonehenge, a shrine dedicated to worship of the Sun God and completed around 2250 BC by thickset, round-headed invaders from the Iberian Peninsula who were eventually absorbed, as so many of their successors were, into the British race.

By this time copper and tin had been discovered in Britain and blended to make bronze which was exported to the continent and thus became the country's first industrial enterprise. A Bronze Age began which lasted from about 1000 BC to around 400 BC; in the meantime, around 650 BC the country was again invaded, this time by the first wave of Celts who introduced the plough. Later waves of Celts, warriors of Indo-European stock originally from the steppes of central Europe, arrived and with their iron swords very easily conquered their bronze-armed predecessors.

They came to Britain from north-eastern France, from the Low Countries and from Brittany, and they settled in Lincolnshire and Yorkshire, at Glastonbury in Somerset and in the Severn and Wye valleys and Wales.

The most warlike and powerful group, the Belgae from what later became Belgium, settled in Hampshire and Wiltshire and had as their tribal stronghold a place later called Venta Belgarum by the Romans, and later still Winchester, the capital of Anglo-Saxon England.

These Celts had chariots and cavalry, and painted themselves blue with woad, to give themselves a more frightening aspect in battle; they were formidable fighters. They were druidic, with magicians and witch-doctors, and they believed in the efficacy of burying a live child in the foundations of a building for good luck, among other forms of human sacrifice.

They were the Ancient Britons of the history books we studied at school.

And when, in August 55 BC, Julius Caesar set sail from northern France with two legions to conquer Britain, it was these Celts who crowded the crests of the cliffs of Dover and drove their chariots out into the surf to repel his advance. Their stout efforts at resistance were useless against the force of Roman arms and discipline, and though Caesar left again after a fortnight, he returned the following year with five legions, and the Romans ran what they called Britannia for over three centuries, introducing to the island civilization in all its disparate details from the long, straight Roman roads and the strict Roman laws to the civilities of centrally heated villas, heated swimming pools and the delicious products of the vine.

They also introduced Christianity (to the Roman Britons) and taxes. The British didn't mind paying taxes, Tacitus reported, provided that they were fair. I think the same thing is probably true today; they certainly do not go to the extreme lengths to which other Community people, such as the Italians, will go to avoid paying taxes.

The Romans only pulled out of Britain when the barbarians started to threaten the Roman capital of Londinium, by which time the country was being invaded by waves of Angles, Saxons and Jutes — Germanic tribes whose warriors rowed across the North Sea in longboats.

In AD 306, the legions of York chose Constantine, a Roman Briton, to defend them from the barbarians. But Constantine proved to be far more of a Roman than a Briton and stripped Britannia of some of its legions to march on Rome to try to secure the capital of the empire for himself. On the march, he embraced Christianity, and soon after his arrival in Rome, set up a rival empire in Byzantium, changing its name to Constantinople (now Istanbul).

The Saxon conquest represented no more than a change of masters for the British as a whole, and the Saxons, and the Jutes and the Angles, from whom the term England (Angleland) evolved, soon became absorbed into the British race, though in the process the invaders injected a new element of Teutonic iron. The Danes, in their turn, were equally easily absorbed, though there were Danish kings on the English throne for nearly forty years. And so too, in their turn, were the Normans, though they changed the face of Britain and of the whole of Europe.

In more recent times, Britain has managed to absorb and assimilate wave upon wave of immigrants — Huguenots, Irish, Middle Europeans, Indians, West Indians, Kenyan Indians,

Pakistanis, Arabs, Greeks, Turks, Cypriots, Italians, Maltese, West Africans, etc., etc. – in such numbers that in some British schools, not only is English a minority language in the playground, but parent–teacher meetings at which parents might reasonably expect to air their grievances about such situations often have to be conducted in Pakistani or Arabic. To suggest that they might be bilingual or even held in English, the language of the country, would be considered 'racist'.

These new immigrants have been arriving at the rate of about 50,000 a year. By 1989 it was reckoned that in the Birmingham area at least one school-leaver in five was black, and the Muslims had started demanding segregated schools and even changes in the law to accommodate Muslim fundamentalist practices.

At the last available breakdown into ethnic groups in 1985, the count was Whites, 50,798,000; Indians, 791,000; West Indians, 503,000; Pakistanis, 355,000; Chinese, 105,000; Africans, 91,000; and Arabs, 69,000. In addition there were 196,000 immigrants of mixed ethnic origins including Indians from Africa and 109,000 others, including Maltese, Cypriots and Malaysians.

What Napoleon described as 'a nation of shopkeepers' is no longer that any more; most people buy their groceries in the supermarket chains and any small shops that still exist are likely to be run, not by the Smiths or the Thatchers, but by the Patels or the Singhs.

HISTORICAL PERSPECTIVE

The French Connection

The French connection which runs through the entire fabric of English history had begun as early as the time of the Viking invasions. The Norsemen had also invaded Ireland, Scotland and northern France, where they had settled down, made Normandy their home, adopted the French language and become the Normans.

One of the Wessex line of Anglo-Saxon kings married Emma, sister of the Duke of Normandy, and fled to Normandy when

Wessex and London submitted to a Danish King Selwyn, father of the celebrated Canute. When her husband Ethelred returned to England, Emma left her children behind in France to be brought up in the Norman court. And on the death of Canute's second son, it was Emma's son Edward who succeeded him and restored the Wessex line, though not for long.

Edward, known as the Confessor, had always been pre-occupied with the Church; and he conceived the idea of converting a modest little monastery beside the Thames into a vast abbey like Jumièges, which he had known in Normandy. Thus began the building of Westminster Cathedral, in which, after the Norman invasion and the Norman victory at the Battle of Hastings in 1066, his own cousin, Le Duc Guillaume de Normandie was crowned King William I of England.

William (the Conqueror) immediately began to build wooden forts and then stone castles in all the towns to secure the country. He introduced a new form of the feudal system, granting his followers the lands of all the thanes (local chieftains) who had fought against him at Hastings, but severely limiting the power of the barons. To secure London's loyalty, he offered it a charter, confirming all the special rights which as a great trading town it had exacted from the Anglo-Saxon kings; but he also built the Tower of London to enable him to keep an eye on the city.

The conquest was over within ten years and the English never again rebelled against their Norman kings. Indeed, they soon looked to the king to protect them from the barons, and William took measures, right from the start, to prevent his barons from becoming as powerful as the barons were in France.

When a tax levied to resist an attempted Danish invasion failed to raise what he considered to be an adequate sum of money, William had an inventory made of every estate in the country. It listed every manor, church, house, barn and hovel and still exists today. It is known as the Doomsday Book because it was no more to be disputed than God's judgement would be upon that day.

William replaced the English bishops with Normans whenever an episcopal death caused a vacancy and in every way tried to bring the Church more firmly under the control of the Pope than it had ever been in Anglo-Saxon times. On the other hand he refused to allow any papal laws — or bulls as they were called — to be brought into effect in England without his permission.

Although King of England, William remained a Duke of Normandy, where he spent much of his time and where he died. But in England he established a strong centralized state with a Great Council composed of his earls and barons, the bishops and great abbots.

And when he died, William the Conqueror left what he regarded as the prime part of his possessions in Normandy to his first son Robert, Duke of Normandy. He was among the first of the European nobles to respond to Pope Urban's call to go crusading, and he financed his trip to the Holy Land by mortgaging all his lands in Normandy to William Rufus, the Conqueror's son.

After the death of William Rufus, his younger brother Henry I had to go to Normandy under arms to claim the mortgaged dukedom. This didn't concern the English very much except that they had to pay for the war. When his only son was drowned at sea in 1120, Henry made his barons swear allegiance to his daughter Matilda, wife of Geoffrey, the Count of Anjou, who, because he wore a sprig of broom (in Latin *planta genista*) in his hat-band, was nicknamed Plantagenet, and gave that name to a dynasty.

This marriage united England, Normandy, Maine and Anjou, and when Matilda's son Henry II married the divorced wife of the King of France, Eleanor brought Aquitaine with her as part of her dowry, thus carrying English influence in France as far east as Burgundy and as far south as the Pyrenees, and inextricably linking the affairs of the two countries for generations.

The only other colonial enterprise of the time was Henry II's annexation of Ireland (see the chapter on the Irish).

At this period the Exchequer (so called because the table on which the taxes were paid was chequered, to make the business of counting the money easier) came into existence; so did the custom of trial by jury, as well as the system of scutage, by which knights who did not wish to go to war could pay scutage (or shield money) instead, to enable the king to hire mercenaries to do the actual fighting.

King John, brother of the crusader Richard I the Lion-heart, although a great law-maker, not only succeeded in losing Normandy to the French, but also managed to get himself excommunicated and England placed under an interdict following a quarrel with the Pope. In the end, he plagued his barons to such an extent that they forced him in 1215 to sign a great charter, the Magna Carta, which established for the first time that custom and the law must take precedence over the king's arbitrary wishes, and became the foundation stone of Britain's unwritten constitution.

During the reign of Edward I (1272–1307), statute law developed to supplement common law; Edward also conquered Wales and made it a principality, passing always to the heir to the throne.

The first parliament had been convened in 1265 by Simon de Montfort during the reign of Henry III. Champion of the country gentlemen of England as well as governor of Gascony, de Montfort was one of the leaders of the infamous 'crusade' against the Albigenses, or Cathar heretics, the Purified Ones, who could not bring themselves to accept such notions as the resurrection of the body, Purgatory or Hell.

According to legend, when de Montfort was besieging one of the Cathar towns in southern France, he was reminded that within its walls there might be many adherents of the true faith.

'Kill them all,' he replied. 'The Lord will take care of his own.'

In 1314 Robert Bruce won independence for Scotland, which in all probability would have remained independent to this day if the reigning family of Scottish monarchs, the Stewarts (later known as the Stuarts), had not succeeded to the English throne in 1603.

Edward III claimed the throne of France in 1327 and started the Hundred Years War with France, remembered in the names of battlefields like Crécy, Poitiers and Agincourt. It didn't come to an end until Jeanne d'Arc, a peasant girl who fancied she heard voices that convinced her that she was destined to lead France to victory, managed somehow or other to persuade the Dauphin (the

French Crown Prince) to allow her to lead the French armies into battle.

Incredibly, she succeeded in throwing the English out of Orléans and Rheims, where the Dauphin was crowned as Charles VII. And although Jeanne d'Arc herself was captured and burned at the stake by the English in Rouen in 1431, she had so stirred up a new kind of patriotism in France that from this time onwards England's power in France began to decline. By 1450 Normandy was lost; in 1451 Bordeaux and Guienne fell to the French; and by 1453 Calais alone (for just over another century) remained out of all the former English possessions in France.

During this period the English were also fighting among themselves in the Wars of the Roses between the Houses of York (white) and Lancaster (red) for the succession; the end came in 1485 when the Welshman Henry Tudor, the only surviving Lancastrian claimant to the throne, defeated the Yorkist Richard III at Bosworth field and became King Henry VII, the first of the Welsh Tudor line which ruled England for over a century.

Henry VIII is probably best-known for his six wives, but what altered the whole course of British history was his quarrel with Pope Clement VII, when the latter refused to dissolve his marriage to Catherine of Aragon so that he could marry one of her ladies, Anne Boleyn. The Pope's hands were tied because Catherine of Aragon happened to be the aunt of Charles V, the Holy Roman Emperor of that period. Henry married Anne without the Pope's permission, made himself head of the Church in England, and dissolved most of the monasteries, confiscating their property.

A few years earlier in Wittenberg in what became Germany Martin Luther had started to 'reform' Christianity by suggesting a return to the Bible for authority on all religious matters, rather than the Pope and the by now highly sophisticated and often corrupt hierarchy of the Roman Church. In the process he opened up the way for a plethora of confusingly different forms of Protestantism.

Although he had refused to accept the Pope's authority on the matter of his divorce, Henry VIII was no Protestant; until the death of his elder brother he was being prepared for a career in the Church and in fact had earned the title of Defender of the Faith, which still appears on British coins, from a previous pope for a tract he had written attacking Luther. Nevertheless, his break with Rome made it much easier for the reformed religion to spread to England; and the use of the vernacular and the return to simple services appealed to the bluff, no-nonsense Anglo-Saxon element in England far more than the arcane ritual of the Latin Mass.

Henry VIII founded the Royal Navy and his flagship, the *Mary Rose*, recently raised from the seabed and now on exhibition in Portsmouth, was part of a fleet which prevented a French attempt to dominate the channel and the English supply routes. It was also during Henry VIII's reign that French finally ceased to be used by the English court.

And it was during the long reign of Elizabeth I, the daughter of Anne Boleyn, that English sailors and explorers began to challenge the Portuguese and Spanish supremacy on the high seas, and in the New World.

COLONIAL CONNECTIONS

The Greatest Empire of Them All

The great British colonial enterprise began in the most inauspicious way. A certain John Hawkins of Plymouth, seeing the way that things were going, conceived the idea of selling Negro slaves from Africa to the new Spanish colonies in America. When, on his third voyage, he was attacked in a Mexican harbour and lost some of his ships, he dropped the whole idea and went into parliament. But his young cousin, Francis Drake, who had accompanied him on his last voyage, continued the good work and carried the matter much further. Taking the Spanish by surprise, he stole large quantities of gold, silver and precious stones from them and proceeded home by way of the East Indies and the Cape of Good Hope in 1580. Eight years later the British defeat of the Spanish Armada prevented an invasion of England by Catholic Spain, and guaranteed religious liberty for English Protestantism.

Drake's successes were followed first by a series of attempts to find a way to the East via the North-East and North-West Passages in Labrador, then by the first British settlements in Newfoundland and Virginia (so-called after the Virgin Queen Elizabeth), and eventually by the despatch of three ships to the East Indies.

At the end of the sixteenth century, a party of London merchants founded the East India Company, which was the beginning of Britain's Indian Empire, the ultimate Jewel in Queen Victoria's Crown.

And Elizabeth's — and subsequently James I's — problems with the Nonconformists led to the voyage of the Puritan Pilgrim Fathers in 1620 and the first successful colonizations of North America, in an area called New England. The British were not, of course, alone in attempting this endeavour; and they had to settle matters with the Dutch (who had established their headquarters at New Amsterdam, later to become New York) and the French who had made Quebec their capital in the New World. Inevitably there was a war between the French and the English for what later became Canada.

After the victory the British government decided to leave 10,000 Redcoats in America to keep the Native Americans quiet and to curb any tendency towards resurgence by the French Canadians. This force had to be financed by the new colonists who had not asked for it and didn't want it. The result was the American War of Independence which ended at Yorktown with the surrender of Lord Cornwallis, the British commander, and a written constitution for the collection of divergent colonies that now became a vigorous new nation with almost unlimited natural and ethnic resources.

In the meantime, back in Britain, the Scottish House of Stuart had succeeded the Tudors, and James VI of Scotland became James I of England, bringing down from Scotland with him the curious doctrine of the Divine Right of Kings which resulted in the only real civil war in British history between the Royalists on one side and the Parliamentarians on the other and ended with the execution of James's son Charles I, in 1649.

After eleven years of Puritan rule under Oliver Cromwell and his son (1649–60), the monarchy was restored with Charles II. In 1707 Scotland was tricked into agreeing to an Act of Union which was the beginning of Great Britain; in 1801 the Irish were bribed into accepting a similar status; and the United Kingdom was brought into reluctant existence.

Before that happened, however, another member of the House of Stuart proved unacceptable to the British; when it looked as if King James II was trying to reintroduce Catholicism, the English replied in 1688 by inviting William of Orange, who was married to James II's elder daughter Mary, to come to England from the Netherlands, take over the monarchy and ensure forever the Protestant succession.

James II fled first to France and then to Ireland, gathered a combined French and Irish Catholic army around him to challenge King Billy; the matter was settled by King Billy's victory at the Battle of the Boyne in 1690.

In the meantime, the project of colonizing the world was going swimmingly. The British Empire spread its tentacles all over India, throughout most of Africa, all over the Middle East, in Australia and New Zealand, in Canada, Singapore, Hong Kong, the Fiji Islands, Samoa and Borneo. Although it was an empire upon which, as they used to say, the sun never set, the sun did indeed eventually set for all time.

It started to fall apart with the Boer War in Africa (between the Dutch settlers and the British colonists) and the Irish Easter Rebellion of 1916, and disappeared dizzyingly in the Wind of Change of the early sixties, though the British still tenaciously hold on to two highly unlikely possessions: the Falkland Islands off the southern tip of South America, and Gibraltar, the rock fortress in southern Spain at the entrance to the Mediterranean.

The German House of Hanover had ascended to the English throne in 1714, when George Louis, the elector of Hanover, and a descendant of James I, became King George I of England. There was a war with revolutionary France, followed by a series of wars with Napoleon, which ended at Waterloo in 1815, and for Napoleon, on St Helena.

Britain was inevitably drawn into World War I as a result of a guarantee to maintain Belgium's neutrality, a professed desire to protect the rights of small nations, and a genuine determination to rid Europe of the menace of Prussian military aggression. It is doubtful whether the Allies would have won without the intervention of American troops and armaments.

Prussian military aggression — now in the guise of a Nazi dictatorship — led to Britain and France declaring war on Germany again in 1939 when the Nazi army invaded Poland.

The British have always been at their very best with their backs to the wall and came out of both wars with unparalleled distinction, surviving the Blitz and everything else that Hitler could throw at them until the Japanese attack on Pearl Harbour forced the Americans to come out of their isolationism and join with the British in securing the destruction of Hitler.

The initial French conception of the European Community was an effort to prevent another war between France and Germany by putting the two countries' armaments manufacturing capacity (their iron and steel industries) under common control, but it very soon developed into an effort to form some kind of United States of Europe. And it should have been no surprise to anybody that Britain's first reaction was to have nothing whatever to do with it. Nor that later, when it began to look as if Britain would have to make the best of it anyway, de Gaulle went on saying 'Non' to the prospect of Britain's entry until he departed from the political limelight.

Margaret Thatcher's stubborn fight to maintain the sovereignty both of the British crown and parliament and of the pound sterling, as well as what remained of Britain's proud insularity, was equally understandable and might well have proved popular with a section of the electorate if she hadn't gone on pushing it a bit too hard and a bit too late.

DEVELOPMENT DIRECTIONS

Nationalization and Privatization

It was probably not by chance that Britain's decline from her position of absolute supremacy as the world's first great industrial exporting nation to her present position just above Italy, Ireland, Spain, Portugal and Greece — but well below the other member-states in the European Community's table of wealth in terms of GDP per head of the population — should have coincided with the final disappearance of her empire.

The possession of a vast overseas empire is not, as the Portuguese discovered long ago, and as other imperial powers have found out more recently, an unalloyed blessing. An unearned income, or in other words an artificially high standard of living achieved at the expense of the colonies in one way or another, can very easily lead to sloth, complacency, arrogance, pride and indolence, and can cushion industrial management into a sense of false security which renders it incapable of coping with competition in an open market when eventually and inevitably it arrives.

In Britain's case, there were other contributory factors. Until the Industrial Revolution towards the end of the eighteenth century, Britain, like the rest of Europe, had been a largely agricultural country with a predominantly peasant population working their own holdings as tenants of the local squire, normally a member of the landed gentry. There were industries, too, of course; to take one example, English woollen cloth and other textiles had been exported to Europe for centuries but the materials were produced by people spinning and weaving in their own homes.

The Industrial Revolution which turned England's green and pleasant land into a place of dark, Satanic mills surrounded by closely packed slum dwellings for the factory workers was the direct result of three developments: the invention of spinning and weaving devices, the discovery of steam-power and the use of coal instead of charcoal for smelting iron. The first industrial machines, originally powered by water-mills, could produce far more cloth at a much lower cost than artisans working in their cottages.

Then came James Watt's invention of the steam engine, which could be used to power the manufacturing machines far more effectively than the old mill stream. This in turn led to the development of the first successful coal furnaces for smelting iron, and as coal furnaces could produce four or five times as much iron as charcoal ones Britain soon had a surplus of iron and steel products to export.

But the net effect of all these developments was to turn independent artisans into wage-earners working for mill and factory and colliery owners, and crowded into slums in the towns; at the same time the introduction of more scientific farming methods turned the tenant peasants into labourers employed by men who controlled enough land to farm it profitably.

There was then, suddenly, a vast explosion of production and population and wealth which resulted in the creation of a huge wage-earning population wholly dependent upon their masters. The latter naturally kept wages as low as possible, and employed women and children at even lower rates in their mills and coal mines and factories, and indeed even on the farms, where children as young as seven were employed to scare away birds, and help in gathering in the hay.

The Industrial Revolution was entirely achieved by private enterprise and it produced a new breed of shrewd, hard-headed proprietors who lived lives of great luxury in surroundings very different from those of the huddled masses whose labour had created their wealth. And when in turn the railways and the ocean steamers arrived they too were developed entirely by private enterprise, as was the electric telegraph, originally operated between Paddington and Slough for the Great Western Railway Company, one of the first big railway companies in Britain.

By the end of the nineteenth century, Britain was the richest and most powerful industrial force in the world. Great ocean liners, cargo boats and warships built in the shipyards on the Clyde, in Belfast and in the industrial north were sailing to the four corners of the earth, and the might of British industry seemed unassailable.

The Great War of 1914–18 was initially very popular as a just war but its horrifying cost in men and materials as it dragged on and on meant that the Britain to which the survivors returned, so far from being a Land Fit for Heroes, was a country torn apart by the ever-widening gulf between the rich and the poor, a gulf soon enhanced by the effects of the Great Depression and the mass unemployment which the latter caused.

The fact that it costs a lot more to win a war than to lose one was again demonstrated when Britain went to war against Hitler in 1939. As Peter Jenkins put it in the *Independent*: 'Half our overseas assets were wiped out, half our export trade lost; we staggered into the post-war era under a huge burden of debt. We won the war but again we lost the peace: during the Long Boom that ran from 1950 to 1973, our economy grew on an average by 3.75 per cent a year while those of defeated Japan and Germany grew by 9.7 per cent and 6 per cent respectively.'

One explanation for this was the simple fact that the industrial plants of the Germans and Japanese had been almost totally destroyed by aerial bombing, a situation which forced them to start from scratch, funded by American aid, so that they were soon competing for world markets again, using brand new, highly efficient industrial plants. Britain on the other hand was still trying to stagger along with outdated, obsolete equipment in Dickensian factories operated by a sullen, strike-orientated workforce and managements which could not bring themselves to come to terms with the realities of the post-war world.

One of these realities was the fact that not only was Britain no longer a great world power, but the British people were in fact far poorer in terms of average gross hourly earnings than the Danes and the Dutch and the Belgians and the West Germans and much, much poorer than the Japanese.

Also, from the beginning of the twenties, Britain had been undergoing another almost silent revolution: in 1924 Ramsay MacDonald formed the first Labour government in Britain, and in the 1945 elections Churchill was defeated and an openly socialist Labour government with a big majority in parliament began an extensive programme of nationalization.

It looked as if the great days of private enterprise were over for ever as the state bought out the shareholders in the Bank of England, the coal mines, the railways and indeed all inland transport, most air transport, several motor car and aeroplane manufacturers, and the companies that provided gas and electricity. At the same time they set up a 'cradle-to-the-grave' welfare state, with a National Health Service to provide free medical care for all, and very generous unemployment and other state benefits.

The National Health proved to be a great success and was for a time the envy of the world, but a succession of short-lived, short-sighted governments with stop—go approaches to any problems that arose combined with trade union militancy which led to endless industrial unrest pushed British industry further into the doldrums. The National Health Service was severely hit by the ever-escalating costs of the new drugs and sophisticated surgical treatments that were constantly being discovered, combined with the arrival of tens of thousands of Commonwealth citizens after World War II and the Wind of Change in Africa had stretched it far beyond its resources.

By the eighties all that was effectively left of Britain's mass market motor car industry was the Rover firm, now partly owned by the Japanese Honda company and manufacturing cars that are far more Japanese in character than British. The once world-famous British motor-cycle industry had totally disappeared and the British civil aircraft industry had been reduced to the role of supplying a few parts for the European Airbus. The shipbuilding industry had also largely disappeared.

Whether the Thatcher programme of reintroducing the concept of private enterprise and denationalizing everything in sight from public transport and road haulage to the provision of light and power and even water − a process described by her critics as massive asset-stripping or 'selling off the family silver' − will work any better in the long run, it remains to be seen.

The Thatcher boom of the eighties was greatly assisted by the fact that in the late sixties and early seventies large deposits of natural gas and oil had been discovered and developed in the North Sea, so that Britain became self-sufficient in energy, and even enjoyed a period − probably a brief one − as a net oil exporting country. The extraction of these gas and oil deposits led incidentally to the creation of a whole series of entirely new technologies, which have also proved highly exportable.

During the same period, many of the old, inefficient industries like coal, iron, steel and textile manufacture were streamlined and adapted to meet new patterns of world trade, and new fields of high-technology industries and services were established and developed. These include satellite communications, robot manufacturing machinery and advanced information processing.

Major exports in 1986 featured machinery and transport equipment, aerospace products, manufactured goods, mineral fuels and chemicals. But the balance of trade was still well over £4 billion in the red in 1987, more than 12 per cent of the labour force was unemployed, and if the growth rate of the GDP was relatively high in the years 1983–88, it was principally because it had been so dismally low before that. By 1991 Britain had the fastest falling rate of employment and the largest rising unemployment in the Community.

Britain's railway system was the first, and for a short period the best in the world, and some of the crack trains like the *Royal Scot* and the *Flying Scotsman* have become a treasured part of transport history. When the four major railway companies (LMS, LNER, GWR and Southern) were nationalized and finally emerged as British Rail, the service became and has ever since remained a joke; the trains frequently overcrowded, the food mostly uneatable, the coaches shabby and continuously vandalized, and the entire enterprise extremely scruffy, ill-maintained and badly managed.

Though not yet reprivatized, British Rail is subsidized to a much lesser extent than rail services elsewhere in Europe, and this is reflected both in the standard of the services and the outrageously high fares.

Bus and coach services have been privatized and vary greatly in quality and frequency all over the country. The London Underground, another first, is sordid, slow and noisy compared with the Paris Metro, and far more expensive.

Britain was much slower than most continental countries to adopt the idea of the autoroute or motorway, and stuck doggedly to the principle that the British were born with an inherent right to travel free on their own roads with the result that the network has always been under-financed and is consequently basically inadequate.

The real trouble of course is that the total area of the United Kingdom is only 244,111 square kilometres as against, say France's 544,000 square kilometres for very nearly the same population. And not only that, but the bulk of Britain's 57 million people are concentrated in heavily built-up areas around the principal cities and industrial areas in the Midlands and north of England, around London and the south-east generally, and in the Bristol region.

The overall population density is 232 people per square kilometre as against France's 101 (though in the London area it's over 1,500), but you can walk for twelve hours in the Scottish Highlands without ever encountering another member of the human race. The population density varies enormously, more so perhaps than in any other European country. So it is perhaps not surprising that road and rail transport in the heavily populated areas present certain almost insoluble problems.

London's chief airports, Heathrow and Gatwick, are impossibly overcrowded, especially at holiday times, but there are frequent and efficient car ferries between Britain and the continent and now a channel tunnel, which will be open for business in a few years and should remove the last vestiges of Britain's island mentality. Alone in Europe, the people of the British Isles (including Ireland) still drive on the left-hand side of the road.

Although many people miss the bright red GPO public telephone booths, nobody complains, because telecommunications, privatized during the Thatcher era, are now among the best in the world.

AFFAIRS OF STATE

Happy and Glorious

The United Kingdom is a constitutional hereditary monarchy.

The royal family is a highly expensive luxury, and many of

Britain's most loyal subjects frequently ask themselves whether this vast expenditure is justified, particularly in view of the fact that Queen Elizabeth II, in her own right as a private person, happens also to be the richest woman in the world; her wealth has been estimated at £6.7 billion and her income, from her investments, at about £1.8 million a day. On top of that, she pays no taxes whatever. A public opinion poll conducted in the *Independent* newspaper, in February 1991, found that 79 per cent of the men and 81 per cent of the women who were polled believed that she should pay tax on her earnings like everybody else.

The entire cast of this mammoth super-show costs the British taxpayers in the region of about £8.84 million a year. According to a *Daily Mail* survey, the Queen herself receives £7.9 million a year from the government; Prince Philip, Duke of Edinburgh, another £360,000 a year; the Duke and Duchess of York £250,000 a year between them; the Princess Royal (Princess Anne), £230,000 a year; and Prince Edward £100,000 a year. The Prince and Princess of Wales don't draw anything from the Civil List, but receive around £1 million a year because Prince Charles as Duke of Cornwall is entitled to the net revenue of the Duchy of Cornwall.

The whole outfit probably has a limited public relations/ advertising value, but it undoubtedly has a considerable prestige value, plus a great ceremonial potential, and since the arrival on the scene of characters like Princess Di and Fergie, the Duchess of York, enormous entertainment value, both to the British public and to thousands of faithful fans of the programme in France, the United States, Japan and indeed all over the developed world. The *Independent* poll mentioned above also asked people if the monarchy should be abolished; only 16 per cent of the people who were asked thought that it should, though the figure rose to 25 per cent in the case of Labour supporters.

Although in theory the Queen merely entrusts her executive power to the leader of the majority party in the House of Commons, Her Majesty's speech at the opening of parliament is always written for her by the prime minister, or by the prime minister's scriptwriters, and the Sovereign has in fact no real power at all, apart from control of all television footage of the family. Even visits to other monarchies still in existence are subject to government approval.

All legislation for the kingdom is initiated in parliament, which consists of the House of Commons and the House of Lords. The 650 MPs (members of parliament) are elected by a simple, first-past-the-post majority in single-seat constituencies, an arrangement which enables a party with only relatively minority support in the country to achieve a massive majority in parliament. In her eleven years of Iron Rule, Thatcher never at any time enjoyed the support of a majority of the electorate.

The 1,000-odd members of the House of Lords are mostly hereditary peers, but also include the life peers, the two archbishops and the senior bishops of the Church of England, as well as the senior law lords. The Lords have the power to delay legislation, but not to defeat it; in practice their principal function is to suggest sensible alterations and amendments which may have been overlooked in the heat of interparty debates in the Commons. Parliament must be re-elected every five years, though in general they tend not to last the full five years.

Britain has no written constitution and the laws are interpreted in the courts on the basis of precedence. The much-vaunted reputation of the British police for fair play has taken a few hard knocks lately, after a succession of inquiries in which it became clear that evidence had been fudged or withheld, false confessions had been extorted or forged, and that nothing like the truth and the whole truth had been told. It is only fair to add that these inquiries were instigated and carried out by the police themselves, and in the end no attempt was made to conceal the truth from the public.

Also, today's police are obliged to cope with extra hazards unimaginable a century ago, such as random bomb explosions in crowded streets and shops, terrorist attacks of all sorts by the IRA and by various extremist organizations as well as with a massive increase in crime generally. Fifty years ago there were 741 crimes per year per 100,000 of the population; the figure is now 7,526. The daily average prison population has risen from 12,629 to 55,178 during a period when the total population has only risen from 47.5 million to 57.2 million. I say 'only' purely in relation to the crime figures, not in any general sense.

There is no compulsory military service, but the United Kingdom has a small, well-armed and highly efficient professional army, navy and air force, co-operating closely with NATO; a total of 306,000 members, 63,500 in the Royal Navy and Marines, 152,000 in the Army and 89,600 in the Royal Air Force, while the Ministry of Defence employs about 142,000 civilians. In the wake of the collapse of communism, the British army is to be cut back by 40,000 men.

The Royal Navy's Polaris force comprises four nuclear submarines carrying sixteen nuclear-armed Polaris missiles; they will be replaced in the mid 1990s by four Trident nuclear submarines, at a cost of about £10 billion.

CULTURE AND LEISURE

Too Many Giants

The established church in England is the Anglican Church; there is no established church in Wales or Northern Ireland and the Church of Scotland, essentially Calvinist in outlook and governed by the Moderator of the General Assembly, is the established church there.

Most British people profess to belong to the Anglican faith or claim to be a part of some other branch of the Church of England but a UK Christian handbook table, published in 1991, revealed the real truth about active religious membership in 1987 and demonstrated that while there were still well over 2 million active Catholics in Britain, the number of active (i.e. regular church-attending) Church of England Protestants was less than 1.6 million, the number of church-going Presbyterians just over 1.2 million, and that of other Protestants just over 1 million.

What this amounts to, given that the population now includes more than 500,000 Muslims, is that over 50,000,000 British people effectively have no religion at all. Nevertheless Britain remains an instinctively Christian country and a lot of people secretly feel it is just possible that the increase in crime, the huge increase of births outside marriage (from 45 per 1,000 of the population fifty years ago to 266 per 1,000 of the population today), and the equally sharp increase in the rate of divorces (from 7.038 in 1938 to 164,105 per year half a century later) may not be unconnected with the disappearance of Christianity from the school curriculum and the general break-up of family life.

Education in England began in Roman times when Latin was the only written language and the invading Saxons and other Pagans were all illiterate. Christianity proved much more than merely a religion; it became a moral code, a way of life, a civilizing agent. The first grammar schools were an offshoot of the cathedrals; the Benedictines and other regular clergy also ran their own educational establishments.

By the beginning of the twentieth century, English education had settled into a firmly formed mould at any rate for those who could afford to pay for their children's education. It consisted of some form of kindergarten or play school and then from the age of seven until around eleven a private prep school, followed by the Common Entrance examination, and a public school like Eton or Harrow, Shrewsbury or Westminster or one of the grammar schools and then university.

The British state system of education aims to provide all children with a free education suited to their particular abilities up to the age of sixteen or eighteen, and free university or vocational education thereafter.

About 90 per cent of the secondary pupils in Britain attend comprehensive schools, which take pupils without reference to their ability or aptitude and 'stream' them in a vocational or an academic direction according to their performance while at school. There are also grammar and secondary modern schools, some partly maintained by grants and some part fee-paying, to which children are allocated after several selection procedures at the age of eleven.

Currently, the British educational system is in a state of total disarray. The curriculum has been changed and changed again over the years; a new National Curriculum is now being phased in which requires 70 per cent of teaching time to be devoted to the core subjects of English, maths and science, as well as the other foundation subjects of history, geography, technology, music, art, physical education and one modern foreign language.

Only about half of Britain's sixteen-year-olds now choose to stay on in full-time education, and by the age of eighteen, the figure drops to 19 per cent, considerably lower than that of our industrial competitors in the Community. One explanation that has been advanced is the low standard of teaching. But a contributory factor may be the failure of parents to involve themselves in their children's schooling and their reluctance to help in any way with homework; they feel that if they have paid their taxes and have worked hard all day themselves, there is no reason why they should work at night, making the teachers' job easier for them. Also, many parents actually encourage their children to leave school at sixteen, pointing out that it never did any harm and perhaps even citing the example of Prime Minister John Major.

In a way, it is a pity that I have to deal with British achievements in art, literature and science before I deal with the achievements in the same fields by the French, Italians and Germans. However, having chosen to deal with the peoples of the European Community in alphabetical order, starting with the Belgians, this was inevitable ...

Because, so far as art, literature and science are concerned, I'm going to be obliged to treat them in the same way. I simply have to. The sheer quantity of output from these countries makes any other approach impossible. In his book *The Italians* (London: Hamish Hamilton, 1964), Luigi Barzini said that merely to list all the famous Italians in one field would take a volume as big as the Milan telephone directory, and the same is true of the British, the French and the Germans. The trouble is that these countries simply produced far too many giants.

So far as English literature is concerned, it would probably be possible to fill at least fifteen pages with names like Shakespeare and Spenser, Bacon and Brontë, Austen and Auden, Milton and Keats and Shelley and all the others over the centuries right up to Graham Greene, and they would all be familiar to most well-educated people.

So far as art is concerned, Britain has probably not produced as many giants as Italy, France, Holland or Germany, but there were Reynolds and Turner and Constable and Gainsborough and Hogarth and hundreds of others. And in music, Elgar and Vaughan Williams, Walton and Benjamin Britten.

And science. You would probably start with people like Watt, who invented the steam engine, and Newton and Darwin, and end up with people like Baird, who invented television, and Whittle, who invented the jet engine. Since 1970 alone, there have been sixteen British winners of Nobel prizes for science.

Food used to be universally bad in British hotels and restaurants and based on a persistent and universal English preference for some kind of hot meat, preferably grossly overcooked, smothered in Bisto, a sort of instant brown sauce, and accompanied by two veg, usually potatoes and carrots or cabbage, and followed by pudding, which one dictionary defines as 'a soft kind of dessert food, usually farinaceous, commonly with sugar, milk, eggs, etc.' Exactly.

However, in recent years, the British passion for foreign travel combined with the arrival in Britain of people from all over the world who didn't know how to do anything other than cook a few of the dishes they had seen prepared back in their country of origin has resulted in a rash of restaurants serving specialities from all over the world and serving them very well.

And apart from all that it has become impossible to turn on the TV in the evenings without encountering a programme telling you how to prepare some continental delicacy and what wine you should drink with it.

In the meantime, the presence in our midst of so many new citizens from the Commonwealth and elsewhere has prompted the supermarkets to display an astonishing array of tropical fruit and vegetables, yams and mangos and papayas and avocados, as well as deep freeze pizza and lasagne and canned cannelloni and quenelles de brochet and escargots and frozen chicken tikka and Thai rice with lemon grass, and so on.

Over the years, the British have started to experiment with all these strange foreign foods and have found, to their own considerable surprise, that they quite like them. In fact Indian and Chinese take-aways have become as common as fish and chips used to be. And as a result, British cooking in homes, hotels and restaurants has improved considerably and it is now possible to get a very good meal almost anywhere in Britain.

Although the Romans introduced the vine to Britain over 1,500 years ago and a couple of reasonable white wines are still produced in Kent and on the Isle of Wight, the arrival of the Anglo-Saxons introduced the British to the bitter blandishment of beer, even for breakfast.

Until the Industrial Revolution, beer was mainly produced in the home by the housewife and was the standard drink even for children. French wines, and in particular burgundies and clarets, were extremely popular in England during the Hundred Years War, and port and sherry (the slightly sweet and highly fortified wines of Oporto in Portugal and Jerez in Spain respectively) soon established themselves as the English *digestif* in the case of port and *apéritif* in the case of sherry.

Whiskey, spelled that way, with an 'e', was an Irish invention and it is on record that Queen Elizabeth I was partial to a drop of the stuff and instructed Sir Walter Raleigh to pick up a 32-gallon cask of home-made Irish whiskey from the Earl of Cork when he stopped off at Youghal on one of his voyages.

But if it was invented in Ireland, it was perfected in Scotland and Scotch (the only correct use of this word by the way; in any other context, it's Scots or Scottish) whisky is now a fashionable and popular drink all over the world.

Broadly speaking, the British are basically about as interested in sport as most other nations in the Community and in mainly the same sports. The English game of bowls, which Drake was playing on Plymouth Hoe when he was called away to repel the Spanish Armada, is a more formal version of French *boules* or *pétanque* and requires turf of the quality only found on the putting greens of the top golf courses.

Hunting fox on horseback, described by Oscar Wilde as 'the unspeakable in full pursuit of the uneatable', used to be very popular in the English countryside. These days, when most of the indigenous peasant population have been ousted by rich city folk pretending to be 'county', most hunts are plagued by animal-loving protesters who try to sabotage them in every possible way.

There is no equivalent to the French *chasse*; the ordinary people in England never had much opportunity to shoot game, as almost all shooting rights are strictly reserved by the royal family and the aristocracy for themselves and their rich friends. So indeed are the angling rights, but about 4 million city-dwellers all over the country spend their Sundays coarse fishing and throwing most of the catch of perch, tench and bream back into the rivers and canals because they're too small to eat and are probably poisoned by pollution anyway.

Darts and snooker are the two great English indoor sports; and television has made them spectator sports. In England, as else-where throughout the Community, and indeed all over the world, watching TV is probably the number one leisure activity. Excluding the satellite television channels, one of which is entirely devoted to sport, the four networks broadcast 2,655 hours of sport in 1989.

In sport, as in so many other fields, Britain has had many firsts and still has a few bests. Although skiing was developed as a mode of transport by the Scandinavians, it was the British who invented winter sports. And despite the fact that it is rarely cold enough to provide much opportunity for practice, ice-skating is a sport (or art form) at which the British have always excelled. British couples have won the world ice dance championships seventeen times and Torvill and Dean, who were world ice champions for four successive years between 1981 and 1984, and who won gold medals at the Olympic Games in Sarajevo in 1984, became popular television entertainers.

And although there is a *jeu de paume* in the Tuileries dating back to Louis XIV, Henry VIII was playing tennis at Hampton Court a century and a half earlier. The modern game originated in England in 1872, the first championships were played at Wimbledon in 1877, and Wimbledon is still regarded as the most prestigious international tournament.

The oldest golf club is the Honourable Company of Edinburgh Golfers founded in 1744, and the ruling authority on the sport is the Royal and Ancient Golf Club at St Andrews, which is also arguably the best golf course in the world.

Squash originated at Harrow School in the 1850s; Badminton takes its name from the Duke of Beaufort's country home, Badminton House, where it was first played last century; boxing in its modern form dates from 1865 when the Marquess of Queensbury drew up a civilized set of rules for what had been a bloody fairground spectacle; and Rugby football takes its name from Rugby School in Warwickshire.

THE DANES

The Land of H.C. Andersen

DENMARK IN PROFILE

Area	43,080 sq km
Population	5,100,000
Population density	119 per sq km
Women	50.7%
Under 15	18.8%
Over 65	14.9%
Language	Danish, German
Religion	98% Lutheran
Labour force	54.5%

Employed in:

Agriculture	7.1%
Industry	26.8%
Services	66%
Women in labour force	45.1%
Unemployment (as % of labour force)	7.6%

Major exports: Foodstuffs (meat and preserved foods, dairy products, fish and fish preserves, etc.) (26.7%); furniture and clothing (25.8%); machinery and transport equipment (24.6%); medicines, pharmaceuticals and other chemicals (8.5%)

Main customers: EC (53.2%); Sweden (11.4%); USA (8.6%); Norway (7.7%)

THE DANES

To anybody who has never been there, the word Denmark immediately summons up a stereotyped vision of tall, tanned, leggy flaxen-haired girls on bicycles, the statue of the little mermaid at Langeline, perched on a rock and gazing wistfully out over Copenhagen harbour, and her creator, the famous writer of children's fairy tales, Hans Christian Andersen.

To those who have been there, the word Denmark still summons up a recollection of those tall, tanned, leggy flaxen-haired girls on bicycles and the little mermaid at Langeline, but after that, other images crowd into the mind. Noble brick buildings with green copper domes; a countryside as docile and domestic as Dorset or the Dordogne, with no vestige of a wilderness anywhere; the carousels and ferris wheels and side-shows of the Tivoli Gardens; snug little yacht harbours packed with lovingly maintained craft which, unlike so many of the boats in the marinas of Britain and France, really do go to sea; and meals which look deceptively simple, but turn imperceptibly into banquets, with course after course, each preceded by a schnapps, or aquavit, which must be knocked back in one breath-taking, stupifying gulp, and accompanied with gallons, it sometimes seems, of Tuborg or Carlsberg beer.

And as for Hans Christian Andersen, as he is known

throughout the rest of the world, people who have visited Denmark will know that there and only there is he known for some reason just as H.C. Andersen: the house where he was born in Odense is called the H.C. Andersen Hus.

The Danes are a big (in every sense of the word), friendly people, who enjoy the good things of life with a very healthy contempt for convention, and a genuine feeling for democracy that is not shared by all of their partners in the Community.

At the height of the German occupation of their country during World War II, the future king, Frederik IX, and his daughters (including the present queen, Margrethe II) used to cycle around the streets of Copenhagen without any armed guards or security men, just like any other Danish family. A German officer asked a Danish citizen, who was standing on the corner of the street watching the royal family cycle by, why they didn't have any bodyguard. 'Who protects the Danish royal family?' he asked. 'We all do,' came the reply. 'The whole Danish nation are their bodyguard.'

And when the Nazis ordered all Danish Jews to wear a yellow star, King Frederik immediately set an example for his people by insisting on wearing a yellow star himself, and soon most of the Danes followed suit and adopted the insignia. This totally fazed the Germans, who knew that there were relatively few Jews in Denmark and that if everyone in the country was going to pretend to be a Jew there wasn't very much they could do about it. In the meantime, most of the 7,000 Jews in Denmark were being smuggled across the Kattegat to neutral Sweden.

The Danes are liberal, perhaps almost to a fault, which is why when a sudden wave of permissiveness swept Europe in the middle sixties, Copenhagen became the pornography capital of the continent. The complete abolition of all restrictions on the sale of pornography to adults was followed by a proliferation of strip clubs and cinemas in which one could watch endless cheaply-shot, badly-made 8 millimetre films of queues of naked men and women (and dogs, sometimes) coupled together in a mind-boggling variety of unlikely, not to say extremely uncomfortable-looking positions.

Then there were the huge (3 metres by 1.2 metres) posters showing vast colour blow-ups of male private parts captured by the camera in moments of obviously urgent excitement — a highly alarming sight with which to be confronted on a cold spring morning in the course of a casual stroll in search of a cup of coffee.

And it's not true that you had to go out of your way to look for them. At one time, if you used any of the pedestrian precincts in the centre of Cophenhagen, they were extremely difficult to avoid. These days, they seem to have receded into the depths of the red light district and you don't have to go there unless you choose to do so.

In any event, too much freedom is probably a good fault; far better than too little, and people all over the world who dislike regulations and taxes must have been cheered by the emergence of one Mogens Gilstrup.

Gilstrup was a successful Danish tax lawyer in the late sixties. He had graduated from university with the highest marks ever awarded to a law student, and when invited to give a talk on Danish TV, he confidently assured the Danish people that they need never pay any further taxes. The important thing was to get a good accountant. His TV appearance caused an uproar; the finance minister was immediately rushed to hospital with a heart attack.

Despite the fact that the tax people instantly raided his flat in an effort to find some evidence of failure on his part to contribute sufficiently to the Danish exchequer, he formed a political party dedicated to the abolition of all taxes. His party's line was that the government could easily balance the books by dropping all expenditure on defence and invest instead in a tape recorder which would continuously broadcast a loop on several wavelengths announcing 'We surrender, we surrender' in Russian.

In the end, the Inland Revenue people got him; like the Mounties, they always get their man. However, after paying a huge fine and serving part of a three-year sentence, he emerged to form a new political party which stressed the importance of individual responsibility. A Danish Margaret Thatcher, Pia

Kjaersgarrd, was finally successful in putting him down, but not before he had formed a third 'Welfare Party'. His firm of account- ants now has one of the biggest cash turnovers in Denmark — higher, I am reliably informed, than some of the banks.

The fates of Denmark and the United Kingdom have long been inextricably linked. The king who believed he could stop the tide from encroaching on the English shore was Canute, or Knut, a Dane; Shakespeare's most famous character, Hamlet, was a prince of Denmark. And every British schoolboy knows that when faced with a command he didn't wish to execute, Nelson was in the habit of putting the telescope to his blind eye as he appeared to focus on the string of flags conveying the signal. What they don't perhaps realize is that on the most famous occasion when this happened, Nelson was in the process of bombarding the Danish fleet at anchor in Copenhagen Harbour, during the Napoleonic Wars. The signal was telling him to stop, but as he was using his blind eye at the time, he didn't see it, and continued. The Danes don't seem to bear the British any ill-will over this inci- dent, and until the notion of a European Common Market started to emerge in the late forties and early fifties, the British were among Denmark's principal trading partners. They still come second, after Germany.

In fact the Danes don't seem to have many hang-ups about the past at all; they are a thoroughly well-adjusted race of people with even tempers and a sense of humour which prevents them from taking anything too seriously, above all themselves.

LAND AND PEOPLE

An Uninvaded Wilderness

Denmark is the oldest kingdom in Europe. Not only that, but in general the people of Scandinavia, with the exception of the Finns, still inhabit lands which belonged to their direct ancestors long before the Greeks and Romans began to create that way of life that we call civilization, around the shores of the Mediter- ranean. And the Scandinavians have enjoyed their lands in complete freedom over the centuries; there is no record or evidence of any movement of any other people on any permanent basis into Scandinavia within the past 4,000 years.

The entire area was a wilderness unknown to the Greeks and the Romans, too cold and dark and wet to appeal to them, and even the early Christian missionaries, formidable explorers though they were, barely ventured further into Scandinavia than the southern tip of Denmark, where the Jutland Peninsula is briefly joined to the European continent.

The first Danes appear to have arrived in the area in the interval between the second and third Ice Ages, around 250,000 years ago. In 1972, some crudely dressed flint instruments were discovered in South Jutland which provided clues as to the identity of the area's first inhabitants. They had been hunters, capable of cutting meat from the game animals they succeeded in felling.

Previously, the earliest evidence of man's handiwork had been fallow deer bones, which had been, expertly for those days, split to extract the marrow some 50,000 years ago. From around 12,000 BC it is possible to trace, during the long, intermittent, reluctant retreat of the ice, the presence of reindeer hunters who used flint knives and fishermen who used harpoons to kill the seal and whales and other animals which abounded at the edge of the Arctic Ocean.

These Stone Age Nordic ancestors of today's Danes were followed in the third century BC by large-scale movements of peasant people from around the Danube and the borders of Asia who made their way into Denmark from the south and settled down in that peaceful, fertile if slightly cold, damp country.

The land itself, Denmark, consists of one peninsula, Jutland, which pushes up northwards from Europe to separate the North Sea from the Baltic Sea, and a collection of islands — estimates vary from 529 in one encyclopedia to 406 in a Danish government hand-out. Of these, ninety-seven — many of them big enough only to feed and maintain one family — are inhabited.

The entire Danish archipelago measures 360 kilometres from north to south, where the sole peninsula shares a sixty kilometre land boundary with Germany, and measures 478 kilometres from east to west with a disproportionately long total coastline of 7,438 kilometres; the total area of Denmark is 43,080 square kilometres. It has no mountains – the highest point, Yding Skorvhog, is only 173 metres high – no great rivers and no lakes of any size.

Throughout the centuries, the people there lived by fishing and farming, and if they didn't experience their Industrial Revolution until the end of the nineteenth century (Britain had hers between 1760 and 1830), the reason is that Denmark has no coal, and because there are no mountains and no rivers of any size, could not develop any hydro-electric power either. The country does have a certain amount of clay for making bricks, and limestone for making cement, but such industries as have developed have all been dependent on imported coal and oil: up until the mid-seventies 85 per cent of Denmark's energy came from imported oil and 15 per cent from imported coal. Since 1972, Denmark has extracted oil and natural gas from the North Sea, and by 1990 very nearly half of the country's energy requirements were being met from this source. But for the foreseeable future, Denmark will remain dependent on imported coal and oil for much of her energy requirements. The Danes have, so far at any rate, resolutely resisted the temptation to utilize nuclear fuel, though they are in the forefront of scientific research when it comes to non-polluting energy sources, notably the huge windmill parks to be found in many parts of the country, and various experiments to harness the tide and exploit geothermal energy.

The language is Danish, one of the Nordic languages, very similar to Norwegian. It looks and sounds very difficult, because it features unfamiliar juxtapositions of consonants like GJ and TV and three unfamiliar vowels, Æ Å and Ø which when pronounced sound rather like someone being strangled. However, most people in Denmark speak English and at least one other European language fluently as well as the other Scandinavian ones; they have to, because almost nobody else speaks any Danish.

The weather is not brilliant (between 0 and 17 degrees centigrade in January and July respectively) and the fact that it very rarely gets totally dark in mid-summer is devastatingly offset by the fact that it very rarely gets bright in the winter: a few hours of murky twilight between noon and about four o'clock in the afternoon is about the best you can normally expect.

The total population is currently just over 5 million people, 80 per cent of whom live in cities. The population of Copenhagen is 1.36 million.

HISTORICAL PERSPECTIVE

Vinland and the Vikings

The first appearance of the word Denmark, or a close approximation of it, occurred about 940 when the Sea-king Gorm the Old inserted a reference to the place in an inscription on his wife Tyre's runic gravestone. But it wasn't until after the arrival of Christianity that the Danes began to make their presence felt in the rest of the known world.

They did this with a vengeance in that extraordinary explosion of the Vikings out of Scandinavia: hordes of stout fighting men in longboats who issued forth from all the countries around AD 800–900 – Swedes and Norwegians and Icelanders as well as Danes – in search of wine and women and more clement climes to conquer and enjoy.

Early in the ninth century the Danes attacked England, established settlements in Northumbria and East Anglia and gradually spread their power southwards until eventually King Canute and two of his sons ruled the whole country for about twenty-five years until 1042.

At the end of the ninth century a Danish Viking from Iceland discovered Greenland by the simple process of being driven ashore there in a storm and within two centuries other parties of Vikings had settled in Greenland and had pushed on to discover Newfoundland, which they called Vinland after the wild vines they found there.

At the zenith of their power the Vikings had established themselves in Ireland, England and in that part of France which came to be called Normandy after them. Finding northern France far more to their liking than their own dark forests and frosty fjords, they settled down there and became the Normans; and it was as the Normans that they dominated the whole history of Europe for centuries, initially from their base in France and then from England, which became their principal kingdom.

And although the Viking Age came to an end in the rest of Europe around the middle of the eleventh century, the Viking spirit remained very much alive in Denmark, where continuing piracy made travel between the islands extremely perilous and where the Viking addiction to good food, strong drink and beautiful women persisted. King Svend, one of the most celebrated of the early Danish monarchs, indulged in much feasting, was married four times and had at least fifteen illegitimate children by different mistresses. Nor were the Vikings prepared to ditch their old gods with the arrival of Christianity: Tyr, Woden, Thor and Frey bequeathed to the English language their names for four of the days of the week.

The history of Denmark, and indeed all Scandinavia, in the period between the Age of the Vikings and the nineteenth century is the history of interminable struggles between Denmark, Norway and Sweden for control of one another and did not impinge very much upon the rest of Europe.

When Britain went to war with revolutionary France in 1793, attacks by British warships on Danish merchantmen trading with France led to a system of armed convoys which in turn brought about the seizure of all Danish ships in British ports.

In 1798, Britain's Admiral Hyde Parker sent his second-in-command, Horatio Nelson, to bombard the Danish fleet in the harbour at Copenhagen in an effort to prevent Napoleon from hijacking it and using it for his proposed invasion of England. The Danes were taken by surprise but put up a stout defence and Nelson withdrew, badly mauled. Then in 1806, when Napoleon banned all trade between occupied Europe and Britain, and the latter in turn banned all overseas trade with French-occupied lands, the Danes entered the war on the French side. In August 1807 British troops landed to the north of Copenhagen, and the city was bombarded for five days during which over 1,000 buildings including the university were destroyed.

After the Napoleonic Wars, Denmark's principal conflict in Europe was about the people of Schleswig-Holstein, partly German-speaking, partly Danish, on the border between Jutland and the united German state which was then emerging; the matter was not finally settled until Bismarck, by that time Chancellor of Prussia, moved German troops into the area in 1864. Subsequently, in 1866, it became a part of Prussia, reducing Denmark's stake in mainland Europe by 40 per cent. A part of the peninsula was returned to Denmark after Germany's defeat in World War I, despite the fact that Denmark had remained neutral.

In World War II, Denmark, again neutral, was invaded by the Germans in April 1940 and occupied for the duration of the war. However, throughout the war, Britain maintained close contact with the Freedom Council (the resistance), and by May 1944 an underground army of 43,000 was ready to assist the Allies when they reached Denmark from the south.

COLONIAL CONNECTIONS

Greenland, Iceland, Bornholm and the Faroes

It would be fruitless to try to trace the changes of ownership of the many islands in the icy northern waters between Newfoundland and mainland Russia in the years between their discovery and recent times. For example, in 1782 Norway, then united with Denmark, was claiming sovereignty over the east coast of Greenland on historical grounds.

Norway was separated from Denmark in 1815, and took over control of Sweden until 1905. It was during this period that Norway claimed the eastern part of Greenland.

This area was in fact almost completely unexplored; the Eskimos who lived there were not discovered until 1884. The dispute was finally settled in 1933, when the International Court at The Hague disallowed the Norwegian claim, and Greenland was an undisputed Danish colony until 1953. It then became a part of Denmark, with equal rights and two seats in the Danish single-chamber parliament known as the Folketing. It was part of Denmark when the latter joined the European Community in 1973, but withdrew after a referendum in 1982; it had been granted internal autonomy in 1979 though it remained, and still does, under Danish sovereignty, so far as foreign affairs and defence are concerned.

Greenland is the largest island in the world, 2,175,600 square kilometres in area, measuring over 1,000 kilometres from west to east at its point of greatest width; this makes it roughly four times the size of France. Its northern tip is well inside the Arctic Circle and its population has risen from an estimated 6,000 at the beginning of the nineteenth century to 12,000 in 1900, 46,000 in 1971 and 53,000 today, of whom 11,000 live in the capital, known as Godthåb or Nuuk, according to whether you speak Danish or Eskimo.

The indigenous population are Eskimos, who incidentally resent being called Eskimos; they like to be known as Green-landers, or Northern Danes. Mostly they now live European-style, park their sledges in the car parks outside the supermarkets where they do their shopping, and have become completely integrated with the 7,000 inhabitants of Danish origin.

The first Eskimos, like all the other Amerindians, came from Asia across the Bering Straits at a remote period in the past; in some areas they still live in traditional igloos, though it's worth noting that the word igloo simply means a house of any kind. A snow house is an igloo-yak and consists of a single room reached through an entrance passage, with a bed at the far end. The walls are covered with sealskins or old newspapers and a ventilation hole or *kignak* ('nose') admits air to the often overcrowded dwelling-space, which combines living room, kitchen, dining room, bedroom and everything else.

Another Danish possession, Iceland (which was completely cut off from Denmark during World War II), opted for independence in 1944. The second largest island in Europe, Iceland measures 103,000 square kilometres. Iceland has a population of only

230,000 people, of whom about 90,000 live in the capital, Reykjavik.

Iceland was created by volcanic activity about 60 million years ago and still has working examples of almost every known type of volcanic activity to be found on the earth. It is famous for its hot springs (the result of all that violent underground volcanic agitation) which are no mere tourist attractions. Over 70 per cent of the population heat their homes, and the better-heeled ones their swimming pools and greenhouses as well, from the hot water from these springs.

Most of Iceland's energy requirements are supplied by hydro-electric schemes, and it has been reckoned that only about 6 per cent of the country's geothermal power potential has so far been exploited.

The island of Bornholm in the Baltic Sea remains a Danish possession and is a favourite haunt in springtime of hay fever victims, since it offers total immunity from all types of allergy caused by pollen, as it consists of a bare rock without any vegetation.

The people of Bornholm are noted for their independence. A Dane who was born there told me: 'Bornholm is an island composed of individuals. If you put five Bornholmers into a boat together, it will probably go on the rocks and sink, because that's what happens when you have five captains in one boat.'

Another Danish possession, the Faroes (an archipelago halfway between the Shetland Islands off Scotland and Iceland), achieved home rule in 1948, though the Danish government still controls the foreign affairs and defence of the islands.

The Danish possessions in the Antilles (West Indies) were sold to the United States and became part of the American Virgin Islands.

DEVELOPMENT DIRECTIONS

From Sailboats to Supertankers

For centuries, Denmark's principal industry was agriculture.

Danish agriculture produces enough food to feed all of Denmark's 5 million people, plus the combined populations of New York and Tokyo (another 17 million).

In the late nineteenth century, when the first cheap grain from North America and Russia began to arrive in Europe and upset the economy of many farming communities, the Danes rapidly revised their agricultural policy, used the imported grain as fodder, and specialized in providing butter, bacon and eggs for England and meat for Germany.

Another basic Danish industry was fishing, and again, Danish fishermen were among the first in Europe to adapt to new demands and concentrate on industrial fish, that is to say, fish to be turned into fertilizers, lubricating oil and so on. By 1987, fish destined for industrial use, rather than for the table, represented 76 per cent of the total volume of the annual catch.

The Danes also moved into industrial production via agriculture, on a very sound and logical basis. Beer, aquavit and sugar were first produced on an industrial scale from grain, potatoes and beet, and from their meat and fish they began to turn out processed foods.

The provision of the machinery needed to process and package these food products led to the development of a new industrial skill which, once acquired, could be expanded and exported: the ability to manufacture and maintain food processing plants.

The processed food had to be stored in refrigerated containers and then exported in suitable ships. This necessity forced the Danes to diversify into refrigeration techniques and into the building of container ships and eventually into ships of all kinds. These ships required sophisticated navigational aids in order to negotiate a sea scattered with 529 (or 406) islands, and the navigational equipment, once developed, was then exported for use in aircraft, airports and even in outer space.

Another characteristic of Danish industry has been its ability to find niches in world markets where originality and individuality could create a demand. The development of Lego is a good example. From Greenland to the Philippines, anybody who has ever spent any time in the company of young children will know all about Lego. It's as universal as Coca-Cola or cornflakes. And it was invented in Jutland, where there is now a miniature town, made of Lego and called Legoland.

In the field of hi fi and television, Bang and Olufsen's flair for distinctive shapes has created a line of products elegant enough to be included in displays of design at the Museum of Modern Art in New York.

By 1985 industry accounted for 75 per cent of Danish exports, as against 17 per cent for agriculture and 4 per cent for fishing. By now, the Danes are manufacturing almost everything, from polyester sailing dinghies to 500,000 tonne supertankers. Danish hardware has been landed on the moon, Danish X-ray equipment for testing seamwelds on aircraft is used worldwide, and there are Danish monitoring devices in hospitals everywhere.

Nevertheless, industry still represents only 29.5 per cent of the GNP as against 52 per cent for the service industries.

Danish State railways and a few private companies cover the country with a dense network of fast, modern trains, supplemented by buses in the more remote areas, and train journeys across Denmark frequently involve crossings by ferry which offer an opportunity to relax and enjoy a meal in more comfort than is possible on a train.

Danish motorways are free and the secondary roads are among the best in the world, and are not crowded. Even what would be described elsewhere as country lanes all have asphalt surfaces.

International through-trains with sleeping, couchette and dining cars connect Denmark with the remainder of the European continent and with Britain, via Esbjerg and Harwich.

About forty airlines have regular flights through Copenhagen, and there are services to other parts of Denmark and to all the major airports in Europe.

Telecommunications are excellent, though it may come as a surprise to people in the United Kingdom and indeed in many European countries that until a couple of years ago, Denmark only had one TV channel, run by the state radio station and financed from licence fees. A second channel opened in 1988.

The first Danish newspaper appeared in 1666, and was written entirely in verse. The oldest of the existing newspapers, *Berlingkse Tidende*, was founded by a Copenhagen printer in 1749. Nearly 2 million newspapers are printed every day, and almost all households in Denmark take a daily paper.

AFFAIRS OF STATE

Freedom and the Folketing

Denmark is a parliamentary democracy with a hereditary constitutional monarchy, which, since 1953, has permitted female succession, and the present queen, Margrethe II, is a direct descendant of the first king, Gorm the Old. Parliament consists of a single chamber, the *Folketing*, with 179 representatives, including two each from Greenland and the Faroes. Everybody over the age of eighteen has a vote, and a system of proportional representation is used. This has at times led to a proliferation of small parties, sometimes as many as eleven, now around nine, including Social Democrats, Radical Liberals, Conservatives and others.

Laws are made by the Folketing which has a prime minister and a cabinet elected by the parliament and not chosen by the prime minister, as in Britain, and Denmark has a written constitution, dating back to 1849, which guarantees inviolable personal liberty to every Dane, including the right to free speech and an assurance that no Danish subject will ever be deprived of liberty on the grounds of political or religious convictions, or of descent.

Censorship is forbidden under the constitution, and the referendum is frequently used to refer important matters to the electorate for a direct decision.

For administration purposes, Denmark is divided into fourteen districts known as *amts* and Copenhagen is divided into two parishes, København and Frederiksberg.

Denmark was among the first fifty states to sign the charter of the United Nations in San Francisco in 1945. Her armed forces consist of an army (19,400 regulars and 9,900 conscripts), a navy (5,400 regulars and 900 conscripts), and an air force (6,900 regulars and 700 conscripts), plus 72,000 reservists. Although small, these armed forces have always been available to contribute to peace-keeping forces, for example in the Middle East and in the Congo, and Denmark is represented in the UN forces stationed in Cyprus. Denmark has been a member of NATO since 1949.

The European headquarters of the World Health Organization (WHO) is in Copenhagen, which also has a vast UNICEF warehouse for the distribution of aid to children in need throughout the world.

About one-third of Denmark's total state expenditure goes to the social services. In 1986, the figure was 64 billion kroner out of a total expenditure of 185 billion kroner, and in addition, all local health services are financed from the county authorities to the tune of another 25 billion kroner. What it amounts to is that roughly UK £1,600 sterling is invested every year in the health and well-being of every Danish citizen.

The public health system entitles every one of the 5 million Danes in the country to choose his own doctor from among the 3,000 or so general practitioners. The GP may refer the patient to a specialist or have the patient admitted to hospital and, as in many Community countries, there is no charge to the patient.

A state pension, enough to pay for basic essentials, is paid from age sixty-seven, and while the general policy aims at trying to care for older people in their own homes, all old people who require special attention are entitled to a private room in one of the state-financed old people's homes, which they can decorate and furnish to their liking.

This level of social security costs a lot of money, and in 1986 the total tax burden — including direct and indirect taxes, capital taxes and social security contributions — amounted to 51 per cent of the GNP, which is very high.

On the other hand, the Danes are among the best-paid people

in the world. In 1985, the average disposable income per capita was the seventh highest in the world. Of just over 1 million homes in Denmark, 91 per cent have TV, 90 per cent have telephones, 62 per cent have washing machines and 60 per cent have cars.

The Danes spend about 22 per cent of their disposable income on food, drink and tobacco, and around 25 per cent on housing, which leaves them more than 50 per cent for leisure activities and holidays. About 59 per cent of the householders own their own homes, while 10 per cent of them also have secondary residences or country cottages.

CULTURE AND LEISURE

The Quiet Hooligans

Denmark is a predominantly, though not passionately, Protestant country; the principal religion is Evangelical Lutheranism. About 92 per cent of the population are listed as Lutherans, though even the Lutheran Church is prepared to admit that not more than 4 or 5 per cent are to be found in church on Sundays and that Christmas Eve is about the only occasion when priests can expect a full house.

It is certainly unlikely that many of them are in any way evangelical: it is against the whole Danish psyche to be evangelical about anything.

A distinctively Danish development in education was the *Folkehojskole* (People's High School), boarding schools of which the prime aim is not the acquisition of knowledge for its own sake, but rather the development of personality through dialogue between teachers and pupils, and immersion in literature and history. There are no examinations, and the idea came originally from the poet-historian Bishop Nikolai Frederick Severin Grundtvig in the early nineteenth century. The first school run on these lines was established in South Jutland in 1844.

School attendance is compulsory for a minimum of nine years. Over 91 per cent of them attend the state-funded *Folkeskole* (People's School), a development of the *Folkehojskole*, where again there are no formal examinations, though at the end of the ninth or tenth year the pupils may voluntarily choose to take an examination, and receive a certificate.

There are also a number of private schools, for which the state provides 85 per cent of the funding.

The country has five universities, the oldest dating from 1479, and hundreds of specialized schools of all sorts; in addition, most industries have comprehensive and lengthy training schemes for apprentices.

It has been said, with a certain amount of truth I believe, that while other countries have culture, the Scandinavians have taste. It is certainly true of the Danes. They have not, I think, produced a single great artist of international standard, or as a Danish government publication puts it, 'Danish art has seldom attracted attention in other European countries.'

One sculptor, Bertel Thorvaldsen (1770–1844), was very successful in Rome, and through him some less talented of his fellow-countrymen were accepted in international art circles. The painter C.W. Eckersberg (1783–1853) studied under Jacques Louis David in Paris, and one of his own pupils, Christen Kobe, became famous for his studies of old Danish churches.

One composer, Carl Nielsen, is widely known outside Denmark. Apart from H.C. Andersen, Danish literature is associated abroad either with the philosopher Søren Kierkegaard, who is generally credited with the invention of existentialism, or with Karen Blixen, who was at least as well known for her lifestyle as for her writing, and whose name is familiar to young people today through a film based on one of her books, *Out of Africa.*

Danish architecture, as represented by castles like Kronborg at Helsingor, and Frederiksborg at Hillerod, Christianborg Palace in Copenhagen and Roskilde Cathedral, is very striking, though no more so than equally well-preserved examples of the same sort of architecture elsewhere. One of the most remarkable modern buildings in the world, the Sydney Opera House, was designed by a Danish architect, Jørn Utzen.

But where the Danes and other Scandinavians have really left their mark on the world is in the design of furniture and textiles, towels and carpets and curtains, chairs and tables, all sorts of things in everyday use.

Tycho Brahe (1546—1601), an archetypal Renaissance humanist, is recognized as the originator with Copernicus of modern astronomy; he laid the basis for Kepler's discovery of the laws governing the planetary movements around the sun.

Thomas Bartholin (1616—80) discovered the human lymphatic system; Nicolaus Steno (1638—86) founded the science of geology; Ole Romer (1644—1710) measured the speed of light; H.C. Orsted (1777—1851) discovered electro-magnetism, as well as that extremely useful element, aluminium; and Niels Bohr (1885—1962), a Nobel prize winner, was one of the pioneers in the development of nuclear energy.

Many foreign visitors to Denmark, accustomed to fairly rigid mealtimes and a definite distinction between lunch and dinner, tend to be puzzled by the Danish attitude to the main meal of the day, which is known as *middag*, and is consumed at whatever time the man of the house returns from work, which is usually the late afternoon.

The object of this arrangement is to enable the Danes to make the maximum use of their long, bright summer evenings, because, although they enjoy their food thoroughly, they don't really take it seriously, as an end in itself, as the French used to do. They'd far rather be out and about, hiking or swimming or sailing.

There is another evening meal, known as *aftens*, a light supper taken after whatever activity has filled the evening hours, before retiring to bed.

The explanation as to how the Danes can manage to last out until the late afternoon for their main meal of the day may lie in the nature of their breakfast. This can, and usually does, include such items as fruit, muesli, cornflakes and other cereals, as well as eggs, several varieties of cheese, a selection of charcuterie, salami and cold meat, with raw herrings in endless guises. Hot meatballs, and salads as well as many kinds of bread, with butter and jam, and Danish pastries are also fairly normal.

After such a breakfast, you are not likely to feel hungry before *middag*, whenever that chances to come along, but if you do, you can always nip into a restaurant and order a *smorrebrod*. The word means simply buttered bread, though there is nothing simple about a typical Danish example of their national gastronomic speciality, the open sandwich. To call it a sandwich would be an insult, except to the extent that somewhere, underneath that enormous pile of delicious food, you will eventually find a slice of bread, and to call it open is confusing except in the sense that they don't attempt to balance another slice of bread on top of it.

Smorrebrod can consist of anything: crab, lobster, smoked salmon, or a combination of any or all of them, fully garnished; or cold turkey or smoked herring or chicken or roast beef; or pork or sausages or salami or cheese; or hard-boiled eggs or curried rice or any known variety of salad or almost anything edible you can think of.

Most Danish seafood is excellent, meals of international standard are obtainable everywhere in Denmark, and Danish cheese producers manufacture convincing if sometimes slightly stronger versions of such international cheeses as Roquefort, Gruyère, Stilton and Camembert.

It's a beer-drinking country, and an expensive one at that, which is a warning that wines are pricey. But who wants to drink Gevrey-Chambertin with pickled herrings?

The Danes make the most of their long summer evenings, and in a country where nowhere is more than a few miles from the sea, spend a great deal of their spare time swimming, sunbathing, messing about in boats, as well as seriously yachting and fishing. They also enjoy cycling, walking, youth-hostelling and, in fact, all so-called sports associated with the open air.

The Danish football team in their red and white jerseys caught the attention of the world when in 1986 they fought their way through to the final rounds of the World Cup championships in Mexico, as the Danish nation came to a standstill. The sport has a huge following, and it is reckoned that there are about 300,000 active players of the game, ranging from six-year-old boys dreaming of joining the national team to star professional players.

Although the whole nation follows the sport, and the team's more ardent followers accompany the players to their away matches, the Danish football fans have acquired an international reputation for quiet, good behaviour. The Danes have a word for it, *roligans*, as opposed to hooligans. The Danish word *rolig* means quiet.

Understandably, the Danes have produced one outstanding international yachtsman, Paul Elvstrom, who won Olympic gold medals in 1948, 1952, 1956 and 1960, but in general they have never made a great name for themselves in athletics or the more fiercely competitive sports like boxing or tennis, and their big marathon, which attracts up to 20,000 participants a year, is not in any sense a race: the purpose is never to win, merely to participate.

The explanation probably lies in the Danish character; they have too strong a sense of humour to take anything very seriously, even themselves, and it is very hard to succeed in the more competitive one-to-one sports unless you take yourself very seriously indeed.

THE DUTCH

A Place for People

THE NETHERLANDS IN PROFILE

Area	41,160 sq km
Population	14,500,000
Population density	349 per sq km
Women	50.5%
Under 15	20%
Over 65	11.9%
Language	Dutch, Frisian
Religion	36% Catholic, 32% Protestant (mainly Dutch Reformed)
Labour force	39.6%
Employed in:	
Agriculture	4.9%
Industry	28.1%
Services	67%
Women in labour force	24.5%
Unemployment (as % of labour force)	12.4%

Major Exports: Minerals (23.6%); finished goods, including textiles (20.8%); vehicles and electrical appliances (19.2%); food beverages and tobacco (17.4%); chemical products (15.4%)

Main customers: EC (75.7%); USA (4.6%); Sweden (1.7%); Switzerland (1.7%)

THE DUTCH

Bicycles occupy a very special position in the Dutch ethos. The Dutch population is approximately 15 million. The number of ordinary, two-wheel push bicycles in the Netherlands is approximately 14 million. It therefore seems that the Dutch population, male and female, between say twelve and sixty years of age, must have two bicycles apiece. Possibly an old bone-rattler for visiting the friends and neighbours, and a brand new mountain-bike (called an ATB – all-terrain-bike – on the continent) for difficult journeys. Except that there are no hills at all in Holland; the whole country is as flat as a pancake and almost half of it is well below sea-level. So why do they need the mountain bikes? Perhaps they need them in the same way that people who live in the tropics need central heating, and people in Iceland need air conditioning; as status symbols.

Status symbols or not, the Dutch seem to use their bicycles a great deal. In 1989, according to the magazine *Euroholland*, the 14 million bicycles then domiciled in Dutch households covered a grand total of 12 billion kilometres as against 11 billion kilometres the previous year. And that's an awful lot of miles when you consider that Holland measures less than 300 kilometres from north to south and only about 200 kilometres from east to

119

west. They must spend an awful lot of time on those bikes.

When I was at school, the only thing we knew about Holland was that a little boy had once saved the country by standing all night with his finger plugging up a hole in the dike. Possibly because in Ireland we were accustomed to the idea of emigration as a solution to most of this world's problems, it occurred to me even then that the little boy would be far better employed hitching a lift to Rotterdam and jumping a boat bound for London or New York where there were better jobs to be had than standing all night with your finger stopping up a hole in a sea wall.

Amsterdam with its canals and tall gabled houses is one of the most attractive cities in Europe, and certainly one of the most tolerant. For centuries a refuge for dissenters and religious and political misfits of all kinds, it is now a mecca for hippies, druggies, beatniks and all the other varieties of -niks.

At one end of the scale, it is a place where the young who need them can get the soft drugs they seem to need so desperately without any fear of legal repercussions. And at the other end of the scale, it is a country which appreciates that in certain circumstances the ability to arrange a swift and dignified departure from the scene is far more important than any set of rules and regulations governing euthanasia and the responsibilities of the medical profession. Holland is a place for people, a place where the rights of people always take precedence, sometimes, perhaps, almost to a fault.

After centuries as the most rigid, orderly, Calvinistic country in Europe, the Dutch now seem to have taken over from the Danes as the most palpably permissive people in the Community. They have legalized the sale and use of soft drugs, they have gone much further than Britain in legalizing and accepting homosexuality, and they have carried sexual equality far further than any other European nation. Towards the end of 1990, according to an article by Angela Lambert in the London *Independent*, they lifted the 'fear of prosecution from children aged between twelve and sixteen years of age who engage in a sexual relationship ... provided it is of their own free will'.

This does not mean that the age of consent has actually been lowered to twelve, though it could have that effect. The sexual act is still, in principle, forbidden to both boys and girls under sixteen years of age, but if there is no complaint from anybody, there will be no prosecution. And even in flagrantly free Holland, there could be pressures on children not to complain.

According to a survey of 11,500 Dutch schoolchildren, only about 6 per cent claimed to have had sex before the age of fourteen. By sixteen years of age that figure had risen to 17 per cent, and by seventeen to 50 per cent. In most cases the sexual partners were contemporaries whom they had met at school or at discos. As far as the other cases are concerned — that is, cases involving older people — one boy, with a more cynical approach to the law, hit the weakness in the system on the head. Even if children can complain to the police, he explained, most of them would be too frightened to do so. So the intended protection hardly exists in practice.

Angela Lambert reported that the acceptance of sexual behaviour was evident throughout Holland. Pornography was displayed at knee level rather than on the top shelf in newsagents; while a basket of blue videos with startlingly explicit covers could be found next to the entrance of a shop. She continued: 'In one government department I regularly visit, a security guard says goodbye to his male friend with a frank, unselfconscious kiss. No one turns a hair. Not surprisingly, perhaps, under the new bill everything that applies to teenage heterosexual couples applies also to two girls or two boys.'

Mrs Maarian Soutendijk, the spokesperson for the Christian Democratic Party during the debate on the bill in parliament, said: 'Where a relationship between two young people is good and beautiful and acceptable to their parents, it should be kept out of the hands of the Law. I think this bill is very civilized; I am very pleased that it has passed.'

And a Dutchman in his seventies commented to Angela Lambert: 'Contraception and legislation have given the young all the opportunities they want. The dam has burst, and it can't be closed up again.'

'Upon a map of the world the Netherlands are but a little speck, an estuary and a chain or two of islands,' wrote Sacheverell Sitwell in *The Netherlands* (London: Batsford, 1974). 'The part they have played in history is out of all proportion to their size. They founded a fabulous empire at the far side of the world, in the remote East Indies, with a native population of some 60 millions. They have possessions in the West Indies and only failed to retain domination in North Atlantic America, in Brazil, at the Cape and in Ceylon. It may be that the Dutch genius is more lasting than her colonies. As a race of artists, they are second only to the Italians.'

Their riches came from the other side of the world, and they grew rich in one generation. They are almost alone among the people of Europe in that the Normans played no part in their history and no Norman blood flows in their veins. They build their homes in red-brick like the English, houses with gabled ends and fanlights similar to those found in many parts of London.

Their capital city, The Hague (Den Haag), is no bigger than a few London squares, surrounded by fairly typical twentieth-century urban development and Sitwell remarks slightly unfairly that the Dutch have no landscape, no country, but that every house in Amsterdam has flowers in its windows.

The English connections are many and varied. The seaside resort of Scheveningen is probably the only continental resort every bit as dreary as Margate or Blackpool; it was from these bleak shores that Charles II embarked upon the adventure of the Restoration of the English Monarchy. Daniel Morot, a Huguenot craftsman and artist, accompanied Prince William III of Orange and his wife Mary, the elder daughter of James II, the last Catholic King of England, when they went to England at the time of the Glorious Revolution (1688–9) to become joint monarchs and secure the Protestant succession. Morot designed the state coach for the Speaker of the House of Commons, and it has been used ever since in the coronation ceremonies of English monarchs.

The Zuider Zee, one of the features of Holland which used to be world-famous, doesn't exist any more; a 30 kilometre dam

connecting the provinces of Friesland and North Holland trans-
formed it in the late thirties into an inland sea which gradually
became a freshwater lake, the IJsselmeer, as the waters brought
into it from the rivers could no longer mix with the open sea. Once
the IJsselmeer had been enclosed, work began on draining four
enormous polders — a total gain of 165,000 hectares of new
land.

Incidentally, the word polder comes from an old Dutch word
pol, meaning stake, because the first dikes were constructed of
rows of stakes, supporting seaweed or grass, building rubble,
sand, gravel, clay or any other available material, which theoretically at least would hold back the sea.

The two oldest polders, the Wieringermeer Polder and the
North-east Polder, are used as agricultural land. The more
recently drained ones in Flevoland are used for housing, industrial
development and recreational facilities to relieve some of the
congestion in the Ranstad conurbation around Amsterdam,
Rotterdam, The Hague and Utrecht.

Holland is probably the only country in the world which has a
museum (at Koog aan de Zaan) exclusively devoted to the history
of windmills. This might seem a bit extreme except that the very
existence of at least one-half of the total area of Holland today is
largely due to the efforts of the windmills. The first mills designed
to drain the Dutch farmlands date back to 1414, and they were
used in rows, as many as sixty mills being required for a fairly
large reclamation project.

People who live in countries where the heaviest downpour
drains away down the sewers overnight find it difficult to understand Holland's problem. More than half the total area of the
country is not merely below sea level but a lot of it is as much as
almost 7 metres below sea level. To reclaim such land, it is necessary to build a series of concentric moats; one windmill will
dispose of approximately 60 centimetres of water into the moat,
where the next windmill will dispose of another 60 centimetres
into the next moat, built on higher ground, and so on, until
eventually, it will have taken the combined power of at least a
dozen windmills and a dozen concentric moats to drain an area at

the lowest level. It would never be worth it, if the Dutch didn't happen to be unlucky enough to live in the most densely populated country in the world.

Their history, like Britain's is inextricably linked with the sea, which is their common causeway with the outside world and which has proved their principal means of earning a livelihood through the centuries. They became one of the great seafaring people of Europe, following the Genovese, the Venetians and the Turks. They sailed the Spanish Main at the same time as the Spaniards, the French and the British. Like the British, they began by specializing in privateering and piracy, and found themselves among the world's leading maritime nations.

LAND AND PEOPLE

Canals and Windmills

Holland (officially Nederland) is part of the north-west European plain and has land boundaries with Germany to the east and with Belgium on the south. The North Sea coastline provides the western and northern frontiers of the country and more than half of the total land area of 41,864 square kilometres is below sea level. The highest point in the Netherlands is only 321 metres above sea level, and the lowest point, a reclaimed polder northeast of Rotterdam, is 6.7 metres below sea level.

Over the centuries, Holland's often uncomfortably close proximity to the sea has had both disastrous and highly advantageous effects on the land and the people. Time and again, vast areas of the country have been flooded, so that one aspect of Dutch history has been concerned with their unceasing battle against the sea. As early as the Middle Ages the Dutch were building dikes not merely to keep the sea out, but also to reclaim land from the sea, and by now all of the land formerly lost to the sea has been reclaimed, developed and populated, but at a considerable cost in time, money and effort.

On the credit side, Holland's maritime connections have

proved extremely useful, first in developing a thriving fishing industry, and later in promoting a flourishing overseas trade which was also stimulated by the fact that three of Europe's major rivers, the Rhine, the Scheldt and the Maas (the Meuse in France) finally reach the sea inside Dutch territory. As a consequence, right from the Middle Ages, the Dutch have had international seaports serving a hinterland that extends right across western and central Europe. These ports proved invaluable not only for trade and communications, but also for the export of agricultural produce, the importation of raw materials and fuel for industry and for the export of finished goods. The high population density – at 434 inhabitants per square kilometre, the highest in Europe – forced the Dutch to look abroad for additional sources of prosperity, and it was Holland's geographical location more than any other factor, and more perhaps than in the case of any other nation, which shaped the character and the destiny of the Dutch people.

The Netherlands lies within the temperate zone, but because of the proximity of both the North Sea and the Atlantic enjoys – perhaps endures would be a better word – a maritime climate with prevailing sea winds; in short, it's usually cold and wet and often windy in Holland. The average temperature in January is two degrees centigrade and in July it rarely gets any hotter than seventeen degrees centigrade. The average number of hours of what the Dutch regard as summer days (with a temperature of twenty-five degrees centigrade or higher) varies from five in the Frisian Islands off the north coast to thirty-five in the southern province of Limburg. And that's per year.

The mild, damp climate (average annual rainfall is 800 milli-metres, slightly more than the west of Ireland's 750 millimetres) makes it suitable for grassland, dairy and livestock farming and for horticulture, particularly near the coast where there is a lower incidence of frost, though the lack of sunshine means that a lot of the cultivation has to be under glass.

The landscape is gentle, undramatic, but quietly pleasing. Geologically the High Netherlands (the area high enough to escape flooding without dikes) consists mainly of sand and gravel, and the Low Netherlands mainly of clay and peat. The most striking features of the landscape are all man-made, notably the cities, towns and villages, and above all the canals and the windmills, 900 of which survive from more than 9,000 which were working — mainly draining the polders, grinding seed for oil or driving sawmills — at the turn of the century.

Natural resources include large quantities of natural gas in the north and in the North Sea, small amounts of petroleum in the North Sea as well and also inland. Coal was mined in parts of Holland until about twenty years ago.

All that remains of the prehistoric inhabitants of the area are some *hunebedds* (giant graves), long dolmens dating back to around 3000–2000 BC in the province of Drenthe, and the remains of some *terps* (mounds) built by settlers some 2,000 years ago in Friesland in an early effort to build their homes above the level of the marshlands and the floods.

When the Romans conquered northern Gaul between 57 and 50 BC, they found there a mixture of Gallo-Celtic and Germanic tribes. These included the Celtic Belgae, whom the Romans conquered; the Frankish (Germanic) Batavi, living among the islands and around the river mouths; and the Germanic tribe of Frisians who lived on the coastal strip north of the Scheldt estuary. In AD 13, Drusus the Roman general managed to bring the Batavi under Roman influence, not as defeated foes, but as allies who provided an invaluable source of recruits for the Roman legions. The Romans left only the remains of one civilian settlement, later fortified (today's Heerlen, in Limburg). Subsequently, there was some Frankish and Saxon penetration of the area, but almost alone of all the countries of the Community, no part of Holland ever came under Norman influence.

Today the population of Holland is about 15 million. It was 2,613,000 in 1830 and 5,104,000 in 1900, and the increase is largely due to improved medical care and hygiene, though recently there has been some immigration. The greatest concentration of people is in the three western provinces of North Holland, South Holland and Utrecht; in fact nearly one-half of the population lives in one-fifth of the country's total area. There are eight times as many inhabitants per square kilometre in South Holland as there are in the most sparsely populated area, the province of Flevoland; yet the average population density of Holland is the highest in the Community, which means that the area around Utrecht, Rotterdam and Amsterdam is as over-crowded as Tokyo.

The Dutch have always emigrated; they were among the first of the Europeans to follow the lead of the Portuguese and the Spanish and look for overseas colonies to develop and exploit on the other side of the earth. Towards the end of the nineteenth century and indeed right up to the fifties of this century, thou-sands of Dutch people emigrated to Canada, the United States, South Africa, Australia and New Zealand. By the sixties, when the political situation in Europe had become stabilized and the economy had recovered from the effects of World War II, the situation was reversed, and a shortage of unskilled labour in Holland led to a vast influx of workers from other European countries.

The population of the Netherlands was also increased by an inflow of people from the former Dutch colonies of Indonesia and Surinam, as well as some 350,000 foreign workers from the Mediterranean countries who settled in the country in the late sixties and in the seventies.

The principal language, Dutch, is of Germanic origin; Frisian, a fairly closely related Germanic language is spoken in Friesland. However, because the Dutch, like the Danes, can find few people who speak their language, many of them speak English, German or French.

The Netherlands Antilles — the islands of Curaçao, Bonaire, Saba, St Eustatius, St Maarten (St Martin) and Aruba in the arc of Caribbean islands lying between North and South America — are an autonomous part of the Kingdom of the Netherlands. Part of the island of St Maarten is French, falling under the jurisdiction of the Department of Guadeloupe.

HISTORICAL PERSPECTIVE

The House of Orange

By the third century the Roman hold on the perimeter of her empire was slackening, and by 466 Clovis, King of the Franks, began to impose his authority upon the various Frankish tribes in the area, most of whom were converted to Christianity. Along the coast, the Frisians maintained their independence and their pagan ways; indeed as late as 630 a Christian church built 130 years earlier was destroyed by the pagan Frisians. But by the end of the sixth century, the Frankish ruler Pepin, with the assistance of a Northumbrian missionary St Willibrod, had established Christianity throughout the Low Countries.

After the death in 814 of the Emperor Charlemagne and the subsequent dissipation of his empire, the Netherlands went through a long series of changes of ownership. The whole area, including what later became the Kingdom of Belgium, consisted of a number of autonomous duchies, such as Gelre and Brabant, and counties, such as Holland and Zeeland, as well as the bishopric of Utrecht.

During the eleventh and twelfth centuries, the towns began to grow in size and strength and started to impose their independence upon the local feudal lords through charters setting down rules on taxation, administration and military obligations. Among the first towns in the Netherlands to break away from the feudal system were the great textile centres of Bruges, Ghent and Ypres, as well as cities such as Amsterdam, Rotterdam, Leiden, Haarlem, Delft and Utrecht.

By the middle of the fourteenth century, five feudal lords had emerged as the principal powers in the Netherlands, apart from the cities and towns; they included the Count of Flanders, the Count of Brabant and Limburg, the Duke of Gelder, the Count of Holland and the Bishop of Utrecht. In 1419, Duke Philip the Good of Burgundy acquired Flanders; in 1421, he bought Namurs, another principality; in 1430, he inherited Brabant, Limburg and Antwerp; in 1433, he took over Hainaut, Holland

and Zealand; and in 1443, he added Luxembourg to his possessions. In 1465, he summoned a States-General in Brussels to represent all his acquisitions, and appointed a Grand Council with supreme authority over the Netherlands.

He was succeeded by Charles the Bold, whose daughter Mary married the Archduke Maximilian of Austria. When Mary was killed in a riding accident in 1482, Maximilian became regent for their son, Philip the Fair.

Maximilian restored order in the Netherlands, but when he was elected Holy Roman Emperor in 1494, he handed the territory over to his son Philip, then aged fifteen. Philip married the Infanta of Spain, Joanna (known as Joanna the Mad). When Philip died in 1506, his wife was declared unfit to rule, and the Spanish succession, plus his Burgundian lands passed to their son Charles, then aged six, initially with Margaret of Austria as Regent.

In 1515, the States-General declared Charles to be of age, and in 1516 he became King Carlos (Charles) I of Spain. In 1519, he was elected Holy Roman Emperor as Charles V. Charles's territories then included the Holy Roman Empire of the German nation (basically Austria), the Netherlands and Spain as well as all the vast Spanish colonies overseas which had been acquired in the years immediately after Columbus's discovery of the West Indies and the American continent.

This period was also marked by the growth of the new reformed Christianity. Luther's Protestantism made an instant appeal to the hard-headed, no-nonsense Dutch and gained a very firm hold in the Netherlands right from the start.

Charles abdicated in 1555 and was succeeded by his son Felipe II (Philip II) of Spain, a ruthless and bigoted defender of the Catholic faith, who introduced the Inquisition, Jesuit priests and Spanish garrisons into the Netherlands in an effort to make the Dutch people conform to his ideas, and finally sent the Duke of Alva with an army of 10,000 tough Spanish soldiers to subdue the country.

In 1568, a number of the northern provinces of the Netherlands rebelled under Prince William I of Orange, known as William the Silent. Incidentally, William could trace his title back to

an ancient Roman town in the south of France, Orange or
Arausio, near the uppermost limit of the first Roman province in
Transalpine Gaul, the *Provincia* from which Provence derives its
name, a place where lizards still bask in the sun on the yellow
stone ruins of one of the finest Roman theatres in Europe.
Orange became a separate principality in Carolingian times, as a
result of the feudal disintegration of the Kingdom of Arles, and in
the first half of the sixteenth century the Orange succession
passed to the House of Nassau, which held scattered possessions in the Netherlands. And it was this William the Silent, the
first Prince of Orange-Nassau, who defied the Spanish monarchy,
the Roman Catholic Church and the Inquisition and began the
struggle to make the Netherlands an independent republic which
became a haven for dissenters of all sorts from all over Europe.
The Peace of Westphalia in 1648 recognized the Republic of the
Seven United Provinces as an independent state.

The Netherlands remained independent until the French
Revolution. In 1795, it became a part of the French Empire as the
Batavian Republic, and in 1810 the country was annexed by
Napoleon. When the French occupation came to an end after
Napoleon's defeat at Waterloo, the Kingdom of the Netherlands
came into existence; it included Holland plus the areas which are
now Belgium and Luxembourg.

The first King of Holland, William I, Prince of Orange-Nassau,
was the son of the last Stadholder, William V, who also happened
to be Grand Duke of Luxembourg. The union of the crowns of the
Netherlands, Belgium and Luxembourg came to an end in 1890
under the Salic Law, which excluded women from the Luxembourg succession, but already long before that, exasperated by
William's recalcitrant insistence on Dutch as the official language
and on religious liberty (which to him meant removing the schools
from Church control), the predominantly Catholic and French-
speaking southern provinces had revolted in 1830 to become the
independent Kingdom of Belgium, with Leopold of Saxe-Coburg
as sovereign.

During World War I, the Netherlands remained neutral, though
neutrality posed many problems with warring countries on its two

land boundaries. By now the country was known by most English-speaking people as Holland, after the two principal provinces in the country, North and South Holland. And the inhabitants of the country were known as the Dutch, after an ancient name for their language.

Holland continued to pursue a policy of strict neutrality right up until the German invasion of Poland. This did not however save Holland from invasion by Germany in 1940, after a blitzkrieg which almost destroyed Rotterdam. In five years of Nazi occupation the Jewish population of Holland was ruthlessly persecuted and virtually annihilated. Queen Wilhelmina left the Netherlands in May 1940 and spent the war years in England.

In 1948, after a reign of 50 years, she abdicated in favour of her daughter, Juliana, who herself abdicated in favour of her eldest daughter, Beatrix, in 1980. Queen Beatrix is married to Prince Claus of the Netherlands, and they have three sons.

COLONIAL CONNECTIONS

The Dutch in the Thames

It was during the period when the Netherlands was known as the United Provinces that the first steps to found an overseas empire were made. And they were made largely under the auspices of two commercial concerns, the Dutch East and West India companies.

When Felipe II of Spain closed the Portuguese ports to Dutch ships, the Dutch sailed directly to Java to collect the spices which previously had reached the country via the Portuguese ports. In 1595, the first ship from the United Provinces sailed around the Cape of Good Hope and founded a Dutch settlement in Java. To regulate and protect trade with the new colony, the States-General set up the Dutch East India Company, run by a board at The Hague. It was given a trading monopoly and complete freedom from import duties, and was also permitted to raise its own armed forces to protect its interests and was authorized to establish colonies abroad.

In the East Indies, the company — like the British East India Company — was in effect the government. Its capital was Batavia (now Jakarta in Java), and using its own armed forces, which in its heyday numbered 10,000 men as well as a fleet of some forty warships, the company succeeded in driving the British out of Malaya and the Moluccas, and the Portuguese out of Ceylon and Malacca. By 1652, another colony had been founded in South Africa, at the Cape of Good Hope, where the settlers became known as the Boers (Dutch for countryman or peasant), and the Dutch had established a network of trading posts right around the world.

The work of the Dutch East India Company was complemented by the Dutch West India Company, set up on a similar basis by the States-General to establish colonies in the new world and to regulate and protect the Dutch contraband trade with the Portuguese and Spanish colonies in Africa and the Americas. The colony of New Netherland with its capital New Amsterdam (on Manhattan Island) was established in 1623, and trading posts set up in Brazil, Curaçao, Aruba, Surinam and in West Africa.

In 1664, the settlers of New England, with the assistance of a British naval squadron, captured the Dutch colony of New Netherland, from which the Dutch West India Company's Caribbean colonies had been ruled by governors, the most famous of whom was Peter Stuyvesant. This action and some quarrels between Dutch and English settlers in West Africa led to a protracted war between the English and the Dutch.

France at that time had an alliance with Holland, based largely on shared hostility to Spain, and when in 1667 King Louis XIV of France seemed to be attacking Spain with some success, the English King Charles II felt justified in using the money voted by parliament to fit out a new fleet to fight the Dutch for his own extravagant personal pleasures. The Dutch admiral de Ruyter, hearing this, sailed up the Thames with his fleet and burnt some warships lying at anchor in the Medway. It was the first and last invasion attempt on England since the Norman conquest.

The war, like so many wars in those days, petered out inconclusively, and under the terms of the peace, the English kept New

Netherland (where New Amsterdam then became known as New York in honour of the Duke of York, the future King James II of England) and the Dutch retained Surinam, on the north-east coast of South America. Surinam remained part of the Kingdom of the Netherlands until 1975, when it became an independent republic.

Curaçao, which was valuable because of its salt pans — the Dutch herring industry depended on salt and by now the country's own supplies of salt were almost exhausted — was seized from the Spanish in 1634 and became a base for the Dutch West India Company's operations against the Spanish in the new world. Salt was also the main attraction of Bonaire which Van Walbeek, a predecessor of Stuyvesant's, seized in the same year. Two years later he took possession of Aruba on behalf of the company.

St Maarten was initially largely used as a base by Dutch pirates in the Caribbean; it changed hands many times over the centuries until 1816 when the southern half reverted to the Netherlands.

St Eustatius was colonized by settlers from Zealand in 1636 and became a big centre for the booming slave trade from West Africa. Later it became the main depot for military equipment for the North American colonists during the American War of Independence. Like St Maarten, it changed hands several times until it finally became Dutch again in 1816.

The Boers, hardy Dutch South African settlers, with their guerrilla tactics and their superior knowledge of the terrain, very nearly defeated the mighty army of the British Empire in the Boer War of 1899–1902.

The Netherlands Antilles now enjoy a considerable measure of autonomy; the Queen and government of Holland are represented by governors.

DEVELOPMENT DIRECTIONS

Tulips from Amsterdam

Although more than 54 per cent of Holland's total area is used for agriculture, and 8 per cent consists of woods, only 4.9 per cent of the working population are involved in agriculture and horticulture as against 28 per cent in industry and 67 per cent in the services sector. The few people who still work on the land today produce more food than ever, on less and less land, and much of the food that Holland produces is exported, mainly to other Community countries.

To say that Dutch agriculture is highly intensive would be a gross understatement. Although the environment with its large areas of grassland is eminently suitable for traditional milk and dairy farming, most Dutch farms are highly mechanized and specialize in artificial insemination, selective breeding, computerized feeding and other scientific 'refinements' which have substantially increased production yields over the years since World War II. The volume of milk has increased so much that the Community has been obliged to impose quotas to limit production. Intensive farming has led to vast surpluses of all kinds including manure, and as the Dutch themselves are the first to point out (in *The Netherlands in Brief*, published by the Dutch Foreign Information Service), intensive farming has also 'highlighted the problem that animal welfare is not necessarily synonymous with optimal production'. Wide-ranging research projects aimed at demonstrating that the Dutch are at least trying to discover ways of reconciling animal welfare with the demands of intensive farming are being conducted, if only perhaps as a public relations operation.

For years Holland has been the principal supplier for the rest of Europe of early tomatoes, cucumbers and lettuce, all grown under glass; in fact Westland, between The Hague, Rotterdam and the Hook of Holland, where much of this type of horticulture is carried out, is known locally as 'the city of glass'.

After the windmills and the dikes, Holland is probably most famous abroad for its tulips, and the growing of tulip bulbs has been an ancient tradition in the area between Haarlem and Leiden, in the mineral-rich soil of levelled sand dunes. The famous tulips, which attract tens of thousands of tourists every year, are only an incidental by-product of the bulb industry. In order not to draw too heavily on the resources of the bulbs, the flowers are cut at a very early stage and mostly they are thrown away. It is the bulbs that are being cultivated to be sold all over the world.

The industrial development of the Netherlands was not, as in the case of most countries, initially the result of the exploitation of her minerals – no metal ores have ever been found in the country – but was instead a result of the country's geographical position. Not unexpectedly, therefore, the iron and steel industry, which was set up in 1918, is located on the coast, near the mouth of the North Sea canal, in an area where iron ore and coke – the latter vital since the last of the Dutch coal mines was closed in 1975 – could be conveniently brought in by sea. The canal, constructed in 1876, cut through a chain of sand dunes, and moles were built out into the sea to maintain a channel deep enough to accept ships of ever-increasing size.

Before World War II, Holland's ports had existed mainly to service transit trade between the outside world and the remainder of central Europe. Rotterdam had to be extensively rebuilt after the German air raids of 1940, and the rebuilding reflected the changes that were then taking place in world trade.

The dockyard area was considerably expanded to accommodate firms specializing in bulk cargoes such as petroleum and metallic ores, transported in the huge ships which had been developed to keep Britain supplied with essential goods during the period between the Fall of France and the Second Front. As a result, Rotterdam became the main European petro-chemical port, with five large oil refineries – including Kuwait's State Oil Refinery – as well as other chemical works not directly connected with petroleum products. Trans-shipment remained a major industry, and the Verolme shipbuilding and repair yard in the area of Rotterdam which became known as Europort played an essential part in the story of Holland's industrial development.

The other area of chemical industry in Holland, in the province of Limburg, owes its origins to the coal which was mined there between 1900 and 1975 on twelve sites (eight private and four state-controlled). One of Europe's largest and most efficient mines, the Maurits State Mine near Geleen in south Limburg, was opened in 1925. However, as a result of increasing mining costs and the huge natural gas discoveries in the north Netherlands and in the North Sea, all the mines were closed between 1966 and 1975, and the Limburg chemical plants now use natural gas and imported oil for fuel, most of the supplies coming by pipeline from the north Netherlands and Rotterdam's Europort.

After the Philips brothers had established their first electric light bulb factory at Eindhoven in 1891, a period of very rapid industrial growth followed. In 1900, Eindhoven had 4,000 inhabitants; today, it is the fifth largest town in the Netherlands, with a population of 190,000 (375,000 if you include the suburbs). The Philips firm employs a total of 345,000 worldwide, 70,000 of them in the Netherlands. Another firm which set up shop in the Eindhoven area is DAF, the motor car and heavy goods vehicle manufacturers.

These two firms, in a sense, represent a macrocosm of the success of Dutch industry during this period. Before the world oil crisis of 1973, there had been a long period of steady economic growth. Between 1960 and 1973, the GNP had risen by an average 6 per cent a year, investment in industry had gone up by 6 or 7 per cent every year, and the unemployment rate was down to 2 per cent.

After the 1973 oil crisis, economic growth slowed in the Netherlands to only about 1 per cent between 1973 and 1983, and industrial investment also fell sharply. At the same time, increased mechanization and robotization made industry a lot less labour-intensive, and with an ever-increasing number of women coming into the full-time job-market, led to a rise in unemployment from 3 to 17 per cent between 1973 and 1983.

In 1983, when world trade started to expand again, private consumption began to increase accordingly, investment recovered, inflation was brought down to almost zero, and unemployment dropped to around the present figure of 9 per cent.

Dutch natural gas is used extensively in the Netherlands, both domestically and industrially; approximately 95 per cent of all

Dutch homes are connected up to the network. Not only that but a large proportion of Holland's electricity is produced from natural gas, which is also exported in large quantities to neighbouring Community countries.

Currently, stout efforts are being made to reduce Holland's dependence on natural gas by experiments with wind power and solar power, and there has been much discussion on the advisability of expanding the country's dependence on nuclear power beyond the two existing stations.

The Netherlands currently produces 20 per cent of all its oil requirements and the search for additional sources of oil is continuing apace. The country currently depends on imports for only 5 per cent of its energy requirements.

Long before the Netherlands had a road network, it had an extensive and efficient system of rivers, lakes and canals to transport goods and passengers. Dutch carriers cope with roughly half of all internal transport by water within the Community. The Dutch have a canal/river fleet of some 6,267 vessels, including barges, carrying a total of nearly 6 million tonnes a year on their 4,800 kilometres of navigable inland waterways.

The Dutch have always been world leaders in the heavy, ocean-going cargo sector. Today more than half the world's total tonnage is controlled by Dutch shipping companies. Rotterdam is the world's busiest seaport, handling 330 million tonnes of exports and imports for the Community, as well as 34 per cent of all shipments of high-technology goods to Western Europe from Japan and 43 per cent from the United States (which, incidentally, has twenty major exporting companies situated in Western Europe, half of them in the Netherlands). Dutch companies also control major shares in shipping-related activities, ship-broking, ship-insurance and banking.

Road transport accounts for much of the total volume of freight transported within the Community, and some 24 per cent of all Community road transport is carried out by Dutch companies.

Dutch railways are clean, quick and convenient. All the major towns are accessible by high-speed rail, and the Netherlands railways system, a state-sponsored company (the state pays roughly half the cost of providing a passenger service), carries around 200 million passengers a year who travel 9 billion kilometres every year. Since so much of the Dutch terrain consists of water, the railway system uses lifting and other types of bridges more frequently than railway systems in other lands. These are gradually being replaced by tunnels.

Understandably, in a small country with the highest population density in the Community, traffic jams and bottle-necks are pretty common, though the ratio of cars to people — 343 per 1,000 — is not abnormally high. However, most of the goods that enter Holland (whether imported, exported, or carried in transit) go at least part of the way by heavy goods vehicles, and at the last count there were 500,000 commercial vehicles on the roads, nearly double the number of private cars. Perhaps that's the reason why so many Dutch prefer to go by bicycle.

On a very local level, Holland has introduced the minibus in places where previously there had been no public transport. Driven by unpaid volunteers, the buses — provided by the state — seat eight people, and run on set routes and at regular intervals with the aim of providing both a local service and a connecting link between mainline services.

KLM (Royal Dutch Airlines) is the oldest airline in the world; it began the first scheduled air service between London and Amsterdam in 1920. As well as manufacturing its own Fokker aircraft, Holland has an interest in the European Airbus.

The Netherlands has had a broadcasting system since 1928. It is unique in that it leaves all responsibility for programme-making to private organizations. The government confines itself to licensing broadcasting companies and sharing out available air time. There are currently three TV channels, which are free to present whatever programmes they choose to produce provided that they do not infringe the law, upset public order or offend good taste, and five national radio stations. Alcohol may be advertised subject to certain provisos, but tobacco advertising is forbidden.

Radio Nederland is an independent radio station which broadcasts short-wave news programmes daily in Dutch, English, Spanish, Portuguese, Indonesian, Arabic, French, Surinam and Papiamento (for the Netherlands Antilles and Aruba).

In the first quarter of 1984 – the last year for which full figures are available – there were eighty-two daily newspapers in the Netherlands with a total circulation of 4,413,000, 60 per cent regional and 40 per cent national. The most popular paper is *De Telegraaf* with a circulation of 702,000, almost double that of the runner-up, *Algemeen Dagblad.* Over 1,800 magazines are published in Holland, many of them catering for specialist interests.

The social and health services in the Netherlands cover the entire population: young people, the family, single persons, old people, even the self-employed and the handicapped.

Virtually all the social services are run by non-governmental organizations. At one time most of the money to run these services came from religious bodies and independent funds, and only a small part from the government; weakening ties with the Church, the greatly increased scope of the social welfare programme, and the increasingly difficult problem of job security in a changing world have resulted in central government being obliged to provide a higher proportion of the funding.

Health care is provided to some extent by the government – basic medical treatment is available to everyone at a reasonable price – but the bulk of the health care facilities are provided by non-governmental and private organizations, many of which began as charities. Nursing was initially undertaken by religious orders; Roman Catholic and Protestant hospitals, services and residential homes still exist, though the denominational character of these facilities has declined considerably in recent years.

AFFAIRS OF STATE

No Trial by Jury

The Netherlands is a constitutional monarchy with a bicameral parliamentary system. As indicated earlier, the royal family has historical links with the Netherlands dating back to the sixteenth century.

The sovereign, who is also head of state, appoints the ministers on the recommendation of the prime minister, and together they appoint the Cabinet which co-ordinates government policy.

The parliament, known as the States-General, consists of two houses: the Upper House of seventy-five members, indirectly elected by the Provincial Councils, and the Lower House, with 150 members elected by universal suffrage of all electors over the age of eighteen.

The judiciary is independent. All courts are presided over by judges appointed for life. There is no trial by jury, and there is a considerable right of appeal.

There is a Council of State, the highest advisory body in the country, to consider all proposed legislation, and a national ombudsman to investigate any complaints from members of the public who feel that they have been unfairly treated by the government.

Holland is divided into twelve provinces, each administered by a Provincial Council, a Provincial Executive and the Queen's Commissioner; the members of the Provincial Councils are directly elected by the inhabitants of the provinces.

Dutch defence policy is closely integrated with NATO. Theoretically, all men in the Netherlands are eligible for conscription, though since 1979 it has been possible to choose whether to start the fourteen to seventeen month period of national service at the age of eighteen, nineteen or twenty. There is a Royal Netherlands Navy (15,500 regulars and 1,400 conscripts plus six submarines and other naval vessels), an army of 65,000 (12,000 regulars and 42,700 conscripts), and an air force (employing 18,000 men, 4,800 of them conscripts).

There are only about 2,300 women in the armed forces, and the government is not considering the extension of conscription to women, despite the existence in Holland of one of the most vociferous women's equal rights movements in the Community.

Holland spends about 14.2 per cent of the total national

budget on defence. As well as the armed forces, there is the Royal Netherlands Military Constabulary, a 4,000-strong force responsible for various aspects of security.

CULTURE AND LEISURE

Middle Class Magic

Today just over one-third of the population of the Netherlands claim to be Roman Catholics as against the 24 per cent who admit belonging to the Dutch Reformed Church and the 32 per cent who claim to have no religion. Interestingly, the Roman Catholic proportion is about the same as it was in 1900, when 49 per cent of the population belonged to the Dutch Reformed Church, and only 2 per cent admitted to having no religious beliefs.

The Dutch constitution, which guarantees freedom of religion, also enshrines the 'freedom to provide education', a rather noncommittal phrase, which reflects a reaction against the strict government control over education which had been a feature of the Batavian Republic of 1795. It was thanks to this policy of central government control that in the first half of the nineteenth century, the Netherlands managed to achieve educational standards which compared very favourably with any other European country.

However, a general social trend towards liberalism and a desire for diversity and independence led to a widespread belief that the state should not have a monopoly of schools or control over education as a whole. The 1848 constitution envisaged a withdrawal by central government from school control and management. Schools set up by private or religious organizations were not then funded by the government until 1917, when private and state schools were put on an equal financial footing.

In the Netherlands today, approximately three-quarters of the educational establishments at primary and secondary level are private and only one-quarter state-run, which explains why the government still has a restricted role in educational issues.

Play schools and pre-school classes do not come under the control of the Ministry of Education and Science. Children may attend primary school at the age of four; from five, it becomes compulsory. At twelve, children go on to secondary education; there is no eleven-plus examination, and the type of secondary school to which a child progresses — general, pre-university or vocational — depends on performance, aptitude and intelligence, as graded by the primary school teachers. The primary school curriculum includes Dutch, mathematics, writing, history, geography, science and social studies, and in their last year primary school students also study English. Vocational education includes such subjects as agriculture, commerce, social services and health care, home economics and nautical training.

Full-time education is compulsory up to the age of sixteen; then for two further years, children are required by law to attend courses for one or two days a week.

Of the 15 million people who live in the Netherlands, about 4 million are in full-time education. Free education is available to all during the entire compulsory period, though many Dutch parents elect to send their children to private, fee-paying schools. The Ministry of Education and Science has the biggest budget of any ministry; the state spends roughly 17 per cent of the national budget (about 3 per cent more than is spent on national defence) on education.

There are five state universities, including Leiden, the oldest, founded in 1575 by Prince William of Orange; one municipal university in Amsterdam (1632); two privately run universities, the Calvinist Free University of Amsterdam (1880) and the Catholic University of Nijmegen (1923); and four state universities of technology, along with one privately run institution, the Catholic University of Technology in Tilburg (1927).

In addition, there are seven theological colleges, which are only partly funded by the state. Holland also has plans for an open university, and provides many evening adult and correspondence courses.

When the Dukes of Burgundy ruled the lands that were to

become today's Benelux countries, the greatest painters of the period were the Van Eyck brothers, Hubert and Jan, founders of the Flemish School. Holland differs from Italy, and to some extent France, in that patronage of the arts was not the preserve of the Church and the ruling classes, but was subsidized by the powerful and influential merchants, with the consequence that the arts, and painting in particular, became essentially bourgeois in character: straight portraits, bland cityscapes and simple studies of flowers, as opposed to the more grandiose visions of the Italian and French Renaissance painters.

Yet even as late as the end of the fifteenth century, Dutch art could be surprisingly medieval, and at the same time almost surrealistically modern in approach; the allegoric visions of Hieronymus Bosch (1450–1516) invite comparisons with the more recent nightmares of Salvador Dali, though they obviously spoke a language instantly clear to his contemporaries. His paintings were enthusiastically collected by Felipe II of Spain, by no means the most far-sighted or imaginative of men. This, incidentally, explains why so many of the best of them are to be found in the Prado in Madrid.

Peter Breughel the Elder (1529–69) had something of the same combination of nightmare fantasy and penetrating realism which has never been in fashion, and yet his works have never been outside the comprehension of people of any period since they were painted.

Franz Hals (1580–1666) painted portraits of the bourgeoisie exactly as they must have looked. Rembrandt carried this gift for portraiture into another dimension as well as bringing it into biblical scenes. Jan Vermeer (1632–75) caught the calm, perhaps even slightly stuffy stillness of an afternoon in middle-class Delft with its sudden glimpses of unexpected beauty – as, for example, when the milk that is being poured from the earthen jug of a rather lumpy young Dutch maidservant suddenly catches the light and gleams dully, as milk does; and you wonder how it was possible for anyone to achieve such an effect with canvas and paint.

And even if painters such as Jacob Van Ruysdael and Pieter

de Hogh, the Van Veldes and Jongkind hadn't intervened, any nation capable of producing a painter like Vincent Van Gogh — given that he learnt a great deal about his chosen trade in Paris and stole the light that bursts from his canvases from the skies of Provence — cannot be regarded as a petty people.

There is no Dutch literature to speak about, because not enough people read Dutch to provide writers with a viable audience, and if the country has produced no composers of music it has certainly produced some fine interpreters, such as, for example, the Amsterdam Concertgebouw Orchestra under its conductor Bernard Haitink.

When Dutch food is described as unimaginative by other nations, the Dutch answer that they do not have to resort to rich sauces or fancy trimmings; their basic food is so good, and such an abundance of meat and fish and fowl, vegetables and fruit is available at such reasonable prices that they can concentrate on enjoying the food itself, rather than its preparation and presentation. Breakfast usually includes several varieties of Dutch cheese, ham and salami, often boiled eggs, followed by rolls or bread or wholemeal biscuits with butter and jam or honey, accompanied by a pot of coffee.

After such a start, lunch tends to be a light meal, often consisting of cold meat and cheese, with possibly one light cooked dish such as an omelette. The main meal, in the evening, is taken early, usually around 6 or 6.30 p.m.

Among the best-known Dutch specialities are *hutspot*, a sort of Dutch hotpot, made of potatoes, carrots and onions and often served with *klapstuk* (beef stew). Herrings in any shape or form are popular at all times, but particularly at the start of the herring fishing season, in May. Many Dutch fish specialities can be sampled at street stalls; they include rollmops (salted raw herrings), and to eat them Dutch-style, you dangle the fish over your mouth, holding it by the tail, and then gulp it down. Smoked eel, mackerel and mussels are also served in the streets, as are various varieties of pancakes and waffles.

And of course Holland's centuries-old connection with southeast

Asia means that there are plenty of Indonesian restaurants in most Dutch cities.

The traditional Dutch drink *jenever* is a very strong aromatic gin, usually knocked back neat and very cold, with a beer chaser. Other Dutch gins are available, flavoured with lemon, black-currant or red-currant and other fruit, but most are too strong and too oily for customers weaned on London Dry.

Other celebrated Dutch drinks include *advocaat*, a rich and slightly sickly form of egg-nog, and Curaçao, named after the Dutch island in the West Indies and flavoured with orange peel. But for day-to-day drinking, most Dutch people prefer to stick to their beer which closely resembles German lager.

According to the State Secretary for Welfare, Health and Cultural Affairs, D.J.D. Dees, over one-third of the Dutch population are active participants in sporting activities of one sort or another. Ever since the Dutch football team in their distinctive orange jerseys became the world champions a few years back, the Dutch interest in football is taken for granted.

Because so much of their land area, so to speak, consists of water, the Dutch are also famous for swimming, rowing, sailing, windsurfing and water skiing, and since a good deal of this water freezes every winter, for speed skating and long-distance skating. The Dutch have been winning gold medals in these and other forms of sport and athletics ever since the Olympic Games were revived. Hockey is another Dutch passion; the Prime Minister, Ruud Luffers, is an enthusiastic hockey player.

But as well as excelling at sports which they share with the rest of the world, the Dutch have a few sporting specialities. *Korfball* is the only game in which men and women play together in teams; it was devised in 1902 by Nico Broeyhuysen, a gymnastics teacher, and it is now played by about 92,000 people. Basically, it is a form of basketball, played by teams of twelve, men and women mixed, divided into three sections of the pitch.

A more ancient Dutch speciality in the field of sport is *kolf*, which dates back to the fourteenth century and on which, many Dutch people believe, the game of golf was based, though others believe that golf was based on *klootschieten*, another ancient Dutch game still played in the east of the Netherlands and in Westphalia in Germany. And there are people in Holland who believe that the game of baseball was invented there and introduced into the United States by the Dutch emigrants of the sixteenth century.

One distinctive Dutch sporting event, rivalling the London marathon in some ways, is the *Elfstedentocht*, a long-distance skating race between eleven towns in the province of Friesland in which, weather permitting, up to 17,000 competitors take part.

THE FRENCH

All Kinds of Everything

FRANCE IN PROFILE

Area	544,000 sq km
Population	55,600,000
Population density	101 per sq km
Women	51.2%
Under 15	21.1%
Over 65	13%
Language	French, Breton, Alsatian, Basque, Corsican, Catalan, Languedoc
Religion	90% Catholic
Labour force	43.5%
Employed in:	
Agriculture	7.9%
Industry	33%
Services	59.1%
Women in labour force	41.6%
Unemployment (as % of labour force)	10.8%

Major exports: Machinery and vehicles (34.6%); manufactured goods (28.2%); foodstuffs (11.8%); chemicals (11.4%)
Main customers: EC (57.8%); USA (7.4%); Switzerland (4.6%)

THE FRENCH

The 55.6 million Frenchmen (and Frenchwomen) into which the French race is divided are agreed only on one thing: that it is better to be born in France than anywhere else.

I say divided deliberately. In 1954, the French journalist Pierre Daninos wrote a book about the differences between the French and the English called *Les Carnets de Major Thompson* (The Notebooks of Major Thompson; Paris: Hachette, 1954). It consisted of the memoirs of an imaginary British major, married for the second time to a French wife and living in France. In the years since the book was first published, France has probably changed more profoundly than any other Community country apart perhaps from Ireland, but in one respect it hasn't changed a bit.

Pierre Daninos pointed out all those years ago that while you could say that England consisted of 49 million souls, or that the United States totalled 144 million people, you would have to say that France *was divided* into 43 million (now nearly 56 million) of French. If you add ten French citizens to ten other French citizens, he went on, the result will never be an addition, it will always be a division, by twenty.

In other words, the French are individualists, every last one of them. From the smoggy mists of Lille and the soggy sugar-beet fields of the Pas de Calais to the sun-flowers turning their backs on the Midi sun, from Giscard d'Estaing and the few other aristos who are left, through all the university professors and the intellectuals and *petits bourgeois* and *fonctionnaires* right down to the *facteur* in the foothills of the Auvergne who cycles up with your mail, the French all have their own ideas, philosophies, politics, views on history, morals and manners, food and drink, and every other subject under the sun, and are agreed on only one thing: that they would far rather be alive and well and living in France and able to argue about such matters — and all other matters — over a good French meal than be anywhere else in the world.

Which is one reason why so few French ever emigrate — there are less than 1.5 million French living outside France, a tiny proportion compared with all the other countries which once had overseas territories on the scale of France's — and why so many French people spend their vacations and buy their *résidences secondaires* not in another country, but somewhere else in France.

And could anybody blame them? With a country that offers a choice of climate and ambience which ranges from the sparkling snows of Mont Blanc to the lazy langour of the Mediterranean littoral, from the frenetic excitement of the Rue de Buci in Paris to the almost audible silence of a Cevennes afternoon as a shepherdess nods off in the gentle spring sunshine while her *troupeau de brebis* (sheep kept only for their milk which is used in the manufacture of several types of blue cheese, the best-known of which is Roquefort) on the tough vegetation of the causses?

From the crisp vigour of the lush green pre-Alpine slopes of the Jura, where pale beige cattle, clanking bells around their necks, lumber about on the hills above cosy Swiss-type chalets, with the snow-covered peaks of the Alps on the horizon, to the sleeping stones of Roman cities, like Arles and Aix and Nîmes, arenas and amphitheatres and all, still spread-eagled in a 500-year siesta under the relentless sun of Provence, the old Roman Provincia, the first external province of the Roman Empire.

From the immense, towering, mind-boggling, hand-built

cathedrals like Rheims and Orlèans and Chartres and Albi to the tentative but curiously convincing graffiti of the Neolithic hunters on the walls of the caves at Lascaux and all over the Dordogne, stippled there 18,000 years ago.

From the almost military precision of the regular rows of vine-yards in Champagne and Burgundy, punctuated here and there by austere grey châteaux; from the sprawling ancient ports that were used by the crusaders and are still overlooked by the same medieval turrets and towers, to the *étangs* of the Camargue, where flamingoes still flock, and wild white horses run with small, savage black bulls in a preserve policed by the *gardiens*, some of the only genuine cowboys left in the entire world, easy riders who with their long stirrups and casual laid-back competence illustrate exactly what the term means. And they were doing it long before the Texans thought up the idea.

From the endless golden beaches of Aquitaine, where the Atlantic rollers thunder ashore and collapse into sparkling effer-vescent patterns of lacy spray around the dancing feet of families of healthy young nudists drunk with the sunshine, to the Neapolitan-style alleys of the old towns of Nice and Menton, where old women in black still sit chatting in the deep shade of the early afternoon, exchanging views on what's gone wrong with everybody these days: whatever you may be looking for, it's all there, somewhere in France, all kinds of everything, as the song says. From the Manche to the Med, from the Atlantic to the Alps, France has everything that anybody could possibly want in this world.

Therefore it is not difficult to see why so many members of the European Community — the Germans, the Danish, the Dutch, the Belgians, the British, the Luxembourgers — are instantly and eternally attracted to France.

Nor is it all that difficult to see why so many of the people from these countries immediately feel totally at home there. The French, after all, consist of such a mixture — the Celts (the ancient Gauls); the Latins (the Gallo-Romans); the Scandinavians (the Normans); the Germanic tribes (the Franks); there are even some Flemish — that almost anybody from anywhere else in Europe must feel completely at home somewhere in France.

The English love France, but tend to dislike or at least distrust the French. This is partly due to language problems, but not entirely. The French, as well as being the most lively, sophisticated and stimulating people in the world, can also be the most awkward, obtuse and exasperating.

I mentioned (in the chapter on the British) that the outstanding quality of the British people is, or certainly used to be, their utter fairness, and their respect for the law. Nobody in their wildest dreams could call the French fair. The English are perfectly prepared to pay any taxes demanded of them, provided they regard them as fair; the French regard it both as a duty and as a diverting game to avoid paying any taxes that can be escaped with impunity. Furthermore, they will invoke claims to evade payment far more persuasive to the average French revenue officer than the needs of the Exchequer: 'But, monsieur, how can I possibly pay my taxes when I have chère Tante Marie-France to support?'

They have no sense of fair play. They will cheat at cards and in games if they see any possibility of getting away with it, and only the exigencies of the supermarket check-out system has forced them to accept the logic of queuing. Previously, they used to fight like *fauves* for places on the buses, until the far-sighted and philosophical people who run the transport services in Paris devised the system of numbered tickets which you tear off a lamp-post and then wait in dignity, appraising a work of art in a gallery window, until your number is called.

The fact that the French seem basically opposed to all standard attitudes to morality was sharply brought home to me when as a young film critic, I saw a re-run of Sacha Guitry's *Le Roman d'un Tricheur* (The Story of a Cheat). The idea that the French could make a hero out of a small boy who had been sent to bed before dinner for lying, and so avoided eating the poisonous fungus that killed the remainder of his family, and survived to become an international card-sharp and con-man, struck me then as unbelievable. It doesn't any more.

In general, the English would rather let a dozen murderers escape justice than imprison one innocent man; George Wolinski of *L'Humanité* may well speak for the majority of the French when he says that he'd rather have the prisons full of innocent people than the streets full of criminals.

The French are chauvinistic when with outsiders, but at home among friends they make no secret of their contempt for the government, the army, the police, the establishment, anyone in authority, in fact. A large part of this attitude may be due to the fact that most French people, fundamentally, are of peasant stock, and I am not using that word in any pejorative way; it is one of the great strengths of France.

'The strength of France is in her soil,' Rudyard Kipling wrote. 'If you stood one hundred Frenchmen on their heads you would find the good plough-mould on the boots of at least seventy-five. They have known in their boyhood the chill before sunrise, and the cool of the evening on the naked chest; the sight, sound and smell of the worked earth; the hot, rustling lowland before the reapers go in; the secrets of the dark and tempting barns. They give *La Terre* the reverence they deny to some other Gods; and she repays their worship.'

It is probably this peasant background which is also responsible for their deep resentment of people clearly far better off than they are, so far as worldly goods are concerned. I cannot do better than quote Daninos: 'An American pedestrian who sees a millionaire pass by in a Cadillac secretly dreams of the day when he will pass by in his own Cadillac. On the other hand, a French pedestrian who sees a millionaire pass by in his Cadillac secretly dreams of the day when he will be able to make the millionaire get out of his motor car and walk, like everybody else.'

In all sorts of minor ways, they are totally at odds with the English. They serve the most marvellous meals on cold plates and then expect you to use the same plates and knives and forks for the second course. To an Englishman, this is outrageous. Daninos spotted the anomaly: 'The English have taught the world the correct conduct at table (*la façon de se tenir correctement à table*); but it is the French who eat.'

There's another thing about which the French and the British disagree fundamentally: it's in the matter of greeting fellow-members of the human race. The British believe that they probably invented the system of shaking hands but are convinced that the French let it get completely out of control.

In Britain, once an introduction has been effected and a limp handshake conducted, that is the end of it; you don't really need to initiate any further personal contact for the duration of your acquaintance.

On the other hand, the French shake hands all the time. Daninos reckoned that a man 'of average importance' spends approximately thirty minutes (more than a whole year out of an average lifetime's expectation of sixty odd years) regularly shaking the hands of all his colleagues at nine o'clock, midday, two o'clock in the afternoon, and six o'clock in the evening. And that is without counting the people he meets in the street, or the people who may turn up when he goes home, visitors, relatives and neighbours who might drop in unexpectedly.

Even more alien to the Anglo-Saxon is the French system of kissing. The English used to be terrified of kissing anybody, in almost any circumstances, but familiarity with the habits of showbiz people, as seen on the telly, has made the custom of the quick, furtive, untidy, sideways kiss fairly common.

In this matter, as in so many others, the French have precise rules which ensure impeccably correct behaviour. Watch a young girl approach a group of fellow-students sitting around a café table on a terrace. She will shake hands with a few casual acquaintances, kiss the people she knows very well; one, two or three kisses according to the degree of her intimacy with them, and always in the same sequence, left cheek, right cheek and left again. Then, if she has decided not to sit down and have a drink with them, she will say goodbye to all of them in precisely the same fashion, right down to the last detail, but in reverse order.

It is usually dangerous to make comparisons between national stereotypes, and there is really no French national stereotype because they're all individuals. But the French and the British love analysing the distinguishing characteristics of the two nations; it is part of the love-hate relationship which exists between them. The libraries in both countries are full of books about the difference between the French and the British, written both by French and English writers.

If the principal British quality is fair-mindedness, the outstanding French characteristic, apart from their staggering but understandable chauvinism, is their practicality. The most practical car in the world is the Citroën 2CV, the Deux Chevaux as it was known during all the years when it was the commonest car on the roads of France.

It was ugly, but it was cheap, economical, versatile and efficient; *pratique*, in other words. It was comfortable enough for four people, and with all the seats except the driver's removed – a task that took only a few moments – it became a capacious van. If the weather was good, or you wanted to carry an awkward load, the canvas roof rolled right back. It could be repaired by any garage mechanic or blacksmith in the whole of France, but in any case its engine was so small and so simple that you could easily take it out and carry it into the house and mend it yourself on the kitchen table.

You could drive it across a ploughed field or up the steepest goat-track in the Cévennes or down on to the shingle beaches of the Riviera. Provided you weren't in too much of a hurry, it would eventually take you (and your family and the dog and all your belongings) anywhere you wanted to go. Only the French could design and build such a car.

The *sapeurs-pompiers* are *pratique*. I drove up from the south of France to Dieppe during the big hurricane of January 1990, when the *camions* were being blown over on their sides all along the route. In Britain, if one heavy goods vehicle goes over on its side, there's a tailback of about twenty miles in each direction for four or five hours at least. In France, the *sapeurs-pompiers* came out with bulldozers and gouged temporary roads through the hedges, across the fields around all the toppled *camions* and back through the hedges and onto the road again, at a point well past the obstruction, while the gendarmes were busy keeping the traffic moving.

The *bidet*, another French contrivance, is eminently *pratique*.

The French are discreet. If you're having an affair with your secretary, it's more convenient all around if your wife never gets to hear about it, so it's *pratique* to be discreet. On the other hand, if she ever does get to hear about it, she won't mention it to anybody either, which is also both discreet and *pratique*.

Another characteristic that separates the French from all other nations is their innate, inherent, incredible inconsistency. The contradictions are all there on the surface, for everybody to see. How does it happen that a nation which has always been ready, anxious even, to embrace all the latest social and economic innovations nevertheless remains so conservative that although the franc was devalued as long ago as 1959, you still meet people including young people who could not possibly even remember the old money, who insist on quoting the price of everything to you in old francs, literally talking in millions; they all do it in the mountains in the Languedoc where we now spend roughly half the year.

How could a people so revolutionary that they beheaded their own king and queen and half their aristocracy without a thought at the end of the eighteenth century remain nevertheless so perversely monarchist that as soon as the military dictator who started to clean things up after the revolution had consolidated his position, they began to treat him like royalty and eventually allowed him to crown himself emperor? How else could you describe a race of people who firmly believe themselves to be socialists but still hang on every idiotic word that the tabloids print about the British royal family and about the poor luckless Princesses Caroline and Stephanie of Monaco, the nearest thing they have to a royal family of their own?

A nation which decapitated the amiable and basically harmless Louis XVI and then tolerated the intolerably despotic de Gaulle? A nation still transfixed with the Glory of the Little Emperor, and prepared to file in silent homage through that vast mausoleum in the Invalides, past his cinders reposing there in spectacular splendour on top of a marble catafalque, but which nevertheless insists on naming a street or a square or a place in every city in the country after the first modern French socialist, Jean Jaurès? How could the coldly logical Anglo-Saxon Britons ever hope to understand them? And yet the French would argue, and rightly, perhaps that they have always been far more logical than the British.

With enormous confidence, in their literature and in their conversation, the French claim the best of all possible worlds.

They have carried, unaided it often seems, the torch of civilization from the time of the Roman Empire until the present day, a direct descent through Charlemagne and Louis XIV the Sun King, through the Emperor Napoleon and President de Gaulle, managing to accommodate en route and without losing any of their sense of continuity, the French Revolution of 1789 and all that followed it, becoming in the process enlightened, altruistic patriots who are also citizens of the world with a mission and a duty to inspire and liberate other less fortunate nations.

LAND AND PEOPLE

Butter Mountains and Wine Lakes

France consists of 544,000 square kilometres of the loveliest and most fertile land in Europe, if not the world, plus the island of Corsica in the Mediterranean, off the west coast of Italy. It has sea frontiers on the English Channel (with a tunnel now in an advanced state of construction underneath to connect the two countries), the Atlantic and the Mediterranean, and land frontiers with Belgium, Luxembourg, Switzerland, Italy, and Spain.

Other natural frontiers include the Jura and the Vosges in the east, the Pyrenees in the south-west, and the Alps in the south-east. It has four magnificent rivers: the Seine which flows through Normandy into the English Channel; the Loire and the Garonne which flow into the Atlantic; and the Rhone which flows into the Mediterranean.

Mountain ranges include the Alps, the Alpes Maritimes, the Vosges, the Jura, the Cèvennes, the Pyrenees, and the Massif

Central. In fact you can find examples of every kind of mountain in France, as well as some of the most extraordinary geological freaks in Europe like the Gorges of the Tarn and the Cirque de Mourèze in the Hérault. It also has six volcanoes and miles of underground caves and caverns, some painted by prehistoric man, some sculpted by time and the persistent dribbling of water, into the most fantastic variety of stalagmites and stalactites. The highest mountain in Europe, Mont Blanc (4,805 metres), lies partly within French territory.

The climate is as varied as the scenery. In the north it is temperate — mild and wet, like Britain — and in the south, obviously, Mediterranean. In the Languedoc it can be as hot as a furnace in summer, and blisteringly cold in the winter. In Savoy and the French Alps, the frequent combination of thick snow and bright sunshine has bred a string of winter sports centres, some in old towns like Chamonix (which reached its peak as a fashionable resort around the turn of the century), some new and purpose-built.

The area has been inhabited since our ancestors pushed their way up out of Africa across a land-bridge which once joined the two continents to see what Europe had to offer in the way of game. There are caves in the Dordogne in which men lived 30,000 years ago, and caves alongside them in which men (and women and children) live very comfortably today: la Roque Gageac is a good example.

At Carnac in Brittany there are menhirs, dolmens, tumuli and cromlechs, the standing stones that are the only relic of a forgotten and unrecorded Megalithic civilization which flourished during a period some 3,000 years before the birth of Christ.

A branch of the Celts known as the Gauls established themselves all over what is now France somewhere around 400 BC. The Visigoths occupied part of the area for a period after the fall of Rome and were in turn conquered by the Salian Franks, another Germanic tribe, in 507 AD. In the ninth and tenth centuries Vikings invaded the north of France and settled in Normandy. So French people are basically a mixture of Celts,

Romans, Franks and Normans. The official language is French, but Alsatian, Breton, Basque, Corsican, Provençal and Languedoc are also spoken in different parts of the country with endless dialectal variations.

The present population figure of 56 million includes 4.4 million foreigners, mainly Algerians, Tunisians and Moroccans, though it also encompasses 850,000 Portuguese, 380,000 Italians and 350,000 Spanish. Three-quarters of the French live in urban areas; a great many of them in three conurbations with over 1 million inhabitants each: Paris, Lyons and Marseilles. The population density in France, as a whole, is 101 inhabitants per square kilometre.

About 90 per cent of France is farmed in one way or another, if you include forestry under the heading of farming; if you don't, it's only just over 50 per cent. Despite the fact that France can drown the Community, and indeed the entire civilized world, with milk and fruit juice and wine, the acreage devoted to vines and orchards accounts for only 2.3 per cent of the total. The rest — arable land and pasture — produces an almost embarrassing abundance of beef, grain and vegetables, as well as dairy produce, embarrassing because of the problems of disposing of the surplus in a Community in which most member-states are in exactly the same boat. Hence all the talk about butter mountains and wine lakes.

In 1850, peasant farmers and agricultural labourers made up 64 per cent of the working population; today the figure is down to 7 per cent. Mechanization and modern farming techniques have depopulated the rural areas and forced people to move from the villages into the towns, almost all of which now have industrial zones. Until after World War II, French farms were worked very much as they had been worked over the centuries; now they are extremely well equipped and heavily subsidized by the state. In 1939, there were, for example, only 35,000 tractors in France; today there are more than 1.5 million.

France has coal deposits in the north, in the east and in the Massif Central, producing 16 million tonnes a year, as compared with 33 million tonnes in 1955. It also has some oil in Aquitaine and in the Paris basin, producing 3.6 million tonnes of crude a year (less than 1 per cent of the country's energy needs) and some natural gas (about 5 per cent of the amount consumed). There are also hydro-electric plants in the mountains producing 2.8 per cent of the country's energy needs.

The energy shortfall was made up with imported oil; until the oil crisis of the seventies France was dependent on imported oil for more than 60 per cent of her energy requirements. The French have now switched over to nuclear power. In 1989, nuclear energy accounted for 67.9 per cent of all the energy produced — the highest rate in the world — and industry pays less per kilowatt hour for power in France than in the United States or any other European country.

After the United States, France is the second biggest producer of nuclear power, with fifty-five stations on line and eight more under construction. But because the raw materials all have to be imported, France remains dependent on imports for 54 per cent of her energy needs.

HISTORICAL PERSPECTIVE

Another Roman Empire

The Gauls — as the Celts were known in France — established themselves there in the fourth century BC and enjoyed a fairly stable existence for about three centuries.

Around the end of the second century BC, the Romans annexed Provence, and in 55 BC Julius Caesar, as we all learned at school, spent three years dividing the rest of Gaul into three parts and putting it under firm Roman control, finally disposing of its troublesome leader Vercingetorix by having him fed to the lions in the Roman arena.

Five centuries of peace and prosperity came to an end when the legions were withdrawn to defend Rome from the barbarians. By the fifth century AD, the Visigoths had occupied France from the Loire to the Pyrenees: then they in turn were defeated and ousted by the Salian Franks, under their pagan leader Clovis. He was converted to Christianity by his wife Clothilde and forged a strong link between France's first dynasty, the Merovingians (so called after his grandfather Merovius) and the Church, which was to play such a key role in France's history.

In the meantime, in Rome, St Peter's successors at the Vatican had survived all the upheavals that had led to the final dissolution of the Roman Empire, and all the invasions and pillages by the Huns. In fact, in a city which had become a benighted wilderness in which all sense of law and order had broken down, only the Roman Church could claim or offer any sort of continuity with the past, and in the absence of other candidates, had come to be accepted as the most significant temporal power in the area, as well as the supreme spiritual one. And with the arrival of fresh invaders from north of the Alps, the rulers of the Vatican now set about looking around for an ally powerful enough to protect their tight little city-state, should the need ever arise.

The Franks seemed the most promising prospect, and before long Rome was making overtures to Pepin, son of the Charles Martel who had defeated the Moors at Poitiers in 732 and had saved Europe — at least for the time being — from the fearsome menace of Islam.

Pepin, as mayor of the palace, had taken over power from the effete Merovingians and had become de facto king of the Franks, but he also wanted to be king de jure and felt that the Pope's imprimatur would take a good deal of the harm out of the coup d'état he had accomplished. Emissaries were sent to Rome to inquire whether the royal title should not go to him since he exercised the supreme authority, rather than to one who merely enjoyed the superficial appearance of authority. The Pope gave his assent to this rather dubious, opportunistic argument and Pepin deposed the last degenerate descendant of the line of Clovis. The Pope endorsed his coronation by anointing him, by allowing the words *dei gratia* (by the grace of God) to be inserted in the coronation ceremony, and by conferring on him the title of Roman patrician. And so the Carolingians became the ruling dynasty in France.

A generation later, Pepin's son Charlemagne became involved in a contract with the Pope which changed the whole course of European history, and resulted in the revival of the old Roman Empire in a very different form.

Charlemagne – who already probably entertained ideas of his own of becoming overlord of the area formerly known as the Roman Empire of the West – went to Rome initially to quell a riot, and whilst attending Mass twenty years later in the ancient basilica of the Lateran Palace on Christmas Day, 800, was suddenly and unexpectedly crowned emperor by Pope Leo III and hailed as Caesar Augustus, Emperor of the Holy Roman Empire of the West. The Holy Roman Empire of the East based at Constantinople and founded by Constantine was still in business.

Whatever Charlemagne's initial intention had been, the Pope by his action had created a new Roman Empire and had placed it in the hands of a Germanic Frankish tribal chieftain who could barely read or write. Charlemagne repaid the debt by capturing Ravenna and a few other scattered cities and adding them to what had now become the Papal States.

After Charlemagne's death, there was a dispute over the succession, and the imperial crown passed from one unworthy successor to another until Pope John XII decided to bestow it upon a Germanic tribal chieftain who became the first Holy Roman Emperor of the German Nation, a title that persevered into the nineteenth century. But Charlemagne had laid the foundations of feudalism, and France thus survived further aggravations from the Moors and the great onslaught of the Norsemen in the course of which the latter turned the northern part of the country into Normandy and themselves into the Normans.

Hugues Capet, Duke of the Franks, became King of France in 987, though he controlled only the area around Paris known as the Ile de France. His successors established the principle of hereditary monarchy and soon became enmeshed, as a result of this decision, with England. Matilda, daughter of King Henry I of England, married Geoffrey, Count of Anjou, an arrangement which united England, Normandy, Maine and Anjou. When

Matilda's son, Henry II, married Eleanor, the divorced wife of King Louis VII of France, who brought Aquitaine with her, the area of France which acknowledged the rule of the English kings far exceeded the remainder of France, and the long love–hate relationship between the two countries began.

It took the French roughly 100 years — from the Battle of Crécy in 1346 to the defeat of the English at Castillon in 1453 — to evict the English from France with the exception of the region around Calais, which the French eventually retook in 1558.

In 1519, the Hapsburgs finally managed to get their hands on the mantle of the Holy Roman Emperors as the result of a persistent process of marrying for money, power and influence. Carlos I of Spain became the Holy Roman Emperor Charles V and a period of bitter animosity began between the French and the Germans which was to continue until the first overtures, just after World War II, which led to the formation of the European Community. The animosity started with a series of wars between François I of France and the Emperor Charles V.

The revocation of the Edict of Nantes in 1685 — which had protected the Huguenots in France from persecution — resulted in some of the most industrious citizens fleeing from the country, and divided the population in many areas until 1774 when religious liberty was finally achieved.

The sheer scale of the extravagance of the French royalty and court also succeeded in alienating the people. In 1648, for the first time though by no means the last, the citizens of Paris began to tear up the cobblestones and fling them at the nearest representatives of the authorities. This revolt, known as the Fronde, because the Parisians used slings (*frondes*) to hurl the stones, was easily suppressed, and was followed by some minor tax concessions, but it could well be regarded as a dress rehearsal for the eventual revolution of 1789.

Wars of aggrandisement upset the balance of power in Europe and provoked Louis XIV's neighbours, England in particular, into taking retaliatory measures. When it looked as if the Spanish king was about to die without leaving an heir — and in those days Spain also controlled the Spanish Netherlands – Louis decided to claim the succession on behalf of his grandson Philip.

This would have given the king of France control of the whole continent from the English channel to the Mediterranean, and as England was not content to see the European balance of power upset in this way, one result was a series of battles culminating in Louis XIV's first real defeat at Blenheim by the Duke of Marlborough. Another result was an increasing burden on the French people's taxes to pay for Louis's wars.

A combination of factors thus prepared the way for the French Revolution. The highly successful revolt of the American colony against the British, the writings of philosophers like Voltaire and Rousseau, the loss of France's Canadian colonies by Louis XVI, even a succession of bad harvests which left many peasants starving all contributed to a general feeling of discontent. France at this period led the world in literature and thought: but as in most nations apart from Britain the king still had absolute power and the nobles were a privileged caste with many of their old feudal rights intact. Also, having assisted the American colonists in winning their freedom from Britain, the French naturally wanted to achieve some freedom from the results of the follies of their own kings.

In May 1789, Louis XVI called a parliament; there hadn't been one since the beginning of the seventeenth century. It was called the Estates-General because it represented the three estates: the nobles, the clergy and the commons. But it was too late; the Third Estate seized power, determined to have a new constitution, and on 9 July 1789 formed the National Assembly. They were supported by the Paris mob, which on 14 July attacked the Bastille to secure the release of some political prisoners. What had begun as a mildly republican effort to limit the power of the king and the nobles gradually turned into a radical revolt against authority in any shape or form. Throughout the country, the peasants burnt down many of the big houses, and the gentry began to flee across the frontier to Germany and elsewhere with tales about the Terror.

The Holy Roman Emperor, by now no more than Emperor of

the Austrians, and the King of Prussia, in what later became Germany, began to feel a bit nervous about their own thrones and formed an alliance against the French revolutionaries, declaring war on them in 1792.

When an Austrian army began to advance on Paris there was great alarm. The Jacobin anti-Royalists and the Paris mob got the upper hand; the palace was stormed, the royal family imprisoned and many of the aristocrats who had not already escaped were imprisoned as traitors.

In September 1792 there was another panic occasioned by an advance of the Prussian army; the Paris mob murdered some 2,000 'suspects' and a republic was proclaimed. Thousands of volunteers flocked to the colours; the Austrians were defeated and the Prussians withdrew to the Rhine. The Jacobins now put Louis XVI on trial.

By 1793, there had been 1,800 executions in Paris and 14,000 in the provinces, and the victims included King Louis XVI and Queen Marie Antoinette, many of the aristocrats unable to escape in time, and, inevitably, most of the initial ringleaders of the revolution.

When the victorious French revolutionary army began to push into Holland, Britain protested and France declared war on Britain. There were uprisings in various parts of France against the revolutionary Convention which had been set up to run the country, and one at Toulon was supported by the British fleet. Toulon was captured by a young Corsican artillery officer, Napoleon Bonaparte, and by autumn the republic was successful on all fronts.

The Terror ended in the summer of 1794, when Robespierre, the leader of the Jacobins, was guillotined, and the Jacobins were overthrown; Paris began to breathe again. The country was peaceful and content. The revolution had given the peasants the land they had formerly farmed for their aristocratic overlords, and a new government was set up under a Directory of five, with young Napoleon Bonaparte as its champion. He was rewarded with the command in North Italy; he crushed Sardinia and drove the Austrians out of Italy. He then contemplated invading

England, and even got as far as assembling a fleet of barges at Boulogne before abandoning the idea for the time being. Next he set sail from Toulon and conquered Egypt, with a view to threatening India; but his fleet was wiped out by Nelson as it lay at anchor off Alexandria.

A fresh alliance between Russia and Austria drove the French back out of north Italy, but the Russians were defeated in Switzerland and made peace. Napoleon then invaded Syria. When he was repulsed at Acre with the help of a British squadron, he returned to Egypt, left his army there, and sailed to France where in a coup d'état he set up a government of three consuls, of which he was the first and, in effect, military dictator. The liberty, equality and fraternity achieved during the revolution had lasted less than ten years.

From first consul to emperor — a title more consistent with French aspirations than military dictator — was a short step, and in 1804 the little corporal took that step. Nor did he even allow the Pope the privilege of promoting him; instead he seized the crown of laurels from the Pope's hands and crowned himself.

Between 1805 and 1812 Napoleon dominated a large part of Europe, but lost mastery of the seas to Nelson at Trafalgar. On land he seemed invincible; the day before Trafalgar, 20 October 1805, he forced an Austrian army to surrender, entered Vienna in November, and in December crushed the main Austrian and Russian armies at Austerlitz. In 1806, he made his brothers Joseph and Louis kings of Naples and Holland respectively, united Bavaria and Württemberg which he forced the Holy Roman Emperor to make into independent kingdoms, and with other German states formed a Confederation of the Rhine under German protection. At this point, the Austrian Emperor gave up all pretence of being head of the Holy Roman Empire of the German Nation and proclaimed himself merely Emperor of Austria.

Napoleon then attacked Portugal and Spain. But when Arthur Wellesley, later Duke of Wellington, invaded the Iberian Peninsula, he suddenly turned on the Tsar of Russia in 1812 and marched on Moscow with an army of over 500,000 men. The

Russian capital fell to his army, but the Russians set fire to it. In October, unable to stay on because of lack of supplies and the approach of winter, he began his disastrous retreat, in the course of which he lost most of his army. And, when British and Austrian armies invaded France, Napoleon's career as an empire-builder ended in 1814. He was allowed to retire as ruler of the tiny island of Elba, off the west coast of Italy.

But the little corporal lived to fight another day; he escaped from Elba in March 1815, rallied his old troops around him, attacked Belgium and faced the Allies — the two armies each about 70,000 strong — at Waterloo near Brussels. Napoleon was routed, abdicated for the second time and was packed off to the island of St Helena, a British possession off the west coast of Africa where he died six years later. Louis XVIII, who had been restored to the monarchy during Napoleon's sojourn on Elba, returned to the French throne.

During the brief intervals in his career when he was not fighting battles, Napoleon introduced many desirable reforms, founded the Bank of France, established a legal code which is still in operation, and restored official recognition of the Church, which had been persecuted during the revolution.

The Treaty of Vienna in 1815 accepted the restoration of the Bourbon monarchy, but they didn't last very long in a country trying to raise the finance necessary to become industrialized and to develop and modernize its transport system.

The Second Empire was presided over by Louis-Napoleon (Napoleon III), a nephew of Bonaparte's, who supported the Italians in their war of independence against the Austrians, supported the Poles in their struggle against the Russians, and alienated Britain by seizing Nice and encouraging the unification of north Germany under Prussian leadership. He was rewarded for this ill-judged intervention by his defeat at the hands of the Prussians at Sedan in 1870, and by the sight of the Prussians victoriously marching down wide boulevards and across vast squares which had been created in the course of Baron Haussmann's spectacular reconstruction of Paris in the 1850s and 1860s.

The Rising of the Commune in Paris in 1871 was put down by the army with horrifying zeal and a total of 18,000 deaths, and it wasn't until 1875 that a true parliamentary republic came into being in France.

The first phase of the third Republic is remembered by financial crises, social unrest, political extremism — and the Dreyfus Case. Nevertheless, it achieved for the workers the right to strike and to belong to trade unions, as well as free, compulsory education for all.

The increasingly militaristic tendencies of the Germans had already led to an entente cordiale between those two highly unlikely allies, the British and the French, and in 1914, when neutral Belgium was invaded in defiance of the British guarantee of neutrality and when the Germans declared war on Russia, committing France to support an earlier agreement with Russia, the Allies together faced up to the Kaiser, and won the war. Later, with US President Woodrow Wilson's assistance, they lost the peace in the endless debates of the Treaty of Versailles held in Louis XIV's château at Versailles.

When the Germans invaded France again in May 1940, and the country was divided in two by the armistice of 22 June, Marshal Pétain moved his government to Vichy in the 'unoccupied zone', while de Gaulle tried to convince Britain that there were still some people in France who were prepared to fight on. When the allied forces invaded Europe in June 1944 and defeated the Germans, General de Gaulle entered Paris at the head of a provisional government which lasted little more than a year.

The Fourth Republic, largely the vision of Jean Monnet, one of the founder-members of the European Community, was dogged by France's difficulties with her colonial empire. Terrorism by Arab nationalists led to drastic counter-measures, and in May 1958 the army assumed power. The Fourth Republic and its government collapsed, and de Gaulle took over as President of the Fifth Republic.

Since de Gaulle's resignation in 1969 (he died the following year), the acceleration in industrial development has continued, while in 1978 the French opted for Giscard d'Estaing's right-of-centre coalition.

Then, in the elections of May 1981, the French voted against Giscard for change, and the veteran socialist, François Mitterrand, was elected as president. He put France on a new course aimed at reducing the inequalities of wealth, which had long been greater in France than in most other European countries, and succeeded in nationalizing the private banks and biggest industrial groups.

COLONIAL CONNECTIONS

Protectorates All Over the Place

The French, like the English, were fairly slow to follow up Portugal's and Spain's lead in exploring and colonizing; the French probably because they regarded France, as indeed they still do, as their principal and perfectly adequate source of wealth.

However, stimulated by the Spaniard del Cano's round-the-world voyage in 1519–20 – the voyage during which Magellan was killed – François I decided to follow the current fashion and to sign on an Italian navigator to do some exploring on France's behalf. He employed the master-mariner Giovanni da Verrazano to look for a passage somewhere between Newfoundland and Florida which would open up the sea route to Cathay.

Verrazano set sail from Dieppe in a 100-ton ship *La Dauphine* with three other ships in 1524 and made a landfall at Cape Fear, the southernmost of North Carolina's three capes, which he wrongly took to be on the same parallel of latitude as Damascus and Carthage. He went ashore in a small boat, spied an inland sea and mistook the Pimlico Sound for the Pacific Ocean, which wasn't nearly as silly as it sounds because nobody at that period had any idea how big America was and Pimlico Sound is so wide anyway that it is frequently impossible to see the mainland from a small boat outside the banks.

Verrazano encountered some Native Americans who greeted him affably enough, and he carried on up as far as the area that is now New York, naming Manhattan Island Angoulême (François I had been Count of Angoulême before he became king), and the bay in which he anchored Santa Margharita in honour of the French king's sister. He then carried on up the coast to Newfoundland, and recrossed the Atlantic in the very good time of a little over two weeks.

This voyage was never followed up because, having just resumed his war with the Emperor Charles V, the French king was by then far too busy for such speculative ventures. Verrazano disappeared off in search of fresh sponsors.

A few years later Jacques Cartier, a master mariner from St Malo in Brittany, was recommended to François I as a suitable successor to Verrazano to look for territories for France to exploit in the new world. Cartier had been as far as the Newfoundland Banks several times with the Breton fishermen who had been casually and unostentatiously crossing the Atlantic to ply their trade there for years before Columbus ever dreamed of pioneering the westward route to Cathay.

Cartier made a brief visit to Newfoundland in 1534, and returned the next year with a fleet of three ships, sailed up the St Lawrence River and came upon Canada. He entertained the Huron chief Donnaconna, saw the great rock of Quebec and visited Stadacone, site of the future city of Quebec, and Hochlega, site of the future Montreal, called after a hill overshadowing the area which Cartier christened Mont Réal. He wintered in Canada, building a fort at Quebec and returned after fourteen months, bringing with him as prisoners Donnaconda and two of his sons – as well as a few young Native American girls – to help convince François I of the existence of this new country he had discovered.

Once again, François was too preoccupied with his wars with Spain to do anything about it straight away. In 1541, however, he sent Cartier back to Canada with Jean-François de la Rogue, Sieur de Roberval, in charge of the expedition, giving the latter permission to grant all lands discovered in feudal tenure to any gentlemen volunteers who might be interested in taking up the offer.

This expedition, like the earlier ones, was not followed up, and it wasn't until the early seventeenth century that serious French attempts to colonize the St Lawrence area were made under Samuel de Champlain, who established New France there with Quebec as its capital. The French also took over Nova Scotia, but the cold and dreary climate of Canada and the lack of good French food did not greatly appeal to the French settlers, who after fifty years hardly numbered more than 2,500. Moreover, the settlers were scattered over a wide area and tended to concentrate on exploration, trapping and prospecting rather than setting up a stable colony; having come from France, they could never seriously think of any other place as home.

In 1699, another French colony was established at Biloxi in southern Mississippi, and the great territory of Louisiana to the west of the British colonies became French with New Orleans as its capital.

The French were far better than the British at establishing good relationships with the native tribes, and before long were using them as highly effective allies in a series of skirmishes which inevitably broke out between the British and French settlers, and soon developed into full-scale warfare.

In 1756, England formally declared war on France, and eleven ships of the line were dispatched to cross the Atlantic to attack the French if they attempted to land troops or venture up the St Lawrence River. Meanwhile, a French force of about 3,000 regulars was sailing for Canada under the cover of French naval vessels.

Early in 1756, the Marquis de Montcalm, the new French commander-in-chief in Canada, crossed the Atlantic with six ships of the line and 1,000 fresh troops. He captured Fort Oswego, the vital British fortress controlling the Great Lakes.

For three years, although they outnumbered the French by about ten to one, the British could make no headway. It was not a kind of warfare in which they had ever specialized, and they suffered terribly in the unfamiliar forests and mountains and from the activities of the Native American guerrillas who did not fight wars according to the finer points of fair play as understood by the English.

In 1759, the armies and navies of France and Britain finally came to grips; Wolfe captured Quebec, Montreal capitulated, and in 1761 France formally ceded Canada to Britain. Louisiana went initially to Spain under a subsidiary agreement, but was retaken by France before long. Napoleon seriously considered it very briefly as the basis of a new French empire overseas, then abruptly changed his mind and in 1803 sold it to the United States in the celebrated Louisiana Purchase, the biggest land sale in history.

When the American colonists rebelled against England, the French entered the war as allies of the colonists in March 1778, but the principal battles in the war between the French and the British were naval ones, fought in the waters around the West Indies; it was not until 1782 that Rodney and Hood won a decisive battle and routed the French navy. France succeeded in retaining a few footholds in the area including half of Columbus's first landfall in the Caribbean, which he had called Hispaniola and which later became Dominica and Haiti (the French half), as well as the islands of Guadeloupe and Martinique.

West Africa had been as constantly and just as casually visited by French mariners from Dieppe as the Newfoundland Banks had been fished by French trawlers from Brittany, but the Portuguese were the first to make any serious territorial claims in the area. However, it wasn't very long before traders from the Netherlands, Spain, France and England began to investigate these potential new sources of wealth.

Three or four French attempts to establish trading posts in West Africa failed before André Brue, chief factor for the French Senegal Company at the turn of the seventeenth century, began to court the Damel of Kayor, a powerful slave-trading chief in Senegal. This courtship was conducted with the aid of two 10-gallon kegs of fine French cognac and Brue managed to get the Dumel so plastered that it was four days before he could get a sober word out of him.

When eventually he succeeded, the words were all favourable and France had established a trading presence in West Africa, venturing much further inland than the Portuguese had ever dared to go.

French overseas colonial adventures were interrupted by the French Revolution and the Napoleonic Wars. But by 1830, a French attack on Algiers marked the resumption of French overseas expansion. This was presented to the world as an attempt to put an end to Algerian privateering, and while the West in general was not displeased to see a Christian country taking over from the Muslims, the British were not entirely happy at the idea of the French installing themselves so firmly in North Africa.

By 1844 the French had defeated Morocco, which eventually became a French protectorate, and had begun to occupy the whole of Algeria, destroying every vestige of national life and culture there, making French the official language and imposing French ideas and customs on the Algerians.

Away on the far side of the globe, a rebellion in Vietnam in 1771 had deposed the emperor and his two *chuas* or hereditary governors. A French Catholic bishop by the name of Piqueau de Behaine somehow managed to raise a European army of mercenaries and helped one of the *chuas*, Nguyan Anh, to defeat the rebels. The latter declared himself emperor, changed his name to Gia Long and in gratitude allowed the European missionaries to proceed with their work unmolested. A combined Franco-Spanish expedition of 1858 captured Tourane and Saigon, before the Spanish withdrew after a quarrel with their French allies, and the French carried on to force the emperor to cede them the three western provinces of Cochin-China. They then annexed the three eastern provinces and became the principal power in the area.

In 1863, the King of Cambodia placed his country under French protection (he was slightly less nervous of the French than he was of the neighbouring Thais) and Laos became a French protectorate in 1893. French Indo-China lasted until the fall of Dien Bien Phu in 1954, when it broke up into North Vietnam, South Vietnam, Laos and Cambodia with results of which the world is still only too acutely aware.

It is probably not much of an exaggeration to say that the French colonial adventure was every bit as disastrous, in the long run, as the British one, and indeed all the others, had been. Yet although all the colonized people who suffered under the British (and indeed most of the others) hate and despise their former conquerors, the people from the former French colonies still have a slightly ambivalent attitude.

All over what used to be French West Africa, while they dislike intensely the whole notion of colonialism, the natives still speak French proudly and perfectly — in sharp contrast to the pidgin English spoken in, say, Ghana; the house numbers are in white on blue tiles, exactly as in Paris, and the street signs say '*Sens Unique*' or '*Sans Issue*' exactly as anywhere in France. From your hotel window you can see small, totally naked black African boys returning from the *boulangerie* with three *baguettes* under their arms, chewing at the end of the loaves, as everywhere in France.

Towards the end of the nineteenth century, the French began to expand in West Africa in a very big way, starting with the River Niger in 1876, the Ivory Coast in 1887 and Dahomey in 1889. Madagascar became a French protectorate from 1885; French West Africa, which included Senegal, Guinea, the Ivory Coast and the Sudan Territories, was created by a decree in 1895; Mauretania (most of it the Sahara Desert) was made a French protectorate in 1903; and Morocco a French protectorate from 1912. Britain, France and Italy all had their eye on Tunisia, and when it went bankrupt in 1896, the three nations assumed joint financial control over it. Later Britain allowed France a free hand in Tunisia in return for French acquiescence over the British acquisition of Cyprus. The French also managed to get control of French Syria (including the Lebanon) and French Guiana on the north-east coast of South America, as well as a number of groups of islands in the South Pacific — in New Caledonia, the New Hebrides, the Marquesas and Tuamotu, including Tahiti.

It all started to fall apart when in Haiti in 1801 Toussaint L'Overture fought for independence against the French. Although he was defeated, continued Creole rebellions forced the French to withdraw.

French Indo-China ceased to exist in 1954; Tunisia became fully independent in 1956; French West Africa ceased to be an administrative unit controlled from France by 1958 and was fully independent by 1960; Madagascar became independent the same year; and in 1962 de Gaulle finally came to accept the inevitability of Algerian independence, though only after the death of 100,000 uniformed Algerians, 10,000 French officers and men, and countless thousands of civilians.

France was left with a few West Indian islands like Guadeloupe and Martinique, Réunion in the Indian Ocean, a few islands in the South Seas, and two (St Pierre and Miquelon) in the Gulf of St Lawrence. And Corsica, of course, the island on which Napoleon had been born.

DEVELOPMENT DIRECTIONS

Mosques, Minarets and Channel Tunnels

France is full of surprises. As you drive through it, it still appears to be basically an agricultural country, yet every car you pass on the road seems to be French. Where do they manage to make all those cars, you wonder. Then as you approach what used to be a sleepy little country town, you find yourself driving for miles and miles along a *boulevard périphérique*, skirting an industrial zone.

France's automobile industry is the fourth largest in the world, after Japan, the United States and what used to be West Germany, and sells more than half of its production abroad. About a century old, France's motor car industry employs 300,000 workers who produce nearly 4 million cars, vans and utility vehicles a year. The two principal firms are Renault, which is nationalized, and PSA (Peugeot-Citroën), which is private.

It is also immediately clear as you drive through France that it has a very healthy building and construction industry. There are new houses, blocks of flats, public buildings and factories everywhere. The roads and autoroutes are magnificent, spanning gorges or tunnelling through daunting mountains. It is no surprise to learn that the building and public works sector employs nearly 1 million workers, mainly building houses.

But a lot of France's most spectacular engineering and

construction projects are not in France at all, but abroad. This is nothing new, of course. It was a Frenchman, Ferdinand de Lesseps, who was responsible for both the Suez and the Panama canals, and Gustave Eiffel, who conceived and built the monstrous but curiously graceful Eiffel Tower in Paris, also built the first metal bridge in Europe over the Douro River in Portugal.

The mosque in Casablanca, designed by the architect Michel Pinseau and built by a French firm right on the sea and completed in 1989, is the tallest religious building in the world. The spire of its minaret rises 200 metres above sea level, and its prayer rooms can accommodate 35,000 with room for another 80,000 in the forecourt.

In the year that the Casablanca mosque was completed, another massive religious building in a different part of Africa was blessed and inaugurated by the Pope. The Cathedral of Yamoussoukro in the Ivory Coast is almost an exact replica of St Peter's in Rome; it took only three years to build as against over a century for the Vatican basilica. Standing on a site between the savanna and the lagoon, it was built by a consortium of French firms. About 2,000 workers from twenty-five different trades worked on the site, some employing the latest technology and labouring alongside craftsmen using techniques that have hardly changed since the Middle Ages.

The highest dam in Africa, the Turkwell dam in north-west Kenya, is now nearing completion. This hydro-electric complex, which will increase Kenya's energy resources by 20 per cent, stands at the foot of Mount Elgon (4,130 metres) in the Rift Valley; it's being built by a French company.

Possibly because the French have managed to maintain fairly good relations with their own former colonies, the latter, and other third world countries, seem to favour France when it comes to handing out contracts for construction work. A French group built the railway link from Ramdam to Djamel and El Milia in Algeria; engineers from RATP (the Paris overground transport system) have installed some 600 kilometres of railway line in ninety towns all over the world, including Mexico City, Santiago in Chile and Caracas in Venezuela.

French firms have also provided rolling stock for underground railway systems in Atlanta, San Francisco, New York and Cairo, while in Chicago and Jacksonville, Florida, a VAL (a French-built light automatic vehicle) links the airports with the city centres.

But to return to France itself, textiles, clothing and footwear, particularly in the luxury band (Paris fashions), are exported all over the world.

France is also the fourth largest producer − after the United States, Japan and Germany again − of electric generators, turbines, transformers and elevators.

France was a pioneer in aviation − was it not, after all, Louis Blériot who by proving in 1909 that it was possible to fly the English Channel, opened up the way for international air travel? Concorde, the first supersonic passenger plane and arguably the most beautiful aircraft ever built, was a combination of French flair and British inventiveness, and the European Ariane unmanned rocket project, initiated and mainly operated by France, has proved more economical, reliable and profitable than America's space-shuttle.

The aerospace industry, partly nationalized and concentrated around Paris and in Toulouse, employs 120,000 people; other outstanding products of this industry include the Mirage jet and the Exocet missile. France is the third biggest exporter of armaments in the world after the Soviet Union and the United States; the arms sector of the industry alone employs 300,000, though whether this is a statistic of which any country should be proud is another matter.

Perhaps to offset this, France has also been in the forefront of the development of 'green' industries; for example, out of the 4 billion francs allocated to the motor industry in the period 1990−4, 'a good part' − the government statistics are no more specific than that − will be devoted to developing 'clean' engines and reducing harmful emissions into the atmosphere.

The French are also among the pioneers of mercury-free batteries for household use, silent household appliances, the recycling of glass, plastics, cardboard and paper, and the development of paints free from pollution-causing ingredients.

The French have made history with their TGV (*train à grande vitesse*) streaking across the country at 515.3 kilometres per hour on 18 May 1990, yet again breaking a world record for rail speed; the British may have invented the railway train but it is the French who have perfected it.

The French, unlike the British, believe in investing in public transportation. Within the current ten-year period, they have invested 300 billion francs for the main roads, 350 billion francs for local thoroughfares, 75 billion for urban transport and the same amount for the Channel tunnel. During the same period, nearly 150 billion francs will be spent on the railways, 50 billion on the canals and other waterways, and 35 billion on air transport.

Nevertheless, the French remain very attached to their motor cars. There are almost 28 million vehicles on the French roads, 23 million of them private cars, in a population of 55 million. France comes fourth after the United States, Japan and West Germany in the table listing the number of cars per head of the population.

Their road network is one of the most comprehensive and efficient in the world: 1.5 million kilometres of roads in all, 18,000 kilometres of them A roads, which include 6,000 kilometres of the best autoroutes in Europe, a total which will be nearly doubled by the year 2000. The autoroutes are almost all toll-roads and are fairly expensive – it costs about 300 francs to drive from Paris to the Riviera – but their very existence makes driving on the ordinary roads a joy, by removing most of the *camions*.

But again unlike Britain, the railways have not been almost entirely superseded by planes and cars. Every day, 13,000 trains run on the 36,000 kilometre network of SNCF lines. SNCF (Société Nationale des Chemins de Fer) employs 210,000 people, and carries 300 million passengers and 140,000 tonnes of goods each year. And the TGV has reduced the train travel time between Paris and Marseilles from an overnight journey to four and a half hours.

The national airline Air France carries 15 million passengers and 670,000 tonnes of freight between 210 stopovers in seventy-nine countries. Its fleet of 113 aircraft includes seven

Concordes. Then there is Air Inter, an internal airline with fifty-two aircraft, and UTA, a private company with forty-three stopovers in thirty-six countries, including Africa and the Far East.

In a world increasingly dominated by TV and visual communication of one sort or another, France remains a resolutely literate society. One French person in two reads a daily newspaper; there are ten national dailies and seventy-seven regional ones. More importantly perhaps, every French person, according to a recent survey, devotes between half an hour and an hour and a half per day to reading books, as against 130 minutes listening to the radio (partly in the car) and who knows how long watching the telly; in 1990, 95 per cent of all households had a TV set.

There are three public channels which receive the licensing fee of 552 francs for a colour set and 355 francs for a black-and-white receiver; and four commercial channels.

French telecommunications are among the best in Europe and were the first to provide a Minitel service. This computerized telephone directory also furnishes all the facilities of the Yellow Pages; provides a terminal through which you can check up on national and international rail, bus and airline services, and if required, make reservations; transacts all the business that you have to do with your bank; and books seats for the theatre, among many other things.

Julius Caesar, writing to his folks back in Rome in 54 BC or thereabouts, remarked that the Gauls 'are a most ingenious people, and very clever at borrowing and adapting ideas suggested to them'.

He was right, and they haven't changed a bit since.

AFFAIRS OF STATE

Time for a Second Thought

France is a republic in which, under the constitution, power is shared between the president, the government and parliament.

The appearance of the president in this trinity dates back only to 1958, when General de Gaulle was recalled from retirement on the collapse of the Fourth Republic to cope with the Arab terrorism stemming from the Algerian struggle for independence. He insisted on providing France with a new constitution and himself with a special role in the republic for which he had designed it.

Under de Gaulle's constitution, the president is elected directly by the people for a term of seven years. France, incidentally, now uses a form of proportional representation with two polls a week apart — to enable people to consider the implications of their first attempt at exercising their franchise and have some second thoughts about it, if they should feel so inclined.

The president is head of the executive and appoints the prime minister, appoints or dismisses other ministers on the prime minister's recommendation, and presides over the Council of Ministers. He is also entitled to dissolve the National Assembly and submit major bills to a referendum.

Parliament consists of two chambers: the National Assembly and the Senate. Up to March 1986, the 577 deputies who make up the National Assembly were elected on a single ballot for five years from lists drawn up by the *départements*. In subsequent elections, the two-round system of majority has been and will be used.

The 305 senators, aged thirty-five or over, are elected by indirect suffrage for a term of nine years; the electoral college is composed of the deputies to the National Assembly, the general (departmental) councillors, the mayors and the municipal councillors.

Bills pass through both chambers, and in the event of disagreement, a joint committee is set up to endeavour to reach a mutually acceptable text; if this fails, the National Assembly has the final say.

The nine members of the Constitutional Council are elected for nine years, one-third by the head of state and two-thirds by the presidents of the two assemblies. Their job is to ensure that laws passed by the National Assembly are constitutional. The French judicial system is independent from parliament; the death penalty, which since the French Revolution had been carried out by means of a portable guillotine, was abolished in 1981, and currently the French, like most of the other nation-states in the Community, is seeking alternatives to detention in prison.

In 1990, defence spending in France amounted to nearly 231 billion francs, or 19 per cent of the entire budget.

The French armed forces comprise 540,000 men, 295,000 in the army, 95,000 in the air force, 65,000 in the navy and 85,000 in the gendarmerie, the state police. France has a system of conscription in which Frenchmen aged twenty are called up for a twelve-month period of military service, or a sixteen-month period of technical aid and co-operation with foreign states who ask for the service.

Ever since de Gaulle broke with NATO in 1966, French defence has been independent and relies on its own nuclear deterrent, tested in the South Seas. However, again enjoying the best of both worlds, France has not altogether left the Atlantic Alliance and still takes part in NATO manoeuvres.

The French have always been extremely proud of their army – is there a country in the entire world with so many monuments to the men who died for the sake of *La Patrie*? – and a recent survey showed that a majority (57 per cent) considered military service 'useful' to young people and 'necessary' for the defence of the country.

So far as health is concerned, the French believe very strongly in *prévention d'abord*, or as we would put it, that prevention is better than cure. Life expectancy in France has increased from forty-seven years in 1900 to seventy-six today, while in the last thirty years infant mortality has dropped from thirty-seven to eight per thousand.

By 1989, the French were spending 8,920 francs per head on health. With 175,000 doctors, 39,700 dentists and 295,000 nurses, France is one of the best-equipped countries in the Community to cope with disease: the ratio of hospital beds is 175 per 1,000 of the population, a relatively high one for such a large and scattered population.

In general, access to France's medical facilities is now on a par with most other Community countries, though prescriptions remain extremely expensive if obtained privately.

The French, following the peasant tradition which prevailed for so long, and eternally aware of the long ears of the revenue commissioners, are extremely discreet about their earnings, let alone their inherited wealth; however, recent surveys have established that by 1990, the average inheritance of a French family was around 600,000 francs (it was only 380,000 francs in 1980) so that there is no doubt that the French are becoming more prosperous.

They save, they invest in real estate (more than half of all French families own their own homes), they gamble on the stock exchange, on the national lottery, on horses. Some 25 million gamblers, or roughly half the total population, spend thirty francs a week hoping to win a jackpot of one sort or another.

In the home, they're spending less on food than they used to: 20 per cent of the total income as against 26 per cent in 1970. And they're spending more on the house itself and on home improvements: 19 per cent today as compared with 15 per cent in 1970. They use the phone a lot: only 12 per cent now write a letter rather than making a phone call.

They devote an increasing part of their overall budget to their motor cars, their leisure activities and their holidays: up to 35 per cent for single people under thirty-five years of age.

There are now only 2 million agricultural workers as compared with 5 million in 1955; and there are about 2.5 million people (or 9.5 per cent of the workforce) unemployed.

The birth-rate is dropping and was described as 'becoming a priority and a national exigence' by a finance minister recently. The average number of births per woman of child-bearing age is 1.9, which is 'insufficient to ensure a renewal of the generations' according to a government statement.

CULTURE AND LEISURE

The Priority of Priorities

About 90 per cent of French citizens are officially Catholic, though that means just about as much or as little as it means elsewhere in the Community. France has been, perhaps, more troubled than most of the other member-states with religious strife; the crusades against the Albigensian Cathars in the thirteenth century, the Inquisition at Toulouse and Montpelier, the massacre of the Huguenots on St Bartholomew's Day in Paris in 1572, the uprising of the Camisards in the seventeenth century, following the revocation of the Edict of Nantes, are all evidence of a race of people with strong views, prepared to kill — or indeed to die — in the defence of those views.

Today, the French people still have very strong views on everything except, perhaps, religion. To get married, a visit to the *Mairie* is essential; a service in the local church is an optional extra. Divorce, contraception and abortion are accepted as unavoidable features of everyday life in the run-up to the twenty-first century, whatever the Pope may think about it.

Paris may have yielded some of its public reputation as the City of Sin to Amsterdam and Copenhagen, but every Frenchman knows perfectly well that he can find whatever he seeks, however *outré*, in his own country, and more than likely in the nearest town; only the British and Germans need to go to Amsterdam and Copenhagen in search of the pleasures of the flesh.

Education in France is free and compulsory until the age of sixteen. It is divided into three periods: kindergarten from three to six years of age; primary school until eleven; and then various systems of secondary education leading to the *baccalauréat* (the higher secondary school certificate). In 1989, 75.5 per cent of the pupils who took the examination passed the bac, and the French education authorities expect an 80 per cent success rate by the year 2000.

More importantly perhaps, in 1990 60 per cent of young

people aged eighteen were still studying, and roughly one-quarter of young people aged twenty to twenty-four – were continuing with their studies after the bac, about 1 million of them at university.

In addition to the state schools there are private schools, which receive a grant from the state; about one-quarter of France's schoolchildren are privately educated.

France rates education as a top priority – *la priorité des priorités* as one government paper calls it – and devotes roughly 20 per cent of the state budget to its 14 million students and their 1 million plus teachers and the institutions in which they spend so much time.

School in France starts at 8 or 8.30 a.m. with a long break for lunch from noon until 2 or even 2.30 p.m.; the afternoon session goes on until 4.30 or 5 p.m. and French children get a great deal of homework to do as well. The long lunch-break is a relic of the days when French families all sat down to the main meal of their day at about a quarter past twelve, and went on eating and talking for the best part of two hours.

These days, in France as in most developed countries, most of the urban housewives go to work, and gangs of school kids can be seen wandering aimlessly around the streets or sitting in the cafés to kill time until school reopens; they can't go home because there is nobody there. It is part of the price that must be paid in societies which regard cars and car phones and dishwashing machines and videos and faxes and all the other expensive paraphernalia with which we clutter up our lives as essential.

What I say about the British and the Italians in relation to their art and literature applies equally to the French; they have produced so many giants that it wouldn't be possible even to list them all in a book of this size. Anybody with even the slightest interest in painting or sculpture could reel off a long string of famous French artists without pausing to think about it. A nation that has produced sculptors like Rodin and Maillol and Bourdel and painters like Monet and Manet and Degas and Poussin and

Toulouse-Lautrec and Boucher and Braque and Corot and Cézanne and Delacroix and Derain, to name but a few at random, has no need for a section introducing its artists in a book of this kind.

It is the same with literature – and particularly philosophy – from Voltaire and Rousseau to Jean-Paul Sartre. Probably more 'isms' originated in France than anywhere else. Just think about it for a second or two: Realism, Impressionism, Post-Impressionism, Cubism, Surrealism, Fauvism, Existentialism, Dadaism, Nihilism; you could go on and on.

So far as music is concerned, the French cannot match the Germans or the Italians, but names like Bizet, Debussy, Fauré, Ravel and Saint-Saëns are not unfamiliar to the music-listening public.

And the same applies to science, where the French cannot match the Germans or the British. Names like Pasteur and Curie leap to the mind but not so many others, unless you include pioneers in photography, cinematography and some aspects of aeronautics.

On the other hand, France is probably putting more effort and more cash into scientific research at the present time than any other member of the Community. Almost 2.5 per cent of the total GDP is devoted to research, which employs 315,000 people. The National Scientific Research Centre, set up half a century ago to develop, direct and co-ordinate research, has more than 1,300 laboratories employing 27,000 researchers working on projects as varied as: the fight against AIDS; the defence of the environment; the study of whatever can be learned from the ice archives of Antarctica; space exploration; and human genetics.

In France, eating and drinking are activities which are taken very seriously indeed. While it is probably not true to say, as somebody did, that while other nations eat in order to live, the French live in order to eat, it is certainly true that it was the French who raised the status of cooking from a domestic chore to a fine art.

Where else, other than in France, would you see a family party enjoying their Sunday lunch, tearing crabs and other crustaceans

apart, devouring the rich liver of geese, relishing the intestines of
various other animals, savouring the delights of guinea fowl, fed
on corn, stuffed with grapes and cooked in wine, followed by one
of the 350 officially recognized varieties of French cheeses, or
one of the 300-odd equally good unrecognized varieties, followed
by a rich dessert; and in the meantime all of them, the old people,
young men and women, teenagers, even tiny tots, talking ani-
matedly and enthusiastically through the entire meal? And the topic
of the conversation? As likely as not they will be discussing other
memorable meals that they had eaten in other places, at other times.

In what other country would you find a dish called after a
battle? I'm thinking of Chicken Marengo, which was invented after
a battle to which Napoleon had brought his chef who was forced,
because the supply vans had been left far behind, to improvise a
dish from what was available on the site.

And what other people, as hard-pressed as the French were
during the Franco-Prussian War when Paris was besieged, could
not only make the decision to kill all the animals in the zoo, but
even produce a recipe book for the best ways to serve an
elephant's trunk or a haunch of bear?

But wild animals were expensive; the hippopotamus survived
because no butcher could afford the reserve price of 80,000
francs. Also, according to Alistair Horne's *The Terrible Year*
(London: Macmillan, 1971), 'even eating domestic animals like
dogs, cats and rats − and during the siege, according to one
contemporary calculation, the French ate 65,000 horses, 5,000
cats, 1,200 dogs and 300 rats − was expensive because of the
lavish sauces required to make them palatable. They were a rich
man's dish; hence the famous menus of the Jockey Club,
featuring such delicacies as *salmi de rat.*'

The French eat everything fearlessly. From the snails in the
ditch and the frogs in the pond to the fungae of the forest, exotic
varieties which the rest of the world would shy away from in terror
(but which the French have sampled and classified so relentlessly
that an illustrated chart showing precisely which fungae are edible
appears in every health food shop and chemist's windows), they
eat everything that dares to grow or walk or fly or swim.

Sauce is one of the secrets of French cooking and it is no accident that of all the many grades of chef, the *chef saucier* is the king. 'Be assured,' said Carême in his *Cusenier Parisien*, 'that no foreign sauce is comparable to those of our great modern cuisine. I have been able to make comparisons; I have seen England, Russia, Germany and Italy and I have met everywhere our cooks occupying the highest posts in foreign courts.'

In England there exist only two types of sauce: white sauce and brown sauce. In France, a minor entry in the *Larousse Gastronomique* lists sixteen columns of white sauces all entirely French in origin; they include Suprême, Tarragon, Ravigote, Vertpré, Béchamel, Financière, Perigeux, Tortue, Matelote, Champagne, Régence, Poivrade Chevreuil, Aigre-doux, Piquante, Salamis, Leveret, Parisienne, Robert, Raifort, Magninaise, Provençale, Bâtard and Caper.

There is the point too that French food is regional. Of course food from various regions is eaten in other regions, and in Paris you can find regional dishes from all over France, and indeed all over the world; but in general the people in the regions prefer their own food, prepared in the traditional way, and by and large they eat whatever is in season locally, rather than out-of-season delicacies from the other side of the world which they can easily buy in the supermarket. We were in France at Christmas 1989, and in the *Midi Libre* headlines about the end of Ceausescu's regime in Romania and the dismantling of the Berlin Wall had to share the headlines with one about a local crisis: the appearance of salmonella in the oyster beds of Bouziges, in the Bassin de Thau.

It is perhaps the sheer variety of French food that makes it unique. The English eat half-a-dozen thick soups and one form of consommé; the French *Larousse Gastronomique* list no fewer than ninety-two hot consommés and six cold ones.

Even vegetables are not just vegetables; the best ones come from certain regions. In the Ile de France area alone, the best asparagus comes from Argenteuil, the best green peas from Clamart, the best French beans from Bagnolet, the best artichokes from Laon, the best cauliflowers from Arpajon, and so on, and in the markets the vegetables from these areas are proudly labelled and fetch a higher price than ordinary vegetables. Driving through a tiny village in the Languedoc in 1990 — I think it was called Paulhin — I was surprised and charmed to see a notice announcing that this was: *Le capital mondial de l'ognion doux.*

So far as drink is concerned, traditionally the French have always taken an aperitif — always Pernod, Ricard or some other pastis in the south, anything from Campari or port to Scotch whisky (very popular with the smart set) in the north; wine and table water with their meals; and a digestif — normally cognac or armagnac in the bigger cities and in the country very often a concoction made from nuts or fruit, wine and eau de vie according to a secret recipe which has been handed down for generations: exactly so many nuts, picked on a specific date, more than likely, so much wine, so much eau de vie and a maturing period of not less than five years. If you are very lucky you may even be offered a tiny glass from a vintage bottle laid down by the grandfather of your host before World War I.

When it comes to French wine, whether it's the vin de table which you can buy from the local co-op in ten-litre vracs that are filled straight from the tank like petrol or the better-known and more expensive varieties which are sold in wine merchants and supermarkets, what can you really say that hasn't already been said, almost ad nauseam?

Because they are such a race of rabid individualists, the French have never greatly excelled at team sports, with the curious exception of that most English of games, Rugby football. This is yet another example of the love–hate relationship which exists between the two countries.

So far as the French themselves are concerned, while it is probably less true today than it would have been fifty or even twenty years ago, to say that what the majority of them — men and women alike — most enjoy doing is eating, drinking, talking and making love, probably in that order, it's still not very far off the mark.

Boules or *pétanque*, an ancient French pastime which consists of throwing a set of larger metallic balls in the general direction of a smaller one, measuring the intermediate distances between the point where they fell with measuring tapes, and arguing interminably, is played in every open space in every French village and town from Calais to Narbonne. The only difference is the climate, the atmosphere and the vegetation. Plane trees, bougainvillaea and gentle civility in the Midi; poplars, geraniums and sharp rivalry in the windy bouledromes of the Pas de Calais.

Cycling is another French passion; even men who have never once thrown a leg across a saddle follow the Tour de France with a savage ferocity; and if you are unlucky enough to be driving anywhere along the route when the event is taking place, however important your mission, you will be waved into the ditch by the gendarmerie, to allow *les cyclistes* the best possible conditions in which to contest the affair.

French bull-fighting, known as *courses libres* and conducted in arenas built on the farms or *mas* of the big landowners in the Camargue and other parts of the Midi, are a joke, so far as both the bull and the bull-fighters, known as *razeteurs*, are concerned; the young bulls are let loose into the ring, and the unarmed boys who jump in to face them have merely to stop the bull for a few seconds and place a rope garland bearing the name of their sponsor around one of its horns.

Other typically French leisure activities are sunbathing, preferably in the nude; there are probably more nude beaches in France than anywhere else in the world, some enjoyed by young families, some mixed and some clearly gay.

There was a time when the British were devoted to dogs and the French merely tolerated them; now so many French people have dogs (usually either very tiny ones like miniature poodles and Yorkshire terriers, or very big ones like Alsatians, retrievers and Great Danes) that dog-owning has almost acquired the status of a national sport; and certainly the task of trying to keep the boulevards and the avenues and the beaches and boardwalks free from the dog's contributions to the world's waste is an activity that requires the fitness and the patience of an athlete.

In France these days, exclusive restaurants which would never dream of admitting a man not wearing a tie will welcome parties accompanied by a dog. And since the French remain paranoid *fumeurs* despite all the health warnings, I suppose all you can say about that is, that if the dogs can stand the smell of the cigarette smoke, they are as welcome to be there as their betters who are paying the bill.

The French are very keen on outdoor sports like sailing, skiing, camping, fishing and, above all, the *chasse*. Every autumn the shops are full of camouflage jackets, cartridge pouches, hunting boots and all the paraphernalia with which the French need to adorn themselves before venturing up the mountains or into the woods for the *chasse* — and mostly, it must be added, returning empty-handed.

THE GERMANS

The Wall in The Mind

GERMANY IN PROFILE

Area	357,041 sq km
Population	78,000,000
Population density	222 per sq km
Women	51.67%
Under 15	21%
Over 60	21%
Language	German
Religion	43% Catholic, 41% Protestant
Labour force	45.91%*
Employed in:	
Agriculture	3.7%*
Industry	40.86%*
Services	37.48%*
Unemployment (as % of labour force)	5.7% West Germany, 12.1% East Germany
Women in labour force	38.91*

*Major exports:** Road vehicles (17.5%), machinery (20%), chemicals (12.8%), electrical appliances (8.5%), iron and steel (6%), food, beverages and tobacco (4.1%)

*Main customers:** EC (50.8%), USA (10.5%), Switzerland (5.9%), Austria (5.3%), Sweden (2.8%), USSR (1.8%)

*These figures refer only to the former West Germany; comparable statistics for the former East Germany not yet available.

THE GERMANS

For all the devastating effect they had upon the rest of the people of Europe for the greater part of this century, the Germans, as a nation, haven't really been around for very long. Only for 120 years, in fact.

There were, of course, those ancient Germanic tribes who broke into the Roman Empire towards the end of Rome's domination of Europe. And although one collection of tribes, the Franks, picked up .the Latin language and interbred with the Gallo-Romans to become the French, most of the other Germanic tribes remained on the far side of the Rhine, adopted the Teutonic tongue when it emerged, and became the Germans, so-called after the tribe of the Germanii, who so impressed the Romans by their skill in battle.

Unfortunately, they didn't have a country, merely a collection of tribal settlements which eventually developed into medieval duchies and principalities with nothing more in common than the German language which gave some cohesion to the country when it officially came into existence as a unified state in 1871. And even then, at that late date, after the notions of liberty, equality and fraternity had been kicking around Europe for over a century, Germany emerged not as a democratic state created by its citizens in defiance of their lords and masters, but as an empire, no less, the second *Deutsches Reich* created by the Prussian Junkers and the German princes and minor monarchs after they had defeated France in battle.

This new imperial state showed a singular lack of concern on the part of the nobility and gentry for the rights of the citizens. And ironically enough, it was born not anywhere in Germany but in the Hall of Mirrors in Louis XIV's Palace of Versailles in France, later to be the scene of the German nation's bitter humiliation after its defeat in World War I. The imperial state had lasted from 1871 until the November revolution in Berlin in 1918, though that came too late to achieve anything for the desperate citizens other than despair, disillusion and economic ruin.

Before that, of course, there had been the Holy Roman Empire of the German Nation which, as Voltaire pointed out, wasn't particularly holy, certainly wasn't in any way Roman, and wasn't in any real sense an empire. Also, at the time it was founded there was no German nation. Nor was there for a long time afterwards. The Holy Roman Empire of the Germans was the accidental by-product of a series of attempts by the papacy to use Rome's status as the former capital of the greatest empire Europe had known in order to grab a slice, so to speak, of the temporal action by allying itself with the strongest of the many warring tribes of Europe in the ninth and tenth centuries. But its very existence, as the first Reich (its title in German was *Heiliges Romisches Deutscher Nation*), gave the German-speaking people, whatever principality or duchy they happened to be living in, a sense of national identity which, for example, the Italians never had until the *Risorgimento*.

The Holy Roman Empire became a political institution manipulated by the Austrian Hapsburgs and towards its end, in the period immediately before the title of Holy Roman Emperor was finally abandoned in 1806, was for a time dominated by the Austrians.

Even when the German forces were besieging Paris in 1871, and obliging the rich Parisians to sample the exotic flesh of the wild beasts from the zoo, and forcing the poor to eat rats, nobody thought of the oppressors of the French as the Germans. They were the Prussians, with their distinctive iron-spiked helmets: the conflict was even known as the Franco-Prussian War. Germany didn't even exist until after the war was won.

And yet in the arts, above all in music, Germany had already established a separate and distinctively German identity from the middle of the eighteenth century, despite the fact that some of the most famous German composers were Austrian or lived and worked, as Beethoven did, mainly in Vienna. Haydn was born in Vienna, and Mozart in Salzburg, but they both wrote unmistakably German rather than Prussian or Austrian or Viennese music.

So when did the Germans acquire their unmistakable identity as Germans? Shortly after the outbreak of World War I, their image became that of an army of grimly efficient, sternly disci-plined, abjectly obedient troops in distinctive field-grey uniforms with pot-shaped steel helmets very unlike the shallow dishes worn by the British and the ridged version of the same dish worn by the French.

By that time, Germany had been a major world power for just over forty years, an imperial state which included within its borders all the principal German-speaking populations of Northern Europe, except those in Austria and Switzerland. But although the Kaiser Wilhelm II and his staff officers were clearly spoiling for a fight and hoping to gain some territory to provide more living space for the country's rapidly expanding population, they had to wait for the assassination of the heir to the Austro-Hungarian Empire in Sarajevo, on 28 June 1914, before they could make the first moves towards war. That incident so far removed, it would seem, from the destiny of the German nation, provided the spark which set the fuse for World War I; its reper-cussions gave the Kaiser the excuse he needed to flaunt Belgium's neutrality and invade France through Flanders in August 1914. The very choice of that flamboyant title Kaiser, harking back to the Roman Caesars, indicates the measure of imperialism upon which the German ruling class had set their sights.

The German troops very quickly established another identity

during World War I — an identity that held far more appeal for the bluff British Tommies than the cool, critical cynicism of the French, who had very little respect for authority. The Germans and the British appeared to understand one another very well. Fritz seemed honest and efficient, not a particularly humorous fellow, but a chap you could trust to do his duty, a man you could do business with in fact, in one of Margaret Thatcher's more memorable phrases, a worthy enemy. The French *poilu*, on the other hand, was not a reliable ally; he was always too ready to sneer at the officers, at the system, at the generals who were running the war, at government, at the whole notion of the war, in fact.

And being the sort of people they were, the British and the Germans, despite having developed a certain mutual respect, went on slaughtering each other enthusiastically and obediently, as instructed, right up until the eleventh hour of the eleventh day of the eleventh month, while many of the French troops made repeated attempts — through desertion and mutiny and even self-mutilation — to put an end to the whole wretched business.

The terms of the Peace Treaty of Versailles, largely dictated by Woodrow Wilson, a dying man who was not strong enough to resist the often disastrous demands of the other victorious delegates and who knew that he would not be around to witness the worst results of all the follies he was condoning, made another war within a generation almost inevitable. The worst folly had been to separate East Prussia from the rest of the Reich by the Polish corridor, detaching Danzig and giving the Poles the province of Posen and a part of Silesia which had been Prussian territory since the partition of Poland in the eighteenth century.

Between the wars — as indeed since very soon after World War II — the phrase 'Made in Germany' was a universal guarantee of quality. Whether the product was a Mercedes Benz or an Adler motor car, a Leica or a Contax camera, or any one of dozens of other makes (Voigtlander, Exacta, Rolleiflex, etc), everybody knew that they would be thoroughly reliable simply because they had been manufactured in Germany. And I daresay the same applied to Liebherr cranes, Mann construction equipment, Siemens electrics and presumably, if you had any occasion to use them, Krupp armaments.

Between the wars, too, Germany acquired yet another image, an image stemming partly perhaps from the youth hostel movement — which had indeed started in Germany — as well as various other superficially attractive German youth movements, a fantasy world in which healthy young people sat around the embers of camp fires in the golden evening light discussing the future of the world, after a hard day's hike through the Black Forest. Germany was 'romantic'. The Rhine with its legends of the Lorelei, the heroic *Götterdämmerung* world of the Wagner operas, even poor, mad Ludwig's fairy-tale castles which looked as if they had been designed by one of Walt Disney's more way-out draughtsmen, the jolly Bavarian peasant folk with their lederhosen and rucksacks, litre tankards of foaming beer in their fists, and their noisy but harmless, or so it seemed, hilarity — all were parts of a dream that soon turned into a nightmare.

Most people in the British Isles were probably pretty slow to realize the extent of the changes that started to overtake Germany in the twenties and thirties, after Hitler's first unsuccessful attempt to seize power in a Munich beer hall in 1923, far slower than other Europeans to see the sinister side of the swastikas, the brownshirted gangs of louts, the hysterical mass rallies, the looted Jewish shops, the festival of broken glass of *Kristallnacht*, the boot-faced troops who came at dead of night to burst into ordinary people's homes and take them away, never to be seen again. Words like *Anschluss* and *Putsch* held no special, instinctive horror for us as yet.

Hitler at times seemed a joke, and not only in Britain; Chaplin made a comedy called *The Great Dictator*. It wasn't until the panzer divisions moved into the Low Countries in the spring of 1940, after a six-month 'phony' war, forced the British out of France via Dunkirk, and then moved quietly and quickly on to enter Paris and occupy a shatteringly easily defeated France that people began to realize exactly what was happening.

And when World War II ended, we were faced with yet another set of images of Germany that were almost impossible to grasp.

First there were those nightmare pictures of what the allied soldiers encountered when they went to liberate the inmates of Auschwitz, Buchenwald and the other concentration camps. Then came the gradual realization of the truly monstrous proportions of the Nazi crimes against humanity, which had included the systematic extermination of 6 million Jews and endless other unimaginably evil atrocities.

By now Germany was a defeated, starving nation, its cities bombed to ruins, the whole country divided into zones controlled by the four occupying forces, the Americans, the British, the French and the Russians. Even as the architects and perpetrators of these monstrosities were being tried for their war crimes at Nuremberg — but who could possibly devise punishments to fit such crimes? — we were seeing another set of almost unbelievable pictures of the *Trummerfrauen* (rubble women), the old ladies of Berlin stealing bricks from the shattered buildings to rebuild their city, while, as we read in the newspapers, younger German women were bartering their bodies for a pack of Camels or a half-pound of coffee.

The capital city Berlin was an island stranded in the heart of the area of Germany controlled by the Russians. More than 60 per cent of the built-up area had been badly damaged or destroyed by Allied bombing, and more than half of the apartments and dwellings were uninhabitable. But the Berliners refused to abandon their city, which was divided up into American, British, French and Russian zones.

During this period, there were people in Britain and elsewhere who felt that at a certain point, the Allies should have called a halt to the Russian advance and forced the communist troops back behind their own frontiers. However, the Allies were stuck with them, policing occupied Germany on an equal footing. Tensions were bound to occur, and in 1948 the Russians tried to force the Allies to abandon their occupation of Berlin by cutting off all food supplies to the city.

The Allies replied with a massive airlift. For eleven months until May 1949, using upwards of 1,000 planes, they flew in 4,000 tons of food a day, together with crucial supplies of coal and other necessities, and the Russian blockade was broken. But so was the whole concept of joint, four-power control of the territory, though they still went through the motions of maintaining British, French and American zones in Berlin.

But what happened in effect was that the Allies turned their three Western zones into a federal republic, with proportional representation to prevent any one party from ever again achieving the power that the National Socialists (Nazis) had before the war. The Federal Republic of Germany, as it was known, also was given a market economy. Shortly afterwards, the Russians turned their zone into a separate, communist-controlled state known as the German Democratic Republic.

As conditions, even in starving, post-war West Germany, seemed to be a lot more attractive than they were in the Communist-controlled East, thousands of Germans started to leave the eastern segment of their country to join friends and relatives or to look for better jobs or a better lifestyle in the Federal Republic.

The Russian answer to this was the Wall, a literal wall — more often two or more, with a No Man's Land in between — cutting right through Berlin with a tightly controlled, 1,378-kilometre frontier isolating East Germany from the Western world. The Wall was heavily patrolled by armed guards with machine guns, Alsatian dogs and floodlights, and border guards and marksmen were employed all along the frontier to ensure that nobody passed from East to West Germany. The Wall and the other forti-fications didn't stop people from trying, and many Germans were killed attempting to get across to visit their families and friends on the other side. Checkpoint Charlie, one of the official crossing points in the Berlin Wall, became for a time the most celebrated spot in Germany and many films were based on the exchanges of spies and other prisoners of war that took place in this grim and unreal setting.

The Wall did not of course stop all movement between East and West Germany, or even between East and West Berlin. Thousands of people had passes which permitted them to move backwards and forwards freely. Others paid for the privilege; by

1989 the price a day tripper from the West paid to visit East Germany was thirty Deutschmarks. There were rail and underground links, mostly paid for by West Germany. And the Wall didn't stop the transfer of political prisoners; according to Andrew Gumbel's *Berlin* (London: Cadogan Books, 1991) — a most fascinating little handbook to the city — East Germany was selling prominent dissidents or citizens caught trying to flee across the fortified frontier for between 40,000 and 100,000 Deutschmarks each, and exporting as many as 2,000 people a year. There was also, according to the same book, a lucrative West German business, run mainly by ex-soldiers, in smuggling East Germans across the frontier, under the back seats of specially adapted cars or through tunnels: the going rate, per head, Andrew Gumber reports, was between 50,000 and 100,000 Deutschmarks. 'The risks were high,' he adds. 'Imprisonment or death; and satisfaction could not be guaranteed even at that price.'

For twenty-eight years, the rest of the world tried to come to terms with this nation which had been split into two, and while many people who didn't think about it too deeply felt that it might well be one way of preventing the Germans from ever precipitating another war, a lot of the people who did think about it realized that Robert Schuman and Jean Monnet had already made a start on solving that problem by pooling France and Germany's armament-manufacturing capacity in the European Iron and Steel Community formed in 1950, which became the Common Market, which became the EEC and which will soon become the new, post-1992 European Community.

The collapse of the Berlin Wall in November 1989 took the world by surprise and perhaps because it had been such a tangible symbol of what had looked like a permanent partition between Eastern and Western Europe, it probably seemed more immediately dramatic than the sudden collapse of Communism in Romania and Bulgaria, in Poland and Albania, even in the Soviet Union itself, around the same time.

But the first pictures on TV of those dazed, slap-happy East Germans crossing over into the West in their clapped-out Trabis to fritter away the Deutschmarks their fellow-countrymen in West Germany had presented them with as a gesture of welcome to the new, united Germany, should have sounded a note of warning. How was the West going to be able to accommodate and absorb and employ such people? More importantly, perhaps, how were such people, conditioned, over more than twenty years, to being employed and housed and fed and clothed and taught and transported and literally moulded and mothered by the state (admittedly not very well, but they had survived), how were they ever going to accommodate themselves to a world in which they would have to learn to do all of these things and many, many more for themselves on their own initiative? How could such people acquire the initiative of the sort that would be needed to survive in a competitive, capitalist society? Is it something that you can even begin to teach?

From the moment the first breach in the Berlin Wall was made on 9 November 1989, which happened curiously enough on the exact anniversary of Hitler's beer hall *Putsch* in Munich in 1923, and also on the precise anniversary of *Kristallnacht* in 1938, the West Germans have been studiously careful to talk and think about themselves and the East Germans as simply Germans, and to pretend that Germany was in effect always one country, one people. But even though the country has been officially reunited for almost a year as I write, and the people from the east and the west freely mix together, many Germans still occasionally find themselves caught off-guard and refer to friends and relations from the other side of the frontier as from *druben* (over there). Reporting from Mecklenberg in what was East Germany a correspondent of the London *Independent* remarked that while the local Eastern traders gathered on one side of the market square, the 'outsiders' (from West Germany) grouped themselves on the other side. 'No one decided it should be this way,' he added. 'It just happened. People wanted to be with those they felt at ease with.'

And the plain truth is that until the two Germanies were reunited on 3 October 1990, a date carefully chosen because it wasn't the anniversary of anything, the history of Germany as a founding member of the European Community must be the history of West Germany.

The first stage in what came to be called the German economic miracle was probably the decision of the Americans to secure an economically stable West Germany as a bastion against the Soviet bloc. American firms invested large amounts of capital in West Germany, which also received US$3.3 billion under the Marshall aid plan.

Elections to the first Federal German parliament were held in August 1949, and Konrad Adenauer became the first chancellor; the German Democratic Republic was set up in East Germany in October 1949. In 1955 when the occupation statute was raised the Federal Republic became a sovereign state. In 1956 it joined NATO and was allowed to rearm.

In the meantime, the economy had been booming. With the same energy and drive which had very nearly won the war for the Nazis, the West Germans set about rebuilding their country and their economy. Before long, West Germany was in third place after the United States and the Soviet Union among the industrial nations of the world. By the end of the fifties it was turning out half of the total industrial production of the European Economic Community, formed in 1957 by the Treaty of Rome.

The Volkswagen motor car became the symbol of West Germany's economic miracle. Designed in 1936 by Ferdinand Porsche as a people's car (literally Volks Wagen), it was originally manufactured in a factory built in 1938 at Wolfsburg, a village in the north-east with 150 inhabitants; today the Volkswagen factory there employs 281,000 and there are other Volkswagen factories. When the original factory, which had been destroyed by Allied bombing, was rebuilt after the war, the ugly but highly distinctive, squat, snub-nosed, rear-engined, air-cooled 'beetle', as it was affectionately known, became extremely popular, and was universally acknowledged as the most sturdy and reliable small car in the world. In its heyday, it was more famous even than Henry Ford's celebrated 'tin lizzy', the Model T. Five million of the cars were exported to the United States and by the time it went out of production a few years ago, the Volkswagen Beetle had been exported to 147 countries and was already regarded as a classic, something that rarely happens to a model still coming off the production line.

There are few countries in the world today where you won't encounter Volkswagen Beetles, some of them twenty-five years old or more, most of them in far better condition mechanically and certainly far fitter as regards the bodywork, than cars four or five years old. There's a Volkswagen Beetle in Bavaria today which came off the production line in 1939. It's still in daily use, with its original engine and 449,000 kilometres on the clock. So much for German efficiency and reliability; the Volkswagen story says it all.

The German balance of payments which showed a deficit of 3,000 million Deutschmarks in 1950 had been turned into a credit balance of 1.2 million Deutschmarks by 1955. The Mercedes, the Porsche, the BMW, the Audi were soon in demand everywhere. As new factories were built and bombed factories rebuilt, the demand for workers exceeded the supply, and foreign workers from Turkey, Italy and the rest of Europe were drafted in to boost the German boom. The Germans were soon making so much money that the first self-service supermarkets in Europe were built to enable the German housewives to spend it more readily. Before long there was a TV set in almost every German sitting room, a dish-washing machine in every luxury fitted kitchen, a car (or two and sometimes a boat as well) in every drive.

Tourism, especially to Italy, increased so rapidly that before long most of the menus pinned up outside the restaurants around Lake Garda were in German and in the heart of the Bardolino country, there were restaurants which no longer stocked wine, only beer, because that was what the Germans, their best customers, liked to drink with their meals.

They travelled down to the Riviera, to Provence, to the Camargue with their motor caravans, or sometimes towing expensive speedboats; they were the new rich of Europe, welcomed even in French villages dominated by memorials to the glorious dead killed by the Germans in two world wars, and to resistance fighters and even civilians executed during the Nazi occupation in World War II. Welcomed even by people who had friends and relatives murdered by the Nazis, an economic miracle of another sort.

One year after reunification, West Germany's economy was still steaming along with a 4.6 per cent growth rate, 'an island of prosperity,' as the London *Independent* put it, 'in a vast economic swampland.' But things weren't so good in the eastern part of the reunified country. Redundancies and forced early retirement were looming up. A job protection agreement covering 1 million workers in the metal and engineering industries expired in July 1991; so did a temporary contract extending the employment of 400,000 former East German civil servants. The trust body set up to oversee the privatization of almost 10,000 state-owned companies expected the 3-million-odd people employed in its companies alone would have to go by the end of 1991, and according to the Berlin-based Institute for Applied Economics, 80 per cent of the 2 million 'short-time' workers (most of whom had been receiving 90 per cent of their wages from the state for doing almost nothing at all in order to keep the unemployment figures down) would have been laid off by the end of 1991. About 600,000 former East Germans are believed to have been forced to take early retirement, and tens of thousands have been pouring into what was West Germany every month in search of work.

In August, 1991, in an attempt to speed up privatization in East Germany, a West German consortium of banks was given the task of selling off nearly one-fifth of the land which had been the communal property of the citizens of the former GDR, and of taking over the management of about 7 million hectares of farm-land and forest.

How Germany will cope with the problem of financing reunification in the middle of a world recession is merely one of the urgent problems facing the country at the moment. The Bonn government has been pouring what the *Independent* called 'hallucinatory amounts of money' into the collapsed east, bringing public borrowing in one year (1990–1) up to 200 billion Deutschmarks, on top of contributing 60 billion Deutschmarks to help Gorbachev solve his problems in the Soviet Union, very largely as a reward for his help in facilitating German reunification.

Six months after German unity, Germany recorded its first monthly trade deficit in nearly a decade, and many economists were forecasting a zero German trade balance for the full year 1991, compared with West Germany's surplus of $57.5 billion for 1990.

There was another important anniversary on 1 July, 1991. Exactly a year earlier, the Deutschmark had become the standard currency of the new united Germany on a one-to-one basis with the former East German Ostmark.

Chancellor Helmut Kohl had assured the people that things would be much better within a year, and that nobody would be any the worse off for political union. But Chancellor Kohl is a politician, and when he made these promises he had an election to win.

Most people in East Germany, who had been accustomed to a fifteen-year wait for a Trabant motor car which was out-of-date even when it was ordered, much less when it was eventually delivered, believed that things really were going to be different. They had real money now, after all, and they would be able to buy goods from the West. And so they were, and so they did, and the result has been the almost total collapse of East Germany's domestic production. It was simply wiped off the shelves by Western goods. As John Eisenhammer pointed out in the London *Independent*, 'it was not, as Bonn politicians kept claiming, the unexpected collapse of the East European export market that brought about the economic disaster, for that accounted for only about 15 per cent of East German output. Rather, it was the brutal disappearance of the domestic market, as the big Western firms took over the supply of the whole retail sector ...

'For those who imagined unification could be accomplished with the gift of a currency and the signing of a treaty, the first year of economic union has been a long, brutal awakening. Few realized just how deep the gulf really is between the two Germanies. The Westerners appear arrogant, impatient, unsympathetic. The Easterners seem confused, resentful and submissive. It is a classic colonial pattern.'

There is a phrase for this mutual incomprehension between

those Germans from one side of the frontier (sometimes jokingly referred to as the Wessies) and those from the *druben*, the other side, sometimes known as Ossies. It is 'the wall in the head'.

By now even the most optimistic of East Germans realize that even if all their other economic problems can be solved, it will take ten years at least to get the wall out of their heads.

LAND AND PEOPLE

The Master Race

The reunified state of Germany consists of the former East Germany, the north-eastern part, 108,174 square kilometres in area, and the former West Germany, 248,454 square kilometres in area.

East Germany had a short coastline on the Baltic, and land frontiers with Poland on the east, Czechoslovakia to the south and what was West Germany on the west.

West Germany had both a North Sea and a Baltic coastline as well as a land frontier with Denmark on the north. Its other land frontiers were − anti-clockwise − with the Netherlands, Belgium, Luxembourg, France, Switzerland and Austria.

The total area of the reunited country is 356,628 square kilometres. The total population is 73 million: 57 million in what was West Germany, where the population density at 246 people per square kilometre was the third highest in Europe, after the Netherlands and Belgium, and 17 million in the former East Germany, with a density of only 156 people per square kilometre. Overall, the population density is 222 per square kilometre.

The national flag is the tricolour of the Federal Republic: three equal horizontal bars of black, red and gold. Black and red were the colours of the old Holy Roman Empire; and in the campaign against Napoleon one Prussian cavalry corps wore the ancient black and red colours with gold buttons, a colour combination taken up by the German unity movement in the mid-nineteenth century. During Hitler's regime, the tricolour was replaced with the swastika.

The German national anthem is the *Deutschlandlied*, the 'song of Germany', based on a poem by Hoffman von Fallersleben. Originally the first verse which started with '*Deutschland Uber Alles*' (Germany over all) was used but this was dropped because, as a German government handout puts it, 'this was widely misunderstood abroad.' Now the third verse of the poem is used. It says, inoffensively: 'Unity and right and freedom for the German fatherland.' The music, by Haydn, was composed for the Austrian emperor: *Gott erhalte Franz den Kaiser* (God Save the Emperor Francis).

Germany has a small slice of the Alps in the Allgau, Bavaria and Berchtesgaden areas; the highest peak is the Zugspitze (2,962 metres). North of the Alps a wide, hilly upland, the Alpenvorland (average elevation 500 metres) slopes down to the Donau (Danube) river (647 kilometres). Other German rivers include the Rhine (865 kilometres) which rises in Switzerland, flows through the Bodensee (Lake Constance) into Germany, then northwards through the Black Forest and the Netherlands to the North Sea; the Elbe (227 kilometres), the Oder, the Main and the Neckar.

The Central Uplands consist of very old hard rocks which, long before the Alps erupted, formed part of a great mountain chain which ran right across Europe from west to east. As this mountain range was itself rising, about 300 million years ago, great swamps were formed on its flanks which later became the rich coal deposits of the Ruhr and the Saar, the fuel which fired Germany's industrial revolution. Much of the lowland area of Germany is extremely fertile. Throughout history the area was always capable of feeding its people and nowadays, West Germany has been able to produce 80 per cent of the food it consumes; and on paper at any rate, the state-controlled farms of East Germany supplied more than enough food for its 17 million inhabitants during its twenty-eight years as part of the communist bloc.

Part of the North Sea coast is below sea-level and requires dikes as in the Netherlands. Germany has one off-shore island, Heligoland, 65 kilometres north of the coast near Denmark; having no vegetation whatever, it is a favourite resort for sufferers from hay fever.

Officially in the temperate zone, the climate of Germany is changeable and turbulent, wet and windy in short. In spring a warm wind known as the *Fohnwind* (snow-devourer) sweeps down from the Alps and in summer it is often hot but also often humid and thundery. The Michelin Green Guide to West Germany laconically remarks that the air is keen on the North Sea beaches, adding that although the air is milder on the Baltic, 'the west winds prevent much lazing on the beaches'. Which probably explains all those German cars and campers and caravans parked bumper to bumper all along the Mediterranean littoral from May to October. The best time of the year in Germany is late October, known as the *Altweibersommer* (old woman's summer).

What used to be East Germany is even less clement; there the average temperature is 8.5 degrees centigrade, ranging from 0.7 to 18 degrees centigrade in January and July respectively. Temperatures rise as high as 33 degrees centigrade in summer, and fall as low as minus 25 degrees centigrade in the depths of winter.

Germany has been inhabited for so long that one of the earlier species of man, *homo heidelbergiensis* (circa 500,000 years ago), is named after the famous German university town.

There are sites where Neanderthal man lived 100,000 years ago near Dusseldorf, and in the Bodensee (Lake Constance), wooden piles have been found which supported New Stone Age lake settlements 8,000 years ago.

There were Celts of the *La Tene* culture in Germany between 800 and 400 BC who became absorbed into the Roman nation, unlike the Germanic Teutonic tribes who were so warlike that the Romans had to build a wall 550 kilometres long known as the Limes Boundary to keep them out. Not that the Romans were successful in doing so, in the end; the Vandals and the Goths were among the Germanic tribes which eventually around AD 400 sacked Rome and brought its empire to an end.

The Germanic tribes which remained on in what became Germany and which in Hitler's Third Reich became known as the Master Race consisted of Saxons, Franks, Bavarians and

Swabians amongst about a dozen others, not related in any way with the ten federal states into which West Germany was divided by the occupying powers after World War II. During the Middle Ages and indeed right up until the end of the nineteenth century, the entire area which then became the Second Reich consisted of a very mixed collection of about 350 towns, duchies, principalities and minor kingdoms with very little in common apart from the German language. Not indeed that the German language is by any means standard; there was Franconian, Saxon and Bavarian before there was German and even today, although TV has spread the use of a standard version of *Hochdeutsch* (formal German), if an Upper Bavarian and a Lower Saxon were to lapse into their local dialects, they would probably not understand each other without an interpreter. Written German dates back only to 770.

A century ago there were only 26 million people in the whole of Germany. By 1986, there were 61 million people in West Germany and West Berlin alone, including nearly 5 million foreigners. The greatest population increase occurred in the years immediately after World War II when more than 14 million refugees from East Germany fled to the West or were expelled from the East. Since the construction of the Berlin Wall and the frontier, the population growth had been almost entirely the result of immigration by foreign workers, mostly Turks. In one year (1974), at the height of the industrial boom, 2,400,000 foreigners entered West Germany on work permits. Germany employs more women than any other country in the Community: currently about 39 per cent of the total labour force.

The population is very unevenly distributed; 9 per cent of what was West Germany's total population lives in 2 per cent of its territory in the industrial Ruhr area, and there are other conurbations around Frankfurt, Stuttgart, Bremen, Hamburg and Munich in the west and around Berlin, Dresden and Magdeburg in the east.

There is one indigenous minority. Slightly less than 1 per cent of the East Germans are Sorbs, a Slav people found mainly in the area around Dresden, with their own language, which is distantly related to Polish.

West Germany has considerable reserves of hard coal, brown coal and iron ore, as well as some petroleum and enough natural gas to supply one-third of demand. Since 1980 about a quarter of West Germany's electrical energy requirements were met with nuclear power. Nevertheless the West Germans still remain dependent upon imports for about 50 per cent of their energy requirements and they need to import such industrial raw materials as copper, bauxite, manganese, titanium, wolfram and tin.

East Germany produced about 30 per cent of the world's total of brown coal, an easily mined but ecologically disastrous fuel. It was also a major world producer of potash, and produced some copper, lead, zinc, tin and nickel in the Ore Mountains, where, after World War II, the Soviet Union developed some uranium mining, and since the seventies some nuclear power has also been developed.

HISTORICAL PERSPECTIVE

An Army With A State

After the break-up of the Roman Empire around 400 one Germanic tribe, the Franks, settled initially in what is now Belgium, then moved down into France, intermarried with the Gallo-Romans and became the French. By the end of the eighth century, their ruler Charlemagne controlled most of Europe including the area occupied by the German-speaking people. He was unexpectedly crowned emperor by Pope Leo III on Christmas day, 800, and hailed by the Pope as Caesar Augustus, an event which could be said to mark the first papal effort to revive the old Roman Empire under its own auspices.

When, after Charlemagne's death, a row over the succession led to division of his empire into East and West Francia with the Netherlands as a buffer-state between them, and in order to prevent the Roman crown from falling into less worthy hands,

Pope John XII decided to offer it to the king of the most powerful of the warring tribes of Europe at the time. This happened to be Otto, King of East Francia and ruler of the territories unified only by the German language. And so began the Holy Roman Empire of the German Nation, though that title was not officially bestowed upon it until the fifteenth century.

From 962 AD until 1806, when the Emperor Franz I of Austria who happened also to be Holy Roman Emperor at that time, decided to drop the meaningless title, nobody could become emperor without first becoming king of the German-speaking people. The kings were traditionally elected by a college of nobles and ecclesiastics, though only a blood relation of the existing monarch was eligible to be chosen.

There remained the delicate question of who took precedence, the emperor or the pope. The attitude of the papacy right from the start was that since it was the pope who placed the crown upon the head of the emperor — and they all were obliged to go to Rome to be crowned — the ultimate power therefore lay in the hands of the pope. However, there were many occasions when the pope needed the support of the emperor and the matter was not finally put to the test until the eleventh century, when Pope Gregory VII introduced new regulations which made it almost impossible for the emperor to control or even influence the investiture of his bishops. This matter was highly important to the emperor of the period, Henry IV, since the foundation of his power lay in the bishops, invested with the crozier and ring by him and therefore holding their power directly from him and acknow-ledging their obedience to him in a way that he could no longer count on the powerful barons to do. Henry replied by instructing his own bishops to repudiate the pope and declare him unworthy of office. Gregory replied by excommunicating Henry and two of his bishops. This was a very serious business in those feudal times since the excommunication of a king or an emperor auto-matically absolved all his subjects from all oaths of allegiance. The German barons and princes, only too anxious to get rid of Henry, invited Gregory to come to Augsburg and help them elect a new emperor.

Gregory left Rome and travelled northwards. Henry, who was no fool, immediately saw the danger in the situation and crossed the Alps in the middle of winter to meet the Pope at Canossa. Gregory kept him waiting for three days in the snow before granting him an audience at which Henry repented his sins and surrendered his authority to the Pope. It didn't settle anything, but to this day the Germans still use the phrase 'a walk to Canossa' to indicate when someone is obliged to eat humble pie.

It was at Wittenberg University in one of the German states in 1517 that perhaps the most divisive event in the entire history of this part of the world since the birth of Mohammed. An Augustinian monk called Martin Luther, disillusioned by the corruption of the Church, launched what became known as the Reformation. By preaching a return to a simpler form of religion, he succeeded in splitting Christianity into two, and ultimately into dozens of bitterly acrimonious splinter groups, the Catholics on the one hand, and all the endless varieties of Protestants on the other.

But he had a far wider impact than that. As William L Shirer put it in *The Rise and Fall of the Third Reich* (London: Secker and Warburg, 1960): 'Through his sermons and his magnificent translation of the Bible, Luther created the modern German language, aroused in the people not only a new Protestant vision of Christianity but also a fervent German nationalism and taught them, at least in religion, the supremacy of the individual conscience. But tragically for them, Luther's siding with the princes in the peasants' risings, which he had largely inspired, and his passion for political autocracy ensured a mindless and provincial political absolutism which reduced the vast majority of the German people to poverty, to a horrible torpor and a demeaning subservience ... it doomed for centuries the possibility of the unification of Germany.'

Luther's achievement also led to the tragic Thirty Years War (1618–48), which started out as a religious war but degenerated into a confused dynastic struggle between the Austrian Catholic Hapsburgs on the one side and the French Catholic Bourbons and the Swedish Protestant monarchy, as well as Protestant England, on the other. During the course of the fighting, the area inhabited by the German-speaking people was devastated and approximately one-third of the population was killed.

At the end of it all, the Treaty of Westphalia established that the ruler of each state could decide the religion of his subjects. However, the Treaty of Westphalia, as Shirer points out, 'was almost as disastrous for the future of Germany as the Thirty Years War had been.

'The German princes, who had sided with France and Sweden, were confirmed as absolute rulers of their little domains ... The surge of reform and enlightenment which had swept Germany at the end of the fifteenth and beginning of the sixteenth century was smothered. In that period the free cities had enjoyed virtual independence; feudalism was gone in them, the arts and commerce thrived. Even in the countryside the German peasant had secured liberties far greater than those enjoyed in England and France. Indeed, at the beginning of the sixteenth century Germany could be said to be one of the fountains of European civilization.

'Now, after the Treaty of Westphalia, it was reduced to the barbarism of Muscovy. Serfdom was reimposed, even introduced in areas where it had been unknown. The towns lost their self-government. The peasants, the labourers, even the middle-class burghers were exploited to the limit by the princes ... civilization came to a standstill.'

Another historian, A.J.P. Taylor, made the comment that the German people during this period were 'artificially stabilized at a medieval level of confusion and weakness'.

Shirer argues that the Germans never recovered from this set-back. The acceptance of autocracy, the blind obedience to officers and princes and petty tyrants became ingrained in the German mind, preventing any hope that the new ideas of freedom and democracy which were starting to spread in Europe at that time would ever get through to the German people.

By the beginning of the eighteenth century two of the German states had begun to emerge as potential great powers. One was Austria, which had repelled the Turks and had acquired Hungary as well as some of the former Turkish possessions in the Balkans.

The other was Prussia, initially the remote frontier state of Brandenburg, east of the Elbe, which had been clawed inch by inch from the Slavs, mostly Poles, who were pushed back along the Baltic. Brandenburg, which had as its capital the town of Berlin, was a poor area, with no resources whatever apart from its princes — the imperious and resourceful Hohenzollerns — and its highly disciplined and formidable army. 'Prussia,' said Mirabeau, 'is not a state with an army, but an army with a state.'

The Prussian officer caste, known as the Junkers, were the first members of what was eventually to become the German nation to think of themselves as a Master Race. They became the owners of the land their army had stolen from the Slavs, and they forced the Slavs to work on the farms as serfs. And although the quaint rules of the Holy Roman Empire of the German Nation did not permit the minor rulers of the various principalities and duchies which comprised it to assume royal titles, in 1701 the son of the Elector of Brandenburg-Prussia, Friedrich Wilhelm, declared himself to be King Friedrich I in Prussia, and the Holy Roman Emperor of the period let him get away with it.

By 1740, Friedrich II, better known as Frederick the Great, had acquired parts of Poland and had sent the army into Silesia to steal it from the Austrians. By this time Prussia had become a major European power.

The defeat in 1815 of Napoleon at Waterloo by the Allied armies, including the English under the Duke of Wellington and the Prussian army under Gebhard von Blucher, added further lustre to the imperious Junkers and when the map of Europe was redrawn at the Congress of Vienna in 1815, a *Deutscher Bund* (German Confederation) was formed to replace the old Reich. It had a federal diet or parliament, the *Bundestag*, whose members were nominated by the officers and ruling classes and not popularly elected and which could act only if the two great powers in the area, Austria and Prussia, agreed. It concentrated on stifling any attempts to achieve German unity and freedom from the tyranny of the petty princes by means of a rigid censorship of newspapers and books and a close supervision of the universities.

In 1830 and again in 1848 there were revolutions in France, which had their counterparts in Leipzig, Dresden and Berlin. By now the whole area occupied by the German-speaking people was becoming industrialized. In 1834, the *Deutscher Zollverein* (Customs Union) had been formed to create a unitary inland market, and the following year the first German railway line was opened. The Communist Party held its first congress in 1847, and the Social Democratic Workers' Party was founded in 1867, but the Junkers were still not listening.

When in 1858 Wilhelm I came to the Prussian throne, he decided that the first thing to do was to make a break with Austria and establish a new unified German state. In doing this he sought the help of Otto von Bismarck, a member of the Junker class, whom he made his minister-president in 1862. He then went to war with Austria, and in 1866 Bismarck's Prussian army defeated the Austrians at Königgrätz. Prussia then annexed the kingdom of Hanover, the principality of Hessen-Kessel, the dukedom of Nassau and the free city of Frankfurt. Schleswig Holstein also became a part of Prussia, and Bismarck a national hero.

Wilhelm I next dissolved the old *Deutscher Bund* and replaced it in 1867 with the *Norddeutscher Bund* (North German Federation), with Bismarck as chancellor and himself as president.

A unified Germany, which had become one of the most highly industrialized and overpopulated countries in Europe, represented an immediate threat to France, right on its borders, and when Wilhelm threatened to put a Hohenzollern on the then vacant throne of Spain, right at France's back, so to speak, the Franco-Prussian War became inevitable. Prussia's invincible army under von Molkte won an easy victory over France at Sedan in 1870, Napoleon III was captured and carted off to Germany, Alsace and Lorraine became part of the new German state, and the vast reparations of 5,000 million francs France was forced to pay fuelled the first Germanic economic boom during which the Ruhr developed into the greatest industrial zone in Europe. The Krupp armaments factory in Essen was soon employing 50,000 workers.

Then in 1871, in the Hall of Mirrors at Versailles, one of the palaces of the defeated French, the German Second Reich was proclaimed with Wilhelm I of Prussia as Kaiser (emperor) and Bismarck as chancellor. (Wilhelm, incidentally, was married to one of Queen Victoria's daughters.) It remained, however, a very loose collection of some twenty-odd principalities, cities and duchies with only the German language and the power of the Prussian army to hold it together.

Bismarck was chancellor for nineteen years and while he succeeded in establishing the Second Reich's place in the new balance of power in Europe, he had no understanding of the democratic views which were gaining ground everywhere at that time. He regarded all political opposition as gross disloyalty to the Reich, and continued to fight the left wing, the liberal middle-classes and the increasingly organized labour movement. In 1890, when Kaiser Wilhelm I had been succeeded by his son, Kaiser Wilhelm II, Bismarck was dismissed.

It would be impossible even to attempt to summarize here all the pacts and ententes and treaties and agreements which turned an isolated action by a Serbian terrorist into a world war. But the bare facts are that on 28 June 1914, the Archduke Franz Ferdinand, heir to the Austro-Hungarian Empire, was assassinated in Sarajevo by a Serbian extremist. The Austro-Hungarian Empire declared war on Serbia. France and Russia mobilized in an attempt to aid Serbia. Germany took Austria's side and invaded France through Belgium, and Britain, which had guaranteed Belgium's neutrality, declared war on Germany. The war that followed went on for four years, cost at least 8 million lives, led to the Russian Revolution in 1917, a revolution in Berlin in 1918 and the overthrow of the Kaiser, who fled to exile in the Netherlands.

A national assembly was elected in Germany to draft a new constitution, but because of unrest in Berlin, the social democratic government was forced to move to Weimar where the Weimar Republic, under Friedrich Ebert as president, was formed in 1919. Germany was now officially a democracy with votes for ordinary men and women, an eight-hour working day, and full recognition of the trade unions.

In the same year, again in the Hall of Mirrors at Versailles, the victorious allies had redrawn the map of Europe. Germany had to restore Alsace and Lorraine to France, lost substantial slices of territory including the Polish corridor to Poland, and was ordered to pay vast reparations which quite clearly it could not possibly afford. The Austro-Hungarian Empire was dissolved, and new nations such as Czechoslovakia and Yugoslavia appeared on the map for the first time.

The Weimar Republic wasn't really a republic and certainly it wasn't socialist: private ownership of industry and agriculture remained untouched, anti-republican judges and civil servants remained on in their previous positions, and the officer caste retained control of the armed forces.

In the confusion of the immediate post-war period, with raging inflation, industrial unrest, and the insult of the occupation of the Ruhr by French troops and the administration of the Saar by the League of Nations, the Weimar Republic didn't really stand a chance. In 1923, the National Socialists (Nazis) under Adolf Hitler — who offered a special brand of German chauvinism, blamed the Communists and the Jews for everything that had happened, and promised revenge for the insults of Versailles — attempted to gain power through a coup in Munich. It failed and Hitler spent about a year in prison writing his political tract, *Mein Kampf* (My Struggle).

But the continued inflation, the mass unemployment of 6 million people in Germany, and the world economic crisis which started with the Wall Street crash in October 1929 favoured Hitler's particular brand of German nationalism, and by 1930 the Nazis were the strongest political party in the country.

By 1933, the leading industrialists, the army officers and even members of the Weimar parliament were beginning to feel that parliamentary government could no longer function, and that the only alternative was to transfer power to the party with the greatest popular support. As many historians have pointed out, the Germans had no one to blame for what happened but themselves.

In January, 1933, Hindenburg, who was now president of the

Weimar Republic, appointed Hitler chancellor. The republic was abolished, and Hitler announced the birth of the Third Reich, which, he said, would endure for a thousand years.

A few weeks after his appointment a fire destroyed the Reichstag building. Hitler blamed the Communists, suspended the constitution, banned all parties but his own, smashed the trade unions, took over the armed forces on Hindenburg's death in 1934 and proceeded ruthlessly, but perfectly legally, to crush all opposition. Germany's brief period of fifteen years of democracy was over.

The events of World War II are so well known that they don't even require a reference here, while what happened after the Allied victory is covered above. Hitler's Reich disappeared in a sordid, modern-dress *Götterdämmerung* in a concrete bunker amid the smouldering ruins of Berlin on 30 April 1945.

The Third Reich had lasted not a thousand years but exactly twelve years and four months.

COLONIAL CONNECTIONS

A Very Brief Overseas Empire

Despite the imperial aspirations of the Second Reich, and the choice of the term Kaiser for its monarch, Germany was a late arrival on the colonial scene and her attempts to establish an empire overseas never got very much above the level of gunboat diplomacy.

From around 1880 German entrepreneurs, tradesmen and troops, sometimes supported by a navy designed to rival Britain's — a great deal of Germany's iron and steel and general industrial capacity was channeled in the last years of the nineteenth and the early years of the twentieth century into the building of a formidable fleet of warships — established trading posts and protectorates and colonies in German South West Africa (today's Namibia), in East Africa in what is now Tanzania, in West Africa (Togoland and the Cameroons), in the South Seas and even in China.

One of the pioneers was a Dr Karl Peters who arrived on the coast of what is now Tanzania and purchased an area as big as Bavaria for a trifling sum from some local chiefs. His plan was to sell tracts of this land to German colonists for development. At first nobody took him very seriously, but he succeeded in convincing the German government that the area had considerable potential and he was granted an Imperial Charter of Protection. As John Gunther put it in *Inside Africa* (London: Hamish Hamilton, 1955): 'The Sultan of Zanzibar, who held theoretical sovereignty over all this territory, was bought off outright with a grant of £200,000 and the German East Africa Protectorate came into being.'

But when they started to advance inland, the Germans soon discovered that not all of the tribes who occupied the area were as disinterested in it as the sultan, and one tribe, the Angoni, fiercely resisted the German advance in an uprising which the Germans put down with typical brutality and efficiency, burning crops, starving villages, and razing the countryside. More than 120,000 Africans died.

German East Africa was conquered by the British – with South African and Indian troops – on the outbreak of war in 1914. Well, not entirely conquered. One German general, Paul von Lettow-Vorbeck who was in charge of a small garrison, held out. He had 218 white officers and 1,542 *askaris* (native troops). When the war ended in 1918 he still had 155 Europeans and far more *askaris* than he had started out with. In the meantime, he had kept 30,000 British and Allied troops who were badly needed on other fronts pinned down in East Africa for the entire duration of the war, during which, as Gunther reports, 'from first to last 130 different generals went into action against him, and he inflicted on the Allies about sixty thousand casualties, including 20,000 dead'.

On one occasion, he crossed over into British East Africa and even threatened Nairobi. At Tanga, the British sent for reinforcements; Lettow lay in wait for them and when they arrived attacked. The Allied casualties were 2,000 for fifty-four of Lettow's men. He was pushed out of German East Africa into Mozambique and then Rhodesia, and still went on fighting. He only gave in when he heard about the armistice; he felt that as a German soldier faithful to the fatherland, he had to honour the armistice. Even then, he didn't surrender. He disbanded his troops and put himself at the disposal of the British commander.

Between the wars Britain effectively ran Tanganyika for the League of Nations, though the stoutly constructed *bomas* (government headquarters) they used were relics of the German regime.

The Cameroons in West Africa, so-called after the local prawns (*camaroes*), was initially Portuguese, then Dutch, then British. The British interest was largely commercial, and although several local tribal chieftains asked for British protection in the nineteenth century, the Foreign Office was reluctant to annex the place. When eventually they decided to do so, and in 1883 sent out an emissary to negotiate a treaty with one of the native chiefs, he arrived in Douala just too late: German agents had already signed a treaty of annexation five days earlier. As elsewhere in Africa, German rule was efficient but extremely harsh, so severe that thousands of Africans fled to nearby French and British possessions. At the outbreak of World War I, a joint British-French invasion force captured the country and afterwards it was split between France and Britain under a League of Nations mandate.

The area now known as Togoland was annexed by the Germans when an agent called Gustav Nachtigal signed treaties with a number of the local coastal chiefs in 1884. The Germans started to build a system of roads in the territory and established the city which is now Togo; after World War I the whole territory was divided between France and Britain under a League of Nations mandate.

Perhaps the most German part of Africa is what used to be called South West Africa, then became a protectorate of South Africa under the League of Nations and the United Nations and has now become the independent state of Namibia. The Germans were attracted to South West Africa because it had copper, zinc, lead and manganese, as well as diamonds (both of the industrial and the fashionable variety) as well as the karakul industry which produced extremely expensive lambskins for fur coats.

One geological oddity of the area is the Caprivi strip which looks, on the map, like a hastily constructed arrow trying to reach the East German colonies on the Indian Ocean across the Namib Desert. It was named after a German chancellor called Caprivi, and it makes no sense at all, except that in these green years, we all need some proposition that can be presented as basically ecological in intention. And it was an early effort at conservation.

The capital, Windhoek, is the one place in Africa which even still has a German flavour. The main shopping street is called the Kaiserstrasse, there are Germanic castles glowering over the town and, until fairly recently, German competed with English and Afrikaans in notices and menus in the shops and cafés. Even today, after all that has happened, 17 per cent of the white population speaks German.

So where else did the Germans establish an empire? One trading post in China, a brief hold on a few islands in the South Pacific — the Marianas, the Carolinas and the Marshall Islands, which were relinquished after 1918 — and a foothold in Morocco which very nearly precipitated World War I.

What happened was this. Shortly after the Germans established the Second Reich, the French sent troops to Fez in Morocco, ostensibly to restore order. Germany affected to consider this action as a violation of an agreement reached at a conference in Algeciras and sent a gunboat, the *Panther*, to safeguard alleged German mining interests in the area. The British immediately rallied to the support of the French, and as the Germans were not yet completely ready to mount a world war, another Franco-German convention was signed which gave the French freedom to pursue their plans in Morocco in return for free access to trade in the area.

Other German overseas adventures were limited to the activities of Rommel and the Afrika Korps in Algeria, Libya and Egypt during the early stages of World War II.

DEVELOPMENT DIRECTIONS

The Ossies and the Wessies

Although it is possible to treat the history of Germany as a whole, when it comes to agriculture, trade and industry, it is still far too early to do so. It is still necessary to look at the achievements of East and West Germany separately, and in the light of the vast differences in forces and circumstances which shaped both states.

Traditionally, until the Industrial Revolution, the duchies and kingdoms and states occupied by the German-speaking peoples were basically small feudal agricultural units and such industries as there were – weaving, for example – were largely craft-based.

In West Germany, as recently as 1950, 20 per cent of the gainfully employed worked on the land; now that proportion is under 5 per cent. Over the same period, the number of farms with more than one hectare of land fell from 1.6 million to 700,000.

Family farms still predominate, almost half of them part-time farms, that is to say the main family income comes from some other source, usually industry. But the number of large farms, over 100 hectares in area, has continued to increase from 2,971 in 1949 to 5,405 in 1985.

The major crops are cereals, potatoes, sugar beet, vegetables, fruit and wine. There are also pig and poultry farms run on modern factory lines which in a country that sees the world increasingly through green-tinted spectacles, have attracted a great deal of criticism from the very vociferous animal welfare groups.

Almost a third of the area of West Germany is covered by forest, a total of 7.4 million hectares. About 30 million cubic metres of timber are harvested, enough to meet about half the domestic demand.

Over-fishing has reduced the deep sea fishing fleet from 110 moderately sized ships to fifteen large factory ships in the years since 1970; the total catches in tonnes per year dropped from 591,400 in 1970 to 161,300 in 1986. Germany for the first time now imports a great deal of fish, mainly from other Community countries.

About 43 per cent of the area of East Germany is agricultural land. The produce is basically similar to that of West Germany, and although some private farms survived throughout the period between 1949 and 1989, the majority of the East German farms were reorganized into collectives. There were three types of collective farm: one in which only the land itself was pooled, one in which only the land and equipment were pooled whilst the farmers retained their own buildings and handled the division of the income among themselves, and the most common type in which all land, livestock, equipment and fixtures were pooled and the combined farms operated as true collectives. The average size of the collective farms increased from 280 hectares in 1960 to more than 935 hectares by 1974, with some of the fully collective farms as big as 1,020 hectares.

Initially the process of pooling created a great deal of disruption and yields tended to be poor. However, increased use of machinery and fertilizers in the late sixties and early seventies meant that by 1980 East Germany was self-sufficient in meat, butter, eggs and sugar and almost self-sufficient in grain. East Germany led all the other Soviet bloc countries in agricultural production and is the one country which made the collective farm work efficiently.

In fact the tightly state-run communist-controlled economy, both in agriculture and industry, which proved such a disaster in the Soviet Union and most of the Soviet bloc countries, very nearly succeeded in East Germany because although the system was rotten, the workers were Germans.

East Germany's forests (a quarter of the total land area) had suffered from severe over-cutting during World War II and in the early post-war years. More recently, imports of wood, mainly from the Soviet Union, enabled felling to be reduced to a level designed to allow the forests to re-establish themselves and the timber yield to be increased in the long-term future.

East Germany had a small fishing industry on the Baltic, and a deep sea fleet, operating in the North Atlantic from the port of Rostock.

Although Germany's industrial revolution did not start until nearly a century after England's, once it started, it developed very rapidly; by 1900 Germany's steel production had outstripped Britain's. By then Germany had acquired advanced technologies in the electricity industry, in the optics trade and, very early in the twentieth century, in the manufacture of motor cars.

Until the end of the World War II, Germany had a controlled economy. The change-over to a market economy, based on entre-preneurial self-responsibility, coupled with the development of the Common Market, led to the West German economic miracle referred to above.

West Germany is now one of the world's greatest manu-facturing powers. Output grew steadily during the whole post-war period, doubling between 1962 and 1974. The iron and steel industry is the fourth largest in the world; the steel is mostly produced in the Ruhr area, where imported iron ore can be easily transported on barges from Rotterdam. As in Britain and else-where, the German steel industry has recently undergone a considerable rationalization process to cope with the general decline in world demand.

West Germany's major industrial strength is in the manu-facture of machinery of all types, particularly road vehicles, machine tools and machinery for industrial plants. Heavy machinery, cranes, bridges and mining equipment are mainly manufactured in the Ruhr. In 1986, mechanical engineering employed a million people and the turnover was 165,000 million Deutschmarks. In the same year a record trade surplus of 58,000 million Deutschmarks was achieved and Germany held first place of all major world exporters in twenty-one out of thirty-seven specialized sub-divisions of mechanical engineering; one in four of West Germany's working population depends on the export market. In 1986 major exports, by category, were road vehicles (17.5 per cent), machinery (20 per cent), chemicals (12.8 per cent), electrical appliances (8.5 per cent), iron and steel (6 per cent) and food, beverages and tobacco (4.1 per cent).

After Japan and the United States, West Germany is the third largest producer of motor cars in the world. In 1986, 4.3 million cars, 300,000 lorries and buses, 66,000 motorcycles and 3.3 million bicycles were produced; and almost 60 per cent of the cars were exported.

The aerospace industry employs 76,000 and turned over 14,600 million Deutschmarks in 1986; its activities are largely in connection with the Airbus, an example of European Community co-operation which has produced the most successful range of passenger aircraft in the world today. German shipyards have been rationalized and now concentrate on highly specialized types of ships and advanced technology.

Other successful German exports include optics and cameras, clocks and watches, domestic electric appliances, radio and television sets, office and data processing machinery.

East Germany's industrial production was hampered immediately after the World War II by three factors. First, the sources in Upper Silesia and the Ruhr of the coal, steel and other basic resources for its manufacturing industries were suddenly outside the boundaries of the new state. Second, many of its existing industrial plants and transport installations were dismantled to be transported to the Soviet Union as war reparations. And third, so far from receiving large sums of Marshall aid and other investment money from the United States to enable its industries to scramble back to their feet, East Germany was forced to pay reparations in cash to the Russians out of current production profits. These factors, aggravated by the confusion caused by the transfer of the major part of the economy to public ownership and state control by mediocre and muddled Soviet bureaucrats, meant that it took the East German economy a long time to get under way again.

However, despite the lack of raw materials and a grossly inadequate infrastructure, by the eighties the East German economy was not nearly as disastrous as Western economists liked to think. It had the second largest production after the Soviet Union of all the Soviet bloc countries; its principal products were metals, chemicals, machinery, electronics and shipbuilding, and it still ranked among the world's most advanced industrial nations. Even the boisterously confident Federal Republic PROs have to admit in an official hand-out about the new, unified Germany, that 'judging economic conditions in the new federal states is made more difficult by a chronic lack of statistical information.'

East Germany was a vital supplier of complete industrial plants, machine tools, computerized tools and precision equipment of all kinds used in the other Soviet bloc countries. The manufacture of motor cars was deliberately restricted to favour railway trains, coaches and freight cars, trucks, farm machinery and ships.

East Germany was also a very big producer of chemicals for the remainder of the Soviet bloc, including ore, sulphuric acid, caustic soda, and above all plastics and resins.

East Germany, deprived of hard coal and other resources, developed the mining of brown coal which can be worked very economically from open cast pits. It was used mainly to produce electricity in the Cottbus area for the electro-chemical and electro-metallurgical industries. Although effective enough the use of brown coal is a major cause of pollution, and it will have to be replaced by other energy sources in the new, green, unified Germany. Natural gas piped from the Soviet Union was also used in East Germany.

Bethel Strousberg, Germany's railway king, was born in East Prussia, worked as a journalist in England, and returned to his native land in 1863, determined to climb on the band wagon of the first industrial boom and build a German railway system on the British pattern. His railway empire – not the first in Germany where the first line was opened in 1835 – extended not only all over East Germany (Poland and Prussia) but deep into the Balkan peninsula. Over-rapid expansion requiring huge investment proved his downfall and he went bust in Romania in 1873, losing fortunes for many of his enthusiastic aristocratic supporters. One of them, Prince Putbus, now became known as Prince Kaputbus.

However, despite this bad start, railway transportation remains the backbone of the German infrastructure, whether east or west. In the west, the largest transport organization is the *Deutsche Bundesbahn* (Federal Railway) with a rail network of 27,500 kilometres (11,400 kilometres electrified) which handles 80 per cent of all rail services and employs 264,000 people.

In the east, inland water transport is important along the Elbe and the canal links to Berlin, but the railway still accounts for 70 per cent of all transport. Steam was not completely supplanted by diesel and electricity in West Germany until as recently as 1977; East Germany still has some steam trains running on the 14,300 kilometres of railroad along with diesel and electric trains.

The West German railway has a high speed train capable of reaching 250 kilometres per hour on the Hanover—Würzburg and the Mannheim—Stuttgart stretches, but as in most Western countries the railway system is deeply in the red; the deficit in 1985 was 3,300 million Deutschmarks which was paid for by the federal government.

Germany's roads, particularly West Germany's, are among the best in Europe; the network of Autobahns (motorways) and secondary routes has grown from 347,000 kilometres in 1951 to 491,000 kilometres in 1986, by which time 8,350 kilometres of the total were motorways. Motor traffic has risen from 1.9 million vehicles in 1950 to 31.7 million in 1986, of which total 26.9 million were private cars.

In East Germany, apart from new highways between Leipzig and Dresden and between Berlin and Rostock, little has changed since World War II and the total classified road mileage is 124,615 kilometres.

As Germany is dependent on both imports and exports for her very existence, inland waterways and harbours are equally important. West Germany has the ports of Hamburg, Bremen, Bremerhaven and Lubeck and a merchant fleet of 1,200 ships with a combined gross registered tonnage of 4.1 million, as well as an inland waterway system of some 4,400 navigable kilometres on the Rhine, and on other rivers and canals. East Germany only had one main port, Rostock, supplemented by Wismar and Stralsund, and was forced to make use of Hamburg and Lubeck in West Germany.

Germany, like Britain, initially believed that the answer to mass air transport would be the dirigible airship and built many Zeppelins. But just as Britain's hopes were dashed by the crash of the R101 at Beauvais in France in 1930, Germany abandoned the airship after the *Hindenburg* burst into flames immediately on its arrival in New Jersey in 1937.

Lufthansa today is one of the best-known and most-successful international airlines. It carries over 15 million passengers and about 600,000 tonnes of freight. In addition 10 million West German passengers have used such charter companies as Condor, LTU and Hapag Lloyd. Berlin, throughout the period that the city was isolated, was served by Air France, British Airways, DanAir and Pan Am through the airports of Tempelhof and Tegel.

East Germany had its own airline, Interflug and its main international airport was Schonefield, about 18 kilometres from Berlin.

In West Germany disposable income rose from 188,000 million Deutschmarks in 1960 to 228,000 million Deutschmarks in 1986. This doesn't mean, however, that every West German household had six times as much spending power in 1986 as in 1960, because prices also rose over the same period. A more realistic assessment of the increase in the standard of living of the West Germans can be gained from studying tables showing the number of hours and minutes of work that would be required to earn enough money to buy certain basics. For example, in 1950 it took 56 minutes work to earn enough money – on average wages – to buy 1 kilogram of sugar; by 1985 it took only 10 minutes work. Coffee? Twenty-three hours and 2 minutes in 1950; 2 hours and 6 minutes in 1964. And what we used to call a push-bike? A total of 121 hours 36 minutes in 1950, as against 30 hours 53 minutes in 1985.

Another useful guide is the proportion of total income spent on such essentials as food, clothing and housing. In West Germany in 1964 these items amounted to 64 per cent of the total average income; by 1985, they only amounted to slightly less than 50 per cent, which meant that by then the average German family could spend approximately half of its total income on consumer durables, cars, dish-washing machines and new kitchens, as well as on leisure and holidays.

East Germany was never a consumer orientated society. Cars were few and far between, clothes were drab and dreary, TV sets and refrigerators were hard to come by, and while some staple foods such as bread and potatoes and probably cabbage were always available, even such relatively mundane exotic foodstuffs as oranges and bananas were largely unobtainable. Most people lived in rented apartments — with rents fixed by the state — of two or three rooms.

On the other hand, the East Germans enjoyed total social security. Well, whether they enjoyed it or not is a moot point; certainly they benefited from it. The combination of a communist-planned economy with its overmanning and therefore an almost perpetual labour shortage meant total job security. Schools were free, university students were sure of scholarships to university, everybody was sure of a retirement pension, free medicine and medicare. The pensions were not all that generous, perhaps, by Western standards, but then the salaries hadn't been all that generous either, and most of the East Germans had learnt not to expect too much from life.

In West Germany, where about half of the working population own their own homes, the high standard of living they have achieved can be maintained only by both husband and wife going out to work, a situation which can cause problems with the children and may cause other problems in the long run.

The old German aristocracy has been replaced by the top managers, high officials, successful doctors and lawyers, property developers and stock brokers. The former bottom-of-the-pile working class has been replaced by new fringe groups of under-privileged citizens who cannot cope with their problems on their own initiative — one-parent families, very large families, elderly people with small pensions and no savings, and the physically handicapped.

By far the largest minority are foreign workers, the *Gastar-beiter* (guest workers) and their dependents. In all they total very nearly 5 million people, more than 60 per cent of whom have been in Germany for ten years or longer, and many of whom have two or more children born in Germany. This is yet another problem looming large on reunified Germany's plate.

For the moment, further immigration of foreigner workers is strictly limited. Foreign workers from outside the Community are not allowed to be recruited, and financial aid is being provided for foreign workers who wish to go home.

Social insurance in Germany dates back to the end of the nineteenth century. It was introduced by Bismarck, not out of any great concern for the fate of the workers in the factories, but in the hope of taking a bit of the wind out of the sails of the rapidly developing communist and socialist labour welfare movements. Nevertheless his legislation willy-nilly became the foundation of a social insurance scheme which served as an example to other industrial countries, if only because it was the only one then in existence.

Today almost all of the inhabitants of what was West Germany are insured against the financial disadvantages of illness, whether as obligatory or voluntary members of various statutory health schemes. Payments to the various schemes average around 12.5 per cent of gross earnings.

The system is very similar to what the British National Health Service turned into under Thatcherism. One quotation from a West German government hand-out says it all: 'No one who falls into material distress in the Federal Republic of Germany need despair. A Social Insurance Act provides a net which catches even those unable to help themselves or unable to obtain the help they need elsewhere, for example from various family members or from the various branches of the social insurance schemes.'

With 154,000 doctors and 34,000 dentists (i.e. one doctor for every 400 inhabitants and one dentist for every 1,800 inhabitants), West Germany is medically one of the best equipped countries in the world. There is also one bed for every 90 inhabitants, another extremely high figure by Community or even world standards.

AFFAIRS OF STATE

Bundestag or Volkskammer?

The Federal Republic of Germany remains the official name of the new unified Germany. According to the latest (1991) figures, it now has a combined population of 78,700,000, an area of 357,000 square kilometres and a GDP valued at 2,712 billion Deutschmarks. The capital is Berlin, and while there is continuing debate as to whether government and parliament should move there, it seems likely that Bonn will remain the administrative centre of the republic for the foreseeable future, if only because of the expense and difficulty of moving the administration to Berlin in the middle of so many other unsolved problems. In the meantime, as a symbol of unity, the head of state, Federal President Richard von Weizsacker, has his second official base in Berlin, a city of nearly 3,500,000 people.

The *Bundestag* (Lower House) has 662 members (as against the 650 in the British House of Commons) and Dr Helmut Kohl heads a coalition government with the Free Democrats which has a majority of 134 over the opposition, mainly the Socialist party.

The *Bundesrat* (Upper House) vets legislation passed by the *Bundestag*, in more or less the same way as the House of Lords operates in England. Its members are representatives of the 16 *Länder* (states) which form the federation.

The former federal republic did not have a constitution as such, but rather a 'basic law'; this was a deliberately temporary device until such time as the two Germanies could again be united. It protected all democratic rights, denied any rights to those who attempted to overthrow democracy and permitted the expropriation or 'socialization' of private property in certain circumstances and made aggressive war illegal.

The president, as head of state, is chosen by the members of the *Bundestag* and by an equal number of delegates chosen by the Länder. His power is very limited — he is not, for example, chief of the armed forces. He can only serve two consecutive, five-year terms, and his principal functions are to appoint a chancellor and to dissolve parliament after a vote of no confidence.

The chancellor is in effect the prime minister and has, broadly speaking, the same power as the prime minister in the United Kingdom. The *Bundestag* is the main chamber of legislature, and a government or cabinet can remain in office only as long as it commands a majority there.

Although West Germany is a federal state, it has a unified legal system. The law is administered by independent judges who cannot be removed and criminal trials are held before a panel of judges — and never before a jury.

West Germany was allowed to rearm when it regained sovereignty in 1955. Compulsory military service was introduced in 1956, and West Germany soon had the biggest army in Western Europe with 345,000 in the army, 39,000 in the navy and 111,000 in the air force, with a frontier guard of 20,000 men and reserves numbering over a million.

Also, although West Germany was forbidden to produce nuclear weapons, its army had eleven battalions equipped with surface-to-surface nuclear missiles, and its air force had the Pershing nuclear rocket, all without warheads.

In East Germany, after World War II, the SPD (Social Democratic Party of Germany) was officially merged with the Russian-inspired KPD (Communist) party to form the SED (Socialist Unity Party), thereby giving the Communists control of all working class organizations. In 1948 a paramilitary police force was set up under the control of the Russians. So-called 'people's congresses' laid down the basis for the new state, and 'elected' a German people's council, though the voters could only say 'yes' or 'no' to the names on a single list, almost all Communists.

On 7 October 1949, those voted to the council became the *Volkskammer* (People's Chamber) of the new republic's parliament and so many changes were subsequently made in the system of representation that it became totally meaningless, as undoubtedly it was intended to become. East Germany was run more or less directly from the Soviet Union. To the extent that the

East Germans could apply any pressure, they were far more successful than any of the other puppet Soviet states, but they, too, frequently fell foul of idiotic Soviet bureaucratic decisions. Looking back on it now, the mystery is not the sudden collapse of the Communist world in 1989 and 1990 but the fact that it held out for so long against all the absurdities it generated.

The first military formations of East Germany were known as the 'People's Police in Barracks', formed in 1952. A real army was not formed until 1956, a few months after the creation of the West German armed forces. Land forces numbered 130,000 in the mid-seventies, not including the 80,000 frontier guards. The air force had 25,000 men and the navy 16,000 and there were 400,000 reservists.

In March 1990, the first free elections for over forty years were held in what had been the GDR and the vote was overwhelmingly for an 'Alliance for Germany', a reunited Germany.

The all-German current account for the first four months of this year (1991) was a deficit of 12,000 million Deutschmarks as against a surplus of 5,400 million Deutschmarks a year earlier. Some of this may be put down to the general recession, but a part of it must reflect the enormous cost of putting East Germany on its feet again. In the period January to April 1990 the German trade surplus of exports over imports was 44,500 million Deutschmarks; by January to April 1991 this surplus had fallen to 5,400 million Deutschmarks.

It will be interesting to see how Germany copes with so many problems, problems which will give the French and the Italians and − despite a lot of initial bungling − possibly even the British, ten to twelve years to catch up with the German economic miracle and perhaps even contain, as the initial Schuman plan was intended to do, any further German military aspirations for the foreseeable future.

CULTURE AND LEISURE

A Protestant People

Despite all the confusion caused by Luther and the first Protestants in the sixteenth century, Germany today is almost exactly divided between adherents to both the Catholic and Protestant versions of the same confusing Christian message.

There was no state church in Germany; the German Protestant Church is an alliance of seventeen Lutheran, other reformed and United Land churches. The population of Germany now also includes some 3 million Muslims with whom, sooner or later, Germany, and indeed the rest of Europe will have to come to terms.

The entire educational system, including all the private schools, comes under state supervision in Germany. School attendance is compulsory from age six to eighteen, during which period, full-time attendance is required for nine years, and part-time attendance at a vocational school thereafter. Attendance at state schools is basically free, though as in other Community countries many parents choose to send their children to schools which charge fees.

The explanation for this is basically the same as it is in Britain: the Germans have a very definite idea of what the notion self-reliance entails, and the education of one's children is an eventuality for which the ordinary, able-bodied citizen is expected to provide.

After primary school, children attend a *Hauptschule* (junior secondary school) until age fifteen, where classes include one foreign language, usually English, and some vocational orientation to ease the transition from school to working life. The majority of students then go into *Realschule* (Intermediate school) where many are streamed into a *Fachschule* (technical school). Many others enter a *Gymnasium*, the German senior high school which prepares students for university.

German universities have a very long history. Heidelberg was founded in 1386, several others are more than 500 years old and more than twenty new universities have been founded since 1960.

In 1950, only six students in 100 expected a university place; nowadays the proportion is more than one in six, and the total number of university students has risen from 511,000 in 1970 to more than 1,360,000 in 1986, including more than 77,000 foreigners.

Despite what they acknowledge as the 'onslaught of television', the sale of German newspapers rose from 13 million in 1954 to 20 million in 1987. Axel Springer's tabloids and the older newspapers such as the conservative *Die Welt* and the Frankfurt-based *Allgemeine Zeitung* are flourishing.

There are nine regional combined radio and TV corporations called *Landesrundfunkstanstalen*, a good example of the German passion for long words.

In the field of science, the Germans were always away out in front. In the comparatively brief period between the establishment of the Second Reich and the end of World War II, ten out of the forty-five Nobel prizes for physics and sixteen out of the forty Nobel prizes for chemistry went to Germans.

So far as art, literature and music are concerned, Germany is such an overwhelming giant that a list of names must suffice: Handel, Bach, Beethoven, Brahms, Goethe, Schiller, Heine, Kant, Marx, Mann, Brecht. Is there any need to go on? And painting? From Dürer to Ernst, the Germans have always produced more than their fair share.

So far as sport and leisure are concerned, the Germans clearly enjoy themselves everywhere, but they also take sport very seriously; they have more than 40,000 public and school sports grounds, 30,000 sports halls for gymnastics, tennis, riding and ice-skating as well as 7,500 indoor and outdoor swimming pools, and have had a consistently high record in the Olympics and other international sports events, like tennis; in 1991 for the first time, both the men's and women's singles championships at Wimbledon were won by Germans.

Football is by far the most popular sport: nearly 5 million

Germans belong to a football club. But runners-up include gymnastics, shooting, tennis, handball, skiing, swimming and angling.

Food and drink? I have tried to be reasonably impartial and fair-minded throughout this book, but for every soul on this earth, there is always something about which it is not really possible to be impartial and fair-minded. In my case, this happens to be a dish known as *Sauerkraut*. I would go even further and say that a nation whose favourite dish is *Sauerkraut* cannot be ranked among the world's great gourmets. Not that the German diet is limited to *Sauerkraut* by any means, but simply that any nation which regards *Sauerkraut* as even remotely edible — much less a delicacy — cannot in my opinion reasonably pronounce on any aspect of cuisine. It would only be tiresome to rub the message in with *Knödel* (dumplings), *Wurst* (sausage) and *Kartoffelensalat* (potato salad). Better to say simply that German food while filling and robust, excellent fare after a hard month's hiking through the *Schwartzwald* or a fortnight pinned to the North Face of the Eiger, seems to me to lack a great deal of the subtle delicacy of French, Spanish or Italian cooking, but on the other hand, can any of these countries offer anything to compare with the Bayreuth festival?

In the end, it all comes down to a matter of taste. The Germans produce several delicate wines from the Moselle area and a great many boringly similar beers, which most of them prefer to wine. As the French say, chacun …

THE GREEKS

They Had a Word For It

GREECE IN PROFILE

Area	131,990 sq km
Population	9,900,000
Population density	75 per sq km
Women	50.8%
Under 15	21.3%
Over 65	13.3%
Language	Greek
Religion	96% Greek Orthodox
Labour force	39.2%
Employed in:	
Agriculture	28.9%
Industry	27.4%
Services	43.7%
Women in labour force	33.7%
Unemployment (as % of labour force)	7.5%

Major exports: Industrial products, including textiles (45%); farm products (28.7%); ores and metals (5.8%); chemicals (3.3%)

Main customers: EC (63.5%), USA (7.1%), Egypt (2.4%), USSR (1.4%); Yugoslavia (1.3%)

THE GREEKS

When you start to think about Greece, your first instinct is to wonder what on earth it is doing as a full member of the European Community. A Balkan country consisting of a peninsula and hundreds of barren, rocky islands in the Aegean, with poor communications, almost no transportation and a very scrappy infrastructure. A country moreover with no common frontier with any other Community member. A country that was never, even in ancient times, able to feed itself, but has always been dependent on food shipped in from abroad. A country which was under Turkish domination for four centuries, and whose history since liberation in 1827 has been marked by a singularly unstable series of governments, and a civil war in the forties and fifties in which at least 125,000 Greeks were killed by their fellow-countrymen, and a period of military dictatorship during which human rights were not scrupulously honoured. A country in which even today very nearly one-third of the population still works in agriculture in what is without any doubt by far the least fertile and most over-exploited land in the whole Community; as long ago as 400 BC Plato noted that the mountain slopes which in his day afforded sustenance only for the bees had once supported trees capable of providing timber for the roofs of even the largest houses, and Homer made several references to the effects of irrational cutting, clearing and over-grazing, as well as to the devastation caused by forest fires. A country with no industries to speak of, few natural resources, no reputation for anything tangible, really. Offhand, can you think of a single distinctive Greek product of any kind that is well known worldwide? The bouzouki, perhaps?

And yet, as you continue to think about Greece, it seems inconceivable that it would not be a member, if not the first member, of any European Community. It was the first farming community in Europe, the first civilization, the first state, the first democracy, the first centre of European sea-trade, the first European Community, in effect.

More than one word in every eight we use in the Western world comes from the Greek; without them we couldn't even begin to explain what our life is all about. Straight off the top of my head, without stopping to think about it for more than a few seconds, I was able to reel off a few English examples: drama, erotic, electric, elastic, geography, gymnasium, government, hour, history, hierarchy, logic, sociology, stadium, theology, technology, tragedy, person, politics, police, place, philosophy, psychology.

And the real point is that it wasn't just these words which came to us from the Greeks, it was the very concepts themselves. Thucydides was the world's first historian, Herodotus the first journalist. Democracy was a Greek idea. So was the theatre. The Greeks introduced the notion of coins to Europe; previously people had reckoned wealth in terms of head of cattle. The first beauty contest was held in ancient Greece. The first university in Europe was established (by the Roman emperor Marcus Aurelius) in Athens in AD 176.

The written word, as we know it, was developed from Greek by the Romans; and two Greek monks from Thessaloniki invented the Cyrillic alphabet which is the basis of Russian and all Slavic languages. They came up with the idea when faced with the problem of converting Slavs to Christianity and first had to translate the Bible into a language that the Slavs could understand. The Olympic Games which had been held every four years from

776 BC to AD 392 at Olympia in Greece were revived in their modern form in 1896. In their original form, not only did women take no part; they were not even permitted to attend as spectators.

Mind you, these and countless other things we take completely for granted were thought up by a very gifted race of people who migrated down into the Balkan Peninsula from somewhere away to the north-east around 2000 BC. They were of Aryan, Indo-European stock, tall and fair-haired. Their civilization was swallowed up in Rome's around the time of the birth of Christ, and they themselves were swallowed up by history.

Many of today's Greeks believe that they are the direct descendants of those classical Greeks who shaped Western democracy and culture, but it just isn't so.

To be fair, it's not their fault that they believe this. They were encouraged to do so by a collection of well-meaning but misguided Europeans like Shelley and Byron who wrote poems and tracts and treatises calling on the Greeks to fight to reclaim their independence from the Turks and exhorting them to re-discover their ancient valour as the direct descendants of the Spartans who had been able, with a mere handful of men, to turn back the hordes of Persia.

The plain truth of the matter is that after the Roman take-over and the eventual break-up of the Greek Empire, what was left of the ancient Greek civilization was subjected to such an endless series of invasions, incursions, intrusions and infiltrations that no race could possibly have kept itself intact and pure, and through no fault of their own the Greeks finally became a mixture of Romans, Albanians, Franks, Slavs, Bulgars, Catalans, Germans, Flemish, Vlachs (a non-Slav people from south-eastern Europe with a language of their own, descended, like Romanian, from the Latin), and Turks.

More than 2 million of today's population of 9.9 million were exchanged for 370,000 Muslims in 1923, in the greatest whole-sale transfer of people ever to take place. It was at the time of Greece's final defeat at the hands of the Turks, after which the Greeks were forced to cede to Turkey that part of Thrace east of the Evros river, as well as all the territories claimed in Asia Minor in which those 2 million hybrid Greek citizens had lived. So there is no way that today's Greeks are in any way very closely related to their ancient forebears.

However, having said that, it is only reasonable to add that the modern Greeks, however murky their genealogy, have somehow managed to retain a certain independence of mind, a curious, almost unique brand of self-respect, an extraordinarily buoyant sense of humour, and a very keen sense of proportion, as well as a deep conviction that they are completely qualified to pronounce on any question of politics, philosophy, morality or manners. And these qualities probably owe far more to what remains in their genes of the serene self-confidence of the ancient Greeks than they do to any of the subsequent strains which have contributed over the years to the Greek character.

It could well be that these qualities stem directly from the nature of the Greek landscape itself. It is probably not insignificant that the first and greatest of the Greek gods, greater even than Zeus, was Gaiea, the Earth Mother. From everything that has been written by and about the ancient Greeks, one simple fact emerges: that they seemed to derive their very character and strength from the barren earth of their country, and from the stunning light which has always come flooding so abundantly from its skies.

Countless visitors to Greece have shared a curious experience there, a sudden feeling that the land is haunted, though not always by anything sinister. It is the sort of feeling you get when you visit a place for the first time and discover that you really know it very well, because you have dreamt about it perhaps, or because you remember it deep down in some lower layer of consciousness. It has happened to hundreds of people, all over Greece, but a great many have experienced this feeling most strongly at Epidaurus, Mycenae and Delphi, among them many writers.

Henry Miller commented in *The Colossus of Maroussi* (published in 1941): 'I never knew the meaning of peace until I arrived in Epidaurus. As I entered the still bowl [of the theatre] bathed now in a marble light, I came to a spot at the dead centre where the faintest whisper rises like a glad bird and vanishes over the shoulder of the low hill, as the light of a clear day recedes before the velvet black of night. Balboa standing before a peak of Darien could not have known a greater wonder than I at this moment. There was nothing more to conquer; an ocean of peace lay before me.'

And Goethe wrote: 'Of all people, the Greeks have dreamt the dream of life best.'

And Lord Kinross: 'The landscape of Greece stares, challenging and tough. Here in the eastern Mediterranean is the hard core of Europe, a land reduced to its essentials of light and form, of rock and sky and sea.'

Nicholas Gage, who has written one of the most penetrating and perceptive modern books about Greece that I have read, *Hellas* (London: Collins Harvill, 1971), believes that the Greek landscape is haunted. He writes about a visit to Mycenae and adds: 'While I sat there I felt such a sense of oppressive evil that I could almost hear the screams of Clytemnestra, Cassandra and the murdered children. Whatever structure once stood here, I came away convinced that to live there for any length of time would surely lead to madness. What explanation is there for such a reaction to an unremarkable collection of rocks? I can only reply that the landscape of Greece is haunted. I have felt it often; many others have remarked upon it, and the Greeks have always known it.'

Writing about Delphi, Gage says that more than eight centuries before the birth of Christ a shepherd sitting on the steep slopes of Mount Parnassos felt a rush of cold air coming from a crevice in the earth and fell into a divine trance, babbling nonsense. From that time on, until four centuries after the birth of Christ, Delphi remained the seat of a divine oracle.

He goes on: 'I think that if man's history were erased, but Delphi itself remained, a passer-by at some future time would again discover divine emanations at the same spot, and would declare it to be the centre of the world. And perhaps he would be right ... The setting at Delphi is so compelling that god and man could hardly have resisted pausing here to talk.'

The Greeks have always been associated with tragedy — and perhaps naturally, since they invented the idea of drama — but perhaps the greatest Greek tragedy for people from elsewhere could be the fact that most of today's nation-states have decided that a classical education is not necessarily an advantage in the modern world. The result of this will be that generations of children are going to grow up regarding Greece merely as one of a number of countries on the Mediterranean littoral where they can readily find reliable sunshine and a secluded sandy beach upon which to spread-eagle their naked bodies in the company of others for the purpose of acquiring a tan.

Unlike most of the other member-states in the Community, which had their religions preached to them or foisted upon them somewhere along the way, the Greeks seem to have arrived upon the European scene with theirs ready-made.

And they appear to have enjoyed an extremely casual relationship with their gods, unlike the Hebrews, Christians and Muslims, who have saddled themselves with extremely awkward, singular, invisible and jealous gods who insist on their adherents having no gods other than them, and expect them to obey the sets of rigid rules which they have laid down.

The Greek gods were simply a larger-than-life extension of the Greek people themselves. They enjoyed the same things, inhabited the same places and, even more importantly, enjoyed sinning the same sins as their subjects.

The Greek gods lived, not in some invisible nowhere place away up in the heavens, but in clearly identifiable spots which you can easily still find with the aid of a map. This made them far more accessible and far less formidable than they became when they had been institutionalized by the Romans, and a lot less formidable and more accessible than Jehovah, God or Mohammed.

The original inhabitants of Greece — the Celts who were there when the ancient Greeks arrived — worshipped the Great Triple Goddess, whose celestial symbol was the moon, and the moon's phases were seen as reflecting one aspect of the human journey. They saw the moon as female, progressing from young maidenhood through mature womanhood to old age, before disappearing altogether, a fairly realistic assessment of what this life has to offer.

I think it is probable that alone of all the people of Europe, the Greeks managed to establish that extraordinary rapport between themselves and their own particular patch of the earth's surface that seems to have been such a feature of the lifestyle of the North American Indians and of the Australian and New Zealand aborigines.

There are all sorts of odd things about the Greeks. The way they dance, for example. Mostly it is the men who dance, sometimes singly, sometimes in groups, sometimes mob-handed, in rings, but always very seriously, almost sadly, with their eyes downcast in deep thought. It is not dancing as the rest of the world understands it. And I don't think that anyone from anywhere else in the world can possibly ever understand why the Greeks dance as they do. Nicholas Gage makes an effort to explain it by quoting Nikos Kazantzakis who tells how his hero Zorba, in great grief at his son's death, suddenly got to his feet and started to dance.

Why did he start to dance? 'Why?' repeats Zorba, and then he goes on: 'The others said, "Zorba's gone mad." But I knew that if I didn't dance at that moment, I would go mad.' That's an explanation?

There are anomalies. Athens is the oldest capital city in Europe, but in another way it is the newest. Apart from that magnificent forest of marble ruins that is the Acropolis, towering over the city, and a few old houses clustered around the foot of it in the Plaka, most of the city of Athens has been built in the last fifty years. In 1834, when it became the capital of the modern state of Greece, it had only about 300 houses and a few churches. The population of the city has increased tenfold since World War II, to 2.6 million.

And if it was the ancient Greeks who taught us so much of what has shaped our very civilization — the gospels, with the possible exception of that of St Matthew, were originally written in Greek — the modern Greeks have been extremely slow in making use of many of the things we have discovered, or rediscovered, more recently. In parts of the country until the middle seventies, plumbing was unknown, electricity was a novelty and most of the roads were unpaved. On many of the islands, donkeys are still the only form of transport.

Greece is also one of the last bastions in the Western world of the male-oriented society. In country districts in Greece, as in Africa, it is the women who do most of the planting and harvesting and marketing, while their men sit in the shade drinking ouzo and playing cards. Even in the cities, it is quite normal to find at a dinner party the women spending most of the time in the kitchen, preparing the meal and then serving it and then washing up after it, while their menfolk sit at the table discussing politics.

Although about one-third of the labour force is now female, it is still considered as a derogatory reflection on a man's virility and on his ability to provide for his family if his wife goes to work. Therefore, even in families where the extra income is essential, there is often a pretence on the part of the woman that she is merely doing it as a hobby because it amuses her and not because they need the money. And however hard she works in the office a Greek woman is still expected to look after the children and do all the housework when she gets home. The father is responsible for disciplining the children but that's all; in no circumstances would a Greek man do any housework or attend to any of the children's other needs.

And yet one of the first and relatively few female poets in the world was burning Sappho, who loved and sang on the island of Lesbos, which gave its name to a way of life in which man played no major role.

So what about the Greek men then?

'The male Greek today,' Henry Miller wrote, 'despite all the variations of type, despite the fact that he no longer has the blood of the gods in him, comes closer to our conception of the Western man than any other in Europe. His manhood reveals itself in the curious fusion of weakness and strength. He is just as curious, just as garrulous, just as susceptible as the Greeks of old. He still weeps openly and unashamedly, like the heroes of Homer.'

eventually it reaches the hearth. The Turf Board, a state-sponsored company set up in 1946 to discover some way of turning this unpromising material into an effective fuel for the Irish, found themselves in effect in the moisture disposal business. They have managed to produce compressed turf briquettes for domestic use, with a moisture content as low as 10 per cent, but their principal achievement has been the generation of electricity from peat in power stations built on the bogs, using turf in powder form. At present the Turf Board's contribution to the country's energy demands is in the region of the equivalent of 866,000 tonnes of oil. But this use of turf was always recognized purely as an interim measure; almost all of the usable turf will be gone by the end of the century.

Happily, in the late seventies, a rich vein of natural gas was discovered in the sea off Kinsale, County Cork, which is now piped up to Dublin as well as serving the entire Cork area. Some oil has also been discovered off the Atlantic coast of the west of Ireland — in the so-called Celtic Sea — but so far not in sufficient quantity or in waters shallow enough to make it viable for immediate development.

Over the past twenty years determined efforts at prospecting for precious minerals have resulted in the discovery of one of the most promising exploration territories in Europe. Zinc-lead deposits found at Navan, in County Meath, have turned Ireland into Europe's largest producer of lead and zinc. At Tynagh, in County Galway, a lead-zinc, copper-silver deposit was worked from 1965 to 1980 and produced in that period a sizeable amount (370,000 kg) of silver. Copper concentrates and zinc and lead have been found in County Tipperary, and copper in Avoca, County Wicklow. In addition to metals, industrial minerals such as barytes, limestone, gypsum and phosphates have all been found in Ireland and make some slight contribution to the GNP of US$21,922 million.

HISTORICAL PERSPECTIVE

A Fair People

Factual Irish history doesn't begin until the Christian era, but it is possible to get a vague picture of life in pre-Christian Ireland from the legends and stories and epics which were passed down verbally from generation to generation and were written down to become literature in the early Christian period; from them we learn that the island was divided into five separate kingdoms, under a High King ruling at Tara, whose supremacy was challenged every bit as often as it was acknowledged. The people were largely nomadic; they didn't build cities, though the kings and High Kings lived in earthwork settlements, surrounded by their courts, their poets and lawyers, their musicians and warriors.

These early rulers of Ireland were the Gaelic Celts, mentioned above. Very little is known about them. Plato referred to them as a race of tall, fair-haired people inclined to drunkenness and much given to fighting, a description which might not be considered inappropriate for their latter-day descendants. They appear to have come from somewhere around the source of the Danube and seem to have spread their considerable influence by peaceful infiltration as much as by forceful conquest, all over Middle Europe, Gaul and Spain, as well as the British Isles.

For some unknown reason the Romans never attempted to extend their empire to Ireland, though they knew all about the place. Perhaps if they had, 400 years of straight Roman roads and strict Roman discipline might have made the Irish a bit more amenable to conquest by the Anglo-Normans when it came and so might have changed the whole course of Irish history.

But before the Normans, there was St Patrick. A Latin-speaking Roman Christian citizen living in Wales, Patrick was captured and carried off to Ireland as a young boy during one of the periodic raids which the Irish Celtic Kings were constantly making on what the Ulster Unionists insist on calling Mainland Britain.

Patrick was sold as a slave and spent the formative years of his young life herding sheep on the slopes of a mountain in County Antrim. Eventually he escaped to the continent, studied for the priesthood, and returned to Ireland in 432, determined to preach Christianity to the pagans amongst whom he had spent his youth.

Even in his wildest dreams, Patrick himself could hardly have foreseen the fanatical zeal with which the mystical and impractical Celts took to the religion he preached. For over 1,500 years — well into the Permissive Sixties — the Irish enjoyed a reputation for fervent piety unequalled in the world outside Poland and Spain perhaps, and certainly not always shared by some of St Peter's successors at the Vatican.

Then the Vikings arrived. While the saints and scholars were busy over their books, the captains and the kings were quarrelling among themselves as usual and fell easy prey to the marauding bands of Danish and Norwegian adventurers who were terrorizing England and Normandy around the same time.

Initially the Danes came to plunder, but they stayed on to settle, to marry Irish women, to build and fortify Ireland's first towns and set up Ireland's first trading posts. For 200 years they occupied large areas of Ireland, mostly along the coastline, near the natural harbours. They pillaged the monastic settlements and exacted tributes in return for undertakings not to plunder, a sort of primitive protection racket. Only in Ulster, the most fiercely Celtic part of the whole island, were the O'Neills and O'Donnells strong enough to keep the Danes out.

Throughout the rest of the country, the Irish kings were still too busy quarrelling among themselves to make any concerted effort to get rid of the Danes until 1014, when a large number of the latter were driven into the sea during the course of a great battle at Clontarf near Dublin. The survivors of the battle were assimilated into the Irish race; the trade they had built up had proved useful to the Irish kings. Needless to say, there were Irish soldiers fighting on the side of the Danes — mostly the men of Leinster who resented the High King's attempts to control them. 'The Irish are a fair people,' Dr Johnson was to remark, centuries later. 'They never speak well of one another.'

So the Irish once again had control of their own affairs and proceeded to restore the monasteries and seats of learning pillaged by the Danes. It was during this period that a king called Malachy — who was later canonized — arranged for the ecclesiastical division of Ireland which persists to the present day, precisely paralleled in the Protestant and Catholic faiths.

And typically, it was yet another row between another king of Leinster and another High King which led to the invasion of Ireland by the Anglo-Normans and started a war between the Irish and their next-door neighbours, the English, which isn't over yet, and doesn't look as if it ever will be.

COLONIAL CONNECTIONS

Nearly a Nation Once Again

Apart from the fact that a relatively small number of Irish Celts moved across the water to Scotland and became the Scotiae, Ireland's only colonial connections have always been at the receiving end, so to speak.

By the middle of the twelfth century, England's Norman barons, searching for new estates and fresh raw material for their armies, were looking hungrily at the undeveloped acres of Ireland.

In 1166, the then King of Leinster, Dermot MacMurrough, defeated and banished by the High King, Rory O'Connor, and determined to avenge himself, travelled to Bristol and sought permission from Henry II to raise an army of auxiliaries.

Dermot brought with him his beautiful daughter and offered her hand in marriage — with the additional bonus of the kingship of Leinster — to any Anglo-Norman baron prepared to lead an expeditionary force against Ireland. Dermot's own private plan was to take over the High Kingship himself, with the assistance of the Norman troops.

A Norman expeditionary force landed at Waterford in 1170 under the command of the Earl of Pembroke, known as Strongbow. He had grown up in Wales, hence the title Pembroke, but he still spoke French and didn't have the makings of a king of Leinster.

Strongbow did, however, conquer Waterford and Dublin. Just

as he was settling in, preparatory perhaps to breaking away from England and establishing his own independent Norman monarchy in Ireland, Henry II landed with an army of knights to prevent just such an eventuality and to ensure that Ireland became part of his own personal kingdom. Completely ignoring the High King and all Irish notions of sovereignty and land ownership, Henry parcelled the island up between various of his Norman knights and the few native provincial kings who agreed to pay annual tributes to him.

He didn't, of course, do this without authority. Pope Adrian IV — an English pope it is true, and the only one indeed, but a pope nevertheless — had issued a bull bestowing the island of Ireland on Henry. He had done this because he was alarmed at the great and increasing divergence between the Church in Ireland and in the rest of Christendom — Ireland alone of all the Christian nations had taken no part in the crusades — and he probably felt that a spell of strong, stern Anglo-Norman government might help to bring the Irish Church back into line. Thus began a political dichotomy between the two neighbouring countries which has never since been resolved.

For a time the Norman conquerors had to fight to hold on to the lands assigned to them by the Crown, and spread their power piecemeal, attempting to reproduce in Ireland the whole feudal structure of manors and abbeys, castles and fortresses. But gradually their presence came to be accepted by the Irish, and the Nomans began to adopt the easy-going and casual Irish habits and customs, and even the Irish language, becoming in a much-quoted phrase that is probably more memorable than it is accurate, 'more Irish than the Irish themselves'.

Certainly, left to themselves, the Anglo-Norman colonists probably would have found a way of adapting their laws and customs to make them more acceptable to the Irish, but their rulers in England persisted in ignoring all Irish traditions, and running Ireland as an English colony.

Before very long many second and third generation Anglo-Norman lords, born and brought up in Ireland, began to regard themselves not as Anglo-Normans any longer, but as Anglo-Irish, a situation which didn't at all appeal to the English monarchs who feared a line-up between these Anglo-Irish barons and the ancient Irish kings and chieftains.

Ireland's first parliament was convoked towards the end of the thirteenth century; and one of its first actions was to issue a series of decrees designed to prevent the colonists from assimilating with the Irish.

It needed only the Reformation to add the disastrously divisive element of religious bigotry to the gulf which now separated the Irish and their Anglo-Norman — by now English — overlords. What had been merely a fundamental difference in race and outlook flared into fanatical hatred when Henry VIII — and, to a much greater extent, some of his successors — tried to impose the customs and practices of the new, reformed Church on Catholic Ireland.

The Reformation also added to the Crown's problems with the English overlords; many of them objected just as strongly as the Irish did to the enforced religious changes and tended to side with the Irish against the Crown. Aware of this, and aware that he could no longer continue to claim to be holding the country on the Pope's behalf since he had so signally failed to recognize the Pontiff's authority in other matters, Henry had the title 'King of Ireland' conferred on him by edict of the Irish parliament; and he made the lords and barons and some of the Irish chieftains surrender their lands to him and receive them back, to be held by knight-service. Some of the Irish chieftains were at this time given English titles which explains how the O'Neills of Ulster — descendants of an ancient Celtic High King — came to hold the English title of Earls of Tyrone.

The stage was now set for a succession of rebellions, insurrections and risings as often as not planned and led by members of the Anglo-Norman Ascendancy who had become Anglo-Irish rather than English in their sympathies. Sometimes these were supported by expeditionary forces from continental countries anxious for one reason or another to get a crack at England, and they were usually followed by vast confiscations of Irish land which was then handed over to English or Scottish settlers, or to the soldiers who had put down the rebellions.

The last stand of the old Gaelic Catholic aristocracy took place in Ulster where the O'Neills of Tyrone and the O'Donnells of Tyrconnell (Donegal) held out for nine years against Elizabeth's forces with the support of some Spanish troops and the majority of the Gaelic chieftains all over the country. When they were defeated, pardoned and reinstated, the disillusioned O'Neills and O'Donnells bought a ship and cleared out to the continent, taking with them into exile ninety-eight other Gaelic Catholic chieftains.

This Flight of the Earls, as it was called, was held to be treason; all their lands were confiscated, and the entire area was re-populated with Scottish Lowland Presbyterians and English Protestants. And it was the introduction of these settlers, utterly different in background, race and religion, and all concentrated in one corner of the country, which laid the foundations for the partition of Ireland 300 years later and for today's troubles in Northern Ireland.

The year 1641 saw the outbreak of another Protestant—Catholic war, during which the new Protestant settlers were subjected to some terrible acts of reprisal; indeed much of the Ulster Protestant mistrust of Catholics stems from this period. Eventually the rebellion was stamped out with zealous efficiency and terrible cruelty by Cromwell's Parliamentary Army; and it was followed by a new policy of clearing as many Catholics as possible out of the three other provinces and herding them all into the harsh and barren wilderness of Connemara, west of the Shannon River.

Things began to look a bit more hopeful when a Catholic king, James II, came to the English throne, but he didn't last very long, and when William of Orange landed in England in 1688 to secure the Protestant Succession, James fled first to France and then to Ireland to raise a Catholic army. William followed him over with an army of 36,000. Naturally enough the recently imported Scots Presbyterians and English Protestants in Ulster rallied to the Orange banner. James was finally routed at the Battle of the Boyne, and another flock of wild geese set out for service on the continent.

In 1795 and again in 1798, a society called the United

Irishmen led by a Protestant lawyer, Wolfe Tone, and one of the old Anglo-Irish aristocrats, Lord Edward Fitzgerald, with some half-hearted French assistance, made efforts at insurrection which were quickly quelled. Then in 1803, Robert Emmet and a tiny band of fanatical followers tried to seize Dublin Castle in the most pathetic attempt of them all. The only concrete result of the affair was the killing, in the confusion, of an elderly and well-intentioned judge. Emmet was hanged, but not before he had made a speech from the dock which was to keep the spirit of rebellion alive for another generation: 'When my country takes her place among the nations of the world,' he said, 'then, and not until then, let my epitaph be written.'

From 1800, Ireland had been ruled directly from Westminster, much as Northern Ireland is now, with 100 (later 105) Irish MPs sitting at Westminster. By 1913, the Irish MPs were very close to achieving home rule, but the Protestant settlers in Northern Ireland formed the Ulster Volunteers to take arms against the United Kingdom if need be, in order to remain a part of it.

The Irish Nationalists very understandably then formed the Irish Volunteers which became part of the Irish Republican Army that took over the General Post Office and other strategic buildings in Dublin during Easter Weekend 1916, and held out against the British forces for nearly a week.

The fifteen executions which followed sickened the world and swung public opinion over to the Irish cause, though it took a terrible guerrilla war which dragged on until the summer of 1920 before the British would finally give in. Even then, the British Prime Minister Lloyd George allowed the Ulster Protestants to pressure him into partitioning off six of the predominantly Protestant Ulster counties. This decision led to a disastrous civil war in the south, the sporadic unrest in Ulster ever since, and the state of affairs at times close to civil war which has gone on in Northern Ireland from 1969 to the present day.

After 700 years, Ireland was no longer a British colony but not yet a nation. Not a nation once again, as the patriotic ballad puts it, only nearly a nation once again.

DEVELOPMENT DIRECTIONS

Cows with Long Horns

There are more cattle in Ireland than people, roughly twice as many.

There can be little doubt that the ancient Gaelic Celts were principally cattle-ranchers; by far the best known of all the sagas of that period which have come down to us is an account of a pre-historic rustling adventure, *The Cattle Raid of Cooley*, and the equivalent in Irish Gaelic of the English proverb 'The Far-off Hills are Green' is: 'There are Long Horns on Cows from Over There.'

For centuries, agriculture was not only Ireland's main industry; it was its only industry. As recently as 1965, 35 per cent of the total Irish workforce was employed in agriculture, a proportion far higher than in most European countries at that period and nine times as high as in England, where agriculture then employed only 4 per cent of the working population.

By the eighties, agriculture still provided employment for 17 per cent of the labour force and contributed 11 per cent of the GNP; and when you add the agriculture-related industries, such as food-processing, agriculture today employs more than 20 per cent of Ireland's workforce and accounts for 25 per cent of all the country's exports. Over half of all agricultural production is exported, and about 70 per cent of all beef production. Some 84 per cent of the value of gross output in agriculture is accounted for by livestock and livestock products, almost all of which derive from cattle and milk. At the last count, Ireland's cattle population stood at 7 million, as against a human population of slightly over 3 million.

Because of the excessively important role of agriculture in the overall Irish economy, the Common Agricultural Policy of the Community proved of vital importance to Ireland, enabling it to begin to solve the problems endemic to most agricultural countries — under-investment, low incomes, uneconomic hold-ings, a declining and aging agricultural labour force, with a tribal memory prejudiced against change of any sort.

You have only to drive around the Irish countryside to see the change. Everywhere there are new houses, big, smart, well-painted ones, often erected beside the rotting remains of the old one, now turned into a cattle barn; new cars, tractors and all the latest farm gadgetry. Whether the Common Agricultural Policy — smothered in surpluses and bogged down with butter mountains and milk lakes — will continue to offer sufficiently favourable returns to the farmers to enable them to pay off the debts they were encouraged by the banks and the government to incur when the going was good is another matter.

But there is no doubt that the going has been good for Irish farmers — and fishermen and all the people engaged in the production of food and processed food — ever since Ireland joined the Community in 1973. Before he went bankrupt in 1990 as a result of expanding too rapidly by borrowing vast sums of unsecured money from banks all over the world, Larry Goodman had become by far the biggest meat-processor in Europe, supplying rations for the British army in Germany, the US forces in Europe, and both armies during the Iran–Iraq War of 1980–8.

At the time the Irish Free State was founded in 1922 with British Commonwealth status, the only industries in existence — apart from the brewing of Guinness and the distilling of Irish whiskey — were small manufacturers, operating largely in traditional sectors such as food and textiles almost exclusively for the home market. And the first few factories which were built in Ireland after 1922 were largely designed to make it selfsufficient, so far as possible, in consumer goods.

In a small and dwindling market faced with competition from a highly industrialized next-door neighbour and advertising in most of the newspapers and magazines read by the Irish consumers, this proved a fairly fruitless course of action.

There was a slight industrial revival during World War II, when the shortage of imported goods in neutral Ireland made it easy for such Irish manufacturers as then existed to sell whatever they could manage to produce. But as soon as the post-war austerity period was over, it became increasingly clear that any plans for industrial expansion would have to be based on manufacture for export.

In 1952, an Export Board was established to promote exports, and the government introduced capital incentive schemes to encourage the promotion of new industries in underdeveloped areas. By this time the twenty-six counties of the Irish Free State, by then known as Eire, enjoyed (if that is the right word) the status of an independent republic after a unilateral declaration to that effect in 1949, which the British simply ignored.

In 1958, an Irish Industrial Authority was set up, and tax incentives, grants and other inducements were offered to encourage foreigners to establish new industries, or new plants for their existing industries, in Ireland.

The signing of an Anglo-Irish Free Trade Agreement in 1965 and Ireland's accession to the Community in 1973 had a profound effect on Irish industry, as did the Irish Industrial Development Authority's decision in the early seventies to pursue a policy of encouraging such high-growth sectors as electronics, light engineering and pharmaceuticals. In the ten years between 1973 and 1983, industrial exports increased by more than 10 per cent per year, and in 1983 Ireland achieved the remarkable growth rate of 15 per cent in a European market growing by 1 per cent a year, a figure far in excess of the EC, UK and US figures. However, it is only fair to add that Ireland had started so far behind the rest of the field that a very slight increase in industrial exports would score a fairly high percentage increase rating.

Still, a GNP for 1988 of nearly US$22 millions (US$6,207 per capita) compares quite favourably with other small, relatively undeveloped states in the Community, US$40 million (US$4,042 per capita) for Greece, and US$29 million (US$2,882 per capita) for Portugal, particularly in view of the fact that Ireland has only been in business effectively for about seventy years.

Ireland has the lowest population density in the Community and the highest level of roads per head, which is one of the things that makes motoring in Ireland such a pleasure. It has only one stretch of roadway of motorway standard — the Naas Road, just outside Dublin — and little need of any more since the 92,000 kilometres of primary and secondary routes and country roads are rarely congested and often empty. A recent decision to switch over to kilometres instead of miles has meant that some of the signposts now give the distances in kilometres and others still in miles, which can be confusing, though no more confusing than the general signposting in rural Ireland. And it is pointless to ask anyone the way; the Irish are so anxious to please that they will confidently send you off in the wrong direction altogether rather than disappoint you by admitting that they don't know.

However, since the rail network has been cut back to a few main lines and in the country districts buses are few and far between, you just have to make the best of it and use the roads, which carry 96 per cent of all the passenger and 90 per cent of all the freight traffic in Ireland. Except, perhaps, in Dublin, where parking is difficult and expensive, and there is a good bus service as well as the DART (Dublin Area Rapid Transit), a fast and frequent commuter electric train system.

By virtue of its position, at the very tip of Western Europe, Ireland became deeply involved in transatlantic aviation right from the very start. Alcock and Brown crash-landed in a field in Connemara after the first heavier than air crossing of the Atlantic in 1919; an Irish airman, Captain James Fitzmaurice, was one of the pilots of the German plane, the *Bremen*, which made the first east-to-west crossing in 1928; and Charles Lindbergh knew that he had 'hit Europe on the nose', as he put it, when he saw the green fields of Ireland on the first solo transatlantic flight in 1930.

Just before World War II, the first transatlantic passenger service — using flying boats — operated between Foynes in the Shannon Estuary and Goose Bay in Newfoundland, and after the war Shannon airport was built as a refuelling stop for the first transatlantic flights using passenger planes which had been developed as American troop transports during the war. By a curious coincidence, Shannon airport was built on an area which these days would be regarded as a bird sanctuary, a place known for centuries in Gaelic as Rinneana, the Gathering Place of the Birds. The Irish government put a lot of money into Shannon, not realizing that, within a few short years, jet planes would be flying non-stop from Los Angeles to London and Paris.

Ireland now has four international airports, Dublin, Cork, Shannon and a new one at Knock, built by the government under pressure from the local parish priest who wanted it for the comfort and convenience of pilgrims anxious to view the scene of one of Our Lady's more recent appearances, to a group of schoolgirls in 1879. To everybody's surprise it has proved a great success, carrying not pilgrims so much as migratory – and some commuting – Irish labourers back and forwards between building sites in Britain, mainland Europe and the Middle East, and their homes in Connemara.

Ireland has a friendly and efficient airline, Aer Lingus, with scheduled services to twenty-nine cities in eleven countries in Europe and North America. The telecommunications service is now fairly efficient and RTE (Radio Telefis Eireann), the national TV station, provides two channels, though many Irish homes still have TV antennae mounted on tall poles, stayed like the masts of the *Cutty Sark*, to filch filthy material transmitted by the British stations. I use the word 'filthy' deliberately, because when book censorship was introduced in Ireland in 1930 (it has now virtually ceased to exist), it was 'to stem the flow of filthy literature from over the water' as one politician put it.

If pop music can be regarded as a form of communication, Ireland has made the grade there too with internationally known groups and stars such as U2, Bob Geldof and the Boomtown Rats, Clannad, Enya, Sinead O'Connor, Chris de Burgh and the Pogues. And British radio and television, certainly forms of communication, have for years been dominated by Irish presenters: Eamon Andrews, Terry Wogan, Gloria Hunniford, Henry Kelly, Frank Delaney, Anthony Clare – the list is endless.

AFFAIRS OF STATE

Second and Third Preferences

Ireland is a parliamentary republic with a constitution composed by Eamon de Valera and adopted after a referendum in 1937, which clearly states that all legislative, executive and judicial powers derive from the people.

Legislation is enacted by the *Oireachtas* (parliament), which consists of a lower house, the *Dáil* (from the Gaelic word for assembly), and the *Seanad* (Senate). The *Dáil* is elected on a very elaborate proportional representation system, with multi-seat constituencies and a single transferable vote, an arrangement which requires several counts before all the seats can be filled and which has often resulted in hung parliaments and stalemates of different varieties.

The Senate is partly appointed and partly elected on a political, professional, academic and vocational basis. The single transferable vote system enables the electorate (everybody over eighteen years of age) to number the candidates on the ballot paper in the order of their preference, and in effect to say, that if my chosen candidate does not need my vote to get into the Dáil, it can go to my second choice for the seat, or my third, and so on, or to my second or third choice if my first preference is eliminated by failing to reach the required quota.

A president is elected by the direct vote of the people every seven years; his function is to sign all legislation before it becomes law, to refer any bill to the Supreme Court if he considers it contains anything repugnant to the constitution, and to act as ceremonial head of state. The supreme command of the armed forces is also vested in the president.

Until fairly recently, Irish politics were dominated by two equally conservative, capitalist parties, *Fianna Fáil and Fine Gael*, which were not in fact two separate parties at all, but two factions of the initial *Sinn Fein* party which won Irish independence, split on the question of partition, and then fought on opposite sides in the civil war. Now, seventy years later, the old bitterness has finally disappeared and the structure of the *Dáil* embraces radical, left-wing and some socialist thinking as well as what might have been described as a combination of race memory, family pride and a thirst for revenge.

No stronger proof of the change that has overtaken Irish political thinking in the last two decades could be found than the election to the office of president, in November 1990, of a liberal, left-wing lawyer who has consistently championed the rights of minorities and challenged conventional Catholic thinking on many fundamental issues — and who also happens to be a housewife in her forties — Mary Robinson.

Ireland has maintained a strictly neutral stance since World War II and has resolutely refused to become a member of NATO or any other military alliance. All the same, as a member of the United Nations, Ireland has frequently provided troops from her 14,000 strong defence forces for peace-keeping missions in the Middle East, the Congo, Cyprus, India and Pakistan. The Irish proved acceptable in most countries throughout the long years of the Cold War because they were demonstrably every bit as anti-Communist as they were anti-colonialist. And they are accepted in Black Africa, where they are known as the White Africans, because, as one African government minister put it to me, 'You Irish were among the first of the colonies to throw off the British yoke'.

Dublin used to be about the safest capital city in the world. Thirty years ago, parents could allow a young daughter of fifteen to cycle home alone from a party in Drumcondra (on the north side of the Liffey) to Dalkey (about nine miles away to the south) without a worry in the world: now it isn't safe for a grown man to drive through the city centre unless he makes certain that his car windows are closed and the doors securely locked. Minor burglaries are a daily occurrence, while one of Dublin's main thoroughfares has a junction known as 'handbag corner' from the frequency with which handbags are snatched. There is also a serious drugs problem, with all its concomitant side-effects, including a high incidence of AIDS.

On the other hand, there is very little organized crime, apart from IRA thefts of cars and raids on banks for operating funds, because in a country where everybody still knows nearly everybody else, somebody would be bound to give the game away; naturally, anybody would think twice before informing on the activities of the IRA.

A third of all central government expenditure in Ireland is on health and social security. The poorest people (35 to 40 per cent of the population) are issued with medical cards which entitle them to most medical and hospital services free as well as limited dental and optical services. People with an annual income of less than 12,500 punts (46 per cent of the population) are entitled to free hospital services and a limited range of other services, and there is a Voluntary Health Insurance scheme which provides free hospitalization and other medical services for contributors. There are children's allowances up to sixteen years of age (or eighteen for those in full-time education) and free travel, television, telephone and fuel for old-age pensioners.

So far as wealth is concerned, a survey made in 1980 established that 76 per cent of all houses in the country were owner-occupied, 11 per cent of the people lived in rented local authority housing, and the remaining 13 per cent in private rented accommodation. It also revealed that about 54 per cent of the households ran one car, and nearly 10 per cent two or more. Over 99 per cent of the people have electricity, 92 per cent have piped water, about 30 per cent have central heating and telephones, and about 93 per cent have TV sets. I mention these figures, which would not be relevant in the case of countries like say, Belgium or Holland, because within living memory (my own, for example), very few people had a car or a telephone, and most homes were rented. Electricity, certainly outside Dublin city, was a bit of a luxury — I remember living as a small boy in a house in Dublin lit by town gas — and central heating was to be found only in hotels, business premises and the few big houses owned by the gentry and the rich.

CULTURE AND LEISURE

Celtic Crosses and Thatched Cottages

I referred above to the extraordinary zeal with which the ancient Celts accepted St Patrick's gift, if that is an appropriate word for it, of Christianity. Throughout the post-Reformation centuries of occupation by the British, and particularly during the period when penal laws were in operation in an effort to stamp out the Roman version of the Christian religion, it was inevitable that the Catholic Church would become identified with the nationalist cause, as it is in Northern Ireland today. For that reason, it is probably true to say that for at least the first fifty years of its existence the Irish state was unduly mesmerized by Maynooth, the principal Catholic seminary, and the country as a whole was, not to put too fine a point on it, totally priest-ridden.

The strict censorship of books and films, the total ban on the sale of contraceptives, the impossibility of getting an abortion or a divorce in Ireland were the first fruits of this domination of the state by the Church. Since the permissive sixties, things have changed a lot, and although 95 per cent of the population are still officially Catholic — in the sense that they have been born into Catholic families — today's young Irish people are no different in their beliefs and their behaviour from the young people in the rest of the Community, despite the fact that it is still not possible to have an abortion or get divorced in Ireland.

And not only has censorship virtually ceased to exist, but television talk programmes in Ireland deal with a staggering variety of sexual, medical and anatomical topics with a candour and indeed often a relish that would take the breath out of a viewer accustomed only to British TV.

Amongst the most outspoken of the participants in these TV debates are the young priests, utterly liberated and fiercely ecumenical. But Ireland is a young country. The percentage of the population aged nineteen and under is 38.9 per cent in Ireland as against 27 per cent in the United Kingdom and 26 per cent in Denmark. And they are being well educated, far more liberally educated than their next-door neighbours in Britain, where standards have to be kept artificially low in order to accommodate the puzzled offspring of the flood of Hindus, Pakistanis, West Indians, West Africans, Cypriots and other immigrants who have been crowding into the United Kingdom since the Wind of Change and the collapse of the British Empire after World War II.

School attendance is compulsory for children in the six to

fifteen age group: in the middle eighties there were nearly 1 million people in full-time education, more than a quarter of the country's total population. First-level schools are state-aided and are run by the parents, teachers and local clergy; most of the funds, including the teachers' salaries, are provided by the government. The present curriculum includes maths, English, Irish, French, history, geography, art, music, crafts and social and environmental studies. There are a few privately run first-level schools which receive no state aid.

Second-level schools include the secondary schools, mostly privately owned, many of them run by various branches of the Church, and the comprehensive and community schools, which are state-owned. There are also Vocational schools to provide technical education, and two universities: the National University of Ireland with constituent colleges in Dublin, Cork, Galway and Maynooth, where St Patrick's College, the old Catholic seminary, has been turned into a co-educational branch of the university; and Trinity College, Dublin, also known as Dublin University, which was founded in 1591.

Ireland has no continuous tradition in the visual arts. The stones at the entrance to the megalithic tombs at Newgrange, County Meath, are decorated with uninteresting arrangements of concentric circles like diagrams of watch springs. The Celtic crosses of the ninth and tenth centuries are decorated with inter-woven patterns of a vaguely geometric character, or figures in bas-relief, also arranged in regular, geometric patterns. The illu-minated Early Christian manuscripts like the famous *Book of Kells* are also very largely composed of endlessly elaborate inter-laced patterns, involuted, interfretted, introverted, clearly the work of uninspired holy men with plenty of time on their hands.

And after that, nothing. The Irish were far too busy over the centuries trying to keep body and soul together to think about putting brush to paper or chisel to stone. And such painters as began to develop in the late nineteenth century all stemmed from British traditions and reflected the tastes of the Anglo-Irish Ascendancy society far more than anything inherently Irish.

Among the best-known Irish portrait painters of this period were Sir William Orpen and Sir John Lavery. The latter's portrait of his wife as the spirit of Ireland, with an Irish landscape complete with round towers in the background, used to grace the back of Irish bank notes from the foundation of the state in 1922 until Ireland succumbed to the current fashion of changing the currency every few years.

The first and only great Irish painter was Jack B. Yeats, brother of the only great Irish poet, W.B. Yeats, and his work was virtually unknown outside Ireland until his death in 1958 because he refused to allow reproductions to be made from the best of his paintings while he was alive.

There is no tradition of Irish architecture. The picturesque thatched cottage of Connemara evolved because it was the simplest and the easiest type of dwelling which could be fashioned from the raw materials locally available, and the dilapidated Georgian glories of Dublin and other Irish cities are a relic of the British occupation.

Early Irish Celtic literature is bewildering and as baffling to most ordinary people as *Beowulf* or the Old Testament, and apart from a few oddities like *The Midnight Court*, a satire on the impotence of Irish husbands and the cupidity of Irish priests, written in the eighteenth century by Brian Merriman, a mathematics master, there was no more Irish literature until Dean Swift, who wrote for an English public. Playwrights like Sheridan and Oscar Wilde and indeed even George Bernard Shaw also depended on English manners and morals for their raw material and English audiences for their livelihood.

The first truly Irish writers – although they wrote in English, they used it like a foreign language – were James Joyce and his secretary and disciple, Samuel Beckett. Sean O'Casey used the Irish Rising of 1916 and the Civil War upon which to peg a quartet of plays which still electrify audiences all over the world, largely because of the way he inserts moments of searing tragedy into scenes of hilarious broad comedy.

Joyce's *Ulysses* made the traditional English novel form obsolete for all time and created a new language based on thought associations, and Beckett challenged everything anybody in the Western world had ever believed: 'It helped to pass the time,' remarks one of the tramps in *Waiting for Godot*, referring to an argument about some aspect of religion. 'It would have passed anyway,' the other replies. After that, what is there to say?

Irish music? The traditional jigs and reels are inexplicably repetitive or richly fascinating, according to the way you feel about such traditional music, and not greatly different in that respect from the traditional music of the Basques or the Japanese. John Field was Irish and may have invented a musical form, the nocturne, which Chopin was later to develop, but Ireland has yet to produce a considerable composer, judged by international standards.

Irish or Anglo-Irish contributors to science include William Rowan Hamilton (1805–65), who invented quaternion calculus; William Parsons (1800–67), who built what the Irish at any rate believe to have been the world's first great telescope; and Ernest T. Walton, who won the Nobel prize for physics in 1951.

There is a firmly rooted notion in the United States that the Irish traditionally eat corned beef and cabbage. Traditionally, the Irish exported most of their beef (or to be more accurate, most of the beef they produced was exported to England), except what little was held back to grace the tables of the gentry. When times were good, the occasional pig might be slaughtered to vary the diet a bit; otherwise it was potatoes and point. A piece of meat was suspended on a string above the table and the diners wiped their potatoes against it, to give them a bit of flavour.

Drisheens, a sort of white pudding made from various un-mentionable parts of the pig, black pudding, made from pig's blood, and crubeens (pigs' feet) are traditionally Irish to the extent that they are eaten in Ireland, though they are eaten elsewhere. Stirrabout (porridge) is probably Scottish in origin; colcannon (mashed potatoes enlivened with chopped greens and onions, and eaten with butter) represents an enterprising effort to vary the potato diet; and potato cakes and boxty (a sort of potato pie, not unlike the English 'bubble and squeak') are also probably Scottish in origin.

Irish stew — which, according to some authorities, originated in Liverpool — is simply an effort to disguise an inferior cut of mutton, or to eke out an insufficient quantity of it, or both, and hardly qualifies for mention as a regional speciality; similar meat stews are made in many countries.

On the other hand, the raw materials in Ireland are very good, and the cooking in Irish restaurants is now well up to internationally acceptable standards. Irish salmon, Dublin Bay prawns (which now come from Galway, because the Irish Sea is hopelessly polluted), oysters and seafood generally are delicious and Irish steaks are every bit as good and as generously proportioned as American ones. But prices are higher, higher even than in London, leaving aside altogether the fact that the punt is usually worth about nine or ten pence less than a pound sterling.

But if Ireland has not produced any gastronomical delight to tickle the palates of the world's gourmets, it has certainly made the grade with a couple of drinks. Guinness, that bitter black stout with its creamy head of foam — a pint of the stuff, showing exactly the correct amount of white collar above the rich black vest, known in some parts of the country as a parish priest — is famous the whole world over.

For about 200 years it has been brewed at St James's Gate in Dublin. It was on sale in London as early as 1794, and by Dickens's time it was well enough known to be featured in an advertisement for the *Pickwick Papers*. As early as 1815 it had reached Belgium; one of Wellington's cavalry officers, wounded at Waterloo, recorded in his diary an unsolicited testimonial to its recuperative properties. By the early eighties about 8 million glasses of Guinness were being drunk every day, in 140 countries, and the advertising slogan, 'Guinness is Good for You', has been translated into twenty-two languages, including Chinese and Esperanto.

It is rarely mixed with anything except champagne, to produce a concoction known as Black Velvet, a great favourite with the racing classes, though the Irish writer Brendan Behan always maintained that 'it wrecked the champagne without doing anything for the Guinness'.

The other Irish drink which made the grade is whiskey. Nobody knows when the art of distilling alcohol from a fermented mixture was discovered — it was known in the time of Aristotle — but the Irish were certainly producing the hard stuff when the troops of Henry II invaded the country in the twelfth century. A large whiskey in Ireland is known as a ball of malt, and a single whiskey is contemptuously referred to as a 'half one'.

There is one other native Irish drink, *potheen* (pronounced potcheen), which roughly corresponds with American moonshine. It is an illicit spirit distilled — usually from potatoes — in parts of the west and south-west of Ireland. It is clear, with a flat taste and a sour smell rather like French *alcohol à bruler*, and it has a kick like slivovitz. If offered it, even by a Civic Guard (as policemen are called in Ireland, and they always seem to have access to the very best of it), resist all blandishments; it is almost lethal.

The Irish claim that all ball games, including golf and croquet as well as tennis and cricket, were developed from the ancient Irish sport of hurling; that Rugby football was introduced to the English public school of that name by a young Tipperary boy and is based on Gaelic football; and for good measure, that the sport of yachting was another Irish innovation.

There is a slight element of truth behind all of these claims, but they need sorting out a bit. There is no doubt that a primitive stick-and-ball game was played in Ireland a very long time ago. There is a reference to hurling in an account of the first battle of Moytura in 1272 BC, before the Celts had even arrived in Ireland, in fact, and most authorities are agreed that the only other serious contender in this area is Persia, where polo probably originated.

The pre-Christian legendary hero, Cuchullain (pronounced Coohullen), was reputed to be an expert with a hurley stick, and there is no doubt that hurling was the principal diversion of the menfolk of Ireland through the centuries. Records of matches go back to the thirteenth century. It is a very wild version of the game of hockey in which more or less anything goes; I think there is a rule which says that you mustn't lift the hurley (a stout, unsprung ashplant) above your head if you are using it to strike a player not actually anywhere near the ball.

Several versions of football were also played in Ireland from the earliest times, in some of which the ball could be bounced, handled and carried for short periods, and it is argued that when William Webb Ellis picked up the football during a match at Rugby School, he was instinctively following the rules of an old Munster version of Gaelic football. Well, perhaps ...

As far as yachting is concerned, probably the oldest yacht club in the world is the Royal Cork, founded in 1720 as the Cork Harbour Water Club by a group of Anglo-Irish sportsmen, and the first one-design class of sailing boats in the world was the Dublin Bay Water Wag, a 14-foot open dinghy; the Wags have been racing in Dublin Bay ever since 1886.

Another traditional Irish sport is road bowling. The bowlers, often carrying heavy bets, hurl small iron balls along lonely country roads. Distance is the principal object of the exercise rather than precise placing, and the aim is to cover a certain number of miles with the minimum number of throws. Although Irish roads are fairly empty by Community standards, the opportunities for playing this game with impunity are, understandably, diminishing.

THE ITALIANS

Not So Much a Country,
More a Performance

ITALY IN PROFILE

Area	301,300 sq km
Population	57,100,000
Density of population	189 per sq km
Women	51.4%
Under 15	19.9%
Over 65	12.8%
Language	Italian, German, French, Slovene, Latin
Religion	Catholic
Labour force	40.2%
Employed in:	
Agriculture	11.2%
Industry	33.6%
Services	55.2%
Women in labour force	33.3%
Unemployment (as % of labour force)	13.8%

Major exports: Machinery and vehicles (33.6%); textiles and clothing (17.6%); chemicals (6.7%); food products (5.2%)

Main customers: EC (53.5%); USA (10.7%); Switzerland (4.5%); Libya (1%)

THE ITALIANS

Most people who have been there have found that arriving in Italy is unlike arriving anywhere else in the world. If it's like anything at all in their experience, it's probably most like their first visit to the theatre.

You cross the frontier and you find the orchestra already tuning up, the curtain trembling a bit because it's just about to rise. And when it rises, when your train bursts out of the Simplon tunnel into the blinding Italian sunshine, it's all there, in front of you. You are suddenly in Italy, a totally different place, even a different state of mind, not so much a country really, more a performance.

As soon as you arrive in Italy, you notice that the sky has become that much bluer, the ruins that much more romantically noble, the women that much more beautiful, really beautiful — *bella figure*, as they say — and even the bit players who for the moment are acting the parts of customs officials and *Carabinieri* and *Guarde Civile* that much more handsome, more evenly tanned, more elegantly uniformed. The vegetation has suddenly become more abundant, the bougainvillaea more dazzling, the cana lilies more extravagantly exuberant.

Italy has always been a magical place, the man-made felicities of Siena and Florence marvellously matching the breathless beauty of the surrounding hills, the fabulous young inhabitants of Venice and Florence and Padua looking exactly as if they had just walked straight out of paintings by Botticelli and Piero della Francesca, the gentle Tuscany landscape looking so strangely familiar. Which can be puzzling until you remember where you have seen it all before; in the background to all those Renaissance nativity scenes and crucifixions and stations of the cross.

When you visited Italy for the first time, it always seemed to be a much simpler, less complicated place than it really is. The people all looked vaguely alike, they all seemed to speak Italian, a beautiful language, they all happily ate pasta three or four times a day, and they all seemed to have an integral unity and a national pride by no means all that common in the rest of the Common Market.

They may have seemed poor, back in the early sixties, by British or American standards, but it didn't seem to bother them. All of these impressions were, of course, quite false.

Then during the eighties you began to notice that the price of meals and drinks and hotel rooms had begun to rise very sharply, and that a lot of the Italian people you met had become very well-dressed and were obviously well-heeled. There were Alfa-Romeos and Lancias and even a few BMWs and Porsches around, and not nearly so many Vespa motor scooters as there had been, and hardly any battered old baby Fiats. What had happened so suddenly?

Well, nothing had happened so suddenly; it had been going on for years, particularly since the beginning of the sixties, but those of us who were accustomed to the old, familiar stereotyped image of Italy had failed to notice the changes that had already taken place.

What had principally happened to change things was the arrival of the Common Market, the European Community. Italy was one of the original six, along with France, Germany and the Benelux countries and the Treaty of Rome was signed in the Italian capital itself. Italy was anxious to get in on it for two reasons; to establish herself finally as a nation state equal in status to Germany and France, and to gain access to the Community's iron and steel.

Nobody who knew Italy well in the fifties, sixties and even seventies would ever have believed for a moment that such a country could benefit greatly from a European single market with open, free competition and binding rules and regulations. The Italians had never accepted any binding rules or regulations about anything, even within their own boundaries, and didn't appear nearly efficient enough to prosper in a free common market.

Everybody knew that Olivetti typewriters and office machines and Fiat motor cars and lorries were among the best in their fields, but how could a nation with so many inherent, internal problems ever hope to compete in a race for material prosperity in a Europe that included not only the other very formidable five but also Britain, Switzerland and the Scandinavian countries.

The Italians were lumbered with one of the most inefficient, unreliable and expensive telephone services in Western Europe; even to call it a service was flattery of a high order. The postal service was slow and expensive. The banking and insurance sectors were more than 50 per cent state-owned and managed to make a profit only because the state saw to it that they did so by carefully controlling the environment in which they operated.

State control ran through the whole fabric of Italian life; and state-controlled industries suffered under the monstrous burden of *lottizzazione*, a system of patronage whereby the best jobs always had to go to political appointees, roughly according to the relative strength of the parties in power, and regardless of the merits of the candidates. Under this system, promotion was automatic and based purely on the number of years served, without any regard whatever for relative ability.

And politically, Italy was a mess. It had staggered along from one coalition crisis to another, bogged down by a combination of circumstances. These included a form of proportional represent- ation which guaranteed government by shaky coalitions; a popula- tion adept in the avoidance of taxation, a practice which they regarded both as an obligation and as a diverting pastime; and the innate political immaturity of the Italian people, many of whom couldn't understand each other's widely divergent dialects and who, until the sixties, may have included up to 5 million illiterates.

Nevertheless, despite all of these and other problems, and despite the fact that Giulio Andreotti's 1991 government was the fiftieth since 1945, they have all been dominated by the Christian Democrats, and most of them were led by a member of that party. Andreotti himself has held a ministerial post in twenty-nine cabinets and has been prime minister seven times.

And throughout this entire period, the country has been dogged by desperate, chronic financial insolvency. The *Cassa per il Mezzogiorno*, Europe's biggest development fund, designed to end, or at least to reduce the desperate imbalance between the prosperous north and the poverty-stricken south, has spent US$17,400 million (actually far more, in real terms, if you take inflation into account) on aid for the 40 per cent of the Italian nation who come from the south, the *mezzogiorno*, the land of the midday sun, an extremely poor area which furnishes Italy with 90 per cent of her total unemployed, as well as with a very high percentage of her not inconsiderable sum total of criminals.

In addition, some US$15–17 million is paid out annually, in the form of welfare benefits and pensions, again mainly to southerners, many of whom openly rejoice in the fact that they have discovered ingenious ways of cheating the system.

It is therefore perhaps not surprising that the government runs a big budget deficit amounting to almost 11 per cent of the total gross domestic product. This deficit is almost entirely composed of overdue interest on past deficits which together amount to roughly 100 per cent of Italy's total GDP. So that on paper at least, there didn't seem to be any way that Italy could ever get out of debt, much less become one of the more prosperous members of the Community.

And yet, this is exactly what has happened. In its 1990 survey of Italy, *The Economist* wrote: 'The greatest surprise of recent years may have been its [Italy's] financial success. For mixed with many an outsider's reverential view of Italy's past civilization has been a somewhat patronizing one about its ability to provide the basic conveniences of modern life: art galleries that may occasionally be open to visitors, airline flights that are not habitually cancelled because of strikes, banks that can cash a traveller's cheque in something less than an hour ... Could such a country, part ramshackle museum, part pastoral time-warp, really be a serious economic force?

'The answer is yes,' *The Economist* concludes. 'This nation is now the fifth biggest economy in the world. Its people are already richer than the British, and it is by no means fanciful to imagine them overtaking the West Germans or the Scandinavians in living standards.'

Italy is both the second oldest and also the second newest country in the Community.

The second oldest after Greece, because both Greek and Etruscan civilizations flourished there long before a couple of communities between the mouth of the Tiber and the Sabine Hills were combined in the eighth century BC to form the Roman capital of the Latin world.

And the second newest because Italian unity was not achieved until 1870, a year before Germany. It is true that Ireland did not acquire even the partial independence from Britain which she now enjoys, if that's the word, until 1922, but the Irish had been fighting for their freedom on and off for 700 years and had always thought of themselves as a distinct and different nation.

Not so the Italians. The assorted collection of kingdoms, duchies, principalities, papal states, republics and city-states which made up Italy until nearly a century and a quarter ago had very little in common, and until the 1850s at the earliest, very little desire whatever to be united; indeed many people would argue that some of them still have no burning desire to remain part of a united Italy.

There were deeper and wider gulfs between different areas of Italy than existed inside any of the other member-states or even, for that matter, between any two of them.

The people from the rich industrial northern part of Italy hate and despise the people from the poor southern half, whom they have been forced to subsidize, and to import into their areas to work in their factories. During the industrial boom, cities such as Turin doubled in size, but there were never nearly enough houses, hospitals or schools to cope with the influx of *terroni* as they are scathingly called. The results were what are usually euphemistically termed 'inner city problems', a phrase that includes over-crowding, graffiti, mugging, drug-trafficking and general lawlessness. The word *terroni* means earth-people, peasants really, but with a much more pejorative flavour than the more usual term, *contadini*.

And the worst feature of it all to the hard-working, hard-headed northerners was the fact that the *terroni*, so far from showing the slightest sign of gratitude for all the jobs and the aid and the welfare benefits, seemed instead to resent the northerners for being in a position to help them. They constantly criticized the government for maladministration of the southern states, though one of the root causes of that maladministration was the poor quality of the civil service. And the civil servants and administrators have always been mainly drawn from the ranks of the southerners who mostly prefer safe steady jobs working for the state to precarious whiz-kid careers in industry which call for enterprise, ambition and energy.

Furthermore the southerners are also forever accusing the northern industrialists of getting government grants ostensibly in order to set up factories in the south to provide employment there, but actually with the intention of going bankrupt and taking their heavily subsidized plant back up north again, to restart the new industries under different names.

For their part, the people of the south regard themselves as a separate nation, which indeed in a sense they are; the Neapolitans in particular think back nostalgically to the eighteenth century when Naples was the third largest city in Europe, after Paris and Vienna.

And there are signs that the split may become more serious. With the arrival of automated manufacturing machinery, the northern industrialists no longer need vast workforces for their factories and they would be very much better off if they didn't have to bear the cost of subsidizing the *terroni*. An indication that this line of thinking is gaining support was the success in the 1990 local elections of the Lombardy League, a right-wing group that tends to favour closer consolidation between northern Italy and the industrial northern countries of Europe accompanied by, if necessary, a complete break with the south.

Despite the imminent approach of January 1993, many of Italy's industries are, like the state-owned banks and insurance companies, still operating in a carefully controlled and protected environment. In a survey on Italy published in December 1990 in the London *Independent*, Isabel Hilton claimed that many would-be foreign entrepreneurs have been discouraged from entering the Italian market by 'a portfolio of bureaucratic obstacles ... To try to open a foreign-owned business in Italy is to enter a thicket from which few emerge with the original purpose intact, let alone fulfilled. So far, such tactics have proved a sufficient disincentive to foreign competition.

'They are combined,' she goes on, 'with the other Italian tactic of adopting EC legislation on such issues as state aid to industry, but somehow failing to implement it, a source of some resentment among Italy's northern partners.

'On the other hand, there is a positive side to Italian ingenuity that could help the country through the challenge of the 1990s ... the opening up of Central and Eastern Europe presents a set of opportunities unlikely to be ignored.

'On the diplomatic front, Italy has responded to the events of 1989 with a flexibility which, if reflected in business dealings, should indicate that the country is well placed to exploit the new Central European markets.'

All a very far cry from *The Economist*'s 'gondoliers, extrovert waiters, chaotic World Cup hosts and black-clad, donkey-borne peasant women straight from central casting' and indeed, from the Dolce Vita of Fellini's Rome.

LAND AND PEOPLE

An Entrance to Hell

Italy is shaped a bit like a boot jutting out from Europe into the Mediterranean with Palermo as the toe and Otranto as the heel. It has an area of 301,300 square kilometres, which includes two large islands: Sicily (25,709 square kilometres), at the toe of Italy, and Sardinia (24,089 square kilometres), just south of Corsica and about halfway between Genoa and the coast of Tunisia in North Africa. It extends for 1,300 kilometres from north to south, and its 7,500 kilometre coastline is washed by the waters of four inner seas: the Ligurian, Tyrrhenian, Ionian and Adriatic. It has land borders with France, Switzerland, Austria and Yugoslavia.

About 80 per cent of the total land area consists of hills and mountains, and its peaks include a segment of Europe's highest mountain, Mont Blanc (4,807 metres), a slice of the Matterhorn (4,477 metres), and its own Monte Rosa (4,634 metres), all in the Alps.

Other mountain ranges include the Appenines, running right down the whole length of the peninsula from Genoa to Palermo, with peaks of around 2,000 metres, and the spectacular Dolomites between Venice and the Austrian frontier.

One of the more restless faults in the crust of the earth coincides roughly with the Italian coast between Naples and Sicily, and earthquakes and volcanic eruptions have occurred at irregular and unpredictable intervals. The most famous earthquake partially destroyed the Roman city of Pompeii in AD 62, and while rebuilding was in progress, an eruption of nearby Mount Vesuvius in 79 buried the city and its inhabitants under six or seven metres of cinders and ash and petrified nearby Herculaneum. Vesuvius is still smoking away sullenly, as are several other volcanoes in the area, including Mount Etna and Stromboli, near Sicily, and there was a severe earthquake near Eboli as recently as 1980.

Italy's longest river is the Po (652 kilometres), which rises in the Alps and flows into the Adriatic through a huge triangular-shaped alluvial plain between Milan, Venice and Bologna, creating the most fertile area in the country and comprising two-thirds of all its arable land.

The rivers rising in the Appenines include the Arno, which flows through Florence, and the Tiber, on the banks of which Rome was built. About 58 per cent of the land surface is cultivated and about 20 per cent of it is under afforestation.

The climate is officially Mediterranean, but because the country is so mountainous, it has one of the most extreme and varied climates in Europe. In winter Venice can be as bleak as London, though it's nearly as far south as Nice, and Turin can be even colder than Copenhagen.

The population now numbers about 57,100,000, which makes it the most densely populated place in Europe after Germany and the Benelux countries, with an average density of 189 people per square kilometre as against 101 per square kilometre in neighbouring France. Here as elsewhere in Europe a population explosion combined with the general flight from the land into urban areas led to massive emigration, mostly to the United States, around the turn of the century. Between 1900 and 1910, some 600,000 Italians emigrated every year. Now the figure has settled down to about 120,000 a year.

Roughly 72 per cent of the population live in urbanized areas. Rome has a population of 2,830,000, Milan has 1,520,000 inhabitants and Naples 1,211,000. Florence has 435,000 people and Venice only 340,000.

The official language is Italian, but German is spoken in the area around the Brenner Pass which Italy gained from Austria after World War I and Slovene is spoken in the area around Trieste. In addition, the whole of Italy is riddled with dialects, descending both from Latin and Greek, and influenced by the languages of all the invaders over the centuries.

I suspect that most of the language problems will be resolved within a generation. Everybody in Italy now watches TV which uses standard (Tuscany) Italian, and so everyone will soon speak standard Italian and the dialects will disappear.

Italy has few mineral resources; some sulphur in Sicily, bauxite and lead ore in the south, and the world-famous marbles of Carrera. It provides about a third of the world's supply of mercury. It also produces a considerable amount of hydro-electric power from the lakes and rivers in the Alps.

A vein of oil was struck near Cortemaggiore in the Po Valley in 1949, and more oil was discovered in Sicily in 1953, as well as some natural gas at Lodi and near Ferrara. Nevertheless, Italy remains 83.9 per cent dependent upon imports for her energy supplies.

Sardinia has many traces of prehistoric human settlements, called *nuraghi*, some of which date back to before 2000 BC and were built of stone without any form of mortar. Thought to be watchtowers, there are over 7,000 of them.

Before the Etruscans and the Greeks arrived in the area, the whole of Italy was occupied by two races of people: the Ligurians, who also occupied parts of Gaul and the Iberian Peninsula, and the Sabellines, who were also probably aboriginal and came down from settlements they had established in the foothills of the Appenines. They were known as the Italic tribes and were among the peoples from whom the Roman civilization was created; and it seems likely that the name *Italia* (Italy) came from these Italic tribes, though some authorities believe it came from a Greek form of the word Vitelia, the land of the calves.

The Phoenicians, a Semitic seafaring race originally from coastal towns like Tyre and Sidon in what is now Syria, had settled in Carthage and set up trading posts all around the Mediterranean by the sixth and seventh centuries BC, and around 800 BC the Greeks founded several colonies on the coast of Sicily and in southern Italy.

The entire collection of Greek settlements was known as *Magna Graecia*, and some of the finest remains of Greek temples in the Mediterranean are to be found in southern Italy — Paestum near Salerno, for example, and those at Syracuse and Agrigento in Sicily.

The shores of southern Italy and Sicily held a strange fascination for the ancient Greeks, possibly because they represented the outer limits of their known world. Many places in Italy feature in a number of the ancient Greek legends: to take just one example, the particular entrance to Hades which Orpheus used when he went down to rescue Eurydice was situated at Lake Averna, near Naples.

Greek civilization in Italy reached its zenith during the fifth century BC, the period when Pericles was establishing Athens as the cultural and artistic capital of the Greek world, and the Parthenon was being built. The Greeks introduced the vine and the olive to the Italians, and the Romans later brought them to Gaul (France) and Britain.

Pythagoras, the Greek mathematician, lived in Sicily; so did Archimedes, who discovered the principle of water displacement in his bath.

In the meantime, from the eighth century BC onwards, the Etruscans — who may have been natives of the area, or could have come from Lydia in Asia Minor — were building a civilization between the Arno and the Tiber which spread into a federation of twelve city-states known as Etruria and included the island of Elba.

They worked iron, copper and silver mines in Elba, were skilled artisans and traded widely all over the western Mediterranean. They had basically the same gods and beliefs as the Greeks, but maintained some peculiar practices (as, for example, their system of divining the future by studying the entrails of animals) which later emerged in the Roman culture, along with their passion for bloodthirsty games in the arena.

Both the Greeks and the Etruscans continued to prosper until the Roman conquest at the end of the third century BC.

According to legend, Romulus had founded the city of Rome in 753 BC from nearby settlements of Latins, Etruscans and Sabines; the city-state was probably initially an Etruscan enterprise, and certainly its first dynasty, the Tarquins, were Etruscans. But before long the newly created Roman nation had taken over, ejected the Tarquins and turned the city-state into a republic with two consuls, elected every year. It later became an empire, ruled by a succession of Caesars, a word which has survived almost into our own times as Kaiser in Germany and Tsar in Russia.

It is even possible, as some historians have suggested, that some discontented refugees from Greece, seeking refuge in a different land after the fall of Troy, may have settled in the area and imported the idea of establishing a new civilization centred on this town on the Tiber. All we know for certain is that Rome became a city which extended the domination of the imperial Roman eagle first all over what is now Italy and then all over the known world from the Scottish border to the Atlas Mountains in North Africa, and from Gibraltar to Arabia.

It lasted until the fifth century AD, when torn apart by civil wars and harried by Huns and other barbarians from east of the Danube, Rome fell to Alaric, King of the Visigoths. The Roman Empire was brought to a formal end in 456 with the deposition of the Emperor Romulus Augustus by Oadacer, chief of the barbarian troops.

It was the end of the story of the Romans and the beginning of the story of the Italians.

HISTORICAL PERSPECTIVE

Republics and City-states

By the time the Roman Empire finally collapsed, Europe had become so accustomed, over the centuries, to the idea of looking towards the city of Rome for authority that the habit persisted for a long time after the barbarians arrived. And in the absence of any other centralized governing power the Popes of Rome, gradually and without any overt temporal claims, began to assume the mantle of the Roman Caesars.

During the sixth century, the Lombards, a Germanic tribe from around the Elbe, moved into Italy, and by the beginning of the seventh century, had conquered most of the country apart from Rome, Ravenna, Naples and the south. But they were a barbaric tribal people and never really attempted to establish any strong centralized government.

When in 774 Rome appealed to the Franks for protection, Charlemagne marched into Italy, declared himself king of Lombardy, and forced the Lombards to surrender twenty-two of their city-states around and near Rome to the Pope. These became the Papal States.

Some twenty-five years later, while Charlemagne was attending

Mass in the Lateran Palace in Rome on Christmas Day, 800, Pope Leo III, without any warning, placed a crown on his head and hailed him as Caesar Augustus. It seems probable that the Pope hoped by this action to forge a link between the already central- ized Church and the strongest secular power in Europe at that period, and felt that this arrangement might prove more accept- able if it took the form of some kind of revival of the old Roman empire of the west. He probably also thought that by this action he was establishing the principle that the crown of this new Roman Empire was the Pope's to bestow or withhold at his plea- sure.

However, on Charlemagne's death, there was a dispute among his grandsons over the succession, and the crown of Caesar Augustus passed from one unworthy head to another until 962 when Pope John XII decided to bestow it upon Otto I of West Francia, the area occupied by the Germanic tribes, who was also king both of Lombardy and Saxony and the most formidable of the many rulers in Western Europe at the time.

In the process he created the unlikely institution known as the Holy Roman Empire of the German Nation which, against all odds, survived until the time of Napoleon.

In the sixth century an Arab camel-driver called Mohammed had started to preach a new religion which soon spread like wildfire throughout the Arab world. The new Muslim religion was not unlike Christianity in its general tenets, but had one big differ- ence: Muslims who died fighting the enemy (i.e. anybody with different religious views) were *guaranteed* a place in the Muslim heaven which offered worldly delights not always readily available to Muslims on earth.

By the end of the eighth century, Mohammed's followers, determined to secure those privileged places in heaven, had hurled themselves on the Mediterranean world with such ferocity that they had soon won North Africa, Egypt, Palestine and Syria from the Constantinople-based Roman empire of the east. Jerusalem was now in Arab hands, and Constantinople was in danger.

When the Byzantine Emperor, Michael VII, appealed to Rome for assistance, Pope Urban II, a Frenchman, launched the crusades, calling on French knights in particular and Christians in general to go out to the Holy Land to reclaim the Holy Sepulchre and other sacred sites from the heathens.

In all, four crusades were launched, and various territories in the Holy Land and in the Byzantine Empire changed hands several times. But from Italy's point of view, the most important feature of the crusades was that after the first two disastrous expeditions had proved that the overland route was both too long and too dangerous, subsequent crusades travelled overland only as far as Italy and the remainder of the way by sea.

A good deal of this very considerable traffic in men and materials was handled by the seafaring city-state of Venice. The latter not only made a fortune from it, but also allowed some of the crusading knights to pay for their passages in kind, by doing a bit of fighting en route, on Venice's behalf. In this way Venice greatly increased her territories along the Adriatic coast, in Greece and in the Aegean. By this time a troop of Norman knights, on their way back from the Holy Land, had established a combined Norman-Arab settlement in Sicily, and the Muslims were ravaging the south of Italy.

The Pope's credibility as Saint Peter's direct successor on earth and Rome's status as the natural capital of the Western world were both greatly weakened by what was called the Great Schism; a period of about thirty years during which there were two rival popes, one reigning from Rome and another from Avignon in France, both claiming the direct succession from St Peter and both freely excommunicating each other and their adherents as heretics.

The immediate effect was a decline in papal power and in the status of the Holy Roman Emperor as well as in that of the city of Rome. It was countered by a corresponding growth in the power of the commercial and secular city-states, run by merchants now sufficiently prosperous to make agreements over the heads of both the bishops and the feudal *seigneurs*; in Italy these included Genoa, Florence, Mantua, Milan, Modena and Venice, and during one period there were as many as 300 of them, frequently at one another's throats.

It was inevitable that sooner or later one of these city-states would invite one of the European great powers to come to Italy to intervene in settling its differences with a rival. In 1492, the year an Italian from Genoa discovered America, the Duke of Milan, then at war with Naples, suggested to Charles VIII of France that the French might like to renew their ancient claim to the throne of Naples — since almost all of the European royal families were closely related, most of the monarchs could lay some sort of a legitimate claim to almost any of the other thrones. It is hard to see what Charles VIII hoped to gain from the exercise, but two years later he invaded Italy with an army of about 25,000 men including German and Swiss mercenaries. He landed at Genoa, marched through Florence and Rome, and eventually took Naples.

Hearing that the Pope, Florence and Venice, with some other dukedoms and principalities, had managed to cobble together some sort of a league of Italian city-states and form an army to free Italy from foreign occupation — this was the last united attempt to do so for many years — the French king decided to return home.

His army had by this time been reduced to about 10,000 fighting men as a result of the combined effects of the dolce vita, desertion, syphilis and other ills to which invading armies are prone. At Fornovo in northern Italy, on 6 July 1495, he was confronted by an army of some 30,000 fresh, well-armed Italian troops.

But things went hopelessly wrong for the Italians, and after less than an hour of confused butchery, Charles managed to escape back over the Alps to France with most of what was left of his army intact.

The lesson — that Italy was clearly not able to defend itself against foreign invasion — was one that was not lost on the other European powers, and as Luigi Barzini put it in *The Italians* (London: Hamish Hamilton, 1964): 'Practically all the available armies in Europe came to Italy in the thirty-odd years after 1495. The Austrians, the Germans, the Burgundians, the French, the Flemish, the Spanish, the Hungarians and sundry others marched down the Alps or landed from their ships. Even the Swiss abandoned their peaceful valleys and their prosperous cows for the Italian battlefields ... The foreigners lost or won in turn. The Italians always lost.'

Also, the Portuguese and Spanish voyages of discovery during the fifteenth century had led to shifts in the world's trade routes which further weakened Italy. From then on for almost four centuries, the whole country was reduced to the level of a mere pawn in the power struggles between the great nations and influential dynasties and dukedoms of Europe.

In 1527, Rome was attacked by a mixed army of 30,000 men, led by the Constable of Bourbon, in the service of the Spanish Hapsburg Emperor, Charles V. It wasn't an army; it was a rabble of Spanish soldiers, German and Swiss and even Italian mercenaries who were not paid, but were expected to reimburse themselves by exacting levies and looting. For nine months Rome was subjected to an orgy of spoilage, torture, rape and general vandalism; and the French and Italian troops who were attempting to repel the invasion behaved no better than the invading army.

Charles V emerged as clear victor; and for the next century and a half Italy lived under the shadow of Spain. The French renewed their challenge again during the reign of Louis XIV, but France was defeated by Austria in the War of the Spanish Succession and, in the end, Italy was divided between France, Spain and Austria. The latter was a new European power which had grown out of the Holy Roman Empire of the German Nation after the powerful Hapsburg family had succeeded in buying and bribing and marrying their way into the lineage.

Victor Amadeus of the House of Savoy became King of Sicily in 1713, and in 1720 managed to persuade the Duke of Savoy to swop Sicily with him for the Kingdom of Sardinia, which also included Piedmont on the mainland.

In 1796, Napoleon crossed the Alps, captured Nice and Savoy, and occupied northern Italy. Supported by Italian liberals fired by the success of the French Revolution, he wiped out five Austrian armies sent down into Italy to defend Austrian interests there, and took over Milan, Genoa, the Papal States and Sicily.

After Napoleon's downfall, the Congress of Vienna restored Sardinia and Piedmont to the House of Savoy (the strongest of the Italian minor dynasties) and incorporated Genoa into that kingdom. Venice and Milan were handed over to Austria; and the Austrian territories in northern Italy became the Austrian Kingdom of Lombardy-Veneto. Various members of the Hapsburg family were given principalities in Tuscany, Parma and Modena, and the Pope was officially recognized as the sovereign of all the possessions of the Holy See. The Kingdoms of Naples and Sicily were combined as one single kingdom, under the French Bourbon King Frederick IV, who now became Frederick I of the Two Sicilies.

The only part of the country with the interests of a united Italy at heart in the early nineteenth century was the Kingdom of Sardinia, now under Victor Emmanuel I. And it was here, in Piedmont and Genoa, that a new movement known as 'Young Italy' began to focus Italian aspirations on a demand for national independence and unity, the *Risorgimento*. The Italian intellectuals and middle-class professionals and businessmen now began to form themselves into secret societies like the *carbonari* and to plot against their foreign rulers.

There were revolutions in Naples in 1820, in Piedmont in 1821, and in the Papal States in 1831, during which the revolutionary red white and green flag of Italy was flown for the first time.

Mazzini and Garibaldi were the leading nationalist republican agitators when in 1848 the whole of Italy from Venice to Sicily rose in a general insurrection against the Austrians. The rebels set up provisional republics in Florence and Venice, and on the accession of Victor Emmanuel II, Cavour, Prime Minister of the Kingdom of Sardinia, realizing that foreign aid would be needed to achieve unity, joined France and Britain in the Crimean War against Russia.

In 1858, Cavour entered into an alliance with Napoleon III of

France: France agreed to rid Italy of the Austrians, in return for Nice and Savoy.

In 1859, France and Piedmont (the Kingdom of Sardinia) went to war with Austria, and the next year the Kingdom of Sardinia annexed Tuscany, Parma and Modena on behalf of the new nation. In the same year, Garibaldi and his Thousand Red Shirts (another revolutionary group) captured Sicily and Naples which were soon added to the territories of the new nation, still being assembled and organized from Piedmont and Sardinia, initially with Turin as its capital. By September 1860, the Papal States had been annexed, and apart from the city of Rome and its immediate surroundings, Italy was now free and united.

The first parliament of the new united Italy met in Turin in February 1861 and included representatives from all the annexed territories. Victor Emmanuel II of Sardinia was proclaimed King of Italy in March, and for a period Florence became Italy's provisional capital.

The Pope's claim to territorial sovereignty in and around the Vatican was supported by all the Catholic powers in Europe, particularly France, which still maintained an army in Rome.

Cavour had died in 1861, and in 1862 Garibaldi and his volunteers gathered in Palermo and decided to march on Rome. After several attempts, the newly formed Italian army succeeded in breaching the walls of Rome on 20 September 1870. In fact Garibaldi and his Red Shirts were forced to surrender shortly after they made the breach in the walls, and it was only as a by-product of the Franco-Prussian War, which resulted in the fall of Napoleon III and the withdrawal of all French troops from Rome, that Victor Emmanuel was able to annex the city and imprison Pope Pius IX in a room in the Vatican.

In October 1870, a plebiscite among the Roman citizens resulted in an overwhelming victory for the annexation of Rome by the Kingdom of Italy. Rome became the capital city of the new nation in July 1871.

To allay worldwide Catholic fears, the Pope was granted full sovereignty over the Vatican and Lateran palaces, personal inviolability, and a state pension for life. Despite these concessions,

Pope Pius IX was not at all pleased with the arrangement, and until the early years of the twentieth century all the members of the successive Italian governments, as well as all the people who had voted for them, were automatically excommunicated.

COLONIAL CONNECTIONS

The Abyssinian Adventure

You would have thought that the Italians, having so lately and with such difficulty managed to achieve unity and independence, would have settled down to putting their own house in order before setting off in search of colonies to conquer, but that was not the way the Europeans thought at the end of the nineteenth century. Any self-respecting nation entitled to call itself that, had to have an overseas empire.

And so in 1882, twelve years after Rome was occupied by the troops from Piedmont, Italy was signing a Triple Alliance with Germany and Austria to mark her arrival upon the international scene as the sixth great power in Europe. Three years after that, the new Italian army had started to claw for footholds in North Africa, in Eritrea and on the Somali coast, and to probe into Ethiopia and along the tributaries of the Blue Nile. By 1890, the Italian Crown Colony of Eritrea had been established and Italian Somaliland occupied; the Italians also had a naval station at Asab Bay on the Red Sea.

Expansion into Tunisia, where the Italians formed the largest body of European immigrants, had been firmly discouraged by the French. The Emperor of Abyssinia (now Ethiopia), Menelik II, initially accepted the Italian presence in his territory, even signing a sort of mutual non-aggression treaty with the Italians. Later, Menelik had second thoughts about the whole situation, and in 1896 at Adowa, his soldiers settled the matter by easily routing a fairly considerable Italian force.

In the early 1900s, a secret understanding was reached between France and Italy by which the latter would be given a free hand in Libya in return for Italian acquiescence in French designs on Morocco. Italy attacked Turkey in 1911 and added the entire Mediterranean coast of Libya, then part of the Ottoman Empire, to her own growing empire, and occupied the Dodecanese Islands, also part of the Ottoman Empire. This action did not enjoy much popular support; and one of those strongly against it was the young secretary of the Italian Socialist Party in Forli, Benito Mussolini.

The Austro-Hungarian Empire's declaration of war on Serbia in 1914 was made without consulting Italy. The Italians took the view that this relieved them of any obligations to Germany and Austria under the Triple Alliance, and allowed them to consider the opportunities which the war offered for settling old scores with Austria while at the same time gaining the support of Britain and France for any post-war colonial adventures they might contemplate.

Not all Italians were in favour of intervention. Mussolini was, and said so in a new newspaper he had started, the *Popolo d'Italia*. So was Gabriele d'Annunzio, World War I air ace, poet and politician, who for a time was a political force in Italy. And so, after the Allies had secretly offered Italy large territorial slices of Austrian territory after the war, were the king and the government. But Italy did not enter the war until May 1915, and then only against the Austro-Hungarian Empire. War was not declared on Germany until a year later.

A badly commanded and poorly equipped Italian army took on the Austrians. After an initial and disastrous battle at Caporetto, it took the Italians over two years to recover sufficiently to defeat the Austrians finally at Vittorio Veneto, in the last year of the war, at an enormous cost in men and *matériel*.

The Italians fared relatively badly during the post-war settlement at Versailles too. They came away from the conference with Trieste, Trentino (an area in the South Tyrol extending down as far as the Brenner Pass), and Istria. These were poor consolation prizes for a country that had mobilized more men than Britain (39 million as against Britain's 36 million), had lost half a million of them, and had run up a disastrous war debt.

In the elections of 1919, proportional representation was used for the first time. The system enabled the Socialists — whose ranks included 156 Marxist Revolutionaries — to emerge as the largest party in the Chamber of Deputies. A new party which failed to make any appearance in the chamber — it had achieved very dismal results at the polls — was the right-wing Fascist Party, formed by the renegade Socialist Benito Mussolini in March 1919.

However, a combination of factors, among them rising inflation and unemployment, serious dissatisfaction with the outcome of the Versailles conference, the encouragement by Socialist leaders of strikes and the occupation of factories, all added up to a growing fear of the Communist menace and had the effect of scaring the daylights out of the property-owning classes. For their own protection, and for the sake — as they mistakenly believed — of stability and security, they turned increasingly to Mussolini's right-wing Fascist Party. This party had its own *squadre* (squads of thugs, like Hitler's Brownshirts) who were always ready to go out into the streets and do something positive about the feared and dreaded Reds.

In an election in May 1921, Mussolini and thirty-four members of his Fascist Party were elected. He immediately stepped up his appeal to the right, watering down his innate anti-clericalism and abandoning his republican stance in favour of ostensible support for the monarchy.

By 1922, the Fascists had become a tough, well-equipped, blackshirted army, ready to march on Rome, which they did in 1922. The terrified Prime Minister, Luigi Facta, pleaded with the king to declare martial law but the latter refused, fearing a civil war. And when Facta resigned the king invited Mussolini, then in Milan, to form a government.

Mussolini's regime began in what appeared to be a fairly harmless way. Apart from the Communists, all the other political parties were represented in the Cabinet: Mussolini himself was content for the moment to take only the folios of the Ministries of the Interior and of Foreign Affairs, though he very soon took over the police and local government and set up his own secret police force. His next move was to introduce an electoral reform bill which automatically gave the party with the largest majority in the Chamber of Deputies two-thirds of the total vote in that house.

When Giacomo Matteoti, a Socialist leader who had dared to protest against outrages during the 1924 election campaign, was murdered by Fascist thugs, the opposition, unable to defeat the government, decided to withdraw, hoping in this way to force the government to resign.

When they didn't, the king refused to take any action until parliament succeeded in securing a vote of no confidence which was impossible under the new electoral laws. Mussolini then disbanded all the opposition parties on the grounds that they had forfeited their seats by withdrawing from parliament and announced a one-party state in which all opposition would be suppressed. Henceforward the country, though remaining a kingdom under Victor Emmanuel III, would be run as a dictator-ship by the Fascist Party and its *Duce* (or leader), Mussolini.

In 1926, Mussolini opened negotiations to heal the breach with the Papacy. A treaty signed in the Lateran Palace in 1929 gave sovereign independence to a small (45 hectares) Vatican State, declared Catholicism to be Italy's sole and official religion, and allowed the Church's views on marriage and other family matters to prevail. Religious instruction was made compulsory at school, and the Papacy received financial compensation for the loss of the Papal States.

Having established his own concept of a new Fascist Imperial Rome, Mussolini began to look around for an empire over which he could preside. He decided first to assuage the disgrace of Adowa by attacking Abyssinia in 1935, in defiance of the League of Nations. In May 1936, the Emperor Haile Selassie fled from Abyssinia to settle in Bath in England, and Mussolini proclaimed the foundation of a new Roman empire: Abyssinia, Eritrea and Italian Somaliland were reorganized into one single unit, Italian East Africa. In the same year, he settled his earlier differences with Adolf Hitler, which had arisen over his efforts to force the German-speaking population of the Tyrol to speak Italian, and together they formed the Rome–Berlin Axis.

When his fellow Fascist General Francisco Franco started a

civil war against the Spanish Republican government in July 1936 and appealed for help, Mussolini responded eagerly, sending Italian soldiers to fight for Franco as 'volunteers'. Mussolini's new ally Hitler also responded enthusiastically to Franco's call for help against the left, anxious to try out his new dive-bombing techniques in preparation for the war with Britain and France that was now clearly coming.

The Spanish Civil War dragged on for nearly three years and drained Italy's never very formidable resources, so that when Hitler started World War II with his attack on Poland in September 1939, Italy remained resolutely neutral until 1940, when it became clear that France was just about to collapse. Then, seeing a chance of getting his hands on a slice of French territory, Mussolini hurriedly declared war on the Allies.

But Italy had no heart in the war; on the contrary, there was a strong body of public opinion against it and against the Germans. Also, the Allied armies proved a very different proposition from the Abyssinians, and by 1943 Mussolini's forces were losing on all fronts, except in Greece where German troops had been sent in to stiffen the resolve of the Italians.

There were strikes and peace demonstrations all over Italy, and in July 1943, after the Allied landings in Sicily, when the Fascist Grand Council, by now far more afraid of the Allies than they were of Mussolini, demanded his resignation, the king dismissed him and had him arrested. Fascism was finally abandoned, and all Italy rejoiced.

In September, Italy signed an armistice with the Allies, and although Mussolini was rescued by the Germans to set up a neo-Fascist Italian republic at Salo on Lake Garda, it wasn't long before it was all over, and Mussolini and his mistress were hanging from their heels outside a petrol station in Milan.

In a referendum in June 1946, the monarchy was defeated by 12 million votes to 10 million, and Umberto II, who had succeeded his father Victor Emmanuel III that year, went into exile. A democratic election, held at the same time, put de Gaspari's Christian Democrats in charge of the new Republic of Italy.

DEVELOPMENT DIRECTIONS

Europe's Japanese

The Allies made peace with Italy formally in 1947. The African colonies were all lost, but the Brenner frontier south of the Tyrol was preserved and Trieste, which became a free territory under the United Nations, reverted to Italy in 1954.

Throughout the centuries, Italy's main industry had always been agriculture. As late as the thirties, agriculture employed nearly half of the workforce and accounted for about as much production as all of Italy's industries combined: now agriculture employs only 11 per cent of the labour force as against the 34 per cent who work in industry and the 55 per cent who work in the service industries, and agriculture's share in the GDP is only 5.2 per cent as against industry's 39 per cent.

Cereals — principally wheat but also corn and rice — are the main crops. Italian farms produce about two-thirds of the cereals consumed by the Italians. Grapes, citrus fruit, olives and almonds are also widely grown, as well as industrial crops like sugar beet, hemp and flax. Italy is among the world's top producers of olive oil and wine, and rears about three-quarters of the beef and veal consumed in the country.

Italy's farms still tend to be very small; as recently as 1982 there were over 3 million of them, some as small as one hectare, and only 120,000 had over 20 hectares. With the help of Community funding, efforts are now being made to introduce technical training, co-operative processing and marketing, soil conservation and more scientific irrigation, and it seems likely that Italian farming in the future will develop along more or less the same lines as in France and the United Kingdom.

Between 1954 and 1979 about 4 million agricultural workers left the land, a large proportion of them moving from the south to the industrial areas around Milan and Turin.

Despite Italy's unusually long coastline (a total of 7,500 kilometres) fishing is almost entirely local and very small-scale, with total catches less than half of France's.

At the time of the *Risorgimento*, although the country lacked the raw materials for an industrial revolution — coal and iron — the population was eager and quick to acquire the skills required for industrialization.

From the turn of the century, modern industrial plants were set up in Milan, Turin and Genoa. Textile and chemical industries were established, an electric power network was installed, and a group of industrialists set up the first motor car assembly plant, Fiat (*Fabbrica Italiani Automobilia Torino*) in Turin in 1899.

The first fifteen years of the twentieth century were remarkably prosperous. Although half a million people emigrated annually, mainly to the United States, jobs in the new factories absorbed a large part of the rapidly growing population, and a number of new industries were set up, some of which are still flourishing. Apart from Fiat, now the sixth largest automobile company in the world, these include Pirelli (motor tyres), Olivetti (typewriters and office machines), Vespa and Lambretta (motor scooters), Guzzi (motor-cycles) and Necchi (sewing machines).

Italy was particularly well-placed to undertake large-scale long-term planning after World War II with American aid totalling US$2.4 billion, and an industrial structure inherited from the Fascist regime in which the state already played a big part. State participation in industry was channelled through IRI (*Istituto per la Ricostruzione Industriale*) a state-controlled holding company founded during the world depression which subsequently gained control of most of Italy's iron and steel, cement, shipbuilding and machinery industries as well as taking over corporations involved in shipping, aviation, road-building and telecommunications. IRI was thus in a position to research and plan on a broad national basis.

After the war, IRI built a new steel plant at Taranto in the *mezzogiorno*, founded Alfasud — a branch of the state-owned Alfa-Romeo car manufacturers — near Naples, and sponsored the extension of the splendid autostrada network which had been started by Mussolini, who built motorways for the same reason that Hitler built his autobahn system, in order to be able to deploy his troops rapidly in the event of war.

By the eighties, IRI had provided about 40 per cent of the new jobs which had been created in the *mezzogiorno*. It also controlled Alitalia, the national airline, and the three official TV channels.

In 1953, ENI (*Ente Nationale degli Idrocarburi*) another state-sponsored body, was formed to investigate and control the exploration and utilization of oil and other primary energy sources. It took over AGIP (*Azienda Generale Italiana di Petroli*) the state-owned petroleum company, and branched out in many directions, including oil refining and petro-chemical manufacturing, as well as prospecting for oil on behalf of foreign governments. AGIP was soon joined by AGIP Nucleare, a company responsible for the development of nuclear power.

Enrico Mattei, initially chief engineer of AGIP and the man largely responsible for the discovery of oil and natural gas in the Po Valley in 1949 and the discovery of oil in Sicily in 1953, became chief of ENI and greatly extended its activities; one of its offshoots mined and drilled for oil, conducted research, and refined and distributed oil in Italy.

In 1957, Mattei succeeded in winning the concession to survey and prospect for oil in Egypt and Iran by offering them a much more favourable deal than any of the big American oil companies. In this way he very soon established a special relationship with a large part of the Arab world, including Morocco, Tunisia and Libya, and in 1959 he made an agreement to import Russian crude oil in return for Italian technology and equipment. He was killed in an air accident in 1962, just after the Italian economy had started to boom, due in no small part to his energy and ingenuity.

'It was in 1956 that it became evident that the Italian economy was beginning to boom,' writes Elizabeth Wiskemann in *Italy since 1945* (London: Macmillan, 1971). 'This was the year when the Italians got the commission to build the Kariba dam in Rhodesia. There is no doubt that ENI's contribution to Italy's development was of fundamental importance. Its own expansion was extraordinary at home and abroad; it included a major construction of pipelines for the transference of its wares. Already it impinged on the great chemical industry of Italy grouped round the huge combine of Montecatini. The latter built a big new plant and a new port at Brindisi, an example of the contribution of southern development to northern expansion. Here at Brindisi oil could be brought in cheaply, contributing to a spectacular increase in the production of plastics.'

The index of growth of the chemical industry rose from 100 in 1953 to 273 in 1961. The production of cellulose and artificial fibres more than tripled in the same period, and the production of paper and rubber doubled.

During the boom period, using the raw materials of the European Coal and Steel Community, steel production greatly increased, and Italy developed a big export trade in specialized products such as pipes for oil pipelines. The steel industry was centred on Cornigliano near Genoa, but IRI also built plants at Bagnoli near Naples and at Taranto.

During this period, which happened to coincide with the great post-war package tourist boom, new hotels were springing up all over Italy. The Riviera dei Fiori and the Adriatic coast soon became unrecognizable, and a by-product of the industrial boom was the sad but inescapable fact that the millions of tourists who crowded the Italian beaches in the sixties and seventies could no longer swim in safety in seas unsullied by pollution.

Right through the sixties a growth rate of 4.7 per cent per year was maintained, and Italy outpaced all Common Market countries except France in industrial production. The expansion of the economy had reduced unemployment from about 2.4 million in the late 1940s to under a million by 1962.

Italy's 'economic miracle' was badly hit by the oil crisis of 1973; the boom had been almost exclusively powered by cheap imported oil, which quadrupled in price between 1973 and 1974, with a corresponding effect on Italy's already delicate balance of payments. Inflation, which had always been a problem, now became an acute one; consumer prices rose by 39 per cent between 1973 and 1975 and then doubled between 1975 and 1980. Economic growth dropped to about 2 per cent, and unemployment increased again. By 1987 it was down to about 14 per cent of the total labour force.

Nevertheless by the end of the seventies, northern Italy had become one of the most advanced industrial regions in Europe, and even after the oil crisis the country continued to progress throughout the recession: in 1983, to take one example, 64,000 new business ventures were launched.

And some of the endemic problems seemed to have been solved. In 1979, Fiat lost 200,000 cars as a result of strike action, and each worker on average was turning out only eleven cars a year, as against twenty-nine in Germany's Opel car plants, and forty-three in Japan's Toyota factories. In 1980, 23,000 workers were laid off and put on the *Cassa Integrazione*, a system by which laid-off workers are regarded as 'temporarily unemployed' and the state pays 80 per cent of their wages. By 1982, each worker in employment was producing thirty-five cars a year, and Fiat was in profit again.

It has been basically the same story with most Italian industries. Italy's major exports are machinery and vehicles (over 33 per cent in terms of value); textiles and clothing (17 per cent) and food products (5.2 per cent). The GDP per head of the population in 1985 was 9,676 ECUs, as against 13,040 in France, 13,543 in West Germany and 10,509 in the United Kingdom.

Many of the Italian industries, like Buitoni and Benetton, started out as small family firms. Buitoni began as a small home-made chocolate business; it is now a vast food-processing company which exports 30 per cent of its production to the United States, mainly pasta and canned food.

Benetton, a name you are almost certain to see over a store somewhere in almost every city in the developed world, also began as a small family business. It now operates world-wide, famous everywhere for its distinctive range of 'united colours' which have made Benetton sportswear so universally popular.

Other small family firms stay small, yet become equally world-famous, like Barsolino (slogan: If you want to get ahead, get a Barsolino). This firm has been manufacturing hats for the famous in Alessandria in Piedmont since the middle of the nineteenth century. Distinguished customers have included most of the royal families, most of the aristocrats, most of the millionaires and many film stars.

The Pope's white *galerum*, Al Capone's fedora, Benito Mussolini's bowler, Maurice Chevalier's *chapeau de paille*, Fred Astaire's topper − all were made by Borsalino. The firm also supplies the fez and the tarbush worn by many Arab leaders, it provided 1,000 top hats for the wedding of the Shah of Iran and still provides most of the hats worn by the matadors in the Spanish bullrings. By 1913, the firm was selling 2 million hats a year.

Production is now down to 300,000 a year, because hats went out of vogue for general wear immediately after World War II, but it is still a safe bet that if you see somebody very rich or very famous wearing a top hat at a society wedding, it will have the name Borsalino in ornate italics on the inner leather headband.

It is hard to give many details of Italy's small industries because most of them do not appear in any of the tables of statistics. Teresa Gorman, writing in the London *Daily Telegraph* in 1983, remarked: 'Naples, with no registered glove factory, exports more than five million pairs of gloves a year.'

Some Italian small industries are no more than workshops where components made by locals in their own homes are assembled and finished. In *Italian Labyrinth* (London: Secker and Warburg, 1985), John Haycraft describes visiting a shoe factory in Tuscany which seemed to have no more than a dozen workers, though it was producing 500 pairs of shoes a day, mainly for export to the United States. The explanation? The parts were all made by local women, working in their homes. In this way the factory avoided paying any social security, the women workers avoided Pay-As-You-Earn tax, and the proprietor was relieved of all his responsibilities under the *Scala Mobile* − which sounds like an opera aria, but is in fact a system by which wages are raised every three months to keep pace with inflation and regardless of how the factory is faring.

All Italian products, whether they come from small family firms or huge industrial giants have style − the Olivetti Lettera portable was as elegant as it was practical, and was probably the most stylish small typewriter ever made. Gucci, Fergamo, Armani – the names speak for themselves. So do names like Bugatti, Maserati, Ferrari and Lamborghini; they have a magic that has never been captured by any non-Italian motor car manufacturer. They exude style.

Because of their new-found ability to work hard, rationalize factory procedures and dramatically increase industrial production, the Italians have been called Europe's Japanese. In the production of textiles, clothes and shoes, which together accounted for 18 per cent of all exports in 1989, Taiwan, South Korea, Hong Kong and China may well be able to beat the Italians in labour costs, but they'll never come anywhere near them when it comes to sheer style.

In Italy, during the last century particularly, there have been thousands of people constantly on the move. Italians from all over, travelling to ports like Genoa and Naples to emigrate to the United States. Italians from the south travelling up to the north to look for jobs. Italians from the south who have found jobs in the north travelling south again to visit their relatives. Businessmen travelling between Milan and Venice, Rome and Turin, Naples and Trento. Italians going on holidays from Milan to Venice, from Rome to the Riviera. Above all tourists, 53,315,000 of them in 1989, travelling all over the place because, in Italy, there is so much to see.

All this constant movement, over terrain that is for the most part very rugged and mountainous, calls for a highly efficient and extensive transportation network, which Italy now enjoys.

It was not always so. When Keats and Shelley visited Italy in the early nineteenth century, they arrived by stage-coach and did most of their exploring on foot, using mules to carry their belongings.

The first railroad in Italy was built in 1830 and covered the ten kilometres between Naples and Portici. At the time of the unification of Italy in 1861 there were only 2,371 kilometres of railroad: 850 in Piedmont, 522 in Lombardy-Veneto; 257 in Tuscany, 101 in the Papal States and the rest scattered throughout the peninsula.

With an energy that was later echoed in the boom of the fifties and sixties of the present century, the new nation made a huge constructional effort and in a little over twenty years had brought this total up to 8,139 kilometres. This comprised some major civil engineering projects, including the Simplon tunnel in 1906, through the Alps between Brig in Switzerland and Iselle, near Lake Maggiore, and the Bologna–Florence express in 1934 which entailed boring a tunnel under the Appenines.

During World War II nearly 60 per cent of the Italian railroad system was destroyed. It was completely rebuilt after the war with new rolling stock and extensive electrification, and now offers 16,163 kilometres of rail travel, more than half of the total electrified. Trains in Italy are not luxurious but they run on time, the coaches are clean and the fares are cheap; about half what a corresponding journey would cost in France, and less than a third of what it would cost in Britain or Germany.

The state-run railway company employs nearly a quarter of a million people and also runs the ferries between the mainland and the islands of Sicily and Sardinia.

The roads in Italy are excellent, and some of the motorways along the Mediterranean coast and through the mountains are spectacular; the network is the second best in Europe, after Germany's. During the period of Italy's economic miracle, the total motorway network was increased from 520 to 6,000 kilometres; and state highways now total 45,000 kilometres.

Alitalia, the state airline, provides scheduled services to all the continents, and there are good internal air services with fewer airport hold-ups and stacking problems than in most European countries.

Telecommunications have probably improved as much in the last ten years in Italy as they have elsewhere in the Community, in France and Ireland, for example. Unlike the rest of the Community, all telecommunication services in Italy are still run exclusively by the state, through the Department of Posts and Telegraphs.

Up-to-date statistics are harder to get in Italy than most other Community countries; where the 'latest available figures' in general refer to 1989 or even 1990, the latest available Italian figures tend to date back to about 1984, or sometimes to 1980, and also tend to vary considerably.

In December 1984 Italy had seventy-nine daily newspapers, selling a total of some 5 million copies a day, a figure which will seem extremely low to people in Britain where the popular tabloids like the *Daily Mirror* and the *Sun* alone each sell nearly 4 million copies per day. The Italians, like the Spanish and the Portuguese, read fewer newspapers than the other members of the Community.

Until 1975, radio and TV were strictly a state monopoly. Private stations have been permitted to transmit programmes locally since then, foreign TV stations like the French Antenne-deux and Tele-Monte-Carlo have been allowed to set up relays to broadcast their programmes inside Italy, and three large commercial TV networks are now in operation.

AFFAIRS OF STATE

Petty Pilfering and Tax Evasion

Italy is a parliamentary republic. The constitution guarantees equality without discrimination on the grounds of sex, race or religion; the inviolability of every citizen and his house; freedom of opinion, of the press, of every means of communication; freedom of assembly, of association, of movement; and the right to private property and economic initiative.

Legislative power is vested in the Chamber of Deputies and the Senate. The 630 deputies are elected for five years on a system of proportional representation which has resulted in coalition governments ever since the end of World War II. The 315 senators are elected regionally, again on a system of proportional representation, and in addition the president can appoint up to five distinguished persons to the Senate.

The president, who is elected by parliament, appoints the president of the Council of Ministers (prime minister) and, on his proposals, the ministers. He is also commander-in-chief of the armed forces, and presides over both the High Council of Defence and the High Council of the Magistrature. His term of office is normally seven years, and he can dissolve parliament at any time except during his last six months in office.

There are about fifteen active political parties in Italy, but the Christian Democrats have dominated all of the coalitions which have been patched together over the years.

Italians are entitled to vote from eighteen years of age, and to stand for election at twenty-five, and military service is compulsory.

The armed services operate within the NATO framework, and in 1980 Italy had an army of 253,000, a navy of 42,000 strong and an air force of 71,000. In that year the defence budget was US$6,750 million.

For administrative purposes Italy is divided into twenty regions, some with considerable autonomy, ninety-five provinces and nearly 8,000 communes. Some of the communes are no bigger than a village, but are responsible for all regional administration.

Leaving aside the Mafia and the Red Brigades which so terrorized Italy in the seventies, there is probably about the same amount of crime in Italy as there is in most other countries of the Community, more petty crime perhaps in the major cities and in the south, where gangs of *scipporati* (snatchers) can be very adept at whipping a wallet or a handbag and disappearing into the crowd.

But crime in general, in Italy as elsewhere, is on the increase, and an additional problem in Italy is the length of time it takes to bring suspects on remand to trial. According to *Italy Today*, a state handbook of facts about the country, an overall reform of the criminal justice process is now underway, 'the aim being to provide more extensive guarantees to the defence, among which would be a drastic reduction in the period the accused can be kept in prison before being brought to trial'.

Among the causes for the delays: the shortage of magistrates, which itself is partly due to the fact that judges are not as well paid as other professions; the slow and antiquated legal procedures

— notes are still taken down in longhand as indeed they are in Britain; and a general shortage of staff. As a result, it can take anything from one to four years between the time a man is arrested and the time when his case can be heard. If the case involves a number of defendants, this time-lag could be doubled.

The total of crimes recorded by the police went up from 1,705.9 per 100,000 of the population in 1961 to 3,546.4 per 100,000 of the population in 1986. Kidnapping, a form of crime which one tends to associate with Italy, is relatively rare; the rate has never been higher than 0.5 per 100,000 inhabitants since the war.

And in Italy, as elsewhere, a great deal of the crime is drug-related; according to John Haycraft, the 7,000 drug addicts in Palermo alone need the equivalent of US$20 a day to keep themselves supplied with drugs, which adds up to a total of US$14,000 every twenty-four hours — which can usually only be obtained through theft, robbery or other petty crimes.

Civil offences, like tax evasion, are another matter; there are so many taxes in Italy that, as Italy's first post-war President Luigi Einaudi remarked, if every Italian paid all the taxes for which he was liable, he would have to pay back to the state about 10 per cent more than he could ever hope to earn. This is one reason why the Italians do not feel that they are being in any way disloyal or anti-social in doing their best to evade paying taxes which they could not possibly pay anyway.

Which leaves the Mafia. The Mafia almost certainly originally developed as a form of Sicilian resistance to centuries of foreign domination; they provided protection, policing of a sort and at a price, and even in a way an ad hoc substitute for government. As Luigi Barzini puts it, 'a man belonging to the Mafia does not know he is doing wrong ... Order has to be preserved. Justice must be observed. Unfortunately, men being what they are, it is often necessary to enforce the will of the Mafia by means of violence.'

What the Mafia have done and what they have become since Italy became a unified state which expects and requires its citizens to obey its laws and its laws only is another story which has been well and frequently told.

The Italian social welfare system is based vaguely on the British pattern and was introduced in the seventies. It now còvers health services, pensions, workmen's compensation, unemployment insurance and family allowances. Social insurance is administered by state-controlled insurance companies and is based on contributions from the state, the employers and the workers themselves, with the employers paying the largest share. The system covers almost all employed and unemployed workers and pensioners, as well as many self-employed people and their families.

The social welfare system is extremely expensive to run because the Italians regard state benefits in more or less the same way as they regard taxation. Because they feel that they have been cheated out of a decent welfare system all their lives, most older Italians believe that they are perfectly justified in cheating the social welfare system if they possibly can.

John Haycraft refers to between 15 and 17 million social security pensioners, many of them registered as 'invalids', though they need only a doctor's certificate to qualify for that distinction. 'There is,' he adds, 'one village in the south where 80 per cent of the inhabitants are invalids. One wonders where those who have to push them around in their state-provided wheel-chairs come from ...'

Health services are similar in principle to those in most other Community countries, but in Italy they are handicapped by a lack of modern hospitals and by the extremely low fees paid by the state to doctors and surgeons working for the national health system. There is also a severe shortage of nurses, due partly to a lack of training facilities and partly to the fact that in Italy, as in other Mediterranean countries like Greece and Spain, nursing is not taken seriously as a profession. Families are still expected to come into the hospitals to feed and look after their sick relatives.

Another problem is that the people from the south, where the hospitals are neither so good nor so numerous, tend to go north if they can for treatment, at the expense of the people who live in the north, yet another cause of friction between the two Italies.

In addition to the social welfare system, a large private hospital system exists, and many of the more prosperous Italians have private medical insurance schemes, as in Britain.

But things are improving. In 1985, Italy had 1,798 hospitals, providing one hospital bed per 1,000 inhabitants, a figure which had not changed greatly since 1961; on the other hand, in the years between 1961 and 1985, the number of doctors had increased from 28,602 to 83,961, and the total of other medical staff had increased from 57,866 to 235,430 over the same period.

CULTURE AND LEISURE

Hedging Their Bets

Not surprisingly, Italy is 99 per cent Catholic, though young Italian people are no more devout than young French or young Belgians and, perhaps as a result of the Pope's presence in their midst, so to speak, many of them are far more anti-clerical than Catholics in Ireland and Spain. Anti-clerical feeling is particularly strong in Emilia-Romagna and the Marche (formerly the Marches, on the Adriatic coast, to the north-east of Rome), areas where memories of papal rule are still fresh. In particular, all Italians are highly suspicious of church interference in politics and education.

The attitude to the Church and its institutions can perhaps be assessed by glancing through the family and population statistics. In 1951, nearly 8 per cent of Italian families numbered seven or more; by 1986, that figure was down to 1 per cent. By 1986, too, more than 21 per cent of Italian families had only one child, as against less than 10 per cent in 1956. Throughout the boom years, the average Italian family was confined to two to three children, despite the Pope's continuing ban on any form of contraception. The Italian birth rate is dropping; at 0.18 per cent the population growth figure is one of the lowest in the Community.

Other relevant statistics: in 1951, 97.6 per cent of all marriages were made in church; that figure had dropped by 1986 to 85.6 per cent, with 14.4 per cent of Italian couples electing to have only a civil ceremony. Even more significantly, there were only 5,196 separations and no divorces in 1951 (and none in 1961 either); by 1986, there were 35,547 separations and 16,857 divorces, as well as 197,260 legal abortions. It is necessary to add perhaps that civil divorce was legalized in 1970 and abortion became legal in 1978, despite the Pope's views on the matter. And it is possible that the reason why these figures are not far higher could lie in the Italian tendency to stick to ancient family traditions, or perhaps, hedge their bets.

Even today, many people who regard themselves as Communists shy away from getting married in a registry office or allowing themselves to be buried without the blessing of the Church, and however anti-clerical they may be, they remain almost superstitiously reluctant to deny their children whatever sort of guarantee they may still feel that baptism affords.

In the *mezzogiorno*, the influence of the parish priest, if not as devastating as it was a century ago, is still very strong.

One table of statistics I have come across gives the literacy rate in 1989 as 93 per cent; which is to say that out of every 100 Italians, there will still be seven who cannot read or write. That seems high compared with most of the other countries in the Community with the exception of Portugal, but it may well be true. Writing in 1964, Luigi Barzini commented: 'Millions of people, between 10 and 30 per cent of the population, are still illiterate. The figure varies according to the definition of illiteracy. Is a man who cannot read and can write only his name literate or illiterate? Is a man who went to school but forgot everything, or who can only occasionally make out a few familiar words on a wall poster, literate or illiterate?'

Another source states flatly that in 1951 5 million Italian people were illiterate, which is nearly 10 per cent of the population. Whatever the truth, the Italian education system has been steadily improving since schooling was made compulsory by law in 1962. Previously it had been compulsory under the constitution, but there was no law to enforce it.

Since the law was passed, the number of pupils between six

and fourteen years of age in full-time education has increased by five times and the number of schools has trebled.

Many of the communes offer crèche facilities (in what is called an *asili nido*) where children can be left when they are a few months old; some of them provide nursery school facilities from 8 a.m. until 6.30 p.m. with dormitory facilities for the siesta. Preference is given to working mothers, and they are not expensive.

Pre-school education at a *scuola di maternità* (kindergarten) is optional; the hours are from 8 a.m. until 1 p.m. with no classes on Saturday.

Primary education at elementary school for children between the ages of five and eleven is now compulsory, as is attendance at the *scuola media* (junior high school) until the age of fourteen. Most of these will be parochial schools since the dominant political force, the Christian Democratic Party, favours state-supported parochial schools.

The *scuola superiore* (senior high school) system includes *licei* (equivalent to the French *lycées*) which provide education in classical, scientific, artistic or linguistic subjects, and technical institutes which provide courses in business, industrial, agricultural or other vocational subjects, as well as in hotel management and tourism.

After what are known as the *maturità* exams (again the nearest parallel is probably the French *baccalauréat*, at any rate in the case of the *licei*), students progress either to one of the old universities, a university institute or a free polytechnic. The university institutes concentrate on one single field of study, and the polytechnics include only the engineering and architectural faculties.

The *maturità* and many other examinations in Italy are largely oral because cheating is not forbidden — cribbing belts with compartments for all the separate subject cribs are widely on sale — and because many Italian teachers feel that only by questioning students closely can you discover whether they really have a firm grasp of the subject.

The number of Italian children in full-time education up to senior high school standard increased from 761,000 in 1961 to

2,508,039 in 1984, and the number of students at university from 268,181 to 1,406,807. At the same time, there has been a drop in the number of elementary school pupils, reflecting the drop in the birth rate.

Italy's forty-seven universities have a student population of over a million. Some free places are awarded to students of promise; fees otherwise are extremely high. Also, only the actual tuition is free. Living grants are available to students whose parents' income is below about 2 million lire a year; otherwise the students have to work to support themselves.

Probably the most incisive book about the Italians is *The Italians*, written by Luigi Barzini, himself an Italian, in 1964. He began by pointing out that it was almost impossible to do justice to Italy in any book of normal proportions.

One of the problems, he remarked, is 'the absurd discrepancy between the quality and dazzling array of the inhabitants' achievements through many centuries and the mediocre quality of their national history. Italians have impressively filled Europe and most of the world with the fame of their larger-than-life famous men. Italian architects and masons built part of the Kremlin in Moscow and the Winter Palace in Leningrad; Italian artists have embellished the Capitol at Washington. They have strewn churches, princely palaces, and stately villas all over Catholic Europe, especially in Vienna, Madrid, Prague and Warsaw; their influence on architecture was felt almost everywhere else, exterior architecture to be sure, designed to impress their visitors and please the onlooker more than to serve strictly practical purposes. They have filled South America with ornate and rhetorical monuments to the local heroes.'

He argues that the list of famous Italians is so awe-inspiring that it is as well to record them right at the outset — he does it in a footnote — as they will scarcely be mentioned in the rest of the book. Here is his list:

The saints: Saint Francis, Saint Catherine of Siena, San Bernardino of Siena, San Luigi Gonzaga, St Thomas Aquinas.

The sinners: The Borgia Family, Cellini, Caravaggio, Cagliostro, Casanova. The political thinkers: Dante Alighieri, King Frederick of the Two Sicilies, Lorenzo de Medici, Machiavelli, Guicciardini, Mazzini, Cavour. The military leaders: Giovanni dalle Bande Nere, Raimondo Montecuccoli, Napoleon, Garibaldi. The admirals: Andrea Doria, Mocenigo, Morosini, Bragadin, Caracciolo. The scientists: Galileo Galilei, Leonardo da Vinci, Volta, Marconi, Fermi. The navigators: Columbus, Vespucci, the Cabots. The thinkers: St Thomas Aquinas, Campanella, Croce, Vico. The poets: Dante Alighieri, Boccaccio, Petrarch, Leopardi, Manzoni. The sculptors: Verrochio, Donatello, Ghiberti, della Robbia, Cellini, Michelangelo, Bernini. The painters: Giotto, Botticelli, Fra Angelico, da Vinci, Piero della Francesca, Perugino, Michelangelo, Raphael, Titian, Tintoretto, Tiepolo, Modigliani. The musicians: Palestrina, Pergolesi, Monteverdi, Vivaldi, Rossini, Verdi, Bellini, Donizetti, Puccini.

As Barzini says, these are all names of the first magnitude. The second and third categories would easily fill a city's telephone book.

In the circumstances, as I have said also in relation to the British, the French, and the Germans, it is quite impossible to do justice to Italian contributions to art, science, sculpture, architecture and music in a book of this kind. On the other hand, there are a few points that might usefully be made.

Barzini's thesis is that when the Italians were conquered and dominated by the Spanish, they didn't try, as the Japanese did after World War II, to beat their conquerors at their own game. They did the opposite. They were far too proud to admit that they had anything to learn from others. What could these barbarians teach them, they argued, who had already taught the world everything? They went on cultivating the very virtues which made them invincible in their own eyes, and drew more closely to the Church that was the sole surviving symbol of their one-time dominance.

Again, to quote Barzini: 'It was after the sack of Rome and the coronation of Charles V in Bologna that Michelangelo painted The Last Judgement in the Sistine Chapel and planned the cupola over Saint Peter's, Cellini cast his Perseus for the Loggia di Lanzi in Florence, Palladio raised San Giorgio from the sea in Venice, Titian painted some of his greatest masterpieces, and Sansovino designed some of his most famous buildings ... Sculptors and architects were in great demand. They reached heights of excellence never seen before. Men like Bernini, Borromini, Juvara and their followers filled Rome with hundreds of *palazzi* and churches, studded the panorama of the city with new and daring cupolas, built St Peter's and the colonnade in front of it, and gave Rome the face it has today.'

Music has always been a refuge and a consolation for oppressed and frightened people, because it enables them to express sentiments and longings which might be regarded as seditious if put in plain words. Heine wrote: 'To poor enslaved Italy, words are not allowed. She can only describe the anguish in her heart through music. All her hatred against foreign oppression, all her enthusiasm for liberty, all the anguish of her own impotence, her longing for her past greatness, pathetic hopes, watching, waiting for help, all this is transposed into her melodies.'

During this period, the main patron of music was the Church and the clerical authorities looked on anything more adventurous than Gregorian chant with some distaste. Palestrina was asked to devise a form of music which would be acceptable to Pope Pius IV and his cardinals, and saved church music — and possibly all Italian music forever — with his *Missa Papae Marcelli* (Mass of Pope Marcellus). If he had failed, Italian music might not have survived.

However, the provision of music suitable only for use in church did not greatly appeal to the Italian composers who wanted to write music about love and jealousy and hate and envy and many other purely human emotions, and so they invented first the Teatro dell'Arte and then Grand Opera.

To return to Barzini: 'Everything ... was done not for itself alone, but principally for the effect it would produce. For two centuries or more, an immense number of men of genius dedicated their incredible talents to the national belief that the show is, *faute de mieux*, a good substitute for reality: they filled the world with masterpieces in order to find compensation for the insecurity, emptiness, disarray, impotence and despair of their national life, to forget their humiliation and shame, to forget their collective guilt.'

Perhaps. Or could it be that they just did it because they were talented Italians and had to get it all out of their system somehow? It doesn't matter. The important thing is that they did it, and the world has become a far richer place as a result.

Amongst the other things that the Italians believe is that they taught the French how to cook. The notion comes from the fact that Catherine de Medici sent for her Italian cooks when she left Florence to marry Henri II of France. But while this is patently untrue, there is no doubt that the Italians have had far more effect on the world's cuisine, particularly as it affects the ordinary man in search of a quick, satisfying meal, than the French or any other nation, much more perhaps even than the Chinese.

It is worth noting incidentally that the pizza — a form of food for which the Italians are probably best-known in most other countries — was not an Italian innovation at all, but was developed by Italian immigrants in the United States, who reckoned it would make an acceptable 'Italian-style' dish for Americans in a hurry, in exactly the same way as the Chinese, looking for a 'Chinese-style' dish which would be acceptable to the Americans, invented chop-suey: nobody in the East has ever heard of chop-suey.

Having said that, it is also fair to add that apart from the Chinese cuisine, Italian cooking has probably proved more exportable than any other style of cooking in the world. There are probably more little Italian trattoria and pizza huts and spaghetti houses in most American and British and German and French cities than there are restaurants serving any other national or regional type of food; and the reason is not necessarily that the Italian food is that much better, but simply that the Italians are by far the most talented *restaurateurs* in the world, and manage to make their customers feel that not only are they briefly back once more in Italy, but also that they are being allowed to take part in a very Italian experience − a meal of the kind that any Italian Mamma would make.

This is what it boils down to, ultimately. The young French boy may appreciate Maman's cooking, but he knows in his heart that when he grows up and can afford to go to the *Trois Gros* or the *Tour d'Argent* or the *Taillevent*, the food will be better, if a lot more pricey. The young Italian boy is convinced, and remains convinced until the end of his days, that Italian food is the best in the world and that there is no better way in which to prepare it than the way Mamma used to make it back home in the *casa*.

So, in Italy, it's still pasta, endlessly varied in shape, but pasta nevertheless and all the time, flavoured with pine nuts, basil, olive oil, parmesan, peccorino, tomato, artichokes, funghi, spinach, onions, garlic ... the list could go on forever.

Of course there are incomparable Italian delicacies − Parma ham, for example, and ice-cream; there is no sorbet in the world remotely like an Italian one. And they cook fish and veal, octopus and funghi of various sorts extremely well, and produce two cheeses that are unlike any others produced elsewhere − Gorgonzola and Parmesan. But, apart from the Italians them-selves, nobody really believes you can eat better in Italy than anywhere else.

And pretty much the same applies to drink. Nobody has produced a better antidote to a hot day in a crowded Italian city than a Campari-soda with a lot of ice and a thick slice of orange, but I can't think of a single Italian wine I would seriously consider as indispensable.

But with such a superb setting and a cast like that, is food and drink all that desperately important?

The Italians have never been great sportsmen. As one Italian put it to me, they are interested in 'sailing, skiing, and motor racing if they're rich enough to indulge in these slightly esoteric, enhanced forms of transport. Otherwise, they cycle or just follow the *calcio* [football]. This is probably an over simplification, but it is basically true that the sport which interests Italians most keenly is the sport of life.

Italians — and also the Maltese and the Greeks and many other Mediterranean people — find it impossible to understand that we have no equivalent in Britain to the seven o'clock promenade. We had two young Italian girls — daughters of friends of ours — staying with us in Kew about a year ago. As the magical hour of seven o'clock approached, the girls, dressed to the nines and made up like film extras, drifted down to the living room. 'Where is everybody?' they asked in dismay. 'Why are you not dressed up? Why are there no people in the streets? Where do the people go for the *passeggiata* in Kew?'

How can you possibly explain to two young Italian girls that in England at seven o'clock in the evening, nobody walks in the streets? That there is no *passeggiata*. That the men shave in the morning, to go to work, not in the evening for the promenade. That women who have been out at work all day change into something more comfortable and sit down and start to watch the telly.

That England isn't a bit like Italy. Nor, for that matter, is anywhere else in the world.

THE
LUXEMBOURGERS

The First Common Market

LUXEMBOURG IN PROFILE

Area	2,586 sq km
Population	366,000
Population density	141 per sq km
Women	51.4%
Under 15	17.6%
Over 65	13.2%
Language	Luxembourgish, French, German, etc.
Religion	95% Catholic
Labour force	44%
Employed in:	
Agriculture	4.2%
Industry	33.4%
Services	62.3%
Women in labour force	33.8%
Unemployment (as % of labour force)	1.5%

Major exports: Steel and heavy-industry products (90%); chemicals; agricultural products
Main customers: EC (70%); USA, Switzerland

THE LUXEMBOURGERS

That is what they call themselves in English: the Luxembourgers. In French, they are the *Luxembourgeois*. They speak French, Dutch or Flemish, and a lot of them also speak English as well as their own language, *Letzeburgish* (Luxembourgish in English), a Moselle/Frankish Germanic dialect with words borrowed from French, Dutch and English, which they have been attempting to revive as a written language over the past ten years or so.

Their tiny country in the centre of the European Community is one of a few surviving principalities out of literally hundreds dotted all over Europe and particularly in the areas which later became Italy, Germany, Belgium, Austria and Hungary; among the others surviving are Monaco, Liechtenstein and Andorra.

To anyone who grew up in Britain or Ireland during the thirties, the word Luxembourg immediately conjures up a dim memory of gentle dance music and assertive commercials. Dance music, because that was the popular music of the period, and the only station on which you could get it regularly, all through the day, was Radio Luxembourg. The BBC in those days limited dance music during the daytime to three-quarters of an hour of Henry Hall between 5.15 and 6 p.m.; to hear any of the other dance bands you had to stay up until about 11 p.m.

And commercials because Radio Lux was the only sponsored station then broadcasting in English that you could receive on an ordinary wireless set, as radios were then called, in the British Isles. They were the first jingles any of us had ever heard; to this day I remember the tune that went with the phrase: 'We are the Ovaltinies ...' and another one that went with Balito (or was it Valito?) Silk Stockings.

It was a place we used to drive through late at night, on the way down to Switzerland and Italy when the children were small, and my abiding memory of it is of a Ruritanian sort of castle perched on a hill above a city. Ruritanian because of the musical comedy, Lehár's *The Count of Luxembourg*, perhaps.

I spent a few days in Luxembourg a couple of years ago and the castle is still there, though it looks a lot less impressive, menaced as it now seems to be by a Dallas-style city of glass and concrete modern office blocks, the headquarters of banks from all over the world and some of the institutions of the Community, on the Kircheberg plateau, just across the river from the old town. It's called Luxembourg from two words which meant Little Fortress in a dialect used a couple of centuries ago.

The original Luxembourg castle was built on the site of a Roman observation tower which was part of the defence system against the Germanic tribes. A strategic and easily defended citadel, at one of the main crossroads of Europe, it has dominated Luxembourg's history for over 1,000 years, just as it has dominated the skyline.

The national motto, ironically, is: *Mir welle bleiwe wat mir sin* (We want to stay what we are). I say ironically, because that is the one thing that the Luxembourgers cannot ever hope to do, despite determined efforts to revive the ancient *Letzeburgish* tongue as their official language since 1985.

Theirs is probably the most cosmopolitan country in Europe; nearly a third of the population consists of immigrants from other parts of Europe, the highest proportion in any Community country. In addition, some 30,000 people commute to work in Luxembourg every day from adjoining countries.

The immigrant workers from Italy, Portugal and Spain helped to solve a chronic labour shortage largely caused by massive emigration from Luxembourg to the United States towards the end of the nineteenth century; before industrialization, the people of Luxembourg were largely dependent on subsistence farming and 70,000 of them, approaching a third of the total population, left the country between 1880 and 1900.

With the lowest birthrate in the Community (0.03 per cent), and a capital city which has become one of the main banking and financial centres of the world, the few Luxembourgers that are left (372,000 at the last count), find themselves surrounded by bankers and businessmen, accountants and auditors, tax advisers and stockbrokers from all over the world, as well as immigrant workers from several European countries.

Nearly half of the 15,000 people who work in the banks and other financial institutions are foreigners, including a great many Japanese; foreigners make up half of the capital city's population of 80,000. So how can the Luxembourgers possibly stay what they were? They are no longer remotely like what they were even in 1952, when Luxembourg was chosen as the provisional headquarters of the first supranational European Community: the Coal and Steel Union, the forerunner of today's European Community, which was founded by Jean Monnet and by one of the very few famous men born in Luxembourg, Robert Schuman.

The country had already been right in at the beginning of the first attempt to form a free trade area within Europe. As early as 1839, it became a member of the German *Zollverein* (Customs Union). It has had a fiscal union with Belgium since 1921, and in 1948 it formed, with Belgium and the Netherlands, the Benelux customs union which was Europe's first true Common Market.

Although Luxembourg built a new headquarters for the European Parliament and the first meetings of that odd institution were divided between there and Strasbourg, since 1981 its sessions have all been held in Strasbourg. The Parliament's secretariat, which has a staff of more than 2,500, is based in three buildings on the Kircheberg, one of them a conference centre where at least three meetings of the EC Council of Ministers are held each year.

I was in Luxembourg a few years back to research material for a newspaper article about the European Investment Bank. I stayed there for about three days with a man who works for that institution in a very senior capacity, meeting people who had lived and worked in Luxembourg for years, and the overwhelming impression I got of Luxembourg then was of a tiny, very comfortable, prosperous country, highly pleased with its sudden prosperity, a little surprised but extremely gratified to find itself at the centre of something as big as the European Community. A country in danger of becoming just a little bit smug, perhaps?

A handbook produced by the Press and Information Service of the Luxembourg government claims that according to statistics released by the World Bank in 1990, Luxembourg then ranked among the richest countries in the world after Kuwait and Switzerland.

Maybe. It has no unemployment, virtually no crime, no terrorism, and has had no strikes to speak of in all its industrial history. According to *Eurostat*, the booklet of statistics produced by the Community, Luxembourg tops the table in terms of the highest quantity of municipal waste produced per head of the population, the highest level of carbon dioxide emission per head of the population from fossil fuels, and the highest GDP per head of the population in terms of volume, though not of value. Its GDP, in money terms, is below that of Denmark, Germany and France, and in many other ways it seemed to me to have much less of general human interest to offer, apart from sheer material prosperity, than almost any other nation-state in the Community.

I suppose it all depends on how you measure wealth.

LAND AND PEOPLE

A Very Small Principality

Luxembourg occupies an area of about 2,586 square kilometres. That is to say it is less than one-hundredth the size of the United Kingdom; in fact, it's not as big as the island of Majorca in the

Balearics (80 kilometres from north to south, 55 kilometres from east to west).

It shares common boundaries with France, Germany and Belgium, and its only access to the sea is via the port of Mertret and the Moselle canal.

Its prehistory is similar to that of Belgium and France. When the Romans built a watch-tower on the site of the future city of Luxembourg, it was on the site of an already existing Celtic settlement, and the Celts in question were probably another branch of the Belgae, who by that time had firmly established themselves in Britain and in the area that was later to be called Belgium after them.

After the collapse of the Roman Empire, the whole area was invaded by various Germanic tribes, among them the Franks, who in time, when they became mixed with the Gallo-Romans and the Vikings who settled there and turned into the Normans, became the French nation.

A Frankish leader, Sigefroi, Count of Ardenne, constructed a new fortress on the site of the Roman lookout near an impregnable outcrop and situated at a vital crossroads between Rheims and Germany. This fortress became the nucleus of a country and a duchy which grew in importance between the fourteenth and fifteenth centuries, during which time its reigning house provided four Holy Roman Emperors.

Their land was largely infertile, and most of the people lived on subsistence farming, though there were some small iron and tin deposits in the south which had been worked by the Celts, with some advice from the Romans. Luxembourg's only other natural resource consisted of some inferior deposits of iron ore, discovered at the turn of the twentieth century.

Luxembourg is currently 99 per cent dependent upon foreign sources for its energy supplies and indeed for its raw materials. It produces a minute amount of hydro-electric power. The climate is temperate, not unlike Britain's.

HISTORICAL PERSPECTIVE

A Pawn for Swapping

It is very hard for those of us who think in terms of countries, or even continents, to imagine what it was like when most of Europe consisted of tiny principalities, many of them no bigger than Luxembourg, with a duke in charge, a total population of no more than a few thousand, a small standing army and a collection of peasants and artisans totally dependent upon the whims of the local *seigneur*.

Soon after the Count of Ardennes had established himself in Luxembourg in 963, the duchy became a pawn frequently swapped in the struggle for dominance between the great houses of Europe.

Seized by Burgundy in 1443, it passed backwards and forwards during the ensuing years between Spain, France and Austria. It was Spanish in 1544; reverted to France in 1684 (when its fortifications were supervised by Vauban); went back to Spain in 1697; reverted to Austria in 1714; and was once more in French hands by 1796. It was part of Revolutionary France until Napoleon's defeat at the Battle of Waterloo in 1815.

Its future was debated at the Congress of Vienna in 1814–15 when Napoleon's conquerors were sharing Europe out among themselves, and eventually it was bestowed, along with the Belgian slice of the Netherlands upon the Dutch House of Orange, as part of a buffer state designed to block French expansionism in the area.

In the 1830s, when the southern provinces of the Netherlands rebelled against Dutch rule, Luxembourg would probably also have voted to become a part of Belgium, but the 1839 Treaty of London specifically detached Luxembourg's French-speaking region, and turned it into a grand duchy in the personal possession of the King of the Netherlands. In 1890, after the death of King William III of the Netherlands, who had no male descendants, the crown of the grand duchy passed to the elder branch of the House of Nassau. Since then, Luxembourg has had its own dynasty.

Despite the international guarantee of neutrality, Luxembourg was occupied by German troops during World War I and again during World War II, when the Luxembourg royal family fled into exile in Britain and in the United States; thousands of Luxembourgers were deported to labour and prison camps or forced to join the *Wehrmacht*. Luxembourg's Avenue de la Liberté briefly became the Adolf Hitler Strasse, and the country suffered its worst damage towards the end of 1944, when its northern area, in the Ardennes, was fought over by the US and German forces during what was known as the Battle of the Bulge.

The return of the Grand Duchess Charlotte and her son Jean restored the identity of a tiny country which has since enhanced its role as one of the founders of the new European Community and as host nation to many of its institutions.

DEVELOPMENT DIRECTIONS

For Export Only

Luxembourg is a very good example of industrial prosperity built purely on export. With a population of only a little over a quarter of a million, a domestic market for manufactured goods was clearly non-existent. Therefore, when deposits of iron ore were discovered, the company which developed this ore into steel products had to think from the outset in terms of export, and those exports formed the basis for Luxembourg's industrial and economic development.

Steel production, under one company, Arbed, became by far the biggest employer in the state, and steel and other heavy-industry products still account for 90 per cent of all Luxembourg's exports.

The recession following the oil crisis in the late seventies forced a complete rethink, and in the last ten years a policy of rationalization and modernization, assisted by the sudden renaissance of steel as a structural building material for bridges, skyscraper blocks and offshore oil rigs, has made Arbed one of the world's top exporters of rolled steel beams, and one of its subsidiaries a leading producer of tracks for today's high-speed railways. Other subsidiaries, based in Belgium, the Netherlands, Germany, France, the United States, Brazil and South Korea, produce sheet metal for car manufacture, wire for all purposes, steelcord for tyres, and super-thin copper-foil for semiconductors used in the manufacture of electronic equipment in Japan.

Interestingly, Luxembourg's industry grew from the low-grade ore discovered in the south of the country towards the end of the nineteenth century, and because it had no coal or coke, used imported fuel; now even the raw materials are imported and the mines of the *Minière* have ceased to be worked.

From the second half of the seventies onwards, the financial and services sector began to dominate the economy. Of the labour force (44 per cent of the population), only 33.4 per cent now work in industry, only 4.2 per cent in agriculture, while 62.3 per cent toil, if that's the word for it, in the financial and services sector.

In 1960, there were only fifteen banks in Luxembourg; today 180 banking companies and twenty-five non-bank financial institutions have their headquarters there, including the European Investment Bank. This rapid growth was partly due to the part Luxembourg played in recycling oil revenues in the late seventies and early eighties; today the main business of the Luxembourg finance houses is in private customer banking.

A vital aspect of this branch of the business is Luxembourg's strict system of banking rules, which make unauthorized disclosure by banks of any information about their customers' activities an imprisonable offence. If there is any question of crime involved, these laws may be relaxed, but otherwise absolute secrecy is ensured, even against the inland revenue authorities of other countries.

Understandably, since Luxembourg was the first country in Europe to develop private broadcasting, it was among the first to diversify into other more advanced forms of communication. In the fields of satellite television, computer setting, state of the art reprography (the in-word for reproduction processes), photocopying, microfilm, audiovisual equipment and scores of modern technologies, Luxembourg is well up with the front runners in the Community.

It will probably not surprise anybody either that Luxembourg was also one of the first European countries to develop the credit card as a form of payment. From credit card pay phones and automated car parking facilities, to the Transac system for the restaurant and hotel sector, everything in Luxembourg can be paid for by plastic.

AFFAIRS OF STATE

A Constitutional Right to Work

The Grand Duchy of Luxembourg is a hereditary constitutional monarchy, with a written constitution adopted in 1868 and since amended about half a dozen times. This constitution, among other things, not only guarantees the right to work, but also *insures* [my italics] to every citizen the exercise of that right (a curious provision, but perhaps not so curious in a country which has had no strikes to speak of since World War II and in which unemployment as a percentage of the civilian labour force has never been higher than 1.5 per cent).

The secrecy of correspondence (in other words, bank accounts) is guaranteed under the constitution, which presumably is the reason why Luxembourg has become one of the prime financial centres of Europe.

The constitution also stipulates that all sovereignty resides in the people, and the referendum is frequently used as a means of discovering what the people think about government proposals. Executive power is exercised by the Grand Duke — currently Jean Nassau-Weilburg, whose mother the Grand Duchess Charlotte abdicated in his favour in 1964 and who is married to Josephine-Charlotte, sister of King Baudouin of the Belgians. But every law he signs must also be countersigned by a member of the government, and he is debarred from suspending or countermanding any legislation, though he can initiate it.

Voting is compulsory, and elections to the sixty-seat single chamber of parliament are by proportional representation, and no party has won an overall majority since World War II. Coalition government is part of the way of life in Luxembourg, and the two main parties are the Christian Socialists and the Socialist Workers.

In 1967, compulsory military service was abolished, and today Luxembourg is a full member of NATO, with armed forces numbering about 600-odd.

CULTURE AND LEISURE

Being a small and very wealthy country, Luxembourg is able to afford a very comprehensive public health service and has the second highest total of hospital beds per head of the population in the Community — 1,130 per 100,000 inhabitants, just behind France's 1,210 per 100,000.

So far as wealth is concerned, although not as rich as they believe themselves to be, the Luxembourgers are extremely well-heeled by most standards. Some additional indicators: as long ago as 1984 they held the second place in the Community in terms of the number of cars per head of the population (400 per 1,000 people as against West Germany's 412), and in terms of telephones (587 per 1,000 people as against Denmark's 719). They boast of the highest per capita consumption of electricity in Europe (whether that's something to boast about is another matter) and, another at least debatable distinction, they claim one of the highest ratios of TV sets per head of the population (360 per 1,000 people). Their tables of statistics also prove that they eat a great deal more food and drink a lot more wine and beer per capita than the rest of the Europeans.

About 95 per cent of the people of Luxembourg are Roman Catholics, and they seem to be roughly as casual in their attitude to religion as most Catholics in the other developed countries. They are extremely highly educated; they are currently attempting to revive the old *Letzeburgish* dialect, despite the fact that their children are obliged to start learning German at six, French at seven and usually one other European language (English or Russian) at eight.

About 55 per cent of pupils leave with a recognized qualification and more than 20 per cent with the coveted *baccalauréat* (university entrance). Luxembourg has a school for children of Community employees as well as American, French, English and Japanese schools.

The Luxembourgers like to think of their food as basically French but with German-sized portions. In such a cosmopolitan country, obviously all possible tastes are catered for, and the food, whether European, Malaysian, or American fast, is very good.

Basically the Luxembourgers enjoy the same sort of sports as the other Benelux countries. There used to be only one golf course in Luxembourg, at Senningerberg, built just after World War II; now there is a second, the Kikuoka Country Club near Luxembourg city, designed by a Japanese architect and built partly with Japanese money.

According to a French journalist who worked in the grand duchy for a couple of years, the principal advantage of Luxembourg so far as sport and leisure are concerned is that it is near enough to France to get back there every weekend and do whatever you choose to do.

THE PORTUGUESE

Westward Ho, Then!

PORTUGAL IN PROFILE

Area	92,082 sq km
Population	10,200,000
Density of population	110 per sq km
Women	51.8%
Under 15	24%
Over 65	11.8%
Language	Portuguese
Religion	Catholic
Labour force	43.7%
Employed in:	
Agriculture	23.9%
Industry	33.9%
Services	42.2%
Women in labour force	40.6%
Unemployment (as % of civilian labour force)	8.5%

Major exports: Textiles and clothing (30.3%); electrical machinery and equipment (15.7%); food and beverages (8.1%); pulp and paper (8.1%); wood and cork (7.1%)

Main customers: EC (68%), USA (7%), Spain (6.7%), Latin America (4.3%)

THE PORTUGUESE

The most interesting thing about the Portuguese is their past.

They are the poorest of the twelve new neighbours, with a gross national product per capita less than half that of the Irish, and the lowest standard of living in the European Community. And this despite the fact that in the fifteenth and sixteenth centuries they had an empire that encircled the globe.

With spices from Ceylon and Indonesia, silks and porcelain from China and Japan, slaves from East and West Africa, they dominated world trade. Their capital, Lisbon, became the most lavishly magnificent city in Europe, and its monarchs, who claimed a 'royal fifth' of the profits of all this enterprise, were for a time the richest rulers in Europe.

Spices, particularly the many varieties of pepper, were greatly valued in Europe in the Middle Ages because, even in the richest households, before any form of refrigeration, most meat was inedible unless liberally sprinkled with something strong enough to disguise the odour of decay.

The collapse of this vast empire, 2 million square kilometres of it, including Brazil and vast areas of Africa, is one of the enigmas of history. That the Spaniards, and then the Dutch and the English, who followed hot upon their heels, were able to consolidate

365

their empires, while the Portuguese seem to have let theirs gradually drift out of their grasp, may well have something to do with the national character of the Portuguese themselves, an innate conservatism combined with a deep respect for tradition which makes them among the most agreeable and least divisive of all the people of Europe — but which didn't help much in the highly competitive world of colonial adaptation and development.

And it is probably relevant that the Portuguese started out at least as poverty-stricken as they have wound up today, after the collapse of the last remnants of their empire in the 1970s. They had already effectively lost the greater part of it long before that, within fifty years of acquiring it, in fact.

When Portugal emerged from the mists of the Dark Ages as one of the first independent kingdoms of Europe in 1139, it was as an extremely poor country. Much of it was uncultivated and remained uncultivated until quite recently, and for the same reason. Most of the land was too rocky and hilly to farm effectively and the soil was so poor that only indifferent crops could be grown, and then only intermittently.

Irrigation was always a problem; the difference in river levels between low water and flood, among the greatest in the world, sometimes reaches 30 metres, which means that Portugal's farmers are constantly faced with either a deluge or a drought.

In these circumstances, the Portuguese were forced to turn to the sea to seek their harvest, and since their share of it happened to be the relentless and formidable Atlantic Ocean, they soon developed a tough breed of skilful sailors who were not intimidated by anything the sea could fling at them.

Fishing, plus a little basic farming, enabled the Portuguese to exist; to prosper, they needed to trade. And in the Middle Ages, almost all trade was waterborne. Since few of Portugal's rivers were navigable for any distance, and all ended up in the Atlantic, trade by river was not feasible.

The Mediterranean could be reached only by venturing out into the Atlantic, and in any event was dominated by Venetian, Genoese and Arab traders. The Portuguese had no other option open to them; if they wanted to trade, it had to be Westward Ho!

and off out into the Sea of Gloom, as it was known in those days.

The Portuguese didn't know, any better than anybody else, what if anything lay out beyond their inhospitable western horizon, though like everybody else in medieval Europe they had listened to legends about Hy Brasil, the Island of the Blessed in mid-Atlantic, and had heard tall tales of the discovery of other islands in the Atlantic by Ireland's St Brendan the Navigator and Scandinavia's Eric the Red and his son Leif Ericcson who got as far as Labrador and Greenland.

So they knew that there were at least some islands out there in the Atlantic which therefore seemed to offer a feasible alternative route to the spices and riches of the Far East.

The Portuguese were in many ways far better equipped than many other seafaring nations of the period to pioneer this route. During the Moorish occupation of their territory between 711 and 1249, the Arabs had introduced them to the astrolabe, an early navigational accessory, originally developed in China. They had also made the acquaintance of the map, developed in Greece in the second century by Ptolemy; and the harsh Atlantic had forced their shipbuilders to construct stout carracks and caravels well able to withstand the rigours of the crossing.

And if they needed to rationalize what was basically a burning greed for material things, gold principally, there was always the Church. That institution was only too willing to bestow its blessing upon any expedition which could conceivably be interpreted as an effort to expand enlightenment, spread the faith and increase the sum total of Christian souls. It was also equally prepared to condone, or at least overlook, any minor sins committed in the course of such an undertaking.

But before tackling the Atlantic, the Portuguese explorers flexed their muscles by heading south in an effort to reach the west coast of Africa and gain access to the gold of Guinea, until then carried by camel caravans across the Sahara. The capture of Ceuta in Morocco in 1415 could be taken as the starting point of the Portuguese imperial adventure. Ceuta lies exactly opposite the Arab city of Ta'Rifa; the word means inventory and has come down to us, via Spanish, as the term so often used in the Community, tariff.

The explorers had yet another aim: to search for the empire of Prester John, a semi-mythical figure whose lost Christian empire was believed to be an earthly paradise somewhere in the dark and dangerous interior of Africa. He turned out, in the end, to be the Black Negus or King of Abyssinia, held by some to be the leader of the lost tribe of Israel, descended from Solomon and the Queen of Sheba, and still the focus today of the Rastafarian faith, so called after Rasta Faria who become King Haile Selassie.

Prince Henry, known as Henry the Navigator, though he never personally navigated much further afield than Tangier, founded a nautical school at Sagres near Cape St Vincent, where explorers, seamen, navigators, shipbuilders and map-makers went to sharpen their skills. The first achievements of this academy included the discovery and colonization of the Canary Islands, Madeira, the Azores and Ceylon.

When Bartholomew Diaz rounded the mysterious Tempest Cape at the tip of southern Africa in 1488, it was renamed the Cape of Good Hope by the Portuguese King João II. Vasco da Gama followed the same route and ventured some distance up the eastern coast of Africa before becoming in 1498 the first European to arrive in India by sea.

In 1519, Magellan, a Portuguese mariner financed and equipped by Portugal's rapidly developing next-door neighbour, Spain, set out to sail to the Moluccas. When he was killed in a local war in the Philippines, so called after Philip II, the son of his master Charles I of Spain, his captain del Cano carried on to be the first man to sail around the world. Less than fifty years after that, the Portuguese became the first Europeans to reach Japan by sea.

In the meantime, of course, in 1492 Christopher Columbus from Genoa, who had a Portuguese wife, had set out to reach China via the Atlantic. He had tried to secure Portuguese support for this enterprise, and when he was rebuffed, sought and secured Spanish sponsorship. During his voyage across the Atlantic he encountered the West Indies, as he called them, believing them to be a part of the Indian continent, situated between Europe on this side of the ocean and Cathay and Zhipangu (China and Japan) on the other.

In subsequent voyages made by Columbus it soon became clear, though never to him, that there must be another continent between Europe and Asia. In 1494, the pope in his wisdom decided to divide whatever lands were still left to discover between Portugal and Spain.

Every subsequent discovery to the east of the fiftieth degree of longitude west of the Greenwich meridian would belong to Portugal, and every discovery to the west of it to Spain – an arrangement which gave the Spanish the entire American continent, apart from Brazil (still undiscovered), and the Portuguese all of the Indies and most of Africa.

In 1500, Pedro Alvares Cabral set sail from Lisbon and arrived in Brazil, a country with an area over ninety times that of Portugal, which soon became the most prized of the Portuguese overseas possessions.

At the end of the sixteenth century, Portugal's colonies included Brazil; the Azores; Madeira; the Cape Verde Islands; Elmina and a sizeable part of what used to be called Guinea, in West Africa; a large area of tropical Africa now known as Angola; Mozambique, on the east coast of Africa, and a wide strip of the African shoreline along the Indian Ocean; Ceylon, Goa and a wide strip of western India all the way from Rajputana to Cochin, as well as the island of Macao in the South China Seas. The Portuguese also had virtual control of the Persian Gulf and the Straits of Hormuz, most of the trade around the Cape of Good Hope, in the Indian Ocean and even in the China Seas, and they had trading bases all over the world.

Given such a head-start, it is difficult to understand how they lost the initiative in the race to secure their overseas discoveries to the Dutch, Spanish, French and, above all, the English.

The answer may well be that the very qualities which had enabled the Portuguese to pioneer the exploration business so successfully became a distinct handicap when rapid adaptation to the totally unforeseen requirements of coping with all the problems of colonizing the new lands which had been discovered began to reveal themselves.

The Portuguese had spent years developing their sturdy carracks and caravels; and they were not lightly going to write them off in favour of some new-fangled notion of a seagoing vessel. The result was that the Dutch and the British were soon building less cumbersome and more easily manoeuvrable ships, far more suited to navigating the shallow creeks and inlets and lagoons they had all started to encounter on the other side of the world.

The painstaking, meticulous manner in which the Portuguese planned their voyages may have ensured their safe arrival in foreign parts but instantly became a hindrance once they had arrived; the Dutch and British mariners who followed them had a more haphazard, ad hoc approach to the problems of seamanship which turned out to be far more useful when it came to exploring and opening up the hinterlands of the new colonies.

Also, the careful attention to detail, which had proved so invaluable when plotting voyages never before attempted, became translated, once the explorers were ashore, into a hidebound bureaucratic approach; the Portuguese seemed unable to adjust or to adapt to the huge change in the world that they themselves had largely brought about.

But the biggest mystery of all was the fact that the acquisition of an empire did not seem to stimulate the Portuguese into strengthening their position in Europe, as it did in the case of the other European imperial powers. As Professor C.R. Boxer puts it in *The Portuguese Seaborne Empire 1415–1825* (London: Hutchinson, 1969): '… even more enigmatic, why did the possession of an empire fail to act as a catalyst in Portugal? In the Netherlands, in Britain, in Spain and in France, the possession of an empire worked like yeast, not only on the economic and political life of the nation, but also on its cultural life, its literature, science and art … the cultural impact of the Portuguese empire, though not negligible, remains oddly slight.'

The refusal of the Portuguese to consider more modern

alternatives to the old carracks and caravels led to the loss between 1521 and 1555 of thirty-two of their ships. The Portuguese population dropped from 2 million to around 1 million as the people — men, mostly — scrambled into boats and set off to make their fortunes in the new colonies.

And although from time to time cargoes of young Portuguese orphan women of marriageable age were shipped out, the bulk of the Portuguese colonials married Goan, Indian and Brazilian women, or the daughters of Eurasian women by earlier Portuguese explorers and settlers, and so failed to establish a stable Portuguese ascendancy in their colonies.

Another explanation of the Portuguese failure to consolidate their empire on a more solid and lasting basis could have been the extremely unhealthy conditions, for Europeans at any rate, in places like Goa and Mozambique; according to Professor Boxer, the records of the Royal Hospital for Soldiers at Goa listed 25,000 Portuguese servicemen who died there during the first thirty years of the seventeenth century, and that figure didn't include those who had died in the barracks or while serving on board ship with the fleet. He adds that although long runs of reliable statistics are lacking, there doesn't seem to be any reason to assume that this wastage of manpower showed any great decline during the next 150 years.

One problem which consistently plagued the Portuguese administration in charge of the colonies was the massive desertion from the armed forces, which consisted for the most part of raw recruits and convicts. Again, firm statistics are hard to come by, but it seems that a vast majority of the conscripted men preferred to become slaves to Muslims or other non-Christians, or even to go native, rather than continue in service as soldiers of the king. One reason for this could have been that the Crown was always in arrears in its payments to its armed forces: *tarde, mal e nunce* (late, or in part, or never) was the current catch-phrase.

There were no barracks to receive the men upon their arrival; they starved in the streets, begged at the church doors or went native, either working for some local *fidalgo* (minor nobility), or finding some willing woman, married or otherwise, who was prepared to support them. It was not a firm basis upon which to establish an empire.

Thus, while the Dutch, the Spanish, the French and the British developed their colonies in an organized and controlled manner — which led in the case of the British colonies in North America to a federation of states which, after a war of independence and a civil war, became the most powerful nation in the world — the Portuguese lapsed further and further into the squalor of un-controlled colonialism. An Italian Jesuit missionary complained to Rome that the Portuguese had adopted the vices and customs of India without reserve, including 'the evil custom of buying droves of slaves, male and female, just as if they were sheep ... countless men buying droves of girls and sleeping with all of them, and then subsequently selling them'.

He added: 'There are innumerable married settlers who have four, eight, or ten female slaves and sleep with all of them ... this practice was carried to excess by one man in Malacca who had twenty-four women of various races, all of whom were his slaves, and all of whom he enjoyed.'

It is, of course, only fair to add that whilst many of the Portuguese overseas officials may have been hooked on this particular form of dalliance, others were working hard to develop the trade between the colonies and the mainland in gold, sugar, rum, tobacco and beef ranching. But the plain truth was that the Portuguese were never cut out to be successful colonists.

The monopoly of the trade with India, which previously had been largely the province of the Turks and the Arabs, mainly trading overland, passed for a period to Portugal. Lisbon took over from Venice, Genoa and the Baltic ports as the chief European centre for overseas commerce.

It was a place where merchants from all over the continent came to trade their goods for African gold and ivory, spices from Molucca, Chinese silks, Persian carpets and the unfamiliar products of the New World, including corn, tobacco and cocoa.

Before long, however, the unexpected riches from the new colonies began to demoralize those who remained at home. So long as their country appeared to have plenty of money to pay for imported wheat, the landowners didn't bother to make their peasant tenant farmers till whatever small amount of land was arable. Ancient crafts and skills were quickly forgotten; and the result was what today would be called runaway inflation.

In a sort of dream, the Portuguese squandered away the wealth of their empire, paying for things they could easily have produced themselves, and not even bothering to defend their homeland.

In 1578, Portugal was invaded and conquered by Spain without much difficulty, and a large part of her overseas territories were divided between Spain and the Netherlands. This was during the period when the Netherlands were part of the Holy Roman Empire of the Spanish Hapsburgs, and although the Spanish domination lasted only until 1688, Portugal's role as a major colonial power had come to an end.

By the seventies of this century, when Portugal lost the last remnants of her empire, parts of the nation were almost as poor as the entire country had been in the thirteenth century. Susan Thackeray, who moved from Canada to the Algarve in the early 1970s, describes the life in one corner of the country in her book *Living in Portugal* (London: Robert Hale, 1985): 'Scraggy chickens and small black pigs foraged amiably together. Goats, *café-au-lait* North African-looking sheep and sleek brown oxen grazed on the hillsides, or in the shade of eucalyptus or mimosa trees. Mules and well-tended donkeys pulled carts together or plodded monotonously in circles to work the rusty water-wheels which looked as if they had been there since the Middle Ages. They had, we discovered later. Introduced by the Arabs during the Moorish occupation of Portugal, along with the rice fields and the fruit farms, the *noras* that still provide many Algarve farms with water are essentially the same as they were more than a thousand years ago.'

Portugal is now a member of the European Community and things are going to change, but not yet awhile, a fact which has been recognized by the Community in the special conditions which the country has been granted in order to give it a bit more time to catch up on the rest of the Twelve, or ten of them anyway;

Greece is nearly as poor as Portugal.

But an indication of how dicey and primitive Portugal's economy still was, even as recently as the late seventies, can be gauged from the fact that one product, cork, represented 16 per cent of the total value of all Portugal's exports at that period. By then the use of inferior cork as a general insulating material for most building construction purposes had been superseded by various forms of plastic, and the cork was exported principally for making stoppers for wine bottles.

Cork comes from the bark of a tree which prospers in only a few places, Portugal and parts of Spain amongst them. It is the only material so far discovered which can efficiently stopper a bottle of wine and keep it from contamination caused by contact with the atmosphere over a long period.

It is very expensive to produce, since cork trees cannot be stripped of their bark for the first time until they are at least twenty-five years old and thereafter can be stripped only about once every eighteen to twenty years. Also, the whole business of stripping the bark is highly labour-intensive and requires a force of workers who know precisely what they are doing.

But when you consider everything that goes into the cost of a bottle of wine — the quality of the soil and the species of vine; the fermentation, maturing and bottling; the transportation and marketing; the rent of the off-licence, and the salary of the shop assistant who sells you the final product; the customs duties and tax — it is clear that the cost of the cork must represent only an infinitesimal part of the entire cost of a bottle of wine. And as an ordinary bottle of wine costs only around a couple of quid, this means that the cork must cost only the merest fraction of a penny.

So if cork represented 16 per cent of Portugal's export trade in the late seventies, is it any wonder that the Portuguese came into the Common Market as paupers despite their great colonial past?

LAND AND PEOPLE

Lusitania and Hispania Ulterior

Traces of habitation have been found in the south-west of the Iberian Peninsula dating from Palaeolithic times, and there is evidence of the existence of shell-gathering communities there after the last Ice Age glaciers retreated around 7000 BC, but settled communities did not appear until the Neolithic period.

The first people to arrive upon the scene seem to have been the Celts, and one tribe of Celts, the Lusitani, gave Portugal its ancient name, Lusitania.

The Phoenicians set up trading stations along the coast around 1000 BC, and from about 600 BC they were joined by Greek traders, in search of precious metals mined inland. Next came the Carthaginians, who conquered the country and held out until 202 BC against the Romans.

The whole Iberian Peninsula was then dominated by the Romans, and Portugal became part of their province Hispania Ulterior. Julius Caesar literally put Lisbon on the map by making it his local capital, as indeed he also did with Paris. Four centuries of Roman rule left the Portuguese a rich legacy, including Christianity; their language, which is Latin-based, though it now contains many Arabic and Teutonic words as well as some Asian words brought back by the explorers and traders; a network of straight main roads; a tradition of urban civilization; and the technology for developing their minerals, mainly iron ore, copper and marble at this stage.

After the fall of Rome, the Iberian Peninsula was overrun by the barbarians. These were Germanic tribes from the eastern frontiers of the empire, among them the Visigoths and the Suevi, who occupied north-western Spain, used Porto, nowadays known as Oporto, as their main seaport, and resisted conversion to Christianity until the seventh century AD.

In AD 711, the Moors invaded the whole area from North Africa and dominated it for over 400 years, leaving an indelible impression on southern Portugal, linguistically, architecturally and to some extent culturally.

Christian attempts to reconquer the area began as early as 718, and for the next 150 years the kings of nearby Asturias-Leon and later of Castile made repeated incursions into the area between the Minho and the Douro, around the town of Porto, a district known as 'the land of the Portucale' — from which the name Portugal was derived. The word literally means the quays of Porto (English 'Oporto'), the harbour at the mouth of the River Douro.

By the eleventh century these rulers were appealing to the Pope and to the bishops and kings of France for help against the Moors. The result of their appeal was a minor crusade to oust the infidel from the area; the fact that the land of Portucale happened to be fairly near the site of one of the main European pilgrimage shrines, Santiago de Compostela, in northern Spain, was probably a contributory factor to the decision to clear the Moors out of that area.

After the Moors had been defeated in 1139, Alfonso Henriques, son of Teresa, the illegitimate daughter of the King of Castile, and of Duke Henry of Burgundy, assumed the title of King of Portugal. His claim to reign over the reclaimed northern part of Portugal was accepted by Castile, and the frontier with Spain was fixed. It was one of the earliest and has proved one of the most stable frontiers in Europe.

The Christian reconquest continued to the south of the land of the Portucale but it wasn't until 1249 that the Moors were finally driven out of the Algarve, the southernmost part of what is now Portugal.

The connection between Burgundy and Portugal's monarchy led to the trial plantation of vines from Burgundy in the area around Porto. They thrived in Portugal's sunny climate and were turned into the port wine which for years was the country's most famous export.

Portugal is roughly oblong in shape, with an area of 92,082 square kilometres occupying the south-western corner (one-sixth) of the whole Iberian Peninsula. It has only one land border, that with Spain.

There are no peaks higher than the Serra da Estrela (2,000 metres) in the northern province of Beira, and few areas of plateau higher than 850 metres, all north of the River Tagus.

Today the population is just over 10 million, with a density of 110 people to the square kilometre; 37 per cent is urban, 63 per cent rural. The climate is maritime temperate, almost Mediterranean in the south.

The word Algarve comes from the Arabic El-Gharb, meaning the other side — it appeared to be 'on the other side' to the Moors, who had conquered Portugal from North Africa. The Algarve is Portugal's Riviera, where the sun shines almost as fiercely and as constantly as it does in Greece. As you go further inland and north-eastwards, the climate becomes more and more extreme; in Beira Alta and on the Alentejo Plains, the winters can be bitterly cold and the summers unbearably hot. This climatic variation has had the happy result of giving the Portuguese an extremely varied and attractive landscape.

To quote Susan Thackeray again: 'It has lush vine-clad valleys and sun-baked prairies. Rice paddies and ski slopes. Subtropical gardens and icy plateaux. Cork forests, citrus groves, neatly terraced hillsides, wide sandy beaches. Fishing villages, farming villages, isolated mountain communities and tranquil little towns that have been standing quietly in the sun since Roman times. Squat whitewashed cottages and stately homes. Brash modern developments and cattle ranches. Flossy resorts and windswept plains. Bleak rocky promontories inhabited only by sea-birds, and cities like Lisbon that have managed to combine the old and the new without spoiling either.'

It has everything, in fact, except a high standard of living for the ordinary people who happen to have been born there.

The land is poor, and prone both to drought and inundation. Since the time of the Romans, other mineral resources, including aluminium, a small amount of coal, some tungsten and uranium have been discovered and are now being mined.

The country's natural resources have not so far included either oil or gas, though some hydro-electric schemes to provide power are being belatedly developed to cope with the industrialization needed to catch up with the rest of the Community. Hydro-electric energy now provides nearly half of the nation's require-ments. Portugal does not yet produce any nuclear energy, though it has the raw materials (mainly uranium) to do so, and is keeping its options open.

HISTORICAL PERSPECTIVE

The End of an Empire

The great period of Portuguese discovery, and in effect almost the whole story of Portugal's Colonial Connections has been covered in the introduction to this chapter.

By 1580, having conquered half the world, the country had exhausted a large part of its resources and was in turn conquered, without much resistance, by Spain under the Spanish Hapsburg, Felipe (Philip) II.

After sixty years of Spanish rule, the Portuguese rebelled under the leadership of the Duke of Braganza, grandson of a female claimant to the throne in 1580. Braganza is a town in the north-west of Portugal near the Spanish border. The Duke of Braganza restored the Portuguese monarchy, becoming João IV. His daughter Catherine of Braganza was married to Charles II of England in 1661. As part of Catherine's dowry, Portugal presented England with Tangier and Bombay, and in return, England formed a new alliance with Portugal.

The two countries already had an earlier Treaty of Alliance dating back to 1373, one of the most ancient alliances in Europe. This treaty was initially signed in London — it was confirmed in 1386 by the Treaty of Windsor — after a battle in which English archers helped King João I of Portugal to beat off the Castilians. Subsequently, English crusaders on their way to the Holy Land were diverted to assist Portugal in sorting out her continuing problems with her neighbours. During World War II, Churchill referred to neutral Portugal as 'our oldest ally'.

In the seventeenth century, Portugal's increasingly ailing empire was further depleted when Ceylon and Malabar were ceded to the Dutch. Brazil, however, remained a Portuguese colony, and gold from that quarter helped to finance the mother country for another three centuries.

The Methuen Treaty of 1703 provided England with port wine at a preferential rate of tariff and later allowed England to dump on Portugal the surplus produce of the cotton mills of the Industrial Revolution. The treaty stimulated the Portuguese port-wine trade in the short term, but in the long run, port turned out to be the ruin of Portugal, encouraging landlords and peasants in the Oporto region to neglect other crops for the easy profits to be made from one of England's favourite tipples.

In fact a combination of dependence on the colonies for gold and other riches, and on England for easy profit from port, resulted in a situation in which Portugal became unable to feed herself and became dependent on overseas markets for 60 per cent of her food; this situation continued almost until the time Portugal joined the Community in 1986.

In 1755, a great earthquake devastated Lisbon, killing about 50,000 people; the city was rebuilt by the first of Portugal's authoritarian statesmen, Sebastiano José Pombal, in the English style known as Queen Anne.

Napoleon's troops occupied Portugal in 1807, because Portugal, faithful to its alliance with England, had refused to close its ports to British ships. The Portuguese royal family fled to South America and reigned from exile in Brazil during what was known in England as the Peninsular Campaign. The Portuguese had called on the British to back up their side of the alliance with some military action, and Sir Arthur Wellesley (later the Duke of Wellington) landed an expeditionary force near the mouth of the Mondego and in 1809 drove the French out of Oporto.

Many Portuguese people, including the bourgeoisie and the military, disliked the idea of the country being ruled from Brazil, and demanded the return of a normal, resident, constitutional monarchy. In the meantime, Brazil declared its independence from Portugal in 1822, and although the Portuguese then concentrated all their attention on their African possessions, Mozambique and Angola, the empire continued to fall apart. Goa,

Portugal's last stronghold in India, was annexed by the latter in 1961.

King Carlos I and his heir were assassinated in Lisbon in 1908, and although a younger son succeeded, a parliamentary republic was established in 1910. Portugal entered World War I on the side of the Allies in 1916.

Antonio Salazar, first as minister for finance and then as prime minister, restored some economic and political stability in the late twenties and early thirties, but in 1933 he proclaimed a 'new state' with a constitution which made him a fascist dictator. During this period many rights, including freedom of assembly, protest and strike were severely curtailed, and a strict press censorship was enforced. He dominated Portugal until 1968, when an accident left him brain-damaged.

His successor, Marcello Caetano, tried to introduce some measure of liberalism which, inevitably, led only to more pressing demands for yet further reforms, while the necessity to carry on the fruitless colonial wars in Africa led to military unrest and the formation of a military junta, known as the Armed Forces Movement (MFA).

It had long been clear that the Portuguese had no great talent for colonizing, and the disastrous débâcle in Angola in the early seventies which marked Portugal's final exit from the imperial scene was perhaps a fitting end to an ill-fated adventure which had brought mainly misery to all those connected with it.

But if the Portuguese never acquired a talent for colonization, they certainly developed a great taste for emigration. For centuries, millions of young Portuguese men and women have emigrated to look for a higher standard of living than they could ever hope to find at home. In the nineteenth century particularly, huge numbers emigrated to Brazil and Venezuela, to Mozambique, Canada and the United States. It is estimated that there are now 1.1 million Portuguese living in Brazil, 437,000 in Canada, 203,000 in the United States and 162,000 in Venezuela. Even since 1960, some 2 million Portuguese people have emigrated, about a quarter of them to the industrialized countries of Europe;

by 1989, there were 786,000 Portuguese in France, 70,000 in West Germany, 65,000 in Switzerland and 38,000 in Luxembourg.

Curiously enough, unlike the Irish and the Italians and the Armenians and all the other great emigrant races, the Portuguese never seemed to take their subculture abroad with them. There are no known pockets of Portuguese anywhere in the world, no great number of Portuguese restaurants anywhere, and no Portuguese ghettoes.

By 1974, all Portugal's African colonies had officially been given their independence, and hundreds of thousands of *retornados* (colonial settlers who now wanted to return to the mother country) began to stream back to Portugal, increasing the population by more than a million people over a very short period.

The sudden arrival of so many returned emigrants immediately in the wake of the final collapse of the empire caused enormous problems for a country whose economy was already sorely overstrained, and in 1974 the junior officers of the MFA overthrew the regime in a coup known as the Carnation Revolution, so called because the MFA soldiers stuck carnations in the barrels of their rifles to indicate that the coup was going to be a bloodless one.

Civil and political liberties were in some measure restored, and to the outside world there seemed to be considerable confusion as Portugal struggled on under one military junta after another until, in 1976, an ex-soldier, General Ramalho Eanes, was elected president and introduced a new constitution restoring democratic pluralism and fundamental rights and liberties for the people.

Heavy reductions in government subsidies, increased taxation and the privatization of state industries made life even more difficult for the hard-pressed Portuguese. In 1987, the Social Democrats (PSD) won a majority in parliament and thus were able to justify the position of Prime Minister Anibal Cavaco Silva on some sort of a democratic basis. This victory by the PSD made them – with 145 of the 250 seats in the Assembly – the first majority party to rule in Portugal since its return to democracy in 1976.

DEVELOPMENT DIRECTIONS

Paying for the Past

In 1986, Portugal joined the Community, which promised US$700 million in aid over the following ten years. This led to a 4.5 per cent growth rate in the Portuguese economy, at that time the highest growth rate in Western Europe, though for the same reason as Ireland's initially abnormally high growth rate: because the two countries started so far behind most of the others.

For more than five centuries, Portugal had ruthlessly exploited its colonies and neglected its own agricultural and industrial development. For the five years since 1986, it has been forced to pay the price of that neglect, and it seems likely that it will continue to have to pay for it for many years yet.

Before Portugal joined the Community it was importing 60 per cent of its food while still employing 45 per cent of its total workforce in agricultural production. Today only 23.9 per cent of the workforce is employed in the agricultural sector, but it's still a very high percentage compared with the rest of Europe. The Community money is certainly helping the Portuguese to modernize their food production, but it will also, as it has every-where else, drive a great many more Portuguese farm workers off the land, forcing them to look for industrial jobs in a market already flooded by waves of emigrants from the country's former colonies.

Over 15 per cent of Portugal's population lived by making or selling wine, despite a fact that a good third of the country, south of the Tagus, is unsuitable for cultivating vines.

Initially, too, a good many of Portugal's industries, like Ireland's, were based on agriculture or fishing. One example was the very considerable export trade in tinned sardines. Today Portugal's fishermen, who constitute only 2 per cent of the workforce, contri-bute 30 per cent of the national consumption of protein of 'animal' origin.

One of the prime causes of Portugal's underdevelopment was that the rate of population growth has always been very high. The population increased from 1.2 million in the middle of the seventeenth century to well over 10,388,000 today, giving a relatively high density of population (110 per square kilometre as against 76 in Spain and 51 in Ireland) despite the massive emigration.

The rate of natural growth remains high (0.68 per cent as against 0.53 per cent for Spain, 0.26 per cent for Greece and minus 0.11 per cent for Ireland) which means that the Portuguese have a young population, and one of their constant problems is finding employment for their young people. Unless about 50,000 new jobs are provided every year a proportion of the population, as in Ireland, will continue to be forced to emigrate though the number of Portuguese obliged to go abroad to find work has recently fallen to around 350,000 a year.

As long ago as 1953 Portugal introduced a phased programme of economic development, concentrating first on improving the infrastructure, then on increasing industrialization, and finally on the development of links with the European Free Trade Association (EFTA) and the Community, and an acceleration in the growth of the GDP.

As a direct result of this programme, there has been a good deal of foreign investment in Portugal since the early sixties. The German iron and steel firm Krupp now has a subsidiary in Portugal. The shipyards of Lisnave at Lisbon are turning out modern ships, largely financed by Dutch and Swedish shipbuilding concerns. The Swedish paper manufacturing company Billerud, in association with CUF (*Companhia Unido Fabril*, a Portuguese private company with factories turning out textiles and chemicals), now runs one of the most modern paper-manufacturing plants in the world at Figuera da Foz in Leirosa, using a raw material with which the Portuguese are extremely well-endowed — timber.

However, despite this programme, and even after Portugal had been in the Community for four years, the primary industrial sector remained weak, its productivity representing only between one-eighth and one-quarter of the Community average. And very few of the factories have achieved a level of technology comparable with that of their Community counterparts.

Small industries employ more than a third of the working population and are responsible for nearly 40 per cent of the wealth produced, but most of them are very small indeed; 75 per cent of them employ fewer than five workers, so you could hardly even call them industries.

Tourism is one industry which brings in a great deal of useful foreign currency, and the Portuguese were sufficiently far behind Spain in developing their tourist trade to be able to avoid some of the more obvious pitfalls into which the Spanish fell; for example, the total destruction of areas like the Costa Brava, by the obliteration of all the features that had made the place attractive to foreign tourists in the first place, under a sea of cement and behind a barricade of high-rise hotels and blocks of flats.

By the late eighties Portugal had over 16 million visitors per year (mostly day-trippers from Spain including foreign visitors to Spain), and receipts from tourism were running at around US$2.2 million.

The tourist industry is currently growing at the rate of 23 per cent a year, but in fact Portugal's earnings from one variety of tourism are probably far higher than they appear to be on paper. This is because a large number of foreigners, particularly English people, now have secondary homes or time-share apartments in Portugal, and the money they spend does not appear in the tourist statistics because they have accounts in Portuguese banks and pay their bills in local currency.

Much of Portugal's tourist development has taken the form of luxury secondary residences and time-share apartments with golf courses, yachting marinas and other leisure facilities designed to attract the older, better-heeled traveller.

Madeira, one of Portugal's last offshore islands, also has a successful tourist industry; in fact, 12 per cent of the total hotel capacity of Portugal is on Madeira.

Driving is the only practical way to see large areas of Portugal. There are car ferry services from Britain and Ireland direct to Spain, and car–sleeper services from most European capitals to Lisbon. But the *Blue Guide*, amongst many others, warns that while it may be convenient to travel to Portugal by rail, Portuguese Railways 'are not recommended as a means of touring, except by enthusiasts'.

Most guidebooks admit that the train is considerably cheaper, but also point out that it is usually quicker to go by bus, and there are local bus services all over Portugal. In Portugal, as in Ireland, the local railway station is often quite a distance away from the town or village that it is supposed to be serving.

The roads in Portugal are of a fairly reasonable standard, though there is only one short stretch of motorway between Setúbal and Lisbon, built by the McAlpine firm of British motorway constructors before their activities were interrupted by the Carnation Revolution of 1974. It remains the only motorway in the country, but the main roads are good and well-maintained, though often busy.

Telephones and telecommunications are rapidly reaching international standards, and TV is by far the most popular pastime; 82 per cent of all Portuguese homes now have a TV set and it is estimated that the programmes attract, on average, a daily audience of 2.5 million viewers, aged from eight upwards.

Radiotelevision Portugaise is a public service, financed from taxation, as well as from the receipts from advertising. State intervention is now limited to the provision of a radio and television service for the public.

The Portuguese government provides a network of health centres and hospitals providing free or substantially reduced medical charges and a discount on prescribed medicines. Medical treatment and medicines are completely free for certain categories – retired people, pregnant mothers, children under one year of age, the handicapped, the chronically ill, and so on.

There is a total of 491 hospitals in the country, with a ratio of one hospital bed for every 203 people. As a comparison with Community countries of similar size, Belgium has 808 hospitals, with a ratio of one hospital bed per 84 inhabitants, while Ireland has 1,832 hospitals, with a ratio of one hospital bed per 104 people. In addition to the state hospitals there are private hospitals, which are extremely expensive.

Portugal also has a social welfare system, financed by contributions from employees, employers and the state to cover illness and unemployment, and to provide for pensions.

So far as wealth is concerned, Portugal is right at the bottom of the list published in *Eurostat*, the handbook of basic statistics prepared by the Community. In a chart showing the average gross hourly earnings of manual workers expressed in terms of current purchasing power in their own currencies, Portugal scores just under four units, against Denmark's ten and a half, Belgium's nine, and Ireland's eight and a half.

AFFAIRS OF STATE

Compulsory Military Service

Portugal is now a parliamentary democracy with a one-camera assembly, called simply the Assembly, consisting of 250 deputies elected for four years by universal suffrage, on a proportional representation basis.

Executive power is shared by the president and the prime minister. The present prime minister is Anibal Cavaco Silva and the president is Mario Alberto Soares.

The president is also elected by popular vote, again using a proportional representation system, for a single five-year term. He appoints the prime minister and the Cabinet from the ranks of the party with the highest number of seats in the Assembly, and on the advice of the members of that party.

Until 1976 and in effect for some years afterwards, a revolutionary council of military officers existed to 'advise' the president; since 1983, the military council has been replaced by a tribunal of judges, a Council of State and a Council of National Defence (to advise on military matters only).

Public affairs are effectively centralized, though the Azores and Madeira have some autonomy. Since the 1976 constitution, habeas corpus has been reintroduced, and free speech and freedom of the press are guaranteed.

Under Salazar army expenditure amounted to more than two-fifths of all government expenditure, and the Portuguese army was 179,000 strong. After 1974, decolonization removed the need for armed forces of these proportions, which were considered a threat to civilian rule. By 1983, although obligatory military service remained in force, the Portuguese army had been reduced to 41,000, with a navy of 13,000, and an air force of 9,500, trained by NATO.

Portugal did not join the United Nations until 1955 (largely as a result of Russian vetoes in the Security Council). The country became a member of EFTA in 1960, entered a limited association with the Community in 1973, applied for full membership in 1977, and was admitted in 1986.

CULTURE AND LEISURE

Highest Illiteracy Rate

Portugal has been a Roman Catholic country since the seventh century. The current official total is 94 per cent Roman Catholic, but Church and State have long been separated and the Church receives no direct subsidy from the state. Only about 5 per cent of the population claims any religious affiliation of any kind these days.

Few people bother to attend Mass on Sunday, and the greater part of the population rarely go to church except for weddings, funerals and perhaps at Christmas and Easter.

Education was only one of the many areas which had fallen into neglect in Portugal, and during the Salazar years, had suffered from a profoundly centralized and highly reactionary system of control.

For years, too, there had been large-scale shortages of qualified staff, books, teaching aids and equipment of all sorts. In addition, most of the school buildings were old, sadly neglected and utterly unsuited for their purposes.

The result, perhaps not surprisingly, is that Portugal has the highest illiteracy rate in the Community: 17 per cent in 1989, according to Global World Computer Statistics. This compares with 7 per cent for Italy, 3 per cent for Spain and 1 per cent for Ireland, Denmark, the Netherlands, France and the United Kingdom. What it means in effect is that seventeen out of every 100 people you meet cannot read or write, i.e. nearly one-fifth.

In the sixties, the public education system, aided by the Organization for European Co-operation and Development (OECD), entered a new phase of expansion with the extension of the period of compulsory schooling increased from four to six years. This meant that instead of ending their period of compulsory schooling at ten or eleven, Portuguese children continued to be educated until they were fourteen or fifteen.

This was a great step forward for Portugal, though it would not be reckoned a very big deal in any of the other Community countries with the possible exception of Greece. School lessons on TV (Teleschool) and subsidies to private schools were utilized to make up for the lack of sufficient government schools to implement these plans.

The bloodless military coup of 1974, and the new constitution of 1976, resulted in much more profound changes in the Portuguese educational system. Official – though optional – pre-school education is now given in kindergartens, and is available for children from the age of three until they are old enough to attend primary school.

Six years of compulsory and free schooling make up the basic educational programme. Between the ages of six and eleven, all Portuguese children must now attend one of the government schools, or, where no government school exists, a private school subsidized by the state.

Secondary education, which is optional, lasts for six years, in two stages: a unified general course covering the years from twelve to fifteen, complementary courses from sixteen to eighteen, and one final year. Evening courses are available for children who have already started to work.

Schooling is free up to the ninth year of unified state education, and there are many private schools, though they tend to be extremely expensive.

At the state universities all places are free and are awarded to students on their performance in examinations. There are also several private universities, which charge high fees.

The Portuguese are a baffling race of people. The sudden explosion out of that tiny country on the Atlantic fringe of Europe into a wild flourish of exploration and colonization during the fifteenth and sixteenth centuries did not, as we have seen, lead to Portugal playing any very decisive role on the European scene.

Similarly in the field of literature and the arts, although the epic voyage of Vasco da Gama around the Cape of Good Hope to India in 1498 was celebrated in *The Lusiads*, written by the poet Luís de Camões, and several historical accounts of his and other Portuguese voyages were written, notably by Fernão Lopes, Caspar Correia and João de Barros, they didn't seem to lead anywhere.

Portugal's poets and writers, like its soldiers and sailors and colonial administrators, seem to have lost all heart after that great initial outburst; indeed, the entire nation appears then to have sunk back into an obscure and unambitious provincialism. Offhand, can you think of one single famous Portuguese writer, or painter, or composer or film star? Apart from Salazar, can you think of a famous Portuguese anything since Magellan and Bartholomew Diaz?

I have been through the 100-odd pages devoted to culture in the handbook of facts about Portugal prepared by the Director-General of Social Communications as part of its preparations for entry into the Single Market Community of 1993, and, although this may well be a reflection upon my own insularity or lack of interest in the work of foreign artists, I didn't come across a single name that I immediately recognized and could associate with any specific work. And in my own defence, I must add that this would not be true of any other country in the Community, except possibly Luxembourg, which is more of a principality than a country really, and could not be expected to have any genuine cultural heritage.

So far as music is concerned, there were the troubadours

similar to those of the Languedoc – the earliest courts in Portugal had their bards and balladeers, their poets and musicians – but little remains of all their efforts other than the curiously intro-verted, sad and monotonous chants known as *fados*, a musical form very difficult to define. You could perhaps describe it as fla-menco without any of the passion or indeed very much of the rhythm.

In Portugal it's difficult to separate art from architecture. Every-where you go in Portugal, the Moorish influence seems very strong. Even Portugal's national style of architecture, Manueline, called after King Manuel I, is a blend of Islamic and Gothic features, with Italian and other Northern European overtones.

When you get right down to it, what Portugal is probably most famous for (apart from canned sardines) is the ceramic tile. *Azulejos*, those tiles that grace so many Portuguese walls, old and new, all around the country, are partly Moorish in design, again with Italian components. The original *azulejos* were in bas-relief; these days they are flat, with glaze designs. They are very elegant and they add greatly to some otherwise undistinguished buildings in Lisbon, but they cannot really be regarded as an art form.

And as for art for art's sake, I quote the *Blue Guide* of 1982: 'The arts of painting and sculpture in Portugal from the sixteenth to the early eighteenth century are distinguished by no well-known names.' The same could be said for the nineteenth and twentieth centuries.

In the field of science Portugal has one Nobel prizewinner, Professor Gras Monizin, and I am reliably informed that in the field of international mathematics, the names of Gomes Teixeira and Mira Fernandes have international prestige.

Another curious thing about Portugal. Until fairly recently they didn't have any word for breakfast. Why? Because, until recently, they didn't eat breakfast.

According to an article about corn flakes in the *New York Herald Tribune* of 18 August 1990, the Kellogg's marketing people 'had to confront the fact that traditionally in Spain and Portugal, you get up in the morning and drink coffee and that's about it'.

Arnold Langbo, President of Kellogg's International Division, was quoted as saying that there is actually no word in Portuguese which means breakfast. In Portuguese-speaking Brazil, the Kellogg people spent five years trying to coin a phrase for breakfast. To support this idea, Kellogg found itself marketing the entire notion of breakfast, something to eat first thing in the morning.

On the other hand, modern guidebooks all refer to breakfast as *pequeno almorco*; a Portuguese friend tells me that this means literally small lunch and for him it never consists of anything more than a cup of tea, without milk or sugar, and maybe two dry pieces of toast. He added that *almorco* (lunch), *cha* (both the drink and the occasion), and *jantar* (dinner) are served at 'normal' English hours, slightly later than in France, but slightly earlier than in Spain.

I mentioned above that to most people who have never been to Portugal, the only direct connection between the Portuguese and food is tinned sardines. Even people who have been there tend to think of Portuguese food mainly in terms of salt cod, fish stew or tripe, all dishes which you would normally associate with a barren country on the edge of an ocean, though the dried ham known as *cazuelas* is delicious.

Eggs, wine and rice all play an important part in the Portuguese cuisine; eggs and wine, probably, because hens are as tough as vines and they both will flourish where no other animal or crop can survive, and rice because the Portuguese acquired a great fondness for it during their voyages to the Far East and many now prefer it to other vegetables. A great deal of olive oil is also used in Portuguese cooking, along with such herbs as sage, rosemary and bay.

Soup is served with most meals and fresh fish is available everywhere. Grilled swordfish (*espada grelhado*) is particularly good.

Apart from port wine, which the English (gentlemen mainly) drink as a *digestif* and the French and other Europeans drink (in a slightly lighter form) as an *aperitif*, probably the best-known Portuguese wines are Mateus rosé and *vinho verde*, both slightly sparkling or *petillant*, as the French say. Incidentally, *verde* refers to the youth of the wine, rather than its shade; it comes both in red and white. Beer is also available everywhere; a small glass is known as a *fino* or *imperial*, and a pint tankard a *caneca*.

Bullfighting is not a sport; it is partly a ritual killing, and partly the last relic of the Roman arena. The Portuguese version, in which the bull is harassed by men on horseback, but not killed, lacks both the historical continuity of the Spanish version, and also its whole raison d'être; the moment of truth when an exhausted man faces a wounded and enraged bull. No question of fair play is involved; the bull will die in any event, and usually in a far more dignified manner than if it met its end, as most cattle do, in an abbattoir.

Without the moment of truth, the Portuguese bullfight lacks excitement, and, since it is extremely difficult to kill a bull cleanly from horseback, the *faena* tends to be protracted and messy, so it is perhaps not surprising that it has largely been superseded in the public favour by football.

In general, the Portuguese tend to be spectators rather than participants in sporting activities. At the last count, out of a population of more than 10 million people, only 255,000 claimed to be actively associated with sporting activities, and of those, 112,000 were mainly interested in camping and caravanning.

Football is the top spectator sport, and in this field at least two world-famous names crop up: Eusebio of Benfica, Lisbon, who won the 'golden boot' in 1968 and 1973, and Fernando Gomes of the football club of Oporto, who won the award in 1983 and 1985.

The Portuguese are also very keen on marathons. Carlos Lopes, considered by many followers of the sport to be the greatest marathon runner in the world, still holds a world record which he achieved in Rotterdam in 1985, as well as an Olympic gold medal which he won in the marathon at Los Angeles in 1984.

Although nearly 85 per cent of Portugal's athletes are male, another Olympic gold medal, again for the marathon, was won by Rosa Mota at Seoul in 1988.

THE SPANISH

The Hidden Land

SPAIN IN PROFILE

Area	504,760 sq km
Population	38,600,000
Population density	77 per sq km
Women	50.9%
Under 15	23.9%
Over 65	11.8%
Language	Spanish (Castilian), Catalan, Basque, Galician
Religion	Catholic
Labour force	34.7%
Employed in:	
Agriculture	16.9%
Industry	32.1%
Services	50.9%
Women in labour force	29.6%
Unemployment (as % of labour force)	21.5%

Main exports: Motor cars (31.4%); iron and steel products; machinery; fruit

Main customers: EC (60.9%); USA (9.3%)

THE SPANISH

Spain is different. Very different in language, for a start. Castilian Spanish has curious clicking 'th' sounds not heard in any other European language. The people have an erect dignity and an arrogant remoteness that doesn't feel the slightest bit European. To the English poet W.H. Auden, Spain appeared to be an island, crudely soldered on to Europe. It seemed like an island to the conquering Moors who, from the beginning of the eighth century to the capitulation of Granada in 1492, occupied most of the country. The Phoenicians, long before that, had called the country Spania, a word which could have meant the land of the rabbits, and probably did, or which may have signified, as some philologists insist, the hidden country.

Hidden it certainly is, behind the Pyrenees, through which, throughout the Middle Ages, caravans of pilgrims filed their way slowly southward to Santiago de Compostela, the first package tour pilgrimage, run by the monks of Cluny from the twelfth century onwards, with starting points all over Europe and a string of hospices and monasteries organized to provide overnight lodgings for the pilgrims en route. The focus of this pilgrimage was the unlikely shrine to St James in Santiago de Compostela just south of Corunna, in the north-west corner of Spain. Unlikely because its existence there is based on a Spanish belief that St

James was preaching Christianity in Spain shortly after the crucifixion and that after his own death in Jerusalem his body was smuggled back to Spain, though there is no evidence that he was ever in Spain at all and certainly none that he was the great warrior Santiago Matamoros (St James the Moorslayer), so frequently portrayed in Spanish paintings, on horseback, smiting the Muslim infidel, since he died centuries before Mohammed was born.

Different in their attitude to suffering. Both the Inquisition and the *corrida* are uniquely Spanish institutions which other nations have imitated but never equalled. The Romans may have introduced the idea of death in the arena as a public entertainment — or maybe it was an idea they had stolen from the Etruscans — but it was the Spanish who developed the ritual of *corrida* and invented the *faena*, the moment of truth when an exhausted man faces an aggravated bull bred for ferocity, and tries to kill the animal with a dignity befitting them both. The English regard it all as highly unsporting, but in no way was it ever intended to be a sport; the bull is destined to die anyway, just as anybody who was unlucky enough to have been called upon to answer a charge of heresy at the *auto-da-fé* was bound to die anyway, however fervent or complete the recantation. The *corrida* is a ritual killing, carried out in the glaring *sol y sombra* of a Spanish afternoon, with garish, tawdry music from a small band.

Jan Morris brilliantly describes the effect this essentially brutal spectacle can provoke in *Spain* (London: Barrie and Jenkins, 1988). As the evening shadow creeps across the ring, she writes, 'you will feel yourself, hour by hour, fight by fight, half united with the fierce multitude by your side. The nobility of death … is the point of the bullfight, the Moment of Truth that comes, in the end, to us all; and before very long you too may feel that, through the bloodlust and the intolerance, something of grandeur emerges … the beast, after one clean, almost imperceptible sword-thrust, sinks slowly to its knees. The matador, as proud and kind as any victorious Marquis, reaches out a gentle hand, in a movement infinitely graceful and brotherly, to touch his dying adversary between the horns.'

It's true. That curious combination of gaudy glitter, savage cruelty and something deep and fundamental and primitive reaches out and touches most people who are prepared to expose themselves to it; naturally members of the various animal rights protection societies will not approach the *corrida* in a frame of mind likely to enable them to appreciate what Jan Morris is talking about.

And there is the added fascination that this is a drama without a script, a performance which cannot be rehearsed. The bull will die, but it doesn't know that; the man may also die, and he knows that only too well. But until the moment when the bull thunders out into the blazing sunlight of the arena, pawing the ground and looking for something to charge, nobody can possibly know exactly what is going to happen, though part of the appeal of the spectacle is that every stage in the ritual is preordained, and if all goes well, the *corrida* should proceed, stage by stage, with the unvarying formality of a *missa solemnis*.

But the days of the *corrida* in Spain are limited. It is being killed, as so many other things are, in other countries all over the world, by TV. In the old days people used to go to their local bullring and watch the village lads chance their luck with young bulls reared by a neighbouring farmer. And if one of the local lads did make it, and was chosen as one of the matadors for the Bilbao Feria d'Agosto, some of the people from the village would go up to Bilbao to cheer him on. Now they sit at home and watch on the telly, the ones who have already made it, the stars fighting in Madrid or Barcelona. As a result, there are fewer people to support the local *corrida*, and consequently, much less new blood coming to Madrid and Barcelona and Seville and Pamplona from the provinces to replenish the cast. So the *corrida* will be destroyed as so many human institutions and diversions have been destroyed by the box in the corner with its non-stop transmission of moving wallpaper.

And the Inquisition was different. There was religious intolerance everywhere and on both sides both before and after the Reformation; but nowhere was it so highly organized and so sedulously carried out as in seventeenth-century Spain. There are no statistics on the number of victims all, in the end, killed — burned at the stake, decapitated, disembowelled or impaled, after hours or days or weeks of unimaginable torture. But there were some 20,000 familiars of the Holy Office scattered throughout Spain and there were informers everywhere, to report lapsed *Moriscos* (Moors converted to Christianity), converted Jews suspected of backsliding or Lutheran heretics. Denunciations of friends and neighbours were as common as they were in Nazi Germany during the height of Hitler's Third Reich. The Holy Office had established an iron grip on the country and maintained it by creating and generating fear of the hooded, impersonal inquisitors.

Before World War II, Spain was different because the Spanish had a civil war about which everybody had strong opinions, one way or the other, and a lot of young men from England and the United States and elsewhere were prepared to go out and fight on the side of the Republicans. And again after World War II, Spain was still different because then it had a strict Fascist dictatorship, coming into full flower just around the period when the Allies had defeated Italy and Germany, and were putting the other surviving European Fascist leaders on trial as war criminals.

There was a puzzling contradiction, too, in the fact that many members of the generation of British people who had fought against Fascism in the war saw nothing wrong with spending their holidays or even their retirement in a Fascist country. The first general elections in Spain for over forty years did not take place until June 1977.

Even after that, each province had a military governor as well as a civil one, and the military and police remained very much in evidence all over a country which on Franco's death in 1975 — and on Franco's express instructions — had become a monarchy again, though Juan Carlos I, who was invested with all the trappings of kingship, realized very well that the crown he was being offered after an interregnum of forty-three years was that of a very limited monarchy.

To anyone visiting Spain for the first time from anywhere else in Western Europe up to say five or six years ago it seemed, despite the luxury hotels and cocktail bars and other familiar appurtenances of modern civilization, a strangely remote, introverted, self-contained place, sealed off from dangerous foreign influences and intellectually isolated from the remainder of Europe. It was hard to believe that this country was once the centre of an empire far greater than that of the Romans and, unlike the Portuguese Empire, almost as efficiently governed as Rome's.

Not only that, but during the centuries the Romans ruled Hispania as they called it, the Spanish were most advanced and civilized of all the Empire's subject races. They had already learned (from the Phoenicians) how to write, to use coins, to mine for minerals. From the Greek trading colonies that had been established along the Spanish coast they had learned to cultivate the vine and the olive. They seem to have been born with a natural talent for the arts of war; it took the Roman legions two centuries to subjugate them in the Punic Wars. The exploits of the Lusitanian *caudillo* Viriathus and the tactics of his troops, the first guerrillas who harassed the Romans for six years until he was assassinated, were celebrated by Roman historians, as was the mass suicide of the population who, rather than submit to Scipio Aemilianus in 133 BC, burnt their homes around them and threw themselves over precipices. 'It was the long resistance of the Spaniards that forced Rome to adopt conscription, and it was from a Spanish model that the Roman armourers copied the famous short sword of the legionaries,' comments Jan Morris.

After the Roman conquest in 201 BC, Spanish soldiers were immediately enlisted in the Roman legions, but the arts of peace flourished in Spain under the Romans as well as those of war, and the Province of Hispania became a prosperous and thoroughly integrated part of the empire – in a way, perhaps that the Spanish have never since been integrated in Europe, not at any rate until the arrival of the European Community.

Seneca lived and wrote in Spain as did the Latin satirist Martian, and the emperors Trajan, Hadrian, Marcus Aurelius and Theodosius all came from Hispania. When the Romans finally pulled out in the fifth century AD — about the same time as they withdrew their legions from England — Spain was a flourishing and cultured Christian country.

In 1519, when the Hapsburg Carlos (Charles) I, King of Spain became also the Holy Roman Emperor Charles V, his dominions included Spain, the Netherlands, parts of France, southern Italy, the whole of South and Central America, most of what is now the United States, the Philippines, and various islands scattered around the globe from the Azores to Sumatra. It was the greatest empire the world had ever known.

Some notion of the scale on which the Spanish monarchs of that period thought and conceived can be gained from the Escorial, that vast castle, half-palace, half-monastery started by Charles V's son Felipe (Philip) II of Spain in 1563 just outside the town of Madrid in Castile, which he had chosen to be the first capital city Spain had ever had. It is as big as a city (in fact it is classed as a *ciudad*) and it includes a monastery, a church, a royal palace, a royal mausoleum and a library. It has sixteen courtyards, 2,673 windows (1,100 of them external), 1,200 doors, eighty-six staircases and 900 square metres of painted frescoes. When Felipe built it, Spain was the richest and most powerful nation on earth, and he ruled the entire empire from this palace, which was completed in 1584. Yet before he died in 1598, he knew that Spain's heyday was over.

But these vast possessions brought no great happiness to him or to any of his family. He himself died in great suffering after months of agony in a room in the Escorial overlooking the chapel. His father, Charles V, had abdicated to spend his last years in a lonely hermitage which he had had built expressly for that purpose near Plasencia in Estramadura, the province from which Cortés and Pizarro had set out to conquer the Aztec ruler Monte-zuma and the Inca ruler Atahulpa and to found two new Spains in what are now Mexico and Peru.

Charles V's mother was Juana la Loca (Joanna the Mad), who spent forty-nine years of her life locked up in a cell in the convent of Santa Clara in Tordesillas near Valladolid, and it is a good example of Spanish isolation and single-minded concern for the past that as (comparatively) recently as 1939, just after Franco had won the Civil War, and eight years after Spain had become a republic, it was still not possible for anyone to visit the convent of Santa Clara without written permission from either the Pope or the King of Spain.

It was at Tordesillas in 1494 that the Borgia Pope Alexander VI, in an effort to prevent war between Spain and Portugal over the territories they had discovered in the new world, divided the remainder of the known (and unknown) world between the two of them, granting to the Spanish everything that had been discovered or might be discovered to the east of the fiftieth degree of longitude west of the Greenwich meridian, known as the Line of Demarcation (or the Division of Tordesillas), and everything to the west of this line to the Portuguese. Thus Spain obtained legal possession (i.e. permission from the Pope to claim possession) of most of Central and South America, while Portugal's legal overseas empire now included Brazil, as yet undiscovered.

Pizarro, the son of a swineherd, is buried in the church of Santa Maria de la Concepción in Trujillo in the Estremadura where he was born; in his lifetime, as Sacheverell Sitwell puts it in *Spain* (London: Batsford, 1975), 'in the Temple of the Sun at Cuzco he saw the twelve golden lifesize statues of the Incas and the Incas' garden planted with golden fruits and flowers. And having seen Trujillo and the secular misery in which he was born, it becomes easier to understand the spirit of the Conquistadores. His descendant, after more than four centuries, the Marquesa de la Conquista, still has a "palace" in Trujillo with a corner balcony of the renaissance, splendid heraldry above, and estates in the neighbourhood.'

Not far away from Trujillo near the wild district of Las Hurdes, believed to be inhabited only by wild boars and devils, Sitwell saw, a few years after World War II, the other side of the coin at a town called La Alberca: 'There is no wheeled traffic of any sort in La Alberca. You can only go into town on horse- or mule-back, or on foot. And La Alberca is decidedly a town and not a village, for there must be between two and three thousand persons living there. It is, certainly, the most extraordinary centre of human habitation in which I have ever set foot. The streets or alleys, which are at the same time open drains, are strewn with enormous stones or boulders in lieu of pavement, and you have to pick your way ... The ground floors of the houses are of granite, with smaller stones above that, but their overhanging top storeys are of great baulks of timber. It is difficult to indicate the degree of darkness of the side alleys, but already one dreads the thought of La Alberca after nightfall.'

He adds that 'the Stygian, Tartarean alleys are lit up with the flaming colours of the cocks and hens,' and in the same book remarks that these barn-door roosters have a brilliant plumage which can be traced back to the fighting cocks brought out to Spain during the Peninsular War by the Duke of Wellington's officers, to while away the time between battles.

It is doubtful that anyone in Spain lives like that these days, though there is still a great deal of both poverty and prosperity. And although Sitwell's book was originally written in 1950, it was revised in 1975; and while he was revising it he became deeply aware that Spain was changing. He was proudly shown over a new hotel in the suburbs of Leon in Asturias, opened in 1964, which had originally been the convent of San Marcos and at one time was used as a barracks by the Knights of Santiago. It was the height of luxury with the latest in kitchens, bathrooms, laundries and 'tipico' rustic restaurants with waiters and waitresses in regional costumes. As to the wisdom of turning such a splendid old building into a modern hotel, he argues that the convent of San Marcos was in very bad condition and had then been put into a state where it might be expected to last for many years; and he quotes a Spanish architect, Don Fernando Moreno Barbera, who said: 'When our living standard catches up with that of other nations, we shall differ from only a few of them as regards climate, but we shall differ from them all in the vast number of fine buildings and monuments we possess.'

Certainly Spain has some magnificent buildings – the cathedral of La Sagrada Familia in Barcelona is both extraordinary and in its way totally unforgettable — but there has been such a rash of modern high-rise hotels and blocks of flats and leisure centres in Spain, particularly all along the Costa Brava, the Costa del Sol, much of the Mediterranean coast in fact, as well as in the Balearics, that at times one does indeed feel that Spain may eventually differ from the other Mediterranean countries only as regards climate.

Spain is different. Its climate is extraordinary: in Castile, as the saying goes, they get nine months of winter and three months of hell. Aragon has been described as Africa without the palm trees. In the south of Spain, the winters are so mild and spring starts so early that Spain has captured Europe's common market for *primeurs* and melons.

Its language — though spoken by 170 million people world-wide, 140 million of them in Latin America — is not like any other European language. Some of its music carries heavy overtones from Africa — though it's called flamenco, according to some experts, from a word that entered the language in derogation of those ignorant northerners, the Flemings, who had come down from the Netherlands to help run the civil service when Spain and the Netherlands were all the one kingdom.

Its pride — a fierce, inbuilt assurance which can appear to foreigners to verge on arrogance — is utterly unlike the cheerful chauvinism of the French or the smug self-satisfaction of the Luxembourgers or the placid complacency of the British, and is unique in Europe. The Spanish believe history only in so far as it reflects credit on them and accept a great deal of what the rest of the Community regards as progress with deep, and perhaps justified, suspicion.

Spain is different. There are bears in Spain still, in the mountains of the north, and wolves as well as wild boar and golden eagles and buzzards and bulls bred purely for their fighting ferocity.

Spain is different. Not until 1835, when Santas Crues and Poblet were sacked by mob violence, were the iniquitous Holy Orders finally expelled from Spain. And yet even today in Seville and Malaga, during the Passion Week processions, the penitents still march, wearing tall conical hoods which come down to their shoulders with only narrow slits for the eyes, in a sort of guilty commemoration of Torquemada's hooded and anonymous torturers.

Since Franco's death, the young people of Spain seem to have embraced the notion of the permissive society with undisguised relish. Girlie magazines are openly displayed on the shelves of the newspaper kiosks, there are queues for the X-rated films, and you will see couples snogging, as it's called in Britain, in the public squares, yet more than 1,500 saints (that's more than four per day) are still celebrated in the Spanish calendar. In dozens of seminaries, to quote Jan Morris again, 'pale students still study Latin, and in many villages on the local saint's day, first communicants [aged six or seven] still walk home from church in bridal gowns and sailor suits.'

Spain is different ...

LAND AND PEOPLE

A Citadel Surrounded by a Moat

With a surface area of 504,760 square kilometres, Spain is the third largest country in Europe, after the Soviet Union and France. This figure includes the Balearic Islands (4,992 square kilometres) lying to the east of the Iberian Peninsula and the Canary Islands (7,447 square kilometres) about 1,000 miles south of Spain just off the west coast of Africa. The territory of Spain also includes two cities in North Africa, Ceuta (18 square kilometres), and Melilla (14 square kilometres), but does not include the town of Gibraltar and its hinterland controlling the straits which connect the Atlantic and the Mediterranean; this territory has remained a British possession since the War of the Spanish Succession in the early eighteenth century, a very sore point indeed with the Spanish.

Because of its position – the furthest point in Europe from

Asia, and the nearest to Africa (only 14 kilometres away) — the Spanish happened to find themselves at one of the principal crossroads of world history. However, the rugged terrain and the relative lack of safe, sheltered harbours made it far less accessible to shipping than either the Italian or the Balkan peninsulas, and the barrier of the Pyrenees — which stretch right across the 435 kilometre land frontier with France, and average over 2,000 metres with peaks up to the 3,404 metres of the highest mountain, the Aneto — proved a formidable obstacle to overland trade and communications. So in a sense it was geography which really dictated Spain's isolation from the remainder of Europe; it is, with Portugal, in many ways like a small, self-contained continent.

The entire Iberian Peninsula is a great massif which the Greek historian and geographer Strabo likened to a bull's hide. The Spanish mainland has a coastline 3,904 kilometres long and an average altitude of 660 metres; 47 per cent of the surface area consists of mountains between 600 and 1,200 metres high, mainly, apart from the Pyrenees, around the coastline with a great central tableland, the Meseta, which comprises almost half the entire territory of the country (211,000 square kilometres) and averages between 600 and 1,200 metres high.

The main mountain ranges, apart from the Pyrenees, are the Cordillera Cantabrica and the Cordillera Iberia in the north-east and the Sierra Nevada in the south. The main rivers, none of them navigable for any great length, include the Ebro (910 kilometres), flowing eastwards into the Mediterranean south of Barcelona; the Guadalquivir (280 kilometres), which rises in the Sierra Nevada north-west of Granada and flows into the Atlantic at Cadiz; and the Duero (922 kilometres), which flows across the Meseta and becomes the Duoro in Portugal. The Tagus (1,082 kilometres) is called the Tajo in Spain and the Tejo in Portugal, where it enters the Atlantic at Lisbon. The only other sizeable river, the Guadiana (820 kilometres) forms, for its last few kilometres, Spain's other land border, with Portugal.

The entire structure has been likened to a fortress or a citadel, guarded by a wall of mountains, with the peaks as watch-towers, and surrounded by a moat.

The climate is officially Mediterranean, but its position on the western seaboard of Europe, its proximity to the Atlantic and its depressions lead to extreme seasonal variations particularly in the Meseta, with frost and low temperatures in the winter (3.5 degrees centigrade is the January average), very hot summers (25 degrees centigrade is the July average), long periods of drought and everywhere a lot of sunshine — an average of 2,000–2,700 hours of sunlight per year. On the southern Mediterranean coast, which is protected by the Sierra Nevadas, the winters are the mildest in Europe and the summers the hottest; here the crops include sugar cane, pineapples and bananas.

The peninsula's first inhabitants, a hunting and food-gathering people who possibly came up from Africa, migrated into the area along the coast of the Mediterranean, mainly around the estuaries of the rivers — there is an important Neolithic site in Almeria, near Granada which has been carbon-dated at around 2500 BC — whilst other prehistoric people moved into the caves near Santander on the Atlantic coast. There are traces of prehistoric man all over Spain, but principally in the caves of Altamira, believed to date back to 12,000 BC.

Subsequently, Spain formed the western extreme of a movement of people from the Middle East, and around the fifth century BC, in the Neolithic revolution, the hunter-gatherers learned how to settle down in one place, cultivate crops and raise domestic animals.

These early people including the Ligurians, who also spread into the northern part of Italy around the same time; the Iberians, who may have come from North Africa; and the Celts (including the Basques) who arrived in Spain via France in the sixth century BC.

Around 1100 BC the seafaring, Semitic Phoenicians, who came from Tyre and Sidon in Syria, set up trading posts in the Algarve in what is now Portugal and at Cadiz on the Atlantic coast of Spain, as well as all along the Mediterranean coast. There the Greeks also established trading settlements from the Ebro estuary up to the Gulf of Rosas; Ampurias, near Rosas, is one of the best preserved Greek cities in this part of Europe.

Spain's population by the end of 1992 will number very nearly 40 million people, with an average density of seventy-seven inhabitants per square kilometre, one of the lowest in the Community; Portugal has 110 and Spain's other next-door neighbour France has 101 per square kilometre. The population is very unequally distributed throughout the country, with a growing tendency to desert the Meseta, apart from the Madrid area and a couple of other cities, and concentrate along the coastal areas. The degree of urbanization is extremely high at about 91 per cent, though there are only two big cities, Madrid with 3.6 million (and a population density of 605 people per square kilometre) and Barcelona with 1.8 million; Seville and Valencia both have around 770,000 inhabitants, Zaragoza 600,000 and the remainder of the cities under 500,000.

This urbanization is relatively recent. In 1900, Spain only had 220 towns with a population of over 10,000 inhabitants; by 1981, the figure had grown to 538. It's probably far greater today, but there are no more recent statistics available.

The population growth rate is low, only slightly exceeding an annual average of 1 per cent over the years from 1920 to 1980; towards the end of the last century, the relatively high birth-rate was offset by a high mortality rate, and mass emigration to South America; more recently the Spanish have also been emigrating to other European countries. Between 1900 and 1935, 700,000 Spanish people emigrated, 500,000 of them between 1939 and 1950; and between 1960 and 1977, about 2.5 million people left Spain to work elsewhere in Europe, though many of them returned after a few years.

Since 1981, the growth rate has dropped to 0.4 per cent, about the same as in France and Portugal. The birth rate has dropped considerably as has the mortality rate, and for the first time in centuries Spanish emigrants are now returning from other countries to live in Spain, because access to the Community has created new jobs and better opportunities. Also, according to an earlier census which included foreigners living in Spain, by 1981 more than 230,000 foreigners — a large proportion of them British — had settled in Spain on a more or less permanent basis.

Unlike many of the Community countries, Spain has no problems with non-indigenous minorities; its minority problems are created by members of its own indigenous population, particularly the separatist Basques. Curiously, there has been no immigration into Spain of people from her former overseas colonies; possibly for the reason that until relatively recently Spain had few job opportunities likely to attract immigrants from her former colonies. As a result the population is almost exclusively Spanish, though 16 per cent of them claim to be Catalan rather than Spanish, 8 per cent claim to be Galician, and 3 per cent Basque. And, of course, many Spanish people have Moorish and Jewish descendents.

The languages are Spanish (Castilian), Catalan, Galician and Basque.

It was the country's mineral resources — silver in Murcia (Cartagena) and in Helva (Andalusia) and gold and tin in Galicia — which first attracted the Phoenicians. They set up trading posts there in the eleventh century BC, and the Greeks did the same, and for the same reason, several centuries later. More recently, the industrial development of the Basque region around Bilbao and Asturias was based on the mineral wealth of the area. Almost every type of mineral is found under the soil of Spain — more than 100 varieties including iron, copper, lead, mercury, pyrites and wolfram among the metallic minerals and dozens of non-metallic minerals such as fluospar and quartz.

Spain also has many of the energy-producing natural resources, though not in any great quantity: some coal, some oil, some uranium and a good deal of natural gas. Hydro-electric power, limited necessarily by seasonal variations in rainfall, provided a useful ingredient in Spain's belated industrial revolution until the 1960s, when nuclear power and geo-thermal and solar energy began to be developed on a large scale. Wind-energy as a power source is also now being developed, a product of Spanish–German co-operation.

Up to 1987, coal provided 42.4 per cent of the country's electricity requirements, and hydro-electric schemes 26.3 per cent; with the opening of the Vandelos II and the Trillo I plants in 1989, nuclear energy began to take over, supplying 35.8 per cent of total electricity requirements in that year.

Spain is currently 60 per cent dependent on foreign sources for her energy needs, notably oil, mainly from the Persian Gulf countries.

HISTORICAL PERSPECTIVE

The Black Legend

Up to the fourth century BC, central Spain was largely inhabited by the Celts, who were nomadic herders. They grazed their flocks on the highlands in the north in the summer, and came down to the southern Meseta in winter. The coastal area from the north-eastern Mediterranean to the Atlantic was inhabited by the Iberians, who by 400 BC had started to form a group of city-states similar to those established by the Phoenicians and the Greeks. The first written records of the peninsula date from this period, and one theory is that Hispania, the Roman name for Spain, had its origins in the Semitic word Hispalis (Seville).

After the Phoenicians and the Greeks came the Carthaginians, who founded two great towns in Spain: Cartagena and Barcelona. Attracted by Spain's strategic position, and by its mineral wealth, the Romans decided to add it to their empire, but first they had to deal with the Carthaginians. When they were pushed out of their former headquarters in Sicily by the Roman legions, the Carthaginians made Spain their main base of operations; it was from Spain that Hannibal set out, elephants and all, to cross the Alps and march on Rome. This adventure led to the destruction of the Carthaginian Empire, and from 218 BC onwards the Romans spent almost two centuries trying to subdue Spain, before turning it into one of the most civilized and cultured of the Roman provinces.

The Hispanic provinces were invaded and devastated by the Germanic tribes of the Franks and the Suevi in the period between AD 264 and 276. The Visigoths, who had come to some sort of terms with the Romans, made an attempt to restore order on Rome's behalf from a base in Toulouse, but when they themselves were defeated by the Franks in what was then still known as Gaul, they set up a military autocracy at Toledo. Christianity was one of Rome's many legacies to Spain, and the 4 million Christian Iberians living along the coast could not easily be controlled by 100,000 pagan Visigoths who didn't believe in mixing socially with their subjects. Even after the Visigoths adopted Christianity as their official religion, the fighting continued.

By the eighth century the Moors, a miscellaneous collection of Arab peoples, with very little in common apart from their fervent Muslim religion, had spread from the Near East right along the northern coast of Africa. They were now ideally placed to take advantage of the disunity in Spain, and in 711 an expeditionary force of some 7,000 Berbers from Mauretania landed at Gibraltar and before long the Moors had gained control of most of Spain and were advancing up through France to conquer Europe when they were defeated by Charles Martel and the armies of the Franks at Poitiers.

The Moors fell back on southern Spain, and settled in, allowing the Iberians to keep their religion provided they paid a capitation tax which was levied on them, and holding the more militant northern Spanish Christians at bay, in the Pyrenees and in the mountains of the north-west, where a few Christian principalities like Leon and Castile survived. Castile got its name from the castles the Christian Iberians built to repulse attacks from the Moors.

Under the tolerant rule of the caliphs, Córdoba became one of the most advanced and civilized cities in Europe with libraries and schools of philosophy and medicine.

The Christian reconquest had begun in the seventh century when the reputed discovery at Compostela of the body of St

James the Moorslayer proved an important factor in the struggle, and brought Christians from all over Europe into Spain to support their cause against the infidel. And after the kingdoms of Leon, Aragon and Navarre – the latter set up by the Basques – were united by Alfonso VIII, the Moors were decisively defeated at Las Navas de Tolosa in 1212, though they were not finally driven out of Spain for almost three more centuries. And, after the rise of the Ottoman Empire, the presence in Spain of an unassimilated minority who had far more in common with the Turks than they had with their Spanish conquerors was a nightmare for Spain's rulers for 300 years.

In 1479, Castile and Aragon, the two most powerful kingdoms in Spain, were united. Under the joint rule of Fernando II of Aragon and Isabel I of Castile, the country was partially unified and the Moors were driven out of Granada in 1492. The Moors who elected to stay on in Spain were confronted with a simple choice between Christian baptism or expulsion; those who accepted the Christian alternative were known as *Moriscos*. Similarly, the Spanish Jews were required to renounce their faith or leave the country. Converted Jews were known as *Conversos* and expelled Jews as *Sefardies*.

Ironically, that was the year that Columbus, the navigator from Genoa, finally managed to persuade Fernando and Isabel to finance his voyage across the Atlantic in an attempt to find a new route to the spices of the East, and accidentally stumbled on the continent of America, the future land of liberty and home of the free as well as a place in which millions of Hispanic Latin Americans would later live in peace and relative prosperity.

While the Conquistadores were taking over, on Spain's behalf, the vast wealth of the Incas and the Aztecs, and opening up the riches of the American continent, Fernando and Isabel were consolidating their position in Europe. Isabel, their eldest daughter, was married to King Manuel I of Portugal; Juana, the second daughter, was married to Philip the Fair of Burgundy, son of the Hapsburg Holy Roman Emperor Maximilian I; and Catherine of Aragon, the youngest, became the first of the six wives of King Henry VIII of England.

When in 1494 Charles VIII of France invaded Italy, the Spanish agreed initially to join the French in exploiting these new territories but they soon quarrelled over the division of the spoils, and the Spanish ended up in complete control of the Kingdom of Naples.

Following the deaths of Isabel in 1504 and of Juana's husband Philip in 1506, Juana la Loca (Joanna the Mad) was declared unfit to rule by a regency council under Cardinal Cisneros, and her son Charles, then only six years old, succeeded her with Fernando of Aragon as his regent (and after Fernando's death in 1516, Cardinal Cisneros). Charles had been born in Ghent and brought up in the Netherlands, and on his accession in 1516 inherited Flanders, the Netherlands, Artois, the Franche-Comté, the Kingdoms of Castile and Aragon, and all the new overseas territories in America.

He was, of course, a complete stranger to his Spanish subjects, and when he arrived in Spain in 1517 with a string of Flemish favourites and began to distribute loot, honours and high offices among them, inevitably there was trouble. His election in 1519 as Holy Roman Emperor only made things worse; it now began to look as though Spain was going to be ruled by a man whose main interests lay elsewhere and who might well leave the administration of Spanish affairs in the hands of his Flemish followers. A revolt by the *communeros* (communes or communities) supported by some of the disaffected nobles was quickly put down, and Charles turned his attention to the problem of the Turks. As Charles V, the Holy Roman Emperor, his mission was to defend the faith against the infidel. As Carlos I, King of Spain, he was only too conscious of the Turkish threat to Spain's garrisons in North Africa and of the depredations of the Berber corsairs all around the Spanish coast and on the high seas, and he was acutely aware of the existence in Spain of a large and potentially subversive *Morisco* population, who, if they decided to rebel, would have the support of the entire Muslim world.

In an effort to sever all contact between the Moors in North Africa and the *Moriscos* at home, he led a successful expedition to Tunis in 1535, and tried but failed to take Algiers. In Europe, he used his Spanish armies in his battles with France and in his war against the German Lutherans. His troops were known throughout the world for their ruthless cruelty; the *leyanda negra* (the Black legend) may have had its origins in Italy where Sicily and Sardinia had been added to the Spanish possessions, but it gained added virulence after some of the worst excesses of the Spanish Inquisition and the exploits of the Conquistadores.

By 1558 Charles had abdicated both the throne of Spain and the Holy Roman Empire and had elected to spend his last years in a monastery in Estramadura. He had tried, without success, to secure the succession of the Holy Roman Empire for his son Felipe (Philip); but the position, if one may put it that way, went to his brother Fernand.

But if Felipe II of Spain did not have to concern himself with the affairs of the Holy Roman Empire, he had plenty of other problems on his plate, including continuing discontent in the Netherlands, where a movement towards national separatism had been fortified by adherence to the new, reformed Christianity as well as the continuing Muslim threat. Born in Valladolid, Felipe was essentially a Spaniard dedicated to defending the faith.

He decided to deal first with the religious troubles in the Netherlands and sent the best of his troops there in 1567 under the Duke of Alba. Then in 1568, at a time when the peninsula had been stripped of its stern Spanish soldiers, the *Moriscos* of Granada rose in revolt. The rebellion of Alpujarras turned into a savage guerrilla war, fought in the mountains behind Granada for nearly five years before a royal army under Ferdinand's illegitimate half-brother, Don Juan (John) of Austria, cleared the rebels from the mountains. To punish them for rebelling, the *Moriscos* were driven from their homes in and around Granada and forcibly dispersed throughout the peninsula.

Felipe's next move was to form a league with Venice and the Pope, and send a combined fleet under Don Juan of Austria and the Genoese Admiral Andrea Doria against the Turkish fleet who were routed in 1571 at the battle of Lepanto.

This victory, however, was not followed up because of increasing problems with militant Protestantism in northern Europe. The northern provinces of the Netherlands declared themselves an independent republic at The Hague in 1581, with the support of Protestant England, though the republic wasn't recognized for another twenty-seven years.

Infuriated by England's support of his Protestant Netherlands subjects, irritated beyond measure by British piratical raids on his galleons returning from the Americas laden with loot, and incensed at the failure of his own plot to secure the English succession for the Catholic Mary, Queen of Scots, Felipe very unwisely decided to invade England. At enormous expense, a great armada of ships was prepared, and was ready to tackle the job by 1588, but bad weather and the greatly superior skill of the English seamen under Sir Francis Drake made short work of the whole enterprise. Many of his warships were destroyed in the Channel, and most of the remainder were wrecked on the Scottish and Irish coasts as they tried to escape by sailing northwards all the way around the British Isles.

Any other nation would have been bankrupted by such a disaster, but by now the colonization of the New World was beginning to pay off handsomely. The Spanish colonists in Peru and Mexico were always looking for supplies of all sorts of things from home, and were prepared to pay dearly for them with the gold and silver they had stolen from the Incas and the Aztecs. From a desk in his new palace the Escorial near Madrid, Felipe ran his vast empire, which by now also included Portugal and its overseas possessions which he had seized on the grounds that his mother was the eldest daughter of King Manuel I of Portugal. Felipe died, after a long and painful illness, in 1598.

His son Felipe III carried on his father's work against the Moors by decreeing the expulsion of some 275,000 *Moriscos* out of the 500,000 still remaining in Spain. During the reign of his son Felipe IV, Portugal broke away from Spain and in 1688 restored its own monarchy.

Felipe IV's daughter, the Infanta Maria Teresa, was married to Louis XIV of France as a symbol of reconciliation between France and Spain. Felipe left only one sickly son, Carlos II, who, childless, bequeathed his throne to Philip, Duke of Anjou, grandson of Louis XIV and Maria Teresa.

The arrival on the Spanish throne of a Bourbon had immediate international repercussions in the form of the War of the Spanish Succession. Britain and Austria contested Philip of Anjou's claim to the Spanish throne, and the Archduke Charles of Austria invaded Spain with a force that included British troops and British naval support. The war went on indecisively until 1711, when the archduke died. By this time Britain had lost interest in the matter; in any event, the British redcoats were needed in North America to keep the French from encroaching any further on the British possessions there.

At the Peace of Utrecht in 1713, Philip of Anjou was recognized as the Spanish King Felipe V, but at a cost to Spain of all her European possessions: the part of the Netherlands that was to become Belgium, Luxembourg, Milan, Sardinia and Naples, as well as Minorca and Gibraltar, which the British retained. The British also insisted on the right to send merchant ships to Spanish America, an arrangement which effectively gave them the monopoly of the very profitable trade in slaves from Africa. Nervous about British activities and intentions in North America, Carlos III, who succeeded Felipe V, used his family ties to secure a pact with the French, and as a result recovered Minorca and Florida.

But the French Revolution and the revolutionary wars and finally the Napoleonic wars presented insoluble problems for Spain. Carlos IV made every effort to save another member of the House of Bourbon, Louis XVI, from the guillotine but failed, and then entered into an alliance with Britain on the general grounds of monarchical solidarity; the immediate result was an invasion of Spain by the armies of revolutionary France in 1793. And when, during the early stages of Napoleon's conquest of Europe, Spain switched her alliance to France and against Britain, the immediate result was the destruction by Nelson and the British navy of the Spanish fleet — along with Napoleon's — at Cape Trafalgar off the south-west coast of Spain in 1805. The long-term result was that Britain, as the strongest naval power, could now cut Spain off from America and gain access to the rich American market.

Popular indignation led first to the overthrow of Carlos IV's despotic minister Godoy, and eventually to Carlos's abdication in 1808. Napoleon initially recognized Fernando VII, Carlos's heir, as king of Spain, but then invaded Spain under the pretext of an invasion of Portugal and forced Fernando VII to abdicate in favour of his own brother, Joseph Bonaparte, known in Spain by the quaint nickname Pepe Botellas (Joe Bottles).

Small pockets of resistance held out against Napoleonic rule throughout Spain − revolutionary juntas had been set up in several of the provinces − and this resistance movement led to the Peninsular War (known in Spain as the War of Independence), initially carried out by the Spaniards mainly on a guerrilla basis. Britain sent an army to Spain under Sir John Moore, not so much to help the Spanish revolutionaries but to get at Napoleon. It was forced back to Corunna in 1809, and was then replaced by a much more formidable force under Arthur Wellesley who became Duke of Wellington during the campaign.

The combined efforts of the British redcoats and the Spanish guerrillas − most of them not trained soldiers, but ordinary citizens − succeeded in driving Napoleon's forces out of Spain. Or it could have been that by this time Napoleon needed his troops in Russia; in any event Joe Bottles withdrew to France and Fernando VII, until then held as a prisoner in France, was restored to the throne his people had won back for him.

In the meantime the Cortes (parliament) had met at Cadiz, convened not by the king as formerly, but by the people, and for the first time Spain had a written constitution; it confirmed Fernando VII as rightful king and established the principle that sovereignty resided in the nation as a whole and that in future the king's power would be strictly limited. But the Cortes also spent a lot of time trying to find an acceptable, constitutional way of holding on to the American colonies which were beginning, one by one, to assert their independence.

As soon as he was safely back on the throne, Fernando VII immediately repudiated this constitution; he also introduced a rigid censorship, revived the Inquisition and readmitted the Jesuits, who had been expelled from Spain by Carlos III in 1767, for encouraging the Madrid mob to protest against the king's minister, Leopoldo de Gregoria.

The inevitable result was an army mutiny in 1820 led by Major Rafael de Riego, which succeeded because Cadiz was full of troops assembled there to reassert, by force if necessary, Spain's claim to her overseas colonies. Most of the rank and file had no desire to go campaigning in South America and were quite happy to support de Riego's rising rather than be sent overseas.

A liberal government ran the country for three years until 1823, when Fernando was again restored, this time with the aid of the troops of another Bourbon, Louis XVIII of France. He immediately proceeded to demonstrate that he had learnt absolutely nothing in exile by reasserting the divine right of kings and resuming his persecution of the liberals.

On his death in 1833, his brother Don Carlos claimed the Spanish throne, basing his claim on the Salic Law which the Bourbons had brought with them from France and which disbarred women from succession. He contested the rights of his niece Isabel II, who was under age and was represented by her regent, her mother Cristina.

In the civil war that followed, Don Carlos was supported by the Church, the reactionaries and the Basques; and Cristina and Isabel by the liberals and the army. A legion from Britain also fought on Cristina's side in the Basque area. The Carlists won, Cristina resigned the regency and for three years from 1836 the country was run by what Salvador de Madariaga quaintly calls a 'military politician'. Madariaga, who was Spanish ambassador both to the United States and France and Spain's representative at the League of Nations in Geneva in the period just before the Civil War, remarks laconically in his brilliant study *Spain: A Modern History* (London: Cape, 1961): 'The ambition of every Spanish general is to save his country by becoming her ruler.' The military politician who took over in 1836 was General Baldomero Esparteres and the principal achievement of this regime was the sale of the Church lands.

In 1844, Isabel II came of age, and a period of total confusion ensued. In 1868, after a rebellion in the south, and a mutiny by the army and navy, she was forced to leave the country. As the Cortes had voted in favour of a monarchy, its representatives were forced to look around Europe for a suitable candidate and finally settled on Amadeo I, Duke of Aosta, of the House of Savoy. Subsequent meetings of the Cortes decided in favour of a republic and then a federation so that in the end Amadeo had to abdicate and General Serrano again took over as a military dictator. Throughout Isabel's troubled reign, five military politicians became involved in running Spain's government, a fact which must have prepared the way for Generalissimo Francisco Franco, when he arrived on the scene. Meanwhile, in the north, a second Carlist War had broken out and the Bourbon dynasty had been restored in the person of Alfonso XII, Isabel's eldest son.

A new constitution was adopted with a bicameral parliament, and in 1898, after a tangle with the United States of America, Spain lost Cuba, the Philippines and Puerto Rico; in addition, her precarious hold on her territories in Morocco was under constant threat.

During World War I, Spain remained neutral, and in 1921 there was an insurrection in the Riff, a Spanish protectorate in the Sahara, which went on until 1926. By this time General Primo de Rivera had established a fairly successful military dictatorship, abolished the Cortes and overhauled local and municipal government. His attacks on privileges enjoyed by the artillery and the engineers in the army — which in his view undermined the unity and efficiency of the army as a whole — led to his undoing. Discontented generals appealed to King Alfonso XIII, who as commander-in-chief of the army sacked Rivera in January 1930, though he did not survive him for very long. When a Republican plot to unseat him in San Sebastian was followed by municipal elections in which all the cities voted Republican three months later, Alfonso XIII left the country.

A second Spanish Republic with a new socialist constitution was declared in 1931, but it didn't really stand a chance. The worldwide depression, the rise of fascism in Germany and Italy and the continued existence of a powerful, authoritarian right-wing in Spain (former supporters of Primo de Rivera) led to mounting tensions with which the government could not cope. There were outbreaks of violence all over the country, between peasants and landowners and between rival political groups. Catalonia opted for complete independence from Madrid, and strong home rule movements developed in the Basque provinces and in Galicia.

An attempted rightist military coup by General Sanjuro in Seville was quickly suppressed and Sanjuro exiled. A much more serious rebellion of leftist miners and factory workers occurred in 1934 in the Asturias; this insurrection was brutally stamped out by generals Ochoa and Yague, acting on directions from General Franco in Madrid.

Another general election in February 1936 solved nothing. Disorders became increasingly frequent and continuous strikes paralyzed all normal activities. José Antonio Primo de Rivera, son of the late dictator and leader of a militant right-wing party the *Falange* − which, incidentally, had not won a single seat in the February elections − was arrested and put in prison.

In July 1936, the *Falange* party retaliated by assassinating a very popular leftist police lieutenant. In revenge, José Calvo Sotelo, one of the leaders of the rightist opposition, was in turn assassinated.

In the same month, the garrison in Morocco under General Franco mutinied, sparking off a military coup which had been simmering for months. The soldiers who opposed the Republican government profoundly distrusted politicians; Primo de Rivera's relatively successful period of dictatorship had convinced them that political problems could be solved fairly simply by military power. Influenced by what had been happening in Germany and Italy, the soldiers believed that the stability of their country was being threatened by such 'destructive' forces as liberalism, free-masonry, communism and pluralist politics, and that it was their duty to rescue it.

When Franco emerged as Generalissimo in 1936, he was in command of the Moroccan legion, the élite corps of the Spanish army, and his mutiny was followed by rightist military risings against the Republican government all over the country. Franco crossed the Straits of Gibraltar from Africa at the head of the Moroccan army, and as soon as he was safely back on Spanish soil, installed himself as head of state and military dictator.

The Republicans believed of course that the road to victory lay in the hands of the proletariat whom they proceeded to organize into a voluntary militia. But however brave and well-intentioned these amateur soldiers might have been, they lacked the discipline and cohesive leadership that was needed to oppose the Spanish army, soon reinforced by German and Italian 'volunteers' who were in fact highly trained professional soldiers and airmen.

Brigades of Republicans from all over Europe and from America fought on the government side, but most of them were amateurs and like the Republican militia were never coherently controlled. Both sides were supplied with arms from abroad, Franco's troops by Germany and Italy, the Republicans mainly by the Soviet Union. Officially Britain and France had a policy of strict non-intervention, though intellectuals like Orwell and Malraux fought on the Republican side and saw the struggle as the last of the romantic wars. Spain became fashionable again, as it had been 130 years earlier during the heroic struggle against Napoleon's troops.

Although the Republicans held on to Madrid to the very end, the government itself withdrew to Valencia. After Franco's troops had captured Málaga in February 1937, the Italian brigades attacked Guadalajara and were routed; however in the north, after the bombing of Guernica by the German Condor Legion in April, Bilbao and Santander fell to Franco. Barcelona capitulated in January 1939, and by the end of March all armed resistance to Franco had ceased.

The reprisals were immediate and barbaric; about 2 million people suspected of having Republican sympathies were imprisoned in concentration camps and, apart from the countless thousands who had been summarily executed during the Civil War, it is generally agreed that Franco confirmed more death sentences than any other man (soldier or statesman, king or conquistador) in the entire history of Spain.

Franco believed that a corporate, Catholic, authoritarian regime would cure Spain of all its ills, and during the isolation imposed on Spain during World War II he had plenty of opportunity to test out his theories. His regime prolonged the climate of the Civil War and was based on the wide and general – and very understand-able – fear of his viciously cruel army. But the country had been devastated, and the level of production achieved during Primo de Rivera's dictatorship was not reached again until the end of the fifties.

In Western Europe during this period, the only totalitarian regimes were Spain's and that of her next-door neighbour, Portugal; in Spain all political parties were banned apart from the *Falange* which had become the *Falange Española Tradicionalista y de las JONS (Juntas de Ofensiva Nacional Sinicalista)*, to incorporate all the political parties which had supported Franco's coup.

In 1971, largely as a result of the deliberations of the Second Vatican Council, the Catholic Church withdrew its support from Franco, and political opposition to his regime began to conso-lidate. The Communist Party, the trades unions, the students, the Basque members of ETA (who assassinated Premier Carrero Blanco in 1973), all now opposed Franco.

At this stage Franco nominated Juan Carlos, grandson of Alfonso XIII and a direct descendant of the Bourbons, as his successor as head of state; Juan Carlos, the grandson of Victoria Eugénie of Battenberg and thus related to Prince Philip, Duke of Edinburgh, had been educated in Spain, and had served in the British navy.

In 1977, the first general elections since 1936 were held and the Central Democratic Union (UCD) had a clear majority. An attempted military coup in 1981 was aborted by the king, and in January 1986 a Spain in which the monarchy had finally accepted democracy and all that it entailed, became a full member of the European Community.

COLONIAL CONNECTIONS

Spain's White Elephant

From ancient times until the end of the fifteenth century, the Venetians and the Genoese had been the great mariners and navigators of the Mediterranean. But Spain and Portugal were seething with a sort of overspill of patriotic fervour which had been whipped up during their long struggle against the Moors and they needed new avenues in which to dissipate all that pent-up energy. Exploration of the unknown world turned out to be the answer to their problem.

Ptolemy, the Egyptian geographer of the second century, had developed a hypothesis to explain the existence of the earth and the apparent movement of the stars which was perfectly adequate for the relatively simple needs of the men of the Middle Ages. His ideas had now been superseded by those of the Polish mathematician Nicolaus Copernicus who became convinced that the world was merely one of a number of round planets circling the sun, though for fear of the Inquisition, he didn't dare to publish the results of his deliberations until the year of his death, 1543. But long before his thesis was published, most intelligent men in Europe had a feeling that the world was probably round and that it might well be possible to set out in a westerly direction and wind up in the Far East.

Also Marco Polo had written about an overland journey he had made in the thirteenth century to the Khan of Cathay (emperor of China) and to the islands of Zhipangu (Japan).

One person who firmly believed the world was round was Christopher Columbus (Italian, Cristoforo Colombo; Spanish, Cristobal Colón), the son of a Genoese wool merchant; he had studied mathematics at the university of Pavia. He followed his father's trade and visited Chios in the eastern Mediterranean and England in the course of business, as well as Iceland where he met some of the descendants of Leif Ericsson, the Norseman who had discovered Greenland and who had briefly established a settlement in Vinland (Newfoundland). The tradition of a vast land on the other side of the Sea of Darkness had survived in Iceland and Columbus listened eagerly to everything they had to tell him.

On his return, he went to Portugal, married the daughter of one of the captains who had served under Henry the Navigator, and tried to persuade the King of Portugal to finance a voyage westwards to try to reach Cathay by sea.

The Portuguese, who by now had secured the eastern route, via the Cape of Good Hope, were not greatly interested, so he tried Fernando of Aragon and Isabel of Castile whose marriage in 1469 had more or less unified Spain. Initially, they were too busy trying to clear the Moors out of Granada, but in 1492, as soon as they had succeeded, he tried again and was successful.

On 3 August 1492 he left Palos with three ships and eighty-eight men, and at two o'clock in the morning on 12 October he sighted land. He called it Hispaniola; it was an island, now divided into two halves and known as Haiti and the Dominican Republic, and he was convinced that it was one of the outlying islands of the Indian continents. For that reason the islands were known as the West Indies and the people he found there Indians.

And although he returned to the area three more times (in 1493, 1498 and 1503) and discovered the mouth of the Orinoco in a country which was later called Little Venice (Venezuela) and Honduras, he remained convinced until the day he died in 1506 that he had discovered a direct overseas route to the Asian continent.

In 1493, the Pope formally entrusted the Spanish Crown with the task of evangelizing the peoples of the newly discovered territories, and in 1494 divided all the newly discovered and all as yet undiscovered lands between Spain and Portugal.

In 1519, four Spanish ships under the Portuguese navigator Fernando Magellan crossed the Atlantic between Africa and Brazil and sailed southwards. He found the narrow channel now called after him and finally reached the peaceful sea, the Pacific, which had first been seen from a peak in Darien (the Isthmus of Panama) not by stout Cortés as in the Keats sonnet, but by Balboa, one of Cortés's officers. Magellan himself was killed in a brawl in the Philippines, but his most senior surviving officer, del

Cano, who was a Basque, carried on to become the first captain to sail around the world. Of the 200 sailors who had set out on this voyage, only eighteen returned to Spain.

In the same year, at the head of eleven ships, 400 Spanish soldiers, 200 Indians, thirty-two cavalrymen (horses had never been seen in America) and eleven pieces of artillery, Hernán Cortés began his attempt to overthrow Montezuma's Aztec empire; by 1521, he had occupied and razed its capital Tenochtiteán which became the future Mexico City. In 1424 Francisco Pizarro, who came from the same province as Cortés, Estremadura, had made his first attempt to conquer Peru. He tried again in 1526, and then finally, with an army of 227 men provided by the king, he succeeded in 1531. In 1534, Mendoza, with fourteen ships, sailed to Argentina and founded a city called Our Lady of the Good Winds, now known simply as Buenos Aires.

By this time, almost every island in the Caribbean and the Gulf of Mexico had been discovered and almost the whole of South America opened up, as well as Florida, New Orleans, Georgia, Arizona, Arkansas and Missouri in North America. The Philippine Islands were also added to Spain's dominions, and Manila was founded in 1570.

But the period of expansion was over; with the Dutch and the French and the British on the high seas in search of colonies of their own to develop and exploit, it was time for Spain — which in 1580 had added Portugal and all her Far East, African and Brazilian territories to the Spanish Empire — to take a defensive stance.

It was an extremely difficult situation. Spain had only effectively been a nation since the union of the crowns of Castile and Aragon in 1479, and the expulsion of the Moors in 1492. Yet within half a century the Spanish government was trying to civilize and develop and administer by far the biggest empire ever known, right on the other side of the world in the face of increasing opposition; for years England's principal foreign policy was the weakening and ultimately the destruction of Spain and her empire.

The initial settlers were all soldiers, explorers and adventurers

— with priests to look after conversion and education of the conquered races — and it is perhaps not surprising that the high-minded principles with which Isabel I of Castile had embarked upon this imperial enterprise were not always maintained in practice.

Colonization took the form of a trust system. Each settler undertook to convert and protect a certain number of natives, and they in turn were obliged to work for him for a salary. Slavery was forbidden, except in the case of cannibals and natives who refused to accept the gift of Christianity and resisted conversion. And whilst the friars and the missionary priests did their best, learning Aztec, Quechua and all the other languages so that they could preach to the people in their own tongues, inevitably under economic and other pressures, the situation deteriorated, and there was undoubtedly a great deal of barbarity and cruelty. The natural reluctance of the Indians in particular to do any work at all undoubtedly aggravated matters.

The Indians, whom the Spanish regarded as minors, were thus exempted from the rigours of the Inquisition, but the loophole in the law which enabled a native who resisted conversion to be made a slave, and the anxiety of the first rough settlers to get the place cultivated as rapidly as possible, undoubtedly meant that a great many Indians were very poorly treated. Also, although many Spanish historians piously ignore this aspect of the matter, if the Spanish colonizers did not make slaves of the native populations on any large scale, they were amongst Britain's best customers for the slaves shipped out from Africa.

There was never any colour bar in the Spanish colonies, and although in the Caribbean no Spanish citizens other than priests were allowed to live in the Indian towns (*pueblos*), the Indians were free to live in the Spanish towns and mix on equal terms with the settlers. And although in the Caribbean the original peoples were treated with barbaric cruelty and consequently dwindled and eventually disappeared, in mainland Spanish America they increased and prospered. Today they constitute the bulk of the population of Mexico, Peru and Bolivia, where Spanish is still the principal language and many Spanish traditions and customs are enthusiastically preserved, something which cannot be said of the former British colonies in India and Africa.

It was largely due to the efforts of the Church and the general belief in religious unity that the natives were welcomed into the fold, so to speak, on an equal basis, and there is no question that the Spanish government was prepared to spend a lot of money on educating them. When the university of Mexico was founded in 1533, there were already several colleges in existence, in Santo Domingo, in Havana in Cuba, in New Granada (now Colombia), in Lima in Peru and in Santiago in Chile. The colonies were ruled by viceroys, who ran them like miniature reproductions of the Spanish kingdom with all the corresponding ranks of courtiers and grandees and dignitaries and bureaucrats and hangers-on.

On the other hand, the early explorers and adventurers were tough and resourceful men, and they developed the territories very quickly and successfully. They brought with them horses, oxen, sheep, pigs and hens, all unknown until then in the New World, and they introduced the cultivation of vines, of sugar and of silk to the areas. It is even possible that the first wheat in America was planted by Pizarro's sister-in-law, Ines Munez, who came across a few grains of wheat in a barrel of rice which had come from Spain. She put them carefully aside, according to legend, and cultivated them in a flower pot.

The Spanish Empire lasted for three centuries, during which time a whole continent lived, more or less in peace, and prospered and, like the British Empire, produced new nations.

Whether, in the end, the empire was good for Spain is another matter. Again, Madariaga writes: 'America, in Spanish history, was a white elephant. To be sure, Spain decorated it wonderfully and reaped a considerable amount of prestige from the possession of so immense and picturesque an animal. No doubt, moreover, the discovery made Spain a universal nation before any other European power, and to a degree unequalled even by Great Britain later. But the greatness of Spain, in so far as it came from the discovery and colonization of America, had something abnormal and almost monstrous about it. It was more in the nature of a diseased growth than an organic development and it contributed greatly to prevent the normal evolution of a foreign policy adequately adapted to the requirements of the nation.'

By the time the Bourbons came to the throne in 1700, Spain was in bad trouble with her empire; the frail Spanish economy was not able to provide the goods required by the settlers and the Creole and Indian populations of her American colonies. England was Spain's great rival in supplying these markets, and after the defeat of the Great Armada Spain never had sufficient naval power to keep the British out of South America. And although Spain helped France to fight for her Canadian possessions against the British, it wasn't long after the American War of Independence that Spain's own American colonies started to demand independence.

Chile repudiated allegiance to Spain in 1810 and established her independence by 1818; Paraguay broke away in 1814; Mexico declared her independence in 1821 and Argentina in 1842. After the defeat of the Spanish navy off Santiago in 1898, when Cuba became nominally independent and Puerto Rico and the Philippines went to the United States, Spain effectively wound up her overseas empire and retired into isolation in the Iberian Peninsula, where the whole adventure had started four centuries earlier.

DEVELOPMENT DIRECTIONS

Tariffs and Subsidies

Spain, like France and Ireland, has always had the ability, by no means universal in the Community, to feed its own people. Traditionally, the Meseta, an essentially agricultural area, produced Spain's essential crops, including winter grains (wheat and barley), vines and olives.

Most of the wine produced was consumed in Spain, or sent out to the colonies, though the fortified wines of Jerez (called sherry in Britain) have been exported for over two centuries and, towards the end of the eighteenth century, brandy from Catalonia was exported to America.

The more recent development of modern farming methods, soil management and scientific irrigation in the Guadiana river valley and in the lands surrounding the Tagus and Duero rivers has resulted in the intensive cultivation of industrial crops and such Mediterranean specialities as vegetable *primeurs* and melons.

The Meseta is now the centre of the livestock trade, producing high-quality lamb and pork, as well as cattle, including the breeding of fighting bulls, an industry centred on Salamanca.

Today Spain's agricultural industry produces — and exports — grain, vegetables, citrus and other fruit, wine, olives and olive oil, sunflower oil and livestock all over Europe.

As elsewhere in the Community, though somewhat later, the modernization of agriculture resulted in a huge movement of the population from the country into the urban areas. As recently as 1960, agriculture represented 22.7 per cent of the GDP and employed 5 million people; by 1989, it represented only 4.2 per cent of the GDP and employed only 1,715,000. Fishing provides employment for 110,000 people and accounts for only 0.4 per cent of the GDP.

Spain's industrial revolution dates back only to the nineteenth century. Earlier there had been a modest Catalan cotton industry, dating back to 1746, which was always sheltered by a prohibitive protectionist tariff, and the slow but marked growth in general industry after 1827 produced both an urban middle class and a working class. In Catalonia, the production of cotton doubled between 1830 and 1840; and later the introduction of steam-power and an eightfold increase in investment turned Barcelona from a seaport into an industrial zone, exporting mainly to Cuba.

Around 1840, a Catalan weaver called Munts founded the Association of Handweavers which led to the first confederation of labour unions created in 1854 under the name *Unión de Clases*. In the same year, a co-operative movement began, founded by a hundred families in Barcelona and known as the Co-operative Association of Consumers, and in 1856 a co-operative called *La Proletaria* was formed in Valencia to develop the silk industry. In Barcelona and Madrid, other co-operatives were set up to develop the printing industry.

The increase in general industrial development around the 1850s came about largely as a result of new banking laws which permitted foreign investment in Spanish enterprise. Belgian capital developed Spain's zinc industry, and French investment created the Spanish rail network, which in turn provided an infrastructure upon which a home market for industrial products could be developed. Textile production expanded; a modern wool industry grew up alongside the ancient Catalan cotton industry.

'Industrial expansion created a significant *haute bourgeoisie* [which became] the most powerful single interest group in the country,' writes Raymond Carr in *Spain: A Companion to Spanish Studies*, edited by P.E. Russell (London: Methuen, 1973). 'The new rich ranged from sober Catalan businessmen demanding protective tariffs to shelter their gains to daring speculators like José de Salamanca (1811–83) who hired Napoleon III's chef and installed the first private bathroom in Spain.'

Towards the end of the century, there was a steep increase in foreign investment in mining, and Spanish copper was in great demand everywhere, particularly Britain. The Spanish cotton industry enjoyed a tremendous boom; and so did the Spanish wine industry after phylloxera had decimated the French vineyards.

Then, in 1867, phylloxera attacked the Spanish vineyards in their turn and the boom collapsed. The Spanish vineyards were abandoned, and the expanding metallurgical industry of Barcelona began to reduce its workforce. The wine producers everywhere, the wheat growers of Castile, the miners and metalworkers of the Basque country, and the mill-owners of Catalonia appealed to the government for help; and all the government could think of was yet more tariff protection and increased government interference in the economic life of the country.

Spain's neutrality in World War II put it outside the scope of such European economic recovery plans as the Marshall aid programme, and increased the already deep sense of total isolation. In the period of austerity which affected the whole of Europe after the war, Spain was forced to introduce rationing. Franco then closed the frontiers to foreign goods, services and capital, in the mistaken belief that the country's economy was sufficiently buoyant to supply all its needs as well as achieving economic development without any help from outside.

This policy of protectionism was accompanied by one of massive state intervention in industry through INI (*Instituto Nacional de Industria*), a public holding company which assumed all responsibilities for industrial development.

When it became clear that Spain had neither the raw materials nor the technology to go it alone, and was not capable of generating sufficient capital investment to finance economic growth, a radical change of policy – the Stabilization Plan of 1959 – opened up the Spanish frontiers again to foreign goods and capital. The short-term result of this abrupt change of policy was a chronic deficit in the balance of trade, which happily (and almost accidentally) was offset by the great Spanish tourist boom of the 1960s and by remittances from Spanish workers who had emigrated to the more highly developed countries of the Common Market. The long-term result was a series of sharp fluctuations between expansion and recession, and the government's indecision was reflected in the maintenance of restrictions on imports and the imposition of high customs tariffs to protect Spanish industry from international competition.

Spain's industries had been successful largely as a result of low production costs: cheap energy, a cheap, unskilled labour force and little or no industrial unrest, the latter a direct result of Franco's sternly oppressive dictatorship. The gradual but progressive decline in Franco's power was reflected in increasing labour militancy, and this, combined with the oil crisis of the early seventies and the fall in the world demand for steel and ship-building, began to pose Spanish industry with very severe problems. Once again, the government could think only in terms of protectionism, and when proved incapable of adapting itself to the new market forces, replied with state subsidies, which naturally led to massive inflation. By 1976, the annual rate of inflation had very nearly reached 25 per cent.

In 1977, the peseta was devalued, and some attempt to impose a firmer monetary policy was made, but Spanish industry remained spectacularly uncompetitive, and its problems were aggravated by the second world oil crisis of 1979.

Spain's first Socialist government was saddled with an economy which had an extremely low growth rate (an increase in the GDP of only 1.2 per cent in 1982), high inflation rates (14 per cent in 1982), a deficit in the balance of payments on current account of US$4,000 million, a public deficit amounting to almost 6 per cent of the GDP, and a high and growing rate of unemployment. After a three-year period of adjustment, along lines proposed by the Community, Spain's industries had been rationalized to cope with all that entry into the Community would entail. Assisted by a fall in the price of crude oil in 1985, a fall in interest rates, and the slow depreciation of the US dollar which had been steadily rising from 1980 to 1985, Spain at long last moved into a period of economic growth which coincided with the country's accession to the Community in 1986.

During the period from 1986 to 1988 (inclusive), the GDP grew by an annual rate of 4.8 per cent in real terms, and industrial investment increased by about 15 per cent a year in real terms. About 375,000 new jobs were created every year, and unemployment fell from 21.5 per cent of the working population in 1986 to 16.9 per cent in 1989; over the same period, the national debt fell from 6.1 per cent of the GDP to 2.1 per cent, and the rate of inflation fell to around 7 per cent.

This second industrial revolution was based on the export of processed foods, textiles, footwear, consumer goods and motor cars; the Seat, produced in co-operation with Volkswagen of Germany, is a good example of modern Spanish industrial success. The older, more basic industries such as iron and steel and shipbuilding have not yet been rationalized.

The service sector saw intense growth during this period; it now represents 59.7 per cent of the GDP and employs 6 million people. This is partly a reflection of Spain's popularity with tourists, who now far outnumber the Spanish population. Tourism represents 10 per cent of all economic activity in Spain. Six million foreigners spent their holidays in Spain in 1960; by 1970, that total had increased to 24 million, and by 1980 to 38 million. Today, on average, 50 million people spend their holidays in Spain, 90 per cent from the Community, 22 per cent from France, 19 per cent from Portugal, 14 per cent from Britain and 12 per cent from Germany.

In addition, a great many foreigners — Britons and Germans mainly — have secondary residences in Spain, and by offering off-season cut rates, Spain has succeeded in attracting large numbers of senior citizens — again mainly from Britain and Germany — during the winter months. The income from tourism — US$14,332 billion in 1988 — largely offsets the traditional Spanish imbalance of payments, which increased sharply when Spain was opened up to imports of consumer goods from the remainder of the Community.

The old Roman roads, the stone roadways built by the Moors between 711 and 1085, and the royal thoroughfares built in the eighteenth century by the Bourbons formed the basis of Spain's internal transportation system until the arrival of the railway in 1848.

Despite a belated flurry of road-building in the early eighties to prepare the country for Community entry, the Spanish average of roadworks is still a lot less than elsewhere in the Community; 25 kilometres of road per 100 square kilometres as against the European average of 55 per square kilometre, and a grand total of 113,200 kilometres of roads, including 2,100 kilometres of motorway.

The road system is basically radial with its centre in Madrid, but is currently being reviewed under a *Programa de Autias* which aims at a road system throughout Spain which will be up to general Community standards. The Spanish roads currently cope with 12 million vehicles, two-thirds of them motor cars and one-fifth heavy goods vehicles. By 1985, the ratio of motor cars to people was one to six, as against one to fifteen in 1970, and one to sixty-eight in 1960.

The railway system covers 14,378 kilometres, most of it run by

RENFE (*Red Nacional de Ferrocarriles Españóles*), a company formed when the railways were nationalized by Franco in 1941; and it is remarkable in that the gauge is 233 millimetres wider than the European standard, though not quite as wide as the British standard gauge of 2.10 metres. A *Plan de Transporte Ferroviario*, approved in 1987, foresees the introduction of high speed trains, travelling at up to 250 kilometres per hour on the international gauge of 1.435 metres, with a line operating from Madrid to Seville by 1992.

Traditionally Spain's imports and exports have always gone by sea, and shipbuilding was among the first of the Spanish industrial enterprises. As recently as 1988, 113 million tonnes of goods were imported, and 43 million tonnes exported by sea, roughly 30 per cent of the total in Spanish ships.

Spanish commercial aviation began in 1919 with a mail service between Madrid and Barcelona. The Spanish state airline, Iberia, was formed in 1940; 51 per cent of the shares in the company are held by the state. Iberia now also has a 40 per cent share in the highly successful South American airline, Aerolina Argentinas.

The great tourist boom which started in the early sixties was very largely generated by charter companies; the traffic through Spanish airports increased from 80,000 in 1940 to 150,000 in 1957 and to 13.5 million in 1973, by which year the charter companies were carrying more than three times as many passengers as the scheduled airlines. By 1989, there were also 14 million passengers using the domestic airlines. Almost all of the charter flights originated somewhere else in Europe, most of them within the Community.

The Spanish telecommunications system is highly sophisticated with electronic lines and switchboards, and possesses the third largest total network of underwater cables in the world: 40,000 kilometres, soon to be augmented by a new fibre optics transatlantic cable which will make Spain a key-point in international communications. The first Spanish communications satellite is due to be launched in 1992, in conjunction with a French firm.

Spanish newspapers have comparatively small circulations. Only about eighty newspapers are sold for every 1,000 inhabitants, a very low rate as compared with most other Community countries. One reason for this is that until fairly recently Spain had a relatively high rate of illiteracy, particularly in the rural areas. The official literacy rate is now 97 per cent, but that total – a journalist who has lived and worked for years in Spain assures me – would include a high proportion of people, particularly old country people who can sign a document or read a road sign but do not spend any sizeable portion of their day reading anything.

There are about 100 Spanish daily newspapers, mostly regional, and one Sunday paper now has the hitherto unimaginable circulation of 1 million (as compared with the *News of the World* which currently sells over 5 million copies in Britain every Sunday).

Radio is still considered a very influential medium in Spain, where as late as 1987, more than 50 per cent of Spanish people over 14 years of age listened to the radio every day, a figure that represents 16 million listeners; again, it was partly a reflection of the high rate of illiteracy. Radio was a godsend for people who could understand the spoken word, but couldn't read the written word. Spanish radio is a mixture of private and public sectors.

In Spain, as everywhere else, TV is rapidly gaining ground over all other forms of entertainment. Almost 87 per cent of Spanish people over fourteen years of age watch TV every day, and nearly 10 per cent watch video films every day, which explains the decline of the cinema and the drop in attendances at local *corridas*. Spain has two TV channels, one state-run and the other run by the Spanish radio station, RTVE (Radiotelevisión Española).

In *Eurostat*, the Community's annual list of basic statistics, there is a table giving the average gross earnings of manual workers in the twelve member-states, expressed in current purchasing power in their own currencies; according to this table, the average Spanish worker is a lot better off than his opposite number in Greece or Portugal, nearly as well off as an Irish worker, but a good deal poorer than workers in Denmark, Germany, the Benelux countries and somewhat poorer than those in the United Kingdom.

Spain has one hospital bed per 207 inhabitants, as against one per 107 in Belgium and one per 167 in Greece, and one physician per 374 inhabitants as against one per 371 in Belgium and one per 795 in Ireland. Spain has in fact the highest proportion of doctors in relation to its population in the whole of the Community, though the proportion of dentists is one of the lowest in Europe, and the number of nurses (370 per 100,000 inhabitants) is relatively low.

Although there has been a public health care system of sorts in Spain since the end of the nineteenth century, compulsory national health insurance was not introduced until 1941. Initially conceived as an insurance policy for industrial workers, it has expanded over the years to cover an increasing sector of the community, until by 1982 it covered 86 per cent of the population and 31 per cent of all hospital beds in the best-equipped hospitals in the country. In addition, 76 per cent of all pharmaceutical requirements are publicly financed.

Spain has adopted a comprehensive health policy designed to achieve the same level of health care for the entire population, financed by state resources, contributions and fees for certain services.

The first step towards any form of social security in Spain was the Law of Labour Accidents in 1900, which made employers responsible for accidents in the workplace. Obligatory old age insurance was not introduced until 1921, when a pension of one peseta a day (approximately one-fifth of the average salary at that period) was paid to people from the age of sixty-five. It was financed by employers' and employees' contributions, with a state contribution and a compulsory surcharge on inheritances.

Spanish pensions are now structured on three levels: the first level for people over sixty-five or disabled people who are not covered by their own contributions; the second level based on previous contributions to the social security system; and a third level for people who wish to augment their state pensions by means of private pension plans. The system covers wage-earning employees, seasonally contracted workers and also the self-employed. The state contribution to social security rose from 4.2 per cent of the total in 1976 to 29 per cent of the total in 1987.

In common with most of the Community, Spain has a growing proportion of old age pensioners. By 1987, there was one pensioner for every two contributors to the system.

Unemployment benefit covers unemployment for periods of over three months and up to two years, and varies according to contributions paid; it can be as high as 80 per cent of the former salary during the first six months of unemployment. In December 1987, 431, 807 people who previously had contributed to the social security system were receiving unemployment benefit, as were 400,417 people who had paid nothing into the scheme. This latter group, which represented 28 per cent of all unemployed, is steadily increasing, a result of persistent, long-term unemployment in Spain. The requirement for previous social security contributions rules out young people looking for their first job, a category which now accounts for close on 50 per cent of Spain's unemployed. Family and children's allowances have not kept pace with the cost of living.

AFFAIRS OF STATE

Old Laws and a New Constitution

The present Spanish state is a parliamentary monarchy with all power devolving from the people, through the monarchy, to the parliament (Cortes) and then to the government, in that order. As head of state, the king symbolizes the unity and permanence of the state, exercises a moderating and revisionary role in the working of the state institutions, and represents the state in its relations with the outside world.

The parliament, called the *Cortes Generales*, consists of two houses. The Congress of Deputies has 350 members elected by a system of proportional representation. There is also an upper house, or Senate, of 208 elected members and forty-six members nominated by the autonomous communities. The Senate, like the British House of Lords, has a limited power to hold up all legislation passed by the lower house for further discussion.

In addition to elections for the *Cortes*, elections are also held in each of the autonomous communities which all have their own assemblies; they include Aragon, Asturias, the Balearic Islands, the Canary Islands, Cantabria, Castilla-La Mancha, Castilla-Leon, Valencia, Extramadura, Madrid, Murcia, Navarra and La Rioja.

Municipal elections, in which the Spanish elect their local councillors, are held at the same time as the general elections in 8,000 municipalities. Spain also elects sixty members of the European Parliament.

All Spanish citizens are entitled to a vote from eighteen years of age.

Under Spain's 1978 constitution, the judiciary is responsible for ensuring that what it describes as 'the public powers' (presumably including the police and the army) abide by the law, and for guarding and protecting the basic freedoms and legitimate interests of the citizens.

The huge increase in litigation (by 134 per cent) between 1970 and 1980 is a reflection of the problems which the Spanish are encountering in adapting legal codes enacted last century to the new freedom the people are enjoying under the 1978 constitution. Spain also has a Constitutional Court, separate from the judiciary, to deal with laws which are not any longer constitutionally acceptable and to settle any conflicts which may arise between the state and the autonomous communities.

The *Cuerpo Nacional de Policía* (National Police Force) are part of the security forces, and the task of their 55,000 members is to cope with crime and deal with terrorism and disorder. The 62,500 members of the *Guardia Civil* are based mainly in rural areas, and are responsible for enforcing traffic regulations and for policing the ports, airports, coasts and borders.

Both police forces are involved in the fight against drugs traffic. Like most Community countries, Spain has a serious drugs problem, particularly amongst its young people. A State Information System on Drug Addiction was set up in 1987, and reported in 1988 that 15,701 drug addicts registered that year for treatment for addiction in various centres. This is not a dramatically high figure in a population of 39 millions, but it represents only the tip of the iceberg, since most drug addicts who can afford to buy drugs in the street do not register for treatment.

Also, in Spain as elsewhere, the wave of drug-addiction has led to a spate of drug-related crimes as well as the spread of drug-related diseases such as hepatitis B and AIDS.

Otherwise, and apart from some burglary and minor thieving in the crowded holiday resorts and new residential centres, the Spanish are on the whole more law-abiding than most Community people.

Spain has been a member of NATO since 1982, but is not incorporated in the latter's integrated military command. Nuclear weapons are not allowed to be installed on Spanish territory, and whilst maintaining the current bilateral defence policy with the United States, the government plans to reduce progressively the American military presence in Spain. Interestingly, the 1991 handbook of facts about Spain prepared for Community use lists the number of officers in the armed forces (58,233) but not the number of troops. The total strength of the armed forces is 285,000 including 210,000 conscripts.

CULTURE AND LEISURE

From Cave Paintings to Cubism

Spain is 99 per cent Catholic, and if the young people are almost as casual about religion as they are elsewhere in Europe, the Church and the feasts of the various saints play a large part in the social life of the communities, particularly in the rural areas.

There are four different levels of education: pre-school, primary and secondary education which includes technical training, and university. Until a new educational system was defined by law, the LGE (*Ley General de Educación*) in 1970, pre-school education was very limited, primary education far from universal and professional training limited to a few industrial courses.

Currently 95 per cent of children from four to five years old are in school, and compulsory education up to fourteen years of age is universal. More than 55 per cent of the children go on to secondary education, and 35 per cent receive professional training. Approximately 30 per cent of the population between twenty and twenty-four years of age — a total of over a million — are registered as university students.

Education at the compulsory level is provided by the state and is completely free, though private schools still exist. Until fairly recently, education at a private school was always regarded as socially desirable, if not essential, and most of the private educational establishments were closely connected with the Catholic Church. During the 1988–9 school year, 35 per cent of the pre-school and primary school students attended private (or church) institutions and 27 per cent of the secondary students were educated in private or church schools.

In an effort to break down a long tradition in which education and class (and relative wealth or poverty) were inextricably linked, the government is giving subsidies to private educational institutions provided that they adhere to standard admission requirements and respect the religious and ideological views of teachers, students and parents. About 99 per cent of the church schools and 90 per cent of the other private schools have accepted this arrangement; the remaining tiny minority excluded itself from state funding by choice. About 5 per cent of public spending on education goes on scholarships to enable the children of less wealthy parents to acquire secondary education; and the number of students receiving financial help is around 16 per cent of the total. English is replacing French as the standard modern language in primary schools and the government plans to make secondary education compulsory as soon as practicable.

The Spanish university system goes back to the Middle Ages. The oldest university is Salamanca, founded in 1218. But more than half of Spain's universities are less than twenty years old and are run on a decentralized, self-governing basis like the French liberal universities. There are thirty public universities in Spain today, and four private ones run by the Church. Of the million-odd students, the greatest number (150,000) are studying law, probably because the huge increase in litigation caused by the wide divergence between the old legal code and the new constitution means that there is always plenty of work for lawyers. Economics comes next with 75,000, then history, languages and medicine. The proportion of students who finish their courses is relatively low; in 1986, only 58 per cent went on to sit for their degree examinations.

Spain also has a *Universidad a Distancia*, which provides correspondence courses for 50,000 students, more than 40 per cent of them over the age of thirty.

Spanish art can probably be taken as starting from around 15,000 BC when the Palaeolithic cave-dwellers of Altamira in Cantabria painted what is regarded as the Sistine Chapel of prehistoric art. There are paintings of a much later age, probably of African origin, depicting human figures in the rock shelters from Lerida in Catalonia to Albacete in Castilla-La Mancha.

The Celts left large animal sculptures like the Guisando bulls in Avila; and the Iberians left the three ladies of Elche, now in Madrid's archaeological museum. The Romans left aqueducts and arches and bridges as well as a splendid theatre at Mérida. The Moors left Granada with its lovely Alhambra, the palace of the Nasrid dynasty, the last Moorish dynasty to leave Spain.

In the north, the route of the pilgrimage to Santiago de Compostela is lined with churches which blend European Romanesque art with Spanish pre-Romanesque, culminating in the city's magnificent cathedral with its Portico de la Gloria.

Spanish medieval literature used themes common in Romanesque literature elsewhere; the anonymous *Song of El Cid*, dated around 1140, has parallels in the epic poems of other European nations.

Spain's vehement reaction to the Lutheran Reformation and

the austerity of the Counter-Reformation probably has its finest monument in the Escorial, the palace-monastery built by Felipe II near Madrid and described above.

The one Spanish work which everybody knows about is Miguel de Cervantes's *Don Quixote*, or *El ingenioso hidalgo Don Quixote de la Mancha* to give the book its full title. Considered by many critics to be the first universal novel, it is among the most-printed books in the world, after the Bible, Shakespeare and various prayer books and missals.

Spanish theatre had its golden age corresponding with the golden age of the English Elizabethan theatre; leading dramatists included Fernando de Rojas, Lope de Vega and Tirso de Molina who in his *El Burlador de Sevilla* (The Love Rogue) created another universal character, Don Juan.

Painting also enjoyed a golden age in the sixteenth and seventeenth centuries, with painters like Francisco de Zurbarán, Murillo and Velázquez. Then at the turn of the seventeenth and eighteenth centuries came Francisco de Goya, whose record of the Napoleonic invasions of Spain (*Disasters of War*) has the impact and involvement of the best of modern war photography.

A century later, the echoes of musical nationalism, which were reverberating through the whole continent of Europe, produced Isaac Albéniz and Enrique Granados, two composers who achieved international recognition. Later Manuel de Falla continued the same tradition.

The twentieth century produced Pablo Picasso, who reinvented the whole art of painting with the first cubist work, *Les Demoiselles d'Avignon*, and who captured the horror of the Nazi bombing of a Basque town during the Civil War in his *Guernica*. Other well-known Spanish painters of this century include the surrealist and specialist in soft watches, Salvador Dali, the cubist Juan Gris and the surrealist Joan Miró. The poet and dramatist Federico García Lorca was assassinated by the Nationalists during the Civil War and has since become a folk hero.

So far as science is concerned, Spain has traditionally had the image of a country with little inclination towards scientific investigation. From the time of the Counter-Reformation, when Felipe II prohibited the entry of foreign literature into Spain, in order to preserve the purity of the Catholic spirit, the country has remained on the margin of European scientific achievements. Nevertheless, working in isolation, Santiago Ramón y Cajal was awarded the Nobel prize for medicine in 1906 for his research into histology (the science of organic tissues). Another Spanish Nobel prizewinner for science was Severo Ochoa, who did his research abroad.

In January 1988, the Spanish Antarctic Base Juan Carlos I was installed on Livingston Island in Antarctica, and Spain became a consultative member of the Antarctic Treaty, yet another step out of the isolation in which the Iberian Peninsula had lived for so long.

While Spanish food does not have the same initial, immediate appeal to foreign palates as the food of France and Italy, Spanish cuisine has both a distinctive strength and a subtlety not present in the traditional dishes of, say, Britain and Germany. The Spanish are more modest about their culinary talent than either the French or the Italians, but are every bit as fiercely proud of their cuisine as they are of all their other traditions. In general, the Spanish tend to take their meals much later than their Community neighbours. Dinner is served in restaurants between 8.30 and 11 p.m. but in private homes they rarely sit down to eat before 10 or 10.30 p.m. In hotels, *desayuno* (breakfast) is served as late as 11 a.m., and lunch rarely starts before 1.30 p.m.; in next-door France the roads are deserted from noon because everybody is inside somewhere, eating.

A felicitous feature of Spanish life is the custom of serving *tapas* (appetizers) along with your *aperitif. Tapas* take many forms, hot and cold, from smoked ham, cheese, olives and nuts of various kinds, to *chorizo* (a dry, highly spiced pork sausage), tuna, sardines, and even elaborately prepared dishes made with eggs, onions, peppers, olive oil and shellfish. In some *tabernas* (bars) the *tapas* are so delicious and so filling that you don't really need to eat lunch, especially in the hot weather.

The most internationally famous Spanish dish is paella, originally made in Valencia and consisting of rice flavoured with whatever can be conveniently garnered from the local seabed,
including lobster (if you're extremely lucky), prawns, mussels,
calamares, many varieties of small fish, and sometimes even the
goggles and rubber fins of the scuba divers (if you're unlucky).
Even at its best, it is not one of the world's great gourmet dishes.

Wine is the national drink (*blanco, tinto* or *rosado*) and apart
from sherry, Rioja is probably the only one which is universally
available. Though not as well known internationally, the best
Riojas are similar to good Bordeaux and Burgundy wines, rich
and *fruité*, as the French say.

Spanish brandy is very good, though quite different from
Cognac and Armagnac. Sangria is a summer cup very popular
with British and other summer visitors — it consists basically of
red wine with lemon juice, soda or mineral water, sugar, brandy or
some other spirit, cinnamon, ice and a lot of garnishing, or anges,
lemons, mint, limes, and so on. It is a pleasantly cooling but often
surprisingly heady concoction.

Light beer is also plentiful in Spain (it is called *cerveza*) and the
northern coast of Spain claims to be the original home of cider
(*sidra*), which was discovered by the Normans and imported by
them to Normandy and to England.

In general, the young Spanish people spend their leisure time
following roughly the same pursuits as the rest of the Community.
They are into do-it-yourself home improvement, they spend hours
watching TV, they follow soccer and the *Tour de France* type of
cycling contest, and they have produced a few great golfers, like
Ballesteros. One reason for this may be that, in an effort to attract
well-heeled tourists, they have built some splendid golf courses;
it's easy in Spain, because they've got the space.

Bullfighting, as it is oddly known in Britain, is not nearly as
popular as it used to be. Nevertheless, during the season, which
lasts roughly from the late spring until the early autumn, there will
be a *corrida* somewhere within a few miles of you, wherever you
happen to be in Spain, always on a Sunday, and usually starting at

about 4.30 or 5 p.m. promptly – about the only thing that is ever on time in Spain.

Today the *corrida* draws its audiences mainly from the better-heeled middle class who believe in preserving all the old Spanish traditions, and from the tourists, above all the Americans nurtured on Hemingway. If the *corrida* manages to survive the impact of TV, its next hazard will be European Community regulations. Currently there is talk of a European Parliament ban on picadors in the bullring; if that happens, it will totally undermine the entire business. The picadors are an essential phase in the whole ritual; they weaken the neck muscles of the bull, so that it has to lower its head. If the bull didn't have to lower its head, the matador would never be able to lean over those dangerous horns and pierce it cleanly through the heart. In their misguided efforts to clean up what they still perversely call a sport, the reformers may well succeed in making it a lot messier.

It's really no wonder the Spanish (like the British) regard the whole concept of the Community a little guardedly.

THE EUROPEAN COMMUNITY III:

How It's Going

A UNITED EUROPE

'In pursuing unification we can understand the Soviet Union's desire to live in security. This will be taken into account in the Vienna negotiations when the question of the military strength of a united Germany is concerned. And there are other possibilities of responding to this security interest. The merging of the two parts of Germany offers us Germans a historic opportunity. Our central position can have a positive influence. German unification must become a contribution towards the creation of a united Europe. Germany not as a source of European discord, not as a source of power politics, but Germany side by side with France and firmly anchored in a democratic community showing the way to the whole of Europe ...'

Hans-Dietrich Genscher, Minister for Foreign Affairs, speaking during the debate on German reunification in the German Bundestag on 21 June 1990

THE EUROPEAN COMMUNITY: III

How It's Going ...

To have succeeded in bringing together into an integrated and united Community such a diverse collection of assorted nations with such widely divergent historical and political backgrounds as all the Europeople described in the previous chapters would have been a considerable achievement over any time-span, in any circumstances. To have done it within half a century during a period which included two oil crises with worldwide repercussions, and to have achieved the relative unanimity which the Twelve showed over the Gulf War and the total unanimity they showed over the Soviet coup and the troubles in Yugoslavia in the summer of 1991 must be counted as a major triumph. And the people of the Community have succeeded in coming together like this without forcing any of the member-states to surrender any appreciable element of their sovereignty.

There is, of course, no real conflict between the national identity of individual members of the Community and their status as corporate members. There is no parallel whatever with the huddled masses who passed through the immigration shed on Ellis Island a century ago into the United States of America.

Before they became fully paid-up members of that nation, they were obliged to learn the language and become good Americans. The French are not one whit less French than they were in 1951 when they signed the treaty establishing the European Coal and Steel Community, which was the start of the whole thing; nor are the Italians any less Italian for being one of *Les Six* from the start.

As Robert Elphick, the Community spokesman in London, put it in an interview with me: 'I reckon that nation-states are not compatible with one another. A nation is one thing and a state is another and the fact that the two are not compatible is now being demonstrated by the Serbs and Croats in Yugoslavia and by the Kurds in Iraq.'

But whether the members of the Community regard themselves as members of a select club or as a federation of separate states with a good many basic interests in common, the principal achievement of the Community so far seems to have been to make them all realize that their future lies in a more integrated Europe than ever existed formerly. They realized, perhaps for the first time, that they needed to create a large single market to survive against competition from the United States and Japan, industrial giants which have the advantages of a very large market as well as a common currency and a common language.

There is the fact, too, that many of the big multinational companies have in fact already pointed the way by becoming in effect supranational. Also modern industrial development had become so highly specialized, so technologically advanced and so grotesquely expensive that nation-states cannot afford to go it alone any longer. The Ariadne space rocket and the European Airbus are two examples of the trend; no single European nation-state would have had the resources to develop and exploit either of them fully. More and more people are also becoming aware that it is unrealistic in today's world to believe that retaining its own separate currency gives a country any real control over its economy. In these circumstances, as speaker after speaker agreed in the BBC debate from the Palace of Westminster on 10 July 1991 on, 'The Future of the Nation-state', it makes much more sense to surrender a measure of sovereignty in order to gain a single but equal voice in a community with a much greater overall sovereignty. As Garret Fitzgerald, a former Irish premier, put it: 'Ireland secured independence from England in 1922 but it wasn't until Ireland joined the Common Market, with an equal voice with all the other member-states, big and small, that independence began to mean anything.' Another speaker made the point that the recent developments in travel, sport, TV and industry have opened up the world to the rest of the world more fully in the past fifty years than in all the rest of history.

The existence of the Community has also made people see the advantages of getting rid of all the artificial barriers to free trade which used to exist. For example, there was *cabotage* (the word originally referred to coastal trade but has since been enlarged to include air and road transport) which gave each country control of all transportation within its frontiers. What this meant was that the taxpayers everywhere were paying for these artificial barriers. From the end of 1991, *cabotage* will not be allowed any longer and there'll be no more lorries coming back from Spain empty, because of local regulations.

Another case in point, though a far more difficult one, is the case of air fares. Air fares in Europe are in general absurdly high because most of the member-states (with the exception now of Britain) own the national airline which is both a flag-carrier and a status symbol, and the member-states are anxious to preserve that situation at almost any cost to themselves and to the fare-paying public. According to Robert Elphick, the Community is determined to get air fares down. It will take time, but eventually they'll do it.

'There is another area in which the Community is going to act,' he went on. 'It's the classic one really. At the moment you can leave England (or anywhere else among the twelve nation-states) with £100 in your pocket, and having travelled through the twelve countries, you can come back with only £50 in your pocket, not having spent a penny on any goods or services or anything else, but having merely changed your money from one currency into another as you passed on your way through the Community. The whole Common Market up until now has been based on this kind of anomaly, on not being a Common Market in fact. Currently the Community is dedicating itself to getting rid of all these types of rip-off practices.

'Now at last, after thirty years in fact, we're going to make it a real Common Market and this will help to reduce prices all round and give a far better choice to consumers, and provide the basis for a far higher standard of living for everybody. And that's one justification for it.

'Also the whole concept is becoming attractive to the outside world. We have applications in from Turkey, Austria, Cyprus, Malta and Sweden. Even Switzerland has been vaguely considering it.

'I don't necessarily regard this aspect of it as more important than the increased industrialization of already existing members, like Spain and Portugal. It's all part and parcel of the same thing, really. There are differing standards in different parts of the Community and some parts of the Community have got to be brought up to some sort of a minimal standard. That's important because otherwise you'd get people migrating from one part of the Community to another, and why should they? It's best if you can provide work where the people live rather than have them migrating all over the place, though one of the achievements of the internal market will be to make it that much easier for them to migrate and set up their homes and families wherever the jobs are.'

Which seems simple enough on the surface. But one of the persistent and possibly chronic problems that is going to dog the Community is the question of coping with immigrants. They can call it illegal entry and fulminate about the terrible social consequences of illegal entry, but what can they do about it practically? Any more than the US government has been able to do anything about the so-called wetbacks coming up from Mexico?

The Community authorities admit that there is no way for the moment of preventing Algerians from entering France and Spain (they can cross in small boats in a very short time and land almost anywhere), and once they have established a foothold in those two countries, they are able to move around Europe as migratory workers or whatever. It may be against the law, but how do you stop it? Once they are here, inside the Community, how do you get rid of them?

Apart from illegal entry, two problems confronting the Community at the present time are economic and monetary union and the question of whether there should be a common defence policy. Most people in the Community believe that economic and monetary union will come about anyway, because the industrialists will demand it. Also, there's nothing revolutionary about it. Last century, when gold was widely used, an Englishman (or anyone else) with a few sovereigns in his pocket could go anywhere in the world without having to go first to a bank to make arrangements for a supply of foreign exchange in various currencies and at considerable expense.

And as far as a common defence policy is concerned, it's becoming increasingly clear that it will probably be dictated by circumstances. It won't be a question of whether it should be done inside or outside NATO, it will suddenly become clear that something has to be done immediately for the sake of European security, and the Community will do it, and in this way the needs of the moment will forge a European common defence policy without first setting down any formal parameters.

The biggest problem of all facing the Community — and indeed all other industrial communities — is the problem of unemployment. Current estimates are talking about a total within the next year or so of 14 million throughout the Community as a whole; the Community's attitude to that is that it's only an estimate, and it might or might not be true, but even if it is, what does it really amount to? About 9 per cent of the total workforce. Of course it's far too high, but without the Community, wouldn't it be a lot higher?

Also, as Robert Elphick was quick to point out, the current levels of unemployment are not in any sense a product of the Common Market. It could be, he would admit, that the Community members were not quick enough in getting into the global market, and that when the first big job losses started to occur as a result of industrial rationalization, increased mechanization, the replacement of workers by robots and computers and so on, they were not able to absorb them more effectively.

On the other hand, the Community has created an enormous number of jobs which had never existed before — as well as soaking up a lot of unemployment that had resulted from the decline of old industries like coal, steel and shipbuilding, and expanding the service industries.

So in what direction is the Community heading at the moment? As indicated above, several countries are in the process of applying for membership, of which Turkey was the first. The procedure is that Turkey first decides that it wants to join. It then submits its application to the Council of Ministers, who hand it over to the Commission. The Commission then spends a lot of time talking to people — industrialists, bankers, politicians, economists, journalists — in the country concerned, and finally the Commission advises the Council as to whether the country's acceptance is feasible or not.

In the case of Turkey, the Commission decided that Turkey's entrance is not feasible for the moment, and currently is trying to think up new ways of associating more closely with Turkey in an effort to iron out the problems of enabling Turkey to meet the standards required for accession to the Community. These include the standard of living, the comparative lack of industrialization, the degree of democracy, the freedom of movement and so on.

Basically there is no freedom of movement for immigrants unless they first become citizens of the Community. This is far easier to state than to enforce. Currently the regulations apply only to people in work and their families; students and the elderly have to prove that they have means to support themselves, otherwise there would be social repercussions. There would be trouble from the people who would have to foot the bills, the tax-payers. But the Community has no clear idea about how it's going to enforce any of these regulations.

And the problem has become enormously more complicated

with the collapse of the communist world and the prospect of accommodating countries like East Germany, Poland, Hungary, Romania, Bulgaria and Czechoslovakia into the Community.

'East Germany is now a part of the Community,' Bob Elphick said. 'And the Germans have done a marvellous job of absorbing 18 million of their own people, taking them into the Deutschmark system, but it's still going to cause enormous difficulties for industries whose markets have disappeared. I met someone the other day who had just been in East Germany and had seen a wonderful ship, still on the stocks, beautifully built by East German workers, for the Soviet Union, but now the Soviet Union cannot afford the Deutschmarks to buy it.

'There's also the point that even if there were a market for the products of all these factories, for all the East German steel mills and shipbuilding yards, environmentally they're quite incapable of even approaching the European Community standards for years. It's a disaster, but we'll all have to wear it because they have the skilled workers there, it's just that their factories are so antiquated and disastrous ecologically.

'We have special schemes to help Poland and Hungary, under a group which includes the United States, Canada and Japan as well as EFTA [European Free Trade Association] and the European Community. We have plans to help Albania and Yugoslavia and even the Soviet Union, though they don't yet even know what they want. We have the European Bank of Reconstruction and Development set up earlier this year in London to provide enterprise funds for them, to invest in any sound ideas they happen to come up with, and there are thirty-five countries involved in that, including the Soviet Union.

'The basic question is this: how are we going to make some of them rich enough to buy consumer goods in sufficient quantity to establish a market economy without making the rest of them — the children, the old people, the unemployed, the disabled — an intolerable burden on whatever funding is available? It may take a generation, who knows? But it will be done because it will have to be done.

'They want to belong to this bigger entity, they want to trade freely with us and we want to trade freely with them, but we know that no one has ever yet changed a communist centrally directed economy into a free market economy. Still, we've got to find a way of doing it.

'For example, the Poles may want to sell steel to us, and we may have to say to them: "Look, we've just gone through all the pain of reducing our own steel overcapacity, so we don't want to take over your problems. What you've got to find out first is how much your steel is costing you. Is it even viable for you to go on manufacturing steel at all at that price? If it is, then maybe there is some case for us buying your steel, but if not, if the industry is overmanned and heavily subsidized, then we're just not having any." And the Poles are going to have to learn to understand this. It's not going to be easy. The Czechs are in roughly the same position but they're more advanced technologically.

'We're surrounded by problems. If the GATT [General Agreement on Tariffs and Trade] talks break down it will be such bad news for everybody that they simply cannot break down, and that's the end of it. I think at least that message has got through to everybody concerned. The CAP [Common Agricultural Policy] also has to be reformed because it's wasteful and there's no more money to keep it going, and that message is starting to get through, too.

'I think one thing the European Community did achieve, or at least helped to achieve, was the elimination of the Iron Curtain. It did that by highlighting the failure of communism.

'But even more important, it has eliminated forever the risk of another war between Germany and France. The genius of the Treaty of Rome was that it devised a way by which the separate interests of these two very disparate nations which have been fighting each other for centuries have now become identical, and so there's no longer any point in them competing for markets or for anything else.'

To have eliminated even this one risk, let alone the removal of the Iron Curtain, it would have been worth paying a very high price. And yet, so far from paying a high price, the members of the Community are enjoying a higher standard of living than ever before and a feeling of security engendered by the fact that as a Community they can stand up industrially and if necessary militarily to any nation or any likely combination of nations in the world.

It is quite clear from the brief historical sections in this book that Europe very largely shaped the rest of the world, and shaped it badly. Through the Community, it may be possible for us Europeople to reshape at least our own part of the world, and get it right this time.

COMMUNITY CHRONICLE

1950	9 May	French Foreign Minister Robert Schuman suggests pooling French and German iron and steel (armaments) industries
	24 October	French Prime Minister Rene Pleven proposes European Defence Community (EDC)
1951	18 April	Benelux countries, West Germany, France and Italy sign Paris Treaty establishing European Coal and Steel Community (ECSC)
1952	27 May	Government of Les Six sign treaty establishing EDC
	10 August	The High Authority under Jean Monnet starts work
	10 September	Paul Henri Spaak becomes President of ECSC and is asked by Les Six to prepare draft treaty for European Political Community
1953	1 January	ECSC levy – first European tax – comes into force

	10 February	Common Market for coal and iron established
	1 May	Common Market for steel established
1954	11 May	Alcide de Gasperi becomes President of the ECSC Assembly which decides to finance housing for workers in coal and mining industries
	30 August	EDC Treaty rejected by French National Assembly. Discussions on political community break down
	21 December	Association agreement between ECSC and United Kingdom signed in London
1955	1 June	Rene Mayer succeeds Jean Monnet as Head of High Authority
	2 June	At Messina foreign ministers of ECSC decide to continue and extend economic integration
1956	27 November	Hans Furler becomes President of High Authority ECSC
	30 May	Foreign ministers of Les Six decide to continue and extend economic integration
1957	25 March	Rome Treaty establishes European Economic Community (EEC) and European Atomic Energy (Euratom)
1958	1 January	Rome Treaties come into force
	7 January	Paul Finet becomes President of High Authority
	19 March	Robert Schuman becomes President of European Parliament
	3 July	Stresa Conference – foundations of Common Agricultural Policy (CAP) established
1959	1 January	Gradual phasing out of customs duties and quotas within EEC begins with 10 per cent reduction of duties
	8 June	Greece requests association with EEC

	31 June	Turkey requests association with EEC
1961	31 July	Ireland applies for EEC membership. United Kingdom follows suit on August 9 and Denmark on August 10
	8 November	Negotiations with United Kingdom begin in Brussels
1962	9 February	Spain seeks negotiation for association with EEC
	30 April	Norway applies for membership
	18 May	Portugal applies for association
1963	14 January	General de Gaulle states United Kingdom not ready for membership
	20 January	First Association Convention signed with seventeen African states and Madagascar at Yaounde, Cameroon
	12 September	EEC-Turkey association agreement signed
	14 October	Trade agreement between Iran and EEC signed
1964	4 May	EEC takes part in Kennedy round of international tariff negotiations in Geneva
1967	9 February	Council agrees on first medium-term economic policy and on introduction of a common VAT system
	1 May	New applications for membership from Denmark, Ireland and United Kingdom (May 10)
	29 September	Favourable opinion from Commission on accession of United Kingdom, Ireland, Denmark and Norway
	19 December	Council fails to agree on resumption of negotiations with applicant countries
1968	1 July	Customs union achieved. Duties between member states eliminated. Common customs tariff instituted for trade with non-member countries
	26 July	Agreement signed between EEC and

		East African Common Market (Kenya, Uganda, Tanzania)
	8 November	Free movement for workers achieved (common labour market)
1969	28 March	Association agreement signed with Tunisia and Morocco
	23 July	Council reconsiders applications from United Kingdom, Ireland, Denmark and Norway
1970	1 January	EEC countries embark on CAP
	19 March	Trade agreement between EEC and Yugoslavia signed
	29 June	Free trade agreement between EEC and Spain signed
	5 December	Agreement with Malta signed
1971	8 November	EEC-Argentina trade agreement signed
1972	22 January	Act of accession signed in Brussels
	21 March	Currency snake introduced to allow exchange rates to vary by no more than 2.25 per cent
	10 May	People of Ireland decide by plebiscite to join EEC
	13 July	British House of Commons approves Community membership
	22 July	Free trade agreement with non-applicant EFTA countries signed
	25 September	Referendum in Norway rejects membership
	2 October	Danes vote in plebiscite to join EEC
	19 October	Nine heads of state in Paris decide to develop Community into European Union and establish timetable for Community
	18 December	Preferential agreement between EEC and Egypt signed
	19 December	Agreement with Cyprus signed
1973	1 January	Treaty of accession for United Kingdom, Denmark and Ireland in force

	19 January	Member states (except United Kingdom, Ireland, Italy) form single currency block
	6 April	European Monetary Cooperation Fund established in Luxembourg
1974	21 January	France leaves currency system and allows franc to float
	10 December	Community Summit Conference in Paris decides on direct elections to European Parliament from 1978, extended powers and creation of a passport union
1975	28 February	Lomé Convention signed between EEC and forty-six developing countries in Africa, the Caribbean and the Pacific
	11 May	First trade agreement with Israel signed
	5 June	Two-thirds majority of UK citizens vote to keep United Kingdom in the Community
	12 June	Greece applies for membership
	10 July	French franc returns to 'snake'
	15 July	Mexico and Sri Lanka sign agreement on trade policy cooperation
1976	25 April	Agreements with Algeria, Tunisia and Morocco signed
	6 June	Agreement with Pakistan signed
	6 July	Canada signs framework agreement on economic and trade cooperation
	12 July	Brussels: EEC decides number of seats for directly elected Parliament at 410
1977	6 January	Roy Jenkins becomes President of the Commission
	28 March	Portugal applies for membership
	28 July	Spain applies for membership
1978	3 April	Trade agreement with China signed
	22 November	First general meeting of Community Youth Forum
1979	17 July	Simone Veil elected President of first sitting of directly elected European Parliament in Strasbourg

	13 March	European Monetary System enters into force. ECU becomes new European currency unit
	31 October	Second Lomé Convention signed governing relations between EEC and sixty-one ACP countries
1980	30 May	Council gives Commission mandate to propose modifications to structure of budget and policies
1981	1 January	Greece becomes tenth member of Community
	19 November	Proposals for European Act and draft statement on economic integration presented by Ministers Genscher and Colombo
1982	23 February	Referendum in Greenland on membership. Majority in favour of seeking new relationship
	27 February	Resolution on Community action to combat unemployment
1984	14 February	Parliament passes resolution on draft treaty establishing European Union
	14 June	Second direct elections to European Parliament
	25 June	European Council at Fontainebleau reaches agreement on principles relating to Community budget and on reform of CAP
	13 July	Franco–German agreement signed on gradual removal of border checks
1985	1 January	European passport introduced in all member states except United Kingdom, Germany and Greece
	30 April	Angola signs third Lomé Convention
	21 May	Five-year trade treaty signed between China and Community

1986	1 January	. Spain and Portugal become eleventh and twelfth members of Community
	17 February	Single European Act signed by representatives of twelve member states
1987	14 April	Turkey applies for membership
	1 July	Single European Act comes into force
	29 July	Ratification of Anglo-French Treaty to finance Channel Tunnel
1988	20 September	Thatcher's Bruges speech described by The Times as 'onslaught on European unification'
1989	17 July	Austria applies for membership
	8 December	Community expresses commitment to German reunification
	18 December	Turkey's application for membership postponed until 1993 at earliest
1990	3 October	Reunification of Germany welcomed
	5 October	United Kingdom decides to join Exchange Rate Mechanism
1991	17 January	Foreign ministers give formal backing to Allied Forces fighting in Gulf
	1 July	Sweden applies for membership
	20 August	Community takes united stand on Russian coup and Yugoslav crisis, and prepares to provide arbitration commission to resolve Yugoslav crisis
	8 September	Welcomes recognition of sovereignty of Estonia, Latvia and Lithuania

VITAL STATISTICS

THE ECU IN RELATION TO COMMUNITY CURRENCIES

The value of the ECU (European Currency Unit) in terms of other Community currencies in alphabetical order at 1985 values and at current values (mid-August 1991).

Country	Code	Value
Belgium	BFR	42.22
Denmark	DKR	7.940
France	FF	6.970
Germany	DM	2.048
Greece	DRA	226.7
Ireland	IRL	0.767
Italy	LIT	1,524.9
Luxembourg	LFR	42.22
Netherlands	HLF	2.312
Portugal	ESC	176.82
Spain	PTA	128.42
United Kingdom	UKL	0.708

TRADE BALANCE

(Net flow in millions of ECUs, 1988)

Belgium	946
Denmark	1,586
Germany (West)	65,404
Greece	−5,134
Spain	−15,233
France	−6,818
Ireland	2,612
Italy	−511
Netherlands	6,913
Spain	−15,233
Portugal	−4,338
United Kingdom	−31,412

WHERE THE MONEY GOES

Consumption per head (ECUs, 1987)

No figures available for East Germany

FOOD AND DRINK	
Belgium	1,616
Denmark	2,609
France	1,670
Germany (West)*	1,585
Greece	1,109
Ireland	1,728
Italy	1,682
Luxembourg	1,872
Netherlands	1,402
Portugal	778
Spain	1,147
United Kingdom	1,114
Euroaverage	1,481

CLOTHING, FOOTWEAR	
Belgium	604
Denmark	531
France	587
Germany (West)*	756
Greece	263
Ireland	276
Italy	682
Luxembourg	569
Netherlands	560
Portugal	215
Spain	326
United Kingdom	443
Euroaverage	484

WHERE THE MONEY GOES

RENT, FUEL, POWER

Belgium	1,390
Denmark	2,437
France	1,574
Germany (West)*	1,779
Greece	328
Ireland	468
Italy	1,056
Luxembourg	1,722
Netherlands	1,388
Portugal	104
Spain	628
United Kingdom	1,244
Euroaverage:	1,176

FURNITURE AND FITTINGS

Belgium	817
Denmark	608
France	690
Germany (West)*	810
Greece	240
Ireland	314
Italy	613
Luxembourg	863
Netherlands	593
Portugal	180
Spain	312
United Kingdom	418
Euroaverage	538

MEDICARE, MEDICINES
(includes public health service medicare)

Belgium	848
Denmark	163
France	738
Germany (West)*	1,375
Greece	113
Ireland	144
Italy	411
Luxembourg	673
Netherlands	946
Portugal	94
Spain	157
United Kingdom	82
Euroaverage	475

TRANSPORT, COMMUNICATIONS:

Belgium	963
Denmark	1,532
France	1,397
Germany (West)*	1,405
Greece	376
Ireland	509
Italy	946
Luxembourg	1,424
Netherlands	861
Portugal	322
Spain	652
United Kingdom	1,039
Euroaverage	952

WHERE THE MONEY GOES

RECREATION, EDUCATION:	
Belgium	505
Denmark	882
France	604
Germany (West)*	852
Greece	188
Ireland	444
Italy	583
Luxembourg	356
Netherlands	718
Portugal	120
Spain	290
United Kingdom	590
Euroaverage	511

MISCELLANEOUS GOODS, SERVICES	
Belgium	1,123
Denmark	953
France	1,067
Germany (West)*	950
Greece	292
Ireland	379
Italy	1,180
Luxembourg	1,112
Netherlands	1,046
Portugal	281
Spain	890
United Kingdom	1,307
Euroaverage	882

MOTOR VEHICLES, PRODUCTION AND ASSEMBLY

	Motor cars		Commercial vehicles	
	Production	Assembly	Production	Assembly
EUR12	12,838,000		1,829,000	
Belgium	345,000	1,164,000	54,000	6,900
Denmark	–	1,000	–	1,000
France	3,455,000	–	550,000	–
Germany (West)	4,312,000	–	294,000	–
Greece	–	9,000	–	4,000
Ireland	–	–	–	–
Italy	1,883,000	–	227,000	–
Luxembourg	–	–	–	–
Netherlands	120,000	–	19,000	–
Spain	1,497,000	–	–	4,000
Portugal	–	75,000	–	44,000
United Kingdom	1,226,000	29,000	318,000	4,000

TELEPHONES AND TELEVISION SETS
Per 1,000 of Population 1987–88

	Telephones	Television Sets
Belgium	356	320
France	455	333
Germany (West)	462	385
Greece	362	175
Italy	350	257
Ireland	236	228
Luxembourg	445	249
Netherlands	438	325
Portugal	180	159
Spain	283	368
United Kingdom	427	347
Euroaverage	396	310

UNEMPLOYMENT RATES
(as annual average percentage of workforce, 1989)

	Total	Men	Women
Belgium	9%	6.1%	12.1%
Denmark	7%	6.1%	8.1%
France	9.6%	7.5%	12.8%
Germany (West)	5.7%	4.7%	7.3%
Greece	7.7%	4.9%	12.5%
Italy	11%	7.4%	17%
Ireland	17.2%	16.6%	18.6%
Luxembourg	1.8%	1.4%	2.6%
Netherlands	9.8%	7%	14.4%
Portugal	5.7%	3.6%	8.5%
Spain	18%	13.4%	26.8%
United Kingdom	7%	7.5%	6.3%
Euroaverage	9.3%	7.4%	12.1%